ON THE EDGE OF HISTORY

The story of the Dabney Family
and their influence on Atlantic history

JOSEPH C. ABDO

Tenth Island Editions

On the Edge of History

Tenth Island Editions

Joseph C. Abdo Unipessoal, Lda.
Rua São João da Mata, 5-3º
1200-846 Lisbon, Portugal

Produced by Maria Esther – Gab. Artes Gráficas, Lda

Dep. legal n.º
ISBN 972-99858-0-4

Table of Contents

INTRODUCTION

Until the time I took a vacation to the island of Faial in the Azores archipelago, I had never known of the existence of the Dabney family. When I visited the Tourist Office in the island's main city of Horta on Faial, the brochure they gave me contained a paragraph with a very brief description of the Dabney family and their life on Faial. In addition, I noticed that one of the main streets just up the road in the center of town was named Rua Consul Dabney. Next, I discovered that there was a special exhibit about the Dabneys in the Municipal Museum celebrating the centennial of the family's departure. However, even after reading the brochure and visiting the museum exhibit, I still only had a vague idea who this family was.

My curiosity was aroused about (as to) why an American family had settled on the island and was considered important enough by the people of Faial to include in their tourist brochure and name a street after one of them. When I asked for more information concerning the Dabneys, I was referred to the Horta Library-Archives and they informed me that there was no book about the family except *The Annals of the Dabney Family in Fayal*, by Roxana Lewis Dabney, which they would not photocopy.

However, the library/archives did suggest references in other documents; however these were mostly short citations on single topics. After I returned to Lisbon, I was still curious and expanded my search to the Portuguese National Library and the Portuguese National Archives in Lisbon, as well as to the U.S. National Archives. After some diligent searching I discovered several sources of the *Annals*, and was able to make a photocopy of one. I also was fortunate in being able to make contact with one of the members of the family, Sally Dabney Parker, who was most helpful in providing access to other documents written by family members, describing what she knew and making suggestions for directions to take and offering assistance when asked.

In summary, the Dabney family that settled on Faial was originally from Boston (with the earlier French origins of the family described in the book text). Despite living in the middle of the Atlantic, they maintained contact with a large number of friends who were important in the New England business, intellectual and literary communities.

The first figure in this family story is John Bass Dabney, who was born 10 years before the Revolutionary War and raised in a period of insecurity. This early experience was helpful in reducing the apprehension of taking chances in business ventures. After completing his education and starting work in a counting room in Boston, he founded his first of several businesses, some of which failed. John Bass Dabney's business ventures eventually took him to Alexandria, Virginia with his wife and they started raising a family. From there he journeyed to Paris during the "Reign of Terror" in the 1790's and started a wine shipping business.

Both the British and French created problems for his ships, so in 1804 he finally decided to give up his business there and his family sailed to America. John Bass sailed back to America separately via a side trip to the island of Faial in the Azores. He returned there in 1806 as the U. S. Consul, appointed by President Thomas Jefferson, and opened up a business. Thus began the 86-year story of the Dabney family. His son, Charles William Dabney, and grandson, Samuel Wyllys Dabney followed John Dabney as U. S. Consuls on Faial and as the heads of the thriving family business and major providers of philanthropy in the Azores.

During their sojourn on Faial, the Dabneys had many visitors, including royalty from Portugal and other European countries, a number of important American visitors, in addition to a few visitors that were out-of-the-ordinary. They were also involved with American and Portuguese political and military activities that affected the archipelago with ramifications that reached both sides of the Atlantic.

On Faial they were known for their philanthropy and were major providers of employment and purchasers of goods from the islanders. They also intervened as arbitrators during more than one Portuguese political difficulty, an undertaking that put them at risk of retribution from one side or the other.

All of this took place in surroundings which visitors considered of great natural beauty and beneficial for the health. Furthermore, most visitors described the Dabney family life as almost idyllic and they were highly praised for their lifestyle and the contributions they made not only financially, but also through personal involvement. After reading how decent and respected they were, I kept waiting for the other shoe to fall and find something negative about them. However, it was a search in vain, except for the rare complaint related to their business or Consular activities. In short, however, that shoe is still up in the air.

Nevertheless, as the years passed the life of the family was forced to change. The number of children became so large that there were not enough positions in the family business or Consulate to absorb them so their only chance for work was to leave the island. Eventually, their business and Consular activities decreased because improvements in ship technology resulted in the Azores being bypassed; petroleum replaced whale oil; and, fruits and products from other countries were cheaper than those from the Azores. In addition, the State Department began to question the need for a Consulate in the Azores and restrictions were put on Consuls' ability to engage in private enterprise. Considering all this, the family decided to sell their properties, and the entire family remaining in the Azores moved to the United States, ending their 86-year stay in Faial.

Yet, despite their involvement with international events and their connections to so many famous people in America and Europe, the Dabney family has remained virtually unknown outside the archipelago. I believe that the main reason for their not being acknowledged as contributors to the history of the 19th century was that they lived in such an isolated location that kept them far from the center of what was going on. In addition, when they did receive recognition in U. S. newspapers, it was not persistent enough to keep their name in people's minds. Furthermore, it was part of the family's character that they never sought out public attention. As a result they maintained a position that was on the edge of the history and life during the 19th century.

The primary information available about the family was the 1,500-page *Annals of the Dabney Family in Fayal*, which was written by Roxana Lewis Dabney, granddaughter of John Bass Dabney. In addition there are references in a few books, periodicals and newspapers. The *Annals* is a collection of information written by Roxana to her nieces and nephews. In 1880 a large number of them were in Fayal and urged her to write a volume about the family starting from their arrival on the island, particularly about their grandfather, Charles William Dabney, the second Consul. Roxana argued that one of her sisters would be a better choice, but after much badgering she agreed to write the document.

The *Annals* is not a biography or chronicle in the traditional sense. Rather, it is a collection of factual narratives tied together with anecdotes and personal reminiscences that, based on her own memory of life on Faial, Roxana pieced together from letters, articles and commentaries that various family members sent her. The *Annals* is somewhat bewildering to use since it assumes some prior knowledge about the family and their friends.

It must have been quite a task to put some order to the mass of papers that she was given, in part because some important pieces were missing and others were only isolated bits of information. Roxana prepared the *Annals* in chronological order and the majority of the events and people she describes follow this logical order. However, sometimes she recalls something and inserts it a hundred pages later than the original event. Other times a letter could mention someone and she veers off on a tangent to describe another incident related to this person, but not connected to the main point she had been focusing on. Making the reading of the *Annals* even more difficult is that Roxana wrote for people who knew each other well, and she often used nicknames and other times she just uses just initials.

Another major source of information about the family is the communications between the Faial Consulate and the State Department. Letters from the State Department contained much less information about events on Faial since they were often general letters sent to all Consuls. Sometimes the State Department material and the *Annals* overlap on a particular topic, which allow for combining slightly different points of view about the same event. While an official account reported the basic facts, the *Annals* often provide a slightly different, more in-depth account, as well as presented personal reactions and opinions about what occurred. Official Portuguese documents are less frequently used, but they have a similar relationship with the *Annals* as the official U. S. documents.

Roxana's *Annals* were started before the family left the Azores, but were not published until a number of years after they returned to America. Her original intent was to write more than one volume, but the *Annals* end just shortly after the death of Charles William Dabney. As a result, most of the story of the third Consul, Samuel Wyllys Dabney is not covered by her nor is it included in many other chronicles. The best sources about the last years of the Dabney family on Faial are *The Fayal Dabneys*, by Samuel's daughter Rose Dabney Forbes, and microfilm from the Massachusetts Historical Society, a large part of which are Roxana Dabney's diaries covering these years. Roxana's diaries continue into the 20th century and describe some of her life in California where part of the family moved and where Samuel Dabney died.

In addition to Roxana and Rose, both William Henry and Francis Dabney wrote books about the family; however, the latter two only cover the first half of the Dabney's life on Faial. Besides the Dabneys' documents, several Portuguese authors included information on the family in chapters, or sometimes only a few paragraphs, in chronicles and compilations of texts about Horta, Faial or even the entire archipelago. The local 4-page newspapers, which began operation around 1840, also provided some information, although they generally focused more on major world happenings and local commercial or political subjects.

On the Edge of History is a synthesis of the material available from the various sources mentioned above. It is not meant to be an academic tome, but rather the story of the Dabney family, emphasizing what I felt was most interesting and revealing about them. However, it is not 100% inclusive, especially in regard to their business activities and minor family events. I also attempted to put the story of the Dabneys on Faial into the context of what was going on in 19th century America and Europe. The choice of what was included and what was left out was mine alone.

Language and Spelling

There have been changes in both English and Portuguese spelling and language use from the 19th century. The original language is maintained where it is used in the quoted material. The text of the book uses the modern spelling conventions and uses Portuguese words for names of persons and places. Prominent among the variations are the current spelling of "Faial" versus the 19th century "Fayal", the habit of translating certain locations, such as São Miguel to St. Michael's, and the use of a mixture of American and British spelling in letters and documents.

Acknowledgments

I greatly appreciate the moral and practical support provided by George Abdo, Judy Abdo, Ellen Bowers, Keith Harle, Anita Israel, Teresa Huerta Parente, Leonor Santimano, Jim Shea, Dee Ulrich, Judith and Chet Yates

Also providing invaluable assistance were staff members at the United States National Archives, the Archives and Library on the Island of Faial, the Núcleo Cultural da Horta, the Massachusetts Historical Society, the New England Historical Genealogical Society, the Boston Public Library the Longfellow House Museum (Cambridge, MA), and The Huntington Library (Pasadena, CA). I owe particular appreciation to U. S. Consul David Scott on the island of São Miguel for his technical assistance and personal support.

My very special thanks goes to those members of the Dabney family who provided information and encouragement, particularly Sally Dabney Parker, Fay Dabney and Lew Dabney.

FOREWORD

The Foreword to Joe Abdo's "The Edge of History", known fondly to him and us as "O Tomo"—Portuguese for "Tome", would be incomplete without our praise being heaped on the author for his diligence, his intellectual curiosity and massive painstaking research. Joe's a scholar, high level hospital administrator, world traveler and actor which led him to uncover gems of the Dabney family's background which few of us knew or failed to uncover because we never really dug into the "Annals". That we are grateful is a colossal understatement.

Joe's *chef d'oeuvre* shows the depth of the Dabney family and its geographic spread across the states, but later generations could not match John Bass's bountiful productivity of 11 kids and son Frederick's nine.

The manuscript of this book has achieved limited distribution beyond the existing family to various libraries such as that of the Massachusetts Historical Society and the N. E. Genealogical Society in Boston, MA, the N.E. Whaling Museum in New Bedford, MA and other such institutions.

There are a number of books on the varied, curious and historic "Atlantic Islands" which seem to have surfaced over the last decade. Works such as Joe Abdo's heighten the value of the studies, and we commend them to thoughtful readers' attention.

Our thanks again to Joe Abdo and enjoy!

Lewis Stackpole Dabney,
November 2004.

LIST OF GRAPHIC MATERIAL

1 – IN THE BEGINNING

Far out in the middle of the Atlantic Ocean, nine peaks extend from the ocean floor up through the surface high above the mid-Atlantic ridge. Nine islands tied to a single culture, but maintaining separate cultural identities; islands whose physical character changes faster through the power of Nature revealed by volcanoes, earthquakes and huge storms than the life style and cultural changes of their population. This is the archipelago of the Azores.

The islands of the Azores have been included on maps available to those wanting to sail westward across the Atlantic since the 14th century. Are they the remnants of the sinking of Atlantis? Were they known to the Phoenicians and other ancient peoples who may have roamed the seas farther than we are aware of? We may never discover the answer. Even today the Azores are relatively unknown to the world at large and their prehistory remains a mystery.

During the first half of the 15th century, Prince Henry the Navigator began sending Portuguese navigators and sailors out into the unknown seas to bring back information that would allow the next of his ships to go even farther. Among the knowledge they brought back was the verification of the existence of these islands far to the west of the European mainland. Although there were no inhabitants on the islands, there was a large number of a type of sea hawk that was mistaken for the goshawk, known in Portuguese as the Açor (Azor). This provided the island chain with its name.

Following his usual policy, Prince Henry sent groups of people to inhabit the islands. In addition to Portuguese, many Flemish and people from other European countries also made their way to the Azores. They settled there and took advantage of the mild climate and volcanic soil to create an economy based on agriculture and fishing. Because of the islands' location half way across the ocean, they also became an important stopping point for ships crossing the Atlantic. Initially these were ships on voyages of exploration. Because of the currents and winds, the return voyage from the south and west Atlantic brought ships past the archipelago. Columbus made his first landfall here on his eastward voyage home – not a pleasant memory for him since he and his crew were imprisoned there.

Later, trading expeditions to and from the four corners of the Earth began. Their number continued to increase and reached a peak when North American trade with Europe began to grow significantly. The importance of the Azores to shipping only declined in the 19th century when steam-powered ships became prevalent and reduced the necessity for mid-Atlantic stops.

Just a little over three hundred years after Columbus stopped in the Azores on his eastern voyage homeward to Europe, John Bass Dabney also stopped there for a visit on his westward voyage home from France to the United States. In late 1804 he spent a few months on the island of Faial and continued his return trip to the United States in the spring of 1805. Summer of 1806 found him back on Faial to stay and establish himself and his family in what was to become a pivotal role in the Azores throughout the 19th century. During the 86 years the Dabney family stayed in the Azores, they were associated with much of what happened in the North Atlantic and among the nations bordering it.

The Dabney family's departure was as sudden as its arrival. On January 2, 1892, the Dabney family remaining on Faial climbed aboard their ship and said farewell to the island and its people, both sides feeling the great sense of loss.

John Bass Dabney's youngest son, William was the member of the family most interested in genealogy and studied and wrote about it. He believed the Dabney family in America traces its descent from the Huguenot leader, Agrippa d'Aubigne. This French Calvinist was a well-known writer and a comrade in arms of King Henry IV of France, who issued the Edict of Nantes in 1598. This edict guaranteed Protestants a degree of religious freedom in Catholic France.[1]

Two generations later, the situation reversed. Agrippa's grand-daughter was Madame de Maintenon, who had converted from being a Huguenot to Catholicism. She was responsible for educating the children that Louis XIV had had by his mistress Madame de Montespan. After the death of Queen Marie-Therese, Madame de Maintenon was secretly married to King Louis and exerted much influence over him particularly in the area of religion. In 1685, Louis XIV revoked the Edict of Nantes and took away the freedom of this group of Protestants to practice their religion. This led to severe persecution and the emigration of 200-300,000 Huguenots. Many of these French Calvinists fled to Britain, including the brothers Cornelius, John and Robert d'Aubigne. Sometime between 1715 and 1717, Cornelius and John d'Aubigne left Wales for Virginia and changed the family name to Dabney. Their brother Robert went to Boston and established the Massachusetts branch of the family. His great-grandson was John Bass Dabney, the principal character in the first part of this story.[2]

William Dabney gives his version of the family history in a letter to his older brother Charles' son Charles.

PROVIDENCE, 5th May, 1853.

My dear Nephew, – I had recently the great pleasure of seeing Clara and Roxa and enjoyed their short visit very much. Clara intimated that you were curious to know about what time our family name became changed from French to English, I have now the pleasure of handing you the most reliable account that I have been able to discover, and in doing this have perhaps inflicted upon you a chapter as familiar to you as to me, if so you may consider yourself a lucky man, for getting no more, as when I get among the old records it is hard to quit them, for believe me, dear Nephew, it is one of my luxuries to retrace past scenes and events even to childhood, and to view the hand of the Lord which has sustained me and rescued me from so many fearfully perilous situations; it is good to feel that we are in the hands of the Lord, else the idea of being in the way in the world would be intolerable.

There is a branch of our family out West, who trace their origin from my uncle, Nathaniel Gardner Dabney, and I see by some paper that the Rev. R. L. Dabney of Lexington Presbytery is elected Professor in the Vir. Theological Seminary, whether he is of that nest or not I can't say. I don't see but that we have a pretty fair right to trace back, and claim as our ancestor a very worthy man, the grandfather of Madame do Maintenon, who was born in 1550 and died in 1630. It is said of him that he was not only a person of condition, but likewise of great merit and was a leading man among the Protestants – in 1619 he fled to Geneva. A French Historian says he was a man of great courage and boldness, of ready wit, of fine taste in polite learning as well as good experience in matters of war. He must have been a worthy man, *I shall claim him.*

I observe what you say in regard to Julia's marriage, and I think she has acted advisedly and that her prospect of happiness is very good; Mr. Labbé is highly respectable, has been Mayor of the City, is at present Judge and what is better than all, his moral character is like that of Caesar's wife. I believe be has a sufficiency of tile world's goods, is very domestic, all kindness and affection in his, family, is kind and indulgent to his slaves, and Julia is there, adored by her husband and nearly so by the daughters and family generally; as one of the daughters wrote me "she twines herself round the affections of all." A few days since I received from Frederick Spalding a few lines announcing the death of his mother on, the 12th of April – poor dear sister, she is now I trust at rest; I believe she was wishing to depart; she had but little comfort, and I can not mourn for her.

Most affectely. Yrs.

W. DABNEY

Great-uncle William further records the following:

Robert and Elizabeth Daubigné resided in Boston in 1723 as appears by the following record: In the City Records is found in August of that year, the birth of John, son of Robert and Elizabeth Daubigné. In the records of King's Chapel, Sept. of that same year we find the Baptism of John, son of Robert and Elizabeth Dabney. It would appear that about this period, the family name was permanently changed in America. Charles Dabney, my Grandfather, was, I presume a son of the above, and born probably in Europe, as this was the first record of Robert and Elizabeth; and he married Elizabeth Gardner (who I find was born in 1717), daughter of Nathaniel and Mary Gardner. I remember seeing her at my father's house in Oxford. My father was the first fruit of this connection, then came Nathaniel Gardner Dabney who was a druggist in Salem, previous to the revolution, a refugee during that period. The tradition is that he was lost in a storm on his way from France to America in 1783. I well remember seeing his widow at my father's, she was very ladylike in manners and dress, and I thought the handsomest person I had ever seen, though *she* had a 'cock eye'. She married twice afterward, and died in Andover I believe in 1834. John was next, he was proprietor and editor of the "Salem Mercury," father of my cousins John Peale and Margaret Dabney. There was another daughter, Mary, who at the age of ten, perished in the flames at the burning of her mother's house in Duxbury in 1765.[3]

Among the Virginia branch of the Dabneys, there is another idea of the origin of at least their part of the family. This alternative traces the family from a distinguished Norman-English line beginning with Sir William d'Aubigne, who accompanied William the Conqueror to England.[4]

The Dabney coat-of-arms is unusual. The Dabney coat-of-arms shield is red (heraldic term is gules) and is a sign of their courage and the blood they spilled in brave actions. In a band across the center are five silver (argent), diamond-shaped lozenges (fusils), each with a blue *fleur-de-lis* in it. The *fleur-de-lis* represents crown grants, but nobody knows why there are five. Above this are three gold (or) martlets. They are without

Figure 1

Coat-of-Arms of the Dabney Family

legs, which is normal for this bird in heraldry. The martlet was a swallow-like bird that was very rare and became extinct around 1300. They also signify the interest of the family in sports since they were highly esteemed as a game bird prior to 1300. The crest is an elephant's head cut off at the neck and is green, which is for decoration and has no reference to Ireland. Study by some scholars indicates that one branch of the Dabney family (probably spelled Daubeney) was driven out of France for various, unstated reasons, none of which the family was proud of at the time, and took up residence in India. Because of this Indian influence, the elephant on the crest is Indian, not African. The motto *"Fidele et Reconnaissant"* (Faithful and Grateful) possibly indicates that the family was held in great esteem and were shown great loyalty by their serfs and that the family was always remarkable in showing gratification for anything that came to pass. Although the coat-of-arms was old when the Dabneys arrived on Faial, the characteristics represented on it also described the 19th century Dabneys.[5]

John Bass Dabney, great grandson of Robert Dabney, was born on December 13, 1766, and was raised in an 18th century Boston experiencing the throes of the pre-Revolutionary War activities that would lead to the establishment of the United States of America. To escape the agitation in the city, his father moved the family to Oxford, Massachusetts in 1775. In April of that year British troops marched on Lexington and Concord and the first shots of the American Revolution were heard. This was followed by the Battle of Breed's Hill and a couple of months later Boston was then surrounded by the American Militia, which was soon converted into the Continental Army under its first Commander, George Washington.

As a result of the troubled times and apparent lack of schools in Oxford, John's early education could not have been what his parents had desired for him.[6] In July 1784, John Bass Dabney was placed in the counting room of Providence, Rhode Island, merchants Thompson and Deblois. Such apprenticeships were a normal occurrence for sons of merchants. The conditions for his apprenticeship were as follows:

For the term of three years and six months, the said Thompson and Deblois promising to give him a good suite of Cloathes of all parts of his Body suitable for an Apprentice, and also one Piece of good linen of the price and Value of one shilling and sixpence Sterling money Yearly and every year of the above said Term, and to give the said Apprentice all the shoes, that shall be necessary for him during the whole of the above said Term.[7]

John remained there only a short time, as he had to leave Thompson and Deblois when his father died in October of his first year. From there he then went to Alexandria, Virginia, to earn a living for himself and to support the other members of his family.[8]

William Henry Dabney gives us a description of his father.

Well I do remember his appearance. He was not a large man, indeed he was under the average height and could not have been much over 5 ft 5 to 6 in. When I knew him he was rather stout. His body was long for his legs, a peculiarity which has been inherited by some of his children and their descendants.

He dressed with scrupulous neatness and wore the Consular uniform of Navy blue, tail coat with lapels behind and standing color. Navy buttons on the front, cuffs and lapels, long trousers, white waistcoat with Navy buttons, voluminous neck cloth, and a silk hat with cockade and eagle in it. He wore his face smoothly shaven, long hair powdered and drawn into a queue behind. This he continued up to his death. I well remember the daily visit of the barber to shave him, tie up his queue and to powder his hair.[9]

John Dabney was known for his industriousness and virtue, as well as for a perseverance that was to be tested more than once. But he was not all work. He added to these qualities his sociable qualities which so distinguished him in later life, and to have had a keen sense of wit, and fondness for joking.[10]

These latter qualities, along with his philanthropic activities, were the ones that endeared him to all those who were acquainted with him. In 1789, he began his first business in Alexandria, Virginia, in partnership with a Mr. Rogerson. They exported American products, such as tobacco, to Europe and brought back wines, most of their trade being done with France.[11]

Business must have prospered because in 1792 John Bass felt secure enough financially to marry Roxa Lewis, a young Massachusetts woman known for her beauty and regal bearing. She was a good match for John Bass, who was also known for his fine appearance and pride in his dress, even using gold eagle coins for the buttons on his wedding coat. They made a striking couple. Contemporary descriptions say that Roxa Dabney greatly resembled Marie Antoinette[12] and John Dabney had a great likeness to George Washington[13] – their own international coalition.

On March 19, 1794, their first son, Charles William Dabney, was born in Alexandria. He was destined to become the main figure of the Dabney family in the Azores, but that is still a couple of decades in the future.

Within two months after his son's birth, John Bass Dabney went to France and established himself in business there. Why he went was never explicitly stated in the documentation available, but his son William suggests some possibilities related to current business needs or speculation in future business opportunities based on what he saw happen in the United States after the Revolutionary War.

> What J. B. Dabney's motive was in going to France so suddenly in such dangerous times we do not know, perhaps to look after property sent over there by his house on account of others, and unpaid for or consigned by them to parties who had failed to account for them for its value. I think, however, that his principal motive may have been to purchase ships of which the ports of France were then full. French ships unable to go to sea on account of the war then going on with England and other powers, and prizes taken at sea by French cruisers and privateers brought into French ports for condemnation and sale, and he may have been invited to come over and make such purchases in conjunction with his

friend George W. Murray of Alexandria, [with who he] did purchase together and with others several large ships.[14]

What induced him to go to France to reside permanently at such a troubled time must have been the great opening for business with America and by American citizens. The continued state of war had stimulated this business and American vessels which had increased prodigiously were, you may say, the carriers of the world. Frenchmen were cautious about engaging in business and merchants of European nationalities were debarred from doing so.[15]

However, whatever the reason for his going to France, he began to purchase ships, either individually or in partnership, and started to export wine.[16] His arrival in France occurred during an extremely turbulent period. It was right at the beginning of the Reign of Terror when the guillotine was severing more than 1,000 heads per month, with that of Robespierre falling in July 1794.

One of his principal associates at this time was Mr. Robert Bennet Forbes, who shared John Dabney's view that troubled times brought opportunities. A long business and personal relationship continued between the two families, with John M. Forbes being a friend of Charles Dabney and John Dabney's great granddaughter Rose marrying John Malcolm Forbes in 1892. In a letter dated November 1, 1794, Robert Forbes tells John Dabney that he had just returned to France from the West Indies and wanted "to talk to [him] in a concise (yet to me interesting) way of Futurity".[17] In addition the idea of making money when the French Revolution ended is pointed out by Forbes.

My plan is rather speculative and I may extend my personal excursion as far as l'Isle de France, this will depend on l'état actuel de la guerre [the present state of the war], which I think will soon be finished. C'es le moment mon cher, pour les jeunes gens de mon caractère de faire des movements rapides, de ramasser quelques Capitaux pour leur établissement après la pais. [It is the moment, my friend, for young gentlemen of my character to move quickly, to pull together some capital for their business after the peace.][18]

Forbes was a little over-optimistic in thinking the war would end soon, but his opinion may have been similar to that of John Dabney.

Internal strife was not the only problem that France had. The country was also at war with most of its neighbors, including Britain. Because they feared British attacks, French merchant ships unable or unwilling to sail filled French ports. Adding to this number were many British ships that had been captured by the French Navy. The surplus of ships in port and the need for ready money must have made for some great bargains, of which John Dabney appears to have taken advantage. By June, 1795, he was the part owner of 12 ships, mostly in partnership with a George Murray.[19]

He traveled back and forth between Paris and the port towns in France and made trips to the Caribbean and the United States checking the ship's cargo, making sure that one had a full crew and following up on various problems and opportunities. Given the strategic location of the Azores as a stopping-off point for trans-Atlantic travel, it would be surprising if John Dabney hadn't visited Faial on at least one of his trips across the ocean.

John Dabney was a tireless worker, an 18th-century workaholic. Because of the endless ideas he pursued, he had acquired the nickname of "*Monsieur Projet*"[20] among those best acquainted with him. "During these years was the golden opportunity for Americans and American vessels which J.B. Dabney improved and by it acquired a fortune".[21]

However, the ships that he owned were not allowed to fly the American flag, as the Committee of Commerce in Paris prohibited him from doing so. In a letter to his wife, John Dabney says, "The Committee of Commerce at Paris decreed last week that the Ships we had bought should not sail under American Colours".[22] In addition, American law did not allow American registration for ships bought overseas.[23] As a result, whenever he sailed he was at risk of attack from British warships, and more than one of his ships was captured or prevented from sailing from foreign ports where they had arrived. About 1796, his ship *Elizabeth* was captured and taken as a prize to Halifax, resulting in a major financial setback for John Dabney. Despite this, the excellent opportunities for American businessmen in France remained attractive and he soon recovered his losses.

With all the insecurity brought about by the conflict, the French were reluctant to get involved in business, and other Europeans were prohibited from engaging in business there. This left a big void with few willing to fill it other than astute, serious non-European businessmen like John Dabney.[24]

In mid-1796, he was back in Alexandria and a half-year later had packed up his wife, left his son Charles with one of Mrs. Dabney's sisters and departed to take up permanent residence in France.

> To escape some French cruisers, the ship on which [Roxa Dabney] went put into a port in England where grandmother excited great curiosity, being the first American the inhabitants had ever see, and they wondered at the whiteness of her skin and that she could speak English.[25]

The Dabney's second son, George, was born in Paris in 1797, but 20 months later he ran across a room and out onto an unprotected balcony from which he fell to his death.[26] Besides his personal grief, John Dabney had to cope with serious problems facing his business. The United States would not join France in the fight against England, refusing to take action against British ships and even going so far as to capture French naval raiders. This, understandably, resulted in equivalent retaliation during a period of undeclared war between France and the United States, which extended from 1798 through 1800.

> In 1798, France commenced bullying her new ally, the United States, and both she and England encroached on the rights of Americans during the European War – the French cruisers reaching the height of audacity, not only capturing British ships in American waters, but actually taking American vessels also.[27]

This laid a basis for the "French Claims" for which the United States asked payment from France and for which John Dabney's son Charles may have had an indirect hand in resolving about 40 years later when the heir to the French throne, the Prince de Joinville, visited Faial. During the Prince's visit, Charles Dabney carried on conversations with Monsieur Verneaux.

> M. Verneaux, as I before mentioned, is a member of the Chamber; in our first conversation he acknowledged that he was opposed to the treaty of indemnity, but previous to his departure, he confessed that he had been convinced of the justice of our claims, and that I might depend on his vote, and that of those over whom he had influence.[28]

The last year of the 18th century saw the disbanding of all of France's revolutionary councils and committees. Control of the country was taken over by three Consuls, the most important of these being the first Consul, Napoleon Bonaparte. Problems between France and Great Britain continued despite these changes and the Treaty of Paris in 1801 that produced a temporary cessation of hostilities.

This time peace did not last long. In 1803, Great Britain once again declared war against France and started seizing French ships on the open seas and in ports. Napoleon, who had himself crowned as Emperor in May 1804, did not just sit idly by. He started a hunt throughout France for British agents who were arrested, and many summarily executed.[29]

We don't know exactly what was going on with John Bass Dabney and his business during this period, but it is likely that he found himself caught between the warring powers. His ships would have been targets for British confiscation since they sailed under French colors. His business also would have been a focus of attention by the French who were seeking British sympathizers and did not discriminate between the countries of origin of native English speakers. Even if they did recognize the difference between Americans and British, the actions against French ships by the new American navy a few years earlier would have provided France with ample justification for seizing American property.[30]

Whatever actually did happen, the result was that John Bass Dabney's business was ruined, and he decided to leave France. As an astute businessman, he knew when to cut his losses and seek opportunities elsewhere. In the latter part of 1804, Mrs. Dabney departed Bordeaux for America, making a stopover in Plymouth, England.[31] She took with her young Charles, who had traveled to France alone in 1801, as well as the three younger children, Roxalina, John Lewis and Nancy, who had all been born in France.

At about the same time as his family sailed, John Bass departed on a different ship and in a different direction, passing through Lisbon and stopping in the Azores.[32] It is probable that this was not a chance visit. As we have seen, he had been involved in trans-Atlantic shipping and knew about these islands. He knew they were an important stopping point in order to supply ships with fresh food and water.

They were also havens from the Atlantic's often-brutal weather. Many ships sank near the Azores, including one in 1797 carrying Mr. Whiting, the husband of Beulah Lewis Whiting, one of Mrs. Dabney's older sisters. Many other ships suffered severe damage and had to stop there for repairs.

In addition to the advantages of their physical location, the Azores was controlled by Portugal, which was a neutral country. The Portuguese tried to keep on good terms with all parties and no ships were refused the opportunity to stop for fresh supplies and water. This was an obvious consideration for John Dabney after his experience in France, the neutrality of the Azores enhancing their commercial and strategic possibilities.

Of the nine islands in the archipelago, John Dabney chose Faial as his destination. The two westernmost islands, tiny *Corvo* (Raven) and beautiful *Flores* (Flowers) had no large population center or safe port. The two islands farthest east are *Santa Maria* (St. Mary), which did not have a good port, and *São Miguel* (St. Michael), the largest and most populated island in the chain. Its major city, Ponta Delgada, had an important port, however it was not well protected. São Miguel attracted visitors to its hot mineral water pools, provided most of the archipelago's exports and already had a small, but thriving, American community.

In the central group of five islands, *Graciosa* (Charming) had a small population and no good port, and *São Jorge* (St. George) was a long, narrow ridge whose steep slopes dropped practically straight down into the sea. *Terceira* (Third), the third island discovered, had a small protected port at the main town of Angra and was the center of the civil government. The remaining two islands were *Pico* (Peak), named for its magnificent 8,000 foot plus volcanic cone, but had no protected port, and Faial, named after the *Faia*, or Beech tree. The principal town of Faial is Horta, which was directly across a six-mile wide channel from Pico. It had a wide, semi-circular bay with high points of land at each end and provided the best protection for ships arriving in the archipelago.

It was here that John Bass Dabney arrived in late 1804 to stay until spring 1805, protected from the winter Atlantic seas and with time to consider the business possibilities there.[33] John Bass Dabney's ship sailed into the crescent-shaped Bay of Horta on the island of Faial. In front of him the town of Horta spread along the shore that swept from the massive sea cliff at the north end of the bay past the town to the small black, volcanic mound at the south end. About six miles east was the island of Pico with its massive, black… peak, the base of which is about twenty miles in circumference, and the mountain is one mile and three quarters in height. It is in the form of a sugar loaf, quite pointed at the top, in which there is a crater frequently sending forth columns of smoke, and sometimes flames. It is the most majestic sight I ever beheld.[34]

When John Dabney arrived there were few other ships at anchor because it was late in the year to challenge the North Atlantic weather. The small town hugged the shore, not extending far up the green hills covered with cultivated fields. Above the initial rise, the land levels out into a broad, rich agricultural area crossed by a small river. The area is named Flamengos after the Flemish farmers brought to Faial in the 15th century who settled in this area.

Protruding from the shore in the center of the town was a small stone fortress, which obviously was not of recent construction.

Next to the fortress the shore sloped gently down to the water and the residents pulled their boats up onto it. When not working, men gathered here exchanging gossip while looking at the ships that entered the bay.

After John Dabney's ship entered the bay, it furled its sails, glided to a halt and dropped anchor. Almost at the same time a longboat bumped up alongside the ship and a rope was thrown down, followed by a rope ladder. An official representing the local bureaucracy climbed on board, and, after what seemed to most foreigners like excessive paperwork and questions, a perpetual complaint about the Portuguese bureaucracy, the passengers were cleared to land.

Most of the town's buildings had two to four stories with smaller houses scattered among the farms on the hill. The buildings in the center of town near the fortress were somewhat higher, but the largest buildings in Horta were the churches that dominated several sections of the town. Their bell towers extended high above the surrounding homes, and some of the churches had massive convent or monastery buildings attached to them.

While they were waiting, the passengers and crew had an opportunity to look around at their destination. On the hill behind the town, rows of small houses marked the location of roads, which went over the top to villages in the interior near Faial's green-covered volcanic peak. The hills joined together toward the right into a ridge whose steep sides were terraced to provide additional land necessary for crops. The patchwork of different crops, vines and trees, each with their own green, was a marvel for John Bass who was used to seeing the ground covered with a blanket of white at this time of year.

Life changed slowly on Faial. As a result, the landscape that Roxana Lewis Dabney describes in her *Annals of the Dabney Family* almost a century after her great-grandfather John Bass Dabney had first arrived, and was probably very close to the one he was used to seeing every day., In fact, some of the locations she describes can still be recognized today.

Intersecting portions of the Islands are low gray stone walls, built to enclose gardens, or to divide off the fields of corn, wheat and Lupin. In the crevices of these walls grow ferns and mosses, and often one sees the tiny red fuchsia clambering over them as if it were a vine.

In the uplands there are masses of heath and heather, while the Genestra (Scotch broom) falls in golden showers by the roadsides. On the northern slopes above Ribeirinha and Cedros are miles of Hydrangea hedges, often twenty feet high. The flower heads are a real cerulean blue, and in the luxuriance nearly hide all green leaves. From Pico, five miles off, one can in July and August discern blue lines running up the Fayal valley and it is hard to believe that they are just masses of flowers.[35]

The boat that had come out to the ship ferried John Bass Dabney to shore, and he set foot on Faial for the first time. There is no documentation describing how he chose Faial as his destination among the nine islands, but given his profession as wine exporter, it is likely that he knew of the island of Pico's reputation for fine wines, which had to be shipped from Faial because of Pico's lack of a safe port. Perhaps it was because the Bay of Faial provided the safest port among the nine islands. Whatever the reason, after having lost his fortune in France he needed to find a less risky course to follow, and he began a visit during which he investigated what the island had to offer.

In February 1805, after he had been on Faial for a few months, John Dabney wrote a letter to Mr. Jesse Putnam, a friend in Boston for "the want of something better to occupy me."[36] In his description of Faial and its main city of Horta, there wasn't much about the people or the way of life that appealed to him.

He was not pleased with the food. Not because of the quality of the products grown or raised and purchased in the marketplace, he just didn't think they knew how to cook very well.

The soil here is quite prolific, most of your garden stuffs and fruits are produced here, and a considerable number that you have not in New England, their poultry and fresh fish are extremely abundant, and tolerably good, eggs, butter, milk, and cream cheeses plenty, and the butchers meats passable, but these people have no idea of uniting the requisites for a comfortable table.[37]

John Dabney was also not very impressed with the cleanliness of the kitchens in Horta, and from his description it's surprising he would eat at all. "If you ever want a strong simile to express the utmost degree of filth and nastiness, speak with confidence of a Portuguese kitchen, and utensils, the cooks, and the cookery."[38]

Even the local table wines did not do anything to improve the meal because "their small wines are generally [sour]."[39] This opinion about the wine was probably limited to the table wines, particularly those produced on Faial since the wine produced and exported from Pico already had a good reputation. Pico's *verdelho* is a semi-dry wine very similar to the *verdelho* variety of Madeira wine, both produced from the same variety of grape. John Dabney's opinion of it must have been better than of Faial's wines because it is not likely that he would decide to export and later develop his own vineyards to produce a wine he did not like.

His comments on the language were also far from flattering. "The Portuguese language is disgusting to a foreigner. I should despise a man that would undertake to learn a syllable of it."[40] This may have been why John Dabney never really learned Portuguese. His granddaughter Roxa said he did all his business in English "for he never mastered this language, even if he tried which I doubt, and he spoke it very badly and probably could not write it."[41] This was not true of his children and grandchildren and makes one wonder at what point he decided not to "despise" those who learned Portuguese. The answer is most likely when its value in negotiating business became clear.

He did not even find the music to his taste. "Their music is a dull monotony of inharmonious sounds, and except some passable harpsichords and spinets their musical instruments are most barbarous, and the music beneath that of the banjos of the Virginian Negroes."[42]

However, none of his feelings kept him from getting involved with the social life on Faial during his visit on the island. He was invited to a number of "tea sips" and balls where he was able to meet the upper levels of society on Faial. This was a mixture of foreigners, involved in some kind of merchant activity, and Portuguese, who lived on their titles. Of the *Morgados*, or Portuguese nobility, he thought, "There are no people on the face of the earth more tenacious of family distinctions, not even the nobility of Italy, some of whom you know have scarcely clothes to their backs."[43]

Other than on social occasions, it is unlikely that he had much to do with the Morgados. This would not have been his choice, but rather theirs since they considered themselves a cut above the merchant class. As for the wives and daughters of the *Morgado's*, "The dresses of the ladies here surprised me...(tho' they parade rather too much finery) their dresses are elegant. They wear their own hair curled in ringlets over their foreheads in a very becoming manner, and their caps and bonnets, tho' made by themselves, resemble very much the French taste." However, "They are seldom seen abroad, but on some festival, public or private." Nor did the men get about much. "The enjoyment of fresh air and exercise abroad, these people, male or female, have not the slightest notion of, never stirring out of their houses but on urgent occasions." If they did go out, however, "There are four or five coaches and cabriolets, but so antique in their construction, they look like "*Anno Domini*" itself. The principal mode of conveyance in paying visits is in sedan chairs, and there is not a genteel family without one."[44]

Rose Dabney gives a more specific description of the classes of people living on Faial.

> The inhabitants of the Azores may be said to be divided into three classes, viz., first (and not necessarily best) the aristocrats, who are usually educated in Lisbon or Paris, proud of being "real blue bloods", and usually averse to much work; second the poorer townspeople who have a certain amount of schooling, but early turn to shopkeeping and other trades; and last, but not least, the peasants, who are to be found in all the villages, and who, with their modest ways, their devotion to friends, and hospitality to strangers, are especially attractive.

(...)
One sees fine looking women with great loads on their heads walking off like queens; oxcarts trundling along over the cobble stones; men, women, and children riding on donkeys (the only means of locomotion excepting for 'shanks mare'); and young boys bearing aloft baskets of fruit.[45]

One of the few things that he did find agreeable were the houses which he thought were "very comfortable for a mild climate. They are built of stone, 2, 3 and some few 4 stories high. The ground floor which I count as one, is occupied by Warehouses, wine cellars, etc."[46] Many of the houses also had a type of wooden screen over their windows facing the street so that the women could observe what was going on without being seen. Rose points out they also had "red tiled roofs" and that many of the more well-to-do natives cover their stones with plaster, tinted in white, pink, or blue."[47]

Since "there is no such thing as an inn or a boarding house in these islands," it was necessary for him to stay as a guest in a home. He enjoyed very much the one he stayed in, which was one of the very large houses, with 128-foot frontage and a depth of 80 feet, near the center of town.[48]

From the tone of his comments about Horta and its inhabitants, it seems surprising that John Bass Dabney even considered returning to Faial, let alone living there. Any ordinary person would not have even thought of going back to some place that they did not find pleasing. However, John Dabney was a man of vision. He knew what he wanted, and he could see the opportunities that existed within the problems and disagreeable situations. He was a man who loved his family and believed that the best thing he could do for them was to be successful in what he did. During his short stay on Faial, he obviously found a situation that presented him with some opportunities that far outweighed any problems he might have had with the way of life there.

Notes:

[1] *Petit Larousse Dictionaire*, Librarie Larousse, Paris, 1989, p. 1100.

[2] *Petit Larousse Dictionaire*, Librarie Larousse, Paris, 1989, p. 1401 & p. 1412.

[3] Roxana Lewis Dabney, *Annals of the Dabney Family in Fayal*, comp., n. p.: The Author, 1900, p. 678-679.

[4] "Descendency from Norman knight", *Virginia Magazine*, vol XLV, nº 2, April 1937, p. 128.

[5] Developed from several sites on the internet and personal communication.

[6] Francis L. Dabney, *Sketch of John Bass Dabney by his son William Henry Dabney of Boston, 1887*, comp., n. p.: The Author, 1971, p. 116-117.

[7] Roxana Lewis Dabney, *Annals*, Annals, p. 2.

[8] Francis L. Dabney, *Sketch*, p. 3.

[9] Francis L. Dabney, *Sketch*, p. 118.

[10] Francis L. Dabney, *Sketch*, p. 5.

[11] Francis L. Dabney, *Sketch*, p. 4-6.

[12] Roxana Lewis Dabney, *Annals*, p. 9.

[13] Francis L. Dabney, *Sketch*, p. 8-9.

[14] Francis L. Dabney, *Sketch*, p. 12.

[15] Francis L. Dabney, *Sketch*, p. 25.

[16] Francis L. Dabney, *Sketch*, p. 12.

[17] Roxana Lewis Dabney, *Annals*, p. 6.

[18] Roxana Lewis Dabney, *Annals*, p. 6.

[19] Francis L. Dabney, *Sketch*, p. 12-21.

[20] Roxana Lewis Dabney, *Annals*, p. 8.

[21] Francis L. Dabney, *Sketch*, p. 26.

[22] Francis L. Dabney, *Sketch*, p. 27.

[23] Francis L. Dabney, *Sketch*, p 27.

[24] Francis L. Dabney, *Sketch*, p. 25.

[25] Roxana Lewis Dabney, *Annals*, p. 9.

[26] Francis L. Dabney, *Sketch*, p. 24-25.

[27] Francis L. Dabney, *Sketch*, p. 26.

[28] Roxana Lewis Dabney, *Annals*, p. 356.

[29] Francis L. Dabney, *Sketch*, p. 27.

[30] Francis L. Dabney, *Sketch*, p. 26-27.

[31] Francis L. Dabney, *Sketch*, p. 27.

[32] Francis L. Dabney, *Sketch*, p. 28.

[33] Francis L. Dabney, *Sketch*, p. 28.

[34] Francis L. Dabney, *Sketch*, p. 32; Roxana Lewis Dabney, *Annals*, p. 14.

[35] Dabney, Rose Forbes, *Fayal Dabneys*, n.p.: The Author, 1931, p. 42-3.

[36] Francis L. Dabney, *Sketch*, p. 29; Roxana Lewis Dabney, *Annals*, p. 11.

[37] Francis L. Dabney, *Sketch*, p. 29; Roxana Lewis Dabney, *Annals*, p. 12.

[38] Francis L. Dabney, *Sketch*, p. 30.

[39] Francis L. Dabney, *Sketch*, p. 29; Roxana Lewis Dabney, *Annals*, p. 12.

[40] Francis L. Dabney, *Sketch*, p. 30.

[41] Francis L. Dabney, *Sketch*, p. 38.

[42] Francis L. Dabney, *Sketch*, p. 30.

[43] Francis L. Dabney, *Sketch*, p. 30; Roxana Lewis Dabney, *Annals*, p. 12-13.

[44] Francis L. Dabney, *Sketch*, p 31; Roxana Lewis Dabney, *Annals*, p. 13.

[45] Dabney, Rose Forbes, *Fayal Dabneys*, p. 43-4.

[46] Roxana Lewis Dabney, *Annals*, p. 13

[47] Dabney, Rose Forbes, *Fayal Dabneys*, p. 43.

[48] Francis L. Dabney, *Sketch*, p. 31; Roxana Lewis Dabney, *Annals*, p. 13

2 – GETTING SETTLED

When John Bass Dabney left Faial and arrived back in Boston in May or June of 1805, he set about doing what was necessary to establish himself in business on Faial, and he most surely contacted the friends and associates with whom he had conducted business over the years. He knew a good number of merchants in Boston from his years in business there, and in France, and it is not likely that the problems with his business in France would have affected these connections. They had dealt with him, had received the exports he sent and knew he was an honest, reliable man. He could not be blamed for the vagaries of war and governments.

His stay in Faial had given him a good idea of what he could export from there and what kinds of products he could send from the United States on the return voyage to sell on the islands. The company he established was for exporting wine, specifically the *verdelho* from the island of Pico. This wine was an international favorite at the time and considered superior to the Madeira variety, but is virtually unknown today except on the islands of Faial and Pico.

John Dabney was perceptive enough to realize that representing the United States in the Azores as Consul would benefit him in his commercial activities on Faial. American merchants liked doing business with someone who had both good business and government connections. Because of this, he took advantage of the fact that U. S. Consuls in the early 19th century could have their own business and perform the functions of Consul at the same time. In addition, the high status and respect accorded him by the people on Faial as the representative of the United States would have taken much longer to attain if he were just a businessman, if he could have attained it at all.

Until John Dabney's appointment as U. S. Consul in Horta, the Azores, or "Western Islands" as they were then called, had a system of American diplomatic representation as poorly organized as the new nation. American Consulate offices were located on the three main islands of São Miguel, Terceira and Faial and were responsible to the Lisbon Consulate.[1] The The U. S. representative on Faial was John Street, who had been appointed by George Washington.[2] He was of English descent[3] and claimed to have been serving in this position since 1790.[4]

On the island of São Miguel, the Vice-Consul was Thomas Hickling, Sr., who had been appointed to this position on July 7, 1795 by John Street.[5] Thomas Hickling was an American who arrived on São Miguel in 1769 to set up business.[6] He had been a U. S. envoy since the Second Continental Congress, as well as during the Articles of Confederation, and at the time of Dabney's arrival was one of the richest men in the Azores.[7] Soon after John Dabney arrived in Faial he visited São Miguel and befriended Thomas Hickling. The Dabneys and Hicklings developed a friendly, close relationship, which resulted in two of John Dabney's grandsons marrying two of Hickling's granddaughters.

In the fall of 1805, John Dabney made application to the United States government "for the Office, of Consul General, for the United States at the Western Islands,"[8] as well as requesting that the post be upgraded to a full consulate. It is likely that John Dabney contacted a couple of uncles who were part of the Virginia branch of the Dabney family for help in supporting his application.[9]

As described in Chapter 1, the Boston and Virginia branches of the Dabney family both claimed descent from a Huguenot family that had fled France for England in the late 17th century. However, after their arrival in the two different parts of America in the early 18th century they had virtually no contact with each other.[10] The Dabneys in Virginia were influential and knew their fellow Virginian Thomas Jefferson, who was President of the United States at the time. Whether they actually influenced the decision or not, John Bass Dabney was appointed the first Consul for the United States in the Azores in 1806. Today it is the oldest continuously active United States Consular post in the world.[11]

Before John Dabney's appointment was finalized, however, it appears likely that he made at least one other trip to the Azores because Roxana Dabney's *Annals* reports that he was making another return to the U.S from Horta in April 1806. On his return he stopped in Baltimore and sent a letter to the State Department saying that he was going to return to Faial in June or July and asking if he could receive his appointment as Consul before he went.[12]

The State Department must have paid attention to his request because he received his appointment in June 1806. In August he arrived back in Faial with his mandate and immediately set about getting a place to live and arranging for warehouse space and wine cellars near the quay for the exportation of Pico wine. However, everything did not run smoothly for him.

Shortly after arriving in Horta, John Dabney called on Vice-Consul John Street and informed him of his appointment and that he would be assuming the position as Consul. Street was obviously not pleased at this turn of events. In a letter to the State Department, John Dabney wrote, "He gave me to understand that he should not give up the Office until my appointment had been sanctioned, by the Court of Portugal".[13] Dabney quickly forwarded his Commission to the Lisbon Embassy for them to apply for his Exequatur, the authorization from a country's head of state to perform diplomatic functions there.

Delays in getting anything done with the Portuguese government were common. Mr. Jarvis, the U.S. Ambassador in Lisbon said his own papers had taken five months to process, and this was without the delays resulting from sending them by ship. Because of this, John Dabney went to the island of Terceira, seat of the civil government in the Azores, and met with the Civil Governor. He requested that he be given a *pro tem* appointment as Consul, but this was rejected and he was told to be patient. The Governor General's advice was reasonable, but hard to comply with for a straightforward, no-nonsense American businessman anxious to get started and resolve the situation of a hostile Vice-Consul.

Eight months later, in April 1807, he still had not received his Commission, although he had indications that it was on its way in the mail. At this point, he wrote a letter in which he stated, "This delay [in having his appointment as Consul accepted] has been highly injurious to some of our citizens".[14] The basis for this statement were problems created by actions that John Street had taken both before John Dabney's arrival and after he had arrived. He wrote a communique to the State Department about the situation and in it implies that he had been aware of the way Mr. Street acted even before applying to be Consul.

> I can now say freely, to Your Excellency (what perhaps it would have been improper for me to say when soliciting this office), that Mr. Street's conduct, for many years past, has exhibited one continued scene of Dilapidation, & Pillage, of American Property. This first is notorious to all Fayal, as well as to many individuals, in the U. States.[15]

This situation had apparently been going on for a while as also indicated by letters sent to the State Department in previous years by other people.[16]

There were three situations during 1806 that demonstrated how Mr. Street carried out his duties as Vice-Consul in Horta. The first began in April just before John Dabney's arrival.

The American ship *Acteon*, with Captain Dryburgh as master, was on its way from Philadelphia to Cadiz, Spain, with a cargo of flour when it put into Horta to repair a leak. After the flour was unloaded to allow for the repairs, the local government decided they needed it to feed the population since Faial was going through one of its periodic famines. They offered Captain Dryburgh $11 per barrel, a price he refused because it was below market price. In order to help the Captain, John Street, as the U.S. representative, went to court a few days later and demanded the money. It was given to him, but he then turned around and, instead of giving it to the Captain, used it for his own purposes.

Captain Dryburgh was very displeased with this and attempted to obtain legal redress on Faial, but was unsuccessful. He then filed a formal complaint with the Embassy in Lisbon. Street learned of this and did what he could to defeat the claim. Unfortunately, even if Captain Dryburgh had been able to win the decision, he would still have lost because Mr. Street had already used the money and had no way to pay it back.[17]

A few months later, the American ship *Pomona*, on its way from Amsterdam to New York, put into the Bay of Horta in distress. The ship was declared unseaworthy and, along with part of its cargo, was sold at auction at sacrifice prices. One of the buyers was Street, even though he should have been looking out for the captain's best interest and helping him get a good price rather than looking for a good buy for himself.

When a ship arrived that could take what remained of the *Pomona's* cargo, Street found a way to prevent it from being shipped. This kept it within his grasp and also protected him from having to pay the balance of the money he owed the owners of the *Pomona*. To add insult to injury, he had given a note for the purchase of the cargo instead of paying in cash and wanted to end up with both the cargo and the money.[18]

Even seamen missing at sea were fair game for Mr. Street. A Captain Nicholas Smith sailed to Boston leaving several trunks of dry goods on deposit with Street, although he took the keys and invoices with him. A few months later, it was learned that the Captain and his ship had disappeared at sea. Shortly after this information had arrived, Street broke the trunks open and sold the contents on his own account.[19]

John Dabney was frustrated in his attempts to control John Street and to make sure that the office of Consul was carried out properly and ethically. In a letter to the State Department, he said:

> Mr. Street declares that my Commission of Consul does not invalidate his of Vice Consul whenever I am out of this Island – and I foresee that He will give me much trouble, by assuming the office of Consul, whenever my Consular duties, as my own concerns, call me to Terceira, or St. Michael, even for a few weeks...[20]

On May 1, 1807, notice came that John Street had died at his home on the island of Pico.[21] However, this did not completely settle John Dabney's problems with his adversary. That same day John Dabney presented a petition to the Juiz da Fora, the judge in Horta, to be appointed Consul *pro tem.* The judge asked to see the documents appointing him to the position, and they were delivered the same day. Several days passed, and John Dabney remained at home sick, but no response was forthcoming from the judge until the morning of May 12 when a friend, Mr. William Greaves, visited Dabney at home.

Mr. Greaves informed him that the judge had issued an order to arrest John Dabney because there was an erasure on the document of appointment. Dabney knew that there were erasures in the document when he received it and recognized that it was simply an error in writing. Erasures were not uncommon and impossible to hide because the ink had to be scraped off the paper leaving an unmistakable mark. John Dabney considered it "a thing of no consequence, as it was well known that I was not an imposter, but an agent of the United States".[22]

On his way to Dabney's home, Mr. Greaves had gone to see Senhor Thomas Ignácio, a good friend of the judge, who had verified that such an order had been issued. Thomas Ignácio told Mr. Greaves that he wasn't going to give the arrest order to the officer to carry out until he had spoken to John Dabney since "matters could be arranged".[23]

Thomas Ignácio arrived at John Dabney's home that afternoon and repeated what Mr. Greaves had said. No arguments, statements of logic or offers of further proof of his right to be Consul had any effect on Thomas Ignácio. "He told me that by the laws of Portugal a Public instrument being so erased was a condemnation in itself, that no evidence could be heard in mitigation, or could be of any avail."[24]

Thomas Ignácio said that the judge believed John Dabney to be an honest man and was prepared not to carry out the sentence on certain terms. These terms had nothing to do with the "crime," but involved a monetary settlement, which, if paid, "the Judge and he would always be my friends," and they would help him all they could. If the money wasn't paid, "the Judge would take any occasion to vex and harass" him.[25]

John Dabney's reaction to this blatant request for a bribe was outrage, and he threatened to denounce the scoundrels. He took a while to calm down and then consider the situation. It was obvious to him that the judge was capable of finding a way to create legal problems and could even have him put in prison until he was accepted as American Consul by Lisbon or could make an appeal to the Regional Government. John Dabney, who was still ill, decided his best option was to listen to Thomas Ignácio's proposal. The next morning they met again, with Mr. Greaves present, and had several more meetings over a period of almost three weeks. John Dabney felt he was bargaining "as I would with a highwayman who had his pistol at my breast."[26] They finally reached a compromise where John Dabney was to pay Thomas Ignácio about $94 in merchandise and to give the judge a note for about $300. For this, the judge would be his "friend" and name him Consul, a promise that was kept immediately.[27]

Within a week after that John Dabney wrote a formal letter of complaint, part of which was quoted above about the actions of the judge and Thomas Ignácio, and indicated that he would try to avoid paying the note. This whole incident lost its importance when Dabney's Exequatur arrived from Lisbon the next month.[28]

It finally looked as if the problems had been resolved for the most part, and life on Faial could proceed normally for John Dabney. He had established his Counting Room near the Custom House; his offices were not far away, and his business was ready to take off; he had rented a home high on the hill above the northern part of the town across from Santo António church, "D. Teresa's place"[29]; he was American Consul for the Azores; and, possibly more important than the rest, his family was soon to arrive.

In September 1807, Mrs. Dabney and the four children arrived on Faial.[30] The family was now one child larger than it had been when they left France with the addition of George, who had been born in Dedham, Massachusetts. He was two years old on his arrival in Faial and had been given the name of the infant son who had died in France.

After having spent more than a year alone in Horta, John Dabney must have been delighted with the arrival of his family. Now their life on Faial could begin in earnest. Mrs. Dabney, who was noted for her efficiency and industriousness, immediately set about getting her household organized and her family settled in the residence at Santo António, "beautifully situated on the top of a hill, overlooking the town of Horta."[31] He described it as "a very comfortable house situated upon an elevation and six acres of gardens filled with tropical and other fruits, a beautiful and romantic place only ten minutes walk from the Custom House."[32]

Roxa Dabney set about getting her family established in life on the island while John Dabney continued his Consular activities on Faial and the other islands in the archipelago. On two of the islands he appointed Vice-Consuls to assist him: his friend Thomas Hickling, Sr., on the island of São Miguel and Mr. William Riggs on the island of Terceira.[33] Hickling had been in charge of the consular post on São Miguel since his appointment by John Street in 1795; however, the appointment had never been forwarded to Lisbon nor had it ever been recognized by the Portuguese crown, a fact which created a problem for John Dabney in 1830.[34]

John Dabney still had not been able to rid himself of the specter of John Street, which hung over him in the form of the ship *Pomona*. Part of the ship's cargo remained after the forced unloading and sacrifice sale, in which Mr. Street had participated as noted previously, and Horta's Customs House was still holding it for uncollected duties. Despite the fact that the cargo had been unloaded only because of massive damage to the ship, the Customs House considered it had been imported into Portugal and would not release it for shipment to its original destination of New York. John Dabney argued against the payment of duties on the cargo. He said its importation was forced by the need to repair the damage to the ship, and it had never been intended for import into Portugal. After much arguing, he succeeded in getting the cargo released, had it loaded onto another ship and finally forwarded to its destination. He also got a foretaste of what it was going to be like dealing with the local bureaucracy.[35]

While life was going on in the relative tranquility of the Azores, the unrest that was affecting much of Europe finally arrived full force in Portugal. The French Army under General Androche Junot marched across Spain and occupied Portugal in order to enforce Napoleon's demands for Portugal to close its ports to British ships. For several years the French had sent a number of requests, demands and threats to the Portuguese, all of which had been refused. Portugal had continually asserted that its position of neutrality allowed the country to deal and trade with whomever it wanted. Napoleon was not pleased with this situation and decided to do something to shut this open door for British ships on the European continent.

Portugal, for its part, was trapped between the fear of a French invasion and a commitment it felt toward its "Oldest Ally." The Portuguese and British had signed a mutual defense treaty, the Treaty of Windsor, in May 1386, ten months after English soldiers and longbowmen under John of Gaunt, the Duke of Lancaster, had aided Portuguese troops in their victory over the Castillians at the Battle of Aljubarrota. This battle assured that Portuguese independence would not be threatened again for almost two centuries and the treaty laid the basis for a long-term alliance. The relationship between the two countries and Royal families was further solidified by the marriage of John of Gaunt's daughter, Phillipa of Lancaster, to Portugal's King João I. This royal couple had several children who became famous, the most notable being Henry the Navigator.

There have been many ups and downs in the relations between the two countries over the centuries, but the treaty is still in effect today, the oldest treaty existing between two countries. The sense of moral obligation derived from the treaty has resulted in mutual support during times of crisis. In addition, strong commercial ties, most notably Port wine and textiles, have enhanced the political and moral ties between the two countries.

When the French entered Portugal in November 1807, the British advised the Portuguese that, despite the treaty, they could not defend them militarily. They suggested that the Royal family depart to Brazil, a Portuguese colony since Pedro Álvares Cabral had landed there in 1500. The Prince-Regent João, who was also

Prince of Brazil, had governed Portugal for several years because his mother, Queen Maria I, was incapable of ruling the country. She was subject to fits of melancholy and nightmares, including an obsession that she had been damned. João followed the recommendations of the British Ambassador, as well as those of his own advisors, and loaded his family, the court and a number of retainers into fifteen ships and sailed to Brazil. He remained there with the court until 1821 when he returned to Portugal as King João VI.

General Junot was upset that the Portuguese Royal family had fled before he arrived, but he had achieved Napoleon's goal. With the French takeover of the country the British were no longer welcome, and all Portuguese ports, except for those in the Azores, were closed to British ships. This action was noted in a letter in December 1807 from John Dabney to James Madison, who was then Secretary of State.

> Information has reached the authorities here from the Government of Portugal of the actual shutting of their Ports against the British Flag, but it is confidently asserted here, that these Islands are to enjoy a kind of Neutrality. Several English vessels are now quietly loading and unloading as in time of profound Peace.[36]

The year 1808 started off sadly for the Dabney family. Roxalina, who was nine, was playing and carrying her 2$^1/_2$ year old brother George piggyback. Suddenly he fell, hitting the ground hard. He seemed not to have been seriously hurt, but that night when his brother Charles was bringing him to the table for dessert as he usually did, George went into convulsions. Over the next few days he had repeated attacks of convulsions. He finally recovered from the seizures, but it was found that his mental abilities were permanently damaged. With no way to give him adequate care on Faial, his parents sent George to Mr. Burnett, a businessman who had moved from São Miguel to England, in August 1809.

> I send in this vessel my poor little son George in the hope that some relief may be found for his disorder either in England

or in Scotland. My former servant José Maria goes with the child, and will accompany him to any place you may designate.[37]

George never returned to Faial and remained in an asylum in Britain where he died in 1822 at the age of seventeen.[38]

The month of May 1808 literally opened with a bang when the volcano on the island of São Jorge erupted. The islands of the Azores archipelago, with the exception of Santa Maria, are volcanic in origin, and periodic earthquakes are constant reminders of this. Although eruptions are an ever-present threat on the islands, they are few and far between, but when they occur, they are a sight viewers never forget.

The island of São Jorge is approximately 20 miles northeast of Faial, and its long, narrow ridge of mountains is easily visible from Horta on clear days. At about 1:00 p.m. on May 1, John Dabney was on the balcony of his house. Hearing booming sounds in the distance, he looked out to sea expecting to find a naval battle in progress. Instead, he saw a column of smoke rising from the center of São Jorge. That night the red glow of the material thrown out of the volcano and the streams of lava that could be seen descending to the sea verified that it was a volcano.

This spectacular event was described in a report that John Dabney wrote and sent to President Thomas Jefferson.[39] In it he describes his visit to São Jorge two days after the eruption with his 13-year old son Charles, the British Consul and a few friends, so they could get a close-up view of "this wonderful exertion of nature." They arrived at Velas, the main town on the island, and found the inhabitants "perfectly panic-struck and entirely given to religious ceremonies and devotions."

The group traveled toward the southeast from Velas for a few miles to where the crater, which covered about 24 acres, was located. The volcano had thrown out a large amount of cinders that, because of the north wind, covered much of the island's rich agricultural land south of it. Because of the strength of the wind, some of the cinders and ash had even reached as far as the island of Pico about 10 miles away. By the time the group from Horta got to São Jorge, the volcano's activity had subsided somewhat. Even so, John Dabney and his fellow adventurers were blocked from visiting it by the "sulphurous smoke it exuded."

However, a second, smaller crater had begun erupting to the north of the first and somewhat closer to Velas, and the group decided to visit it. As they walked toward their destination, they "found the earth rent in every direction" and had to jump over or find ways around the chasms that had opened up. In later years Charles Dabney told his family "about jumping back and forth, over the streams of running lava"[40] during his visit to São Jorge. They got to within about 200 yards of the smaller crater.

> The mouth of it appeared to be about fifty yards only in circumference, the fire seemed to be struggling for vent, the force with which a pale flame issued forth resembled a powerful steam-engine multiplied a hundred fold. The noise was deafening, the earth where we stood had a tremulous motion, the whole island seemed convulsed. Horrid bellowings were occasionally heard from the bowels of the earth and earthquakes were frequent.[41]

The dauntless volcano explorers returned to the town of Velas where they spent the night. Most of the town's residents were frightened of more earthquakes and had moved out of their homes and were living in tents. The visitors from Faial got up the next day, after what was probably not a very relaxed night's sleep, and set off by boat down the coast to the town of Urselina, located in an area which was being covered in cinders. Even today the results of the volcanic activity can still be seen here, and modern Urselina is built over the layer of lava and cinders through which the square tower of a church sticks out of the ground and acts as a tombstone for the former Urselina completely covered by the volcanic activity.

That same day the group of visitors returned to Faial. During the next few days on São Jorge, more craters opened, Their activity gradually died down, but then the main crater once again "burst forth like a roaring lion with horrible belchings distinctly heard 12 leagues distant, throwing up prodigious stones and lava and illuminating at night the whole island." The view from Faial at night must have been sensational with "the awful yet magnificent spectacle of a perfect river of fire running into the sea." After all was over, the crater on São Jorge was about 3,500 feet high. The town of Urselina had virtually disappeared, and around sixty persons had been injured or killed by the volcano. "In short this island heretofore rich in cattle, corn and wine for exportation, is nearly ruined and a scene of greater desolation and distress has seldom been witnessed in any country."

John Dabney sent the report he wrote describing the volcanic eruption on São Jorge and its effects along with a sample of lava and cinders to President Jefferson. Because of the Embargo Act of 1807, however, direct contact with the United States was not possible, and the document and accompanying material had to be sent by an indirect route. He also sent a copy to a friend on the island of São Miguel who deceived him and sent it to England where it was published in London before the original had reached Jefferson. Needless to say, John Dabney felt betrayed by this action, especially since it was by someone he had considered a friend, an affront he never forgot.[42]

Thirteen-year old Charles Dabney's education on Faial was not limited to visiting volcanoes and leaping over fiery chasms. He had been boarded with a Dr. Roque so that he could learn the Portuguese language. John Dabney had obviously changed the opinion that he had expressed when he first arrived about despising anyone who would learn Portuguese.[43] Charles had already become quite fluent in French during the years the family lived in France and soon was fluent in both spoken and written Portuguese. Throughout his life he was recognized and respected for his multilingual skills.

However, his education on Faial was not considered sufficient. Therefore, on May 20, not long after the eruption had subsided, Charles Dabney was sent by his family to a Mr. Wheaton in the United States to serve "as an apprentice to learn business in his counting room".[44] This was the usual way to prepare a young man for entering a career in business during the early 19th century among families like the Dabneys. In addition to teaching Charles business skills, Mr. Wheaton was charged with watching over his morals and was asked to find a handwriting teacher. His father felt that "[b]y changing from French to American and Portuguese masters, he has lost his handwriting".

Charles Dabney's future activities show that there is no question he learned excellent skills in business and developed an exemplary moral life. However, his handwriting always left something to be desired. Anyone who has worked with the original documents written by Charles Dabney can attest to this. Even his daughter Roxana, who wrote the family annals, found "his microscopic handwriting so hard to decipher at times."[45]

Notes:

[1] Francis L. Dabney, *Sketch*, p. 33.

[2] Consul William F. Doty, American Consular Service: St. Michael's Azores, "Copy of the Historical Sketch of Office transmitted to the Dept. Under Cover of Consulate's Despatch Nº 402", Feb. 29, 1928, p. 1.

[3] Francis L. Dabney, *Sketch*, p. 33.

[4] Document 6, United States Archives, Microfilm T203, Roll 1, March 4, 1795-November 28, 1832.

[5] Consul William F. Doty, p. 1.

[6] Francis M. Rogers, *Atlantic Islanders of the Azores and Madeira*, Christopher Publishing House, Hanover, MA, p. 145.

[7] Personal communication, U.S. Consul David Scott, São Miguel, Azores.

[8] "Applications and Recommendations for Public Office 1801-1869" (photocopy), United States Archives, Baltimore, April 24, 1806.

[9] Francis L. Dabney, *Sketch*, p. 1.

[10] Francis L. Dabney, *Sketch*, p. 1.

[11] "Commemorating the two hundredth anniversary of United States-Portuguese diplomatic relations" 102d Congress, 1st Session, S.J.Res 55.

[12] "Applications and Recommendations for Public Office 1801-1869" (photocopy), United States Archives, Baltimore, April 24, 1806.

[13] Document 11, United States Archives, Microfilm T203, Roll 1, March 4, 1795-November 28, 1832.

[14] Document 11 United States Archives, Microfilm T203, Roll 1, March 4, 1795-November 28, 1832.

[15] Document 11, United States Archives, Microfilm T203, Roll 1, March 4, 1795-November 28, 1832.

[16] Documents 3 and 7, United States Archives, Microfilm T203, Roll 1, March 4, 1795-November 28, 1832.

[17] Document 11, United States Archives, Microfilm T203, Roll 1, March 4, 1795-November 28, 1832.

[18] Document 11, United States Archives, Microfilm T203, Roll 1, March 4, 1795-November 28, 1832.

[19] Document 11, United States Archives, Microfilm T203, Roll 1, March 4, 1795-November 28, 1832.

[20] Document 11, United States Archives, Microfilm T203, Roll 1, March 4, 1795-November 28, 1832.

[21] Roxana Lewis Dabney, *Annals of the Dabney Family in Fayal*, comp., n. p.: The Author, 1900, p. 16

[22] Roxana Lewis Dabney, *Annals*, p. 16; Francis L. Dabney, *Sketch*, p. 34.

[23] Roxana Lewis Dabney, *Annals*, p. 17; Francis L. Dabney, *Sketch*, p. 35.

[24] Roxana Lewis Dabney, *Annals*, p. 17; Francis L. Dabney, *Sketch*, p. 35.

[25] Roxana Lewis Dabney, *Annals*, p. 17; Francis L. Dabney, *Sketch*, p. 35.

[26] Roxana Lewis Dabney, *Annals*, p. 18; Francis L. Dabney, *Sketch*, p. 35.

[27] Roxana Lewis Dabney, *Annals*, p. 18; Francis L. Dabney, *Sketch*, p. 35.

[28] Francis L. Dabney, *Sketch*, p. 37.

[29] Francis L. Dabney, *Sketch*, p. 37.

[30] Francis L. Dabney, *Sketch*, p. 38.

[31] Roxana Lewis Dabney, *Annals*, p. 41.

[32] Francis L. Dabney, *Sketch*, p. 62.

[33] Francis L. Dabney, *Sketch*, p. 39.

[34] "Letter saying Hickling's appointment not recognized", Torre de Tombo, Ministério de Negócios Estrangeiros, Cx (Box) 412, Correspondência das ligações estrangeiras em Lisboa, Estados Unidos da América, 1820-1833, p. 50

[35] Francis L. Dabney, *Sketch*, p. 39; Document 11, United States Archive, Microfilm T203, Roll 1, March 4, 1795-November 28, 1832.

[36] Roxana Lewis Dabney, *Annals*, p. 20.

[37] Francis L. Dabney, *Sketch*, p. 51.

[38] Francis L. Dabney, *Sketch*, p. 40.

[39] Francis L. Dabney, *Sketch*, p. 42-43; Roxana Lewis Dabney, *Annals*, p. 22-25.

[40] Roxana Lewis Dabney, *Annals*, p. 25.

[41] Francis L. Dabney, *Sketch*, p. 43.

[42] Francis L. Dabney, *Sketch*, p. 41.

[43] Francis L. Dabney, *Sketch*, p. 30.

[44] Francis L. Dabney, *Sketch*, p. 44.

[45] Roxana Lewis Dabney, *Annals*, Introductory, p. 2.

3 – TURBULENCE IN THE ATLANTIC

Volcanoes weren't the only source of noise and heat in the Atlantic during the early 19th century. France and Britain continued beating the drums of war. To increase chances of victory they were doing their utmost to destroy the other's trade. Britain was the more aggressive on the high seas, stopping any ship they thought was heading toward continental Europe. As a consequence, many American ships, despite America's neutrality, were stopped and their cargoes confiscated. This resulted in American--British relations deteriorating and heading toward the brink of war.

President Thomas Jefferson considered the British actions on the high seas as violations of international law, a field which was still in its infancy. He believed that a ship flying a neutral flag should be able to sail into any port, an idea the British did not agree with. In addition, unlike the usual procedure of stopping ships near the blockaded coast, in this case near France, the British were stopping ships wherever they found them, even in the seas close to the American coast.

In October 1807, President Jefferson asked Congress to establish an embargo against American ships delivering goods to foreign ports. He hoped that with the warring countries running short of supplies, cutting off one of their main sources of trade would force them to recognize American rights to free trade. This was, in effect, a blockade of the American ports and had the negative effects of almost ruining the American shipping industry, eliminating markets for American farm surplus and damaging the economy. This affected not only America's international trade, but also trade within the country since much interstate commerce at this time went by sea because America's road network was still poorly developed.

In Portugal, the French General Androche Junot was ruling the country. He had declared that the royal house of Bragança, which had fled to Brazil, was no longer in power and that Napoleon ruled the country in the person of Junot. He set about applying a mixture of repressive measures and rewards in an attempt to maintain a peaceful French occupation of Portugal. Despite his efforts, the Portuguese rebelled in many parts of the country and took much of it back.

The Portuguese, along with British troops under Sir Arthur Wellesley, who was later made the Duke of Wellington, engaged the French near the town of Vimeiro in the rolling hills about 35 miles north of Lisbon in August of 1808. French battle losses were great and they decided to negotiate for a peaceful withdrawal from Portugal. The parties to the conflict met in the town of Sintra, about 20 kilometers from Lisbon, and drew up the Convention of Sinetra. The Convention allowed the French to leave with the items they had looted, a provision that angered the Portuguese, as well as many British.

The Portuguese royal family, however, decided to remain in Brazil. Prince-Regent João gave the British officer William Beresford the rank of Marshal, put him in command of the army and asked him to reorganize it. Beresford took this appointment and interpreted it as broadly as possible, in effect putting himself in command of Portugal

The effects of the war and embargoes on the European and American continents were greatly magnified in the Azores. The islands depended on receiving a large part of their essential supplies from the outside. In addition, their export economy was heavily dependent on shipping the islands' agricultural products and other items produced there to a larger market. Needless to say, the Dabney's shipping ventures were also adversely affected.

As an example of what was going on in the Atlantic during this period, an event that took place in Faial during 1808 is described in a letter from John Dabney, dated July 27, 1808, to Thomas Pinckney, Envoy Extraordinary from the United States to the Court in London.[1] In it Dabney describes how he tried to ship "a quantity of Jesuits Bark"* to Gibraltar on the British Schooner *Experiment*, Captain James Saunders commanding.

---

*The bark of the cinchona tree from which quinine was extracted

The ship had come to the Azores from Gibraltar "to load provisions and return thither." Mr. Thomas Parkin, the British Consul on Faial, was going to accompany the ship full of provisions on its way to Gibraltar. There he was going to try to set up a contract with the British Army and Navy and bring the ship back with merchandise to sell. He suggested that John Dabney ship some of the Jesuits' bark in Parkin's care to be sold in Gibraltar.

Just as the *Experiment* was getting ready to sail, the British Naval Frigate *Undaunted* entered the bay. Mr. Parkin went on board to talk with its commander, Captain Maling, who told him about a revolution against the French in Spain. Parkin thought that this would increase the price of Jesuit's Bark and went to John Dabney and suggested that he increase the amount that he was going to ship. Captain Maling agreed with Parkin's assessment of the favorable sales situation because the Jesuits' bark "would arrive there ere any could come from England" and he also knew that John Dabney was shipping an additional amount of bark.

The Schooner *Experiment* set sail on July 23, but an armed boat from the *Undaunted* immediately pursued and captured it and brought it back to port. Mr. Parkin was "thunderstruck at such conduct." When he went on board the *Undaunted* to complain, "Captain Maling treated him in the most contemptuous and abusive manner, called him an enemy to his country, and unworthy to hold his office." Because the bark belonged to John Dabney, an American, "he was convinced that it was enemies' property and that he was basely taking it under his protection."

Captain Maling's action antagonized everyone on the island. The Governor sent his son, the Commander of the Citadel, with a letter of complaint to Captain Maling and received "an evasive, contemptuous answer." John Dabney wrote the Captain, "in the most temperate manner and polite manner," asking for his property back, taking the responsibility for the shipment of the bark and saying that the only assistance he had was from the Portuguese pharmacist from whom he had bought the bark. He received no response at all. As a final move, Captain Maling "forceably sent off the [*Experiment*] to Gibraltar, and Mr. Parkin was not allowed to go in her."

John Dabney wrote Thomas Pinckney that "I am ignorant of any laws or orders of Council that renders this transaction legal." He said that the Captain "evidently affects all this rage against Mr. Parkin, in order to weaken and destroy his credit, and the report which attaches to his office to render his testimony in my favor negatory; that he may be the more secure of his prey." He concludes by asking Pinckney to "interfere in this business" if he felt it appropriate.

This situation came about as the result of an American, whose country was neutral, tried to ship merchandise that the British needed on a British ship from a neutral port to a British controlled port. It is not surprising, then, that a very large number of American ships coming from American ports with American merchandise were being stopped on the high seas under the pretense of seeing if they were carrying contraband. A number of these ships had their cargo seized regardless of what it was or whether they were in the right.

In the first part of 1809, the French again invaded Portugal, this time under General Nicolas Jean de Dieu Soult, and Wellesley's British and Portuguese troops once again chased them out of the country, this time into Spain. Wellesley and the British continued the chase into Spain, In July he won the Battle of Talavera, about 80 miles southwest of Madrid, after which he was made the Duke of Wellington. However, he could chase the French no farther into Spain. He was short of supplies and a long way from his supply base, so he returned to Portugal. He went to the area of Torres Vedras, a short distance north of Lisbon, where he had his troops establish a defensive complex of towers and artillery emplacements in preparation for another French advance into Portugal.

The continued absence of the Portuguese Royal Family also created problems when John Dabney appealed local governmental decisions. The Portuguese government was run by a council headed by General William Beresford, and many Portuguese wanted to get him out of this position. John Dabney presented his problems in a letter to Henry Hill who was the U. S. Consul to the Portuguese court in Brazil.

And since H.R.H. the Prince left Lisbon, there seems to be no mode of obtaining redress; for the Royal Junta, in Lisbon is recognized by the Royal Junta at Terceira and to petition this latter Body, is in the present situation of things a perfect waste of time and paper.[2]

Jefferson's embargo was very unpopular in America, and Congress passed a repeal to take effect on March 3, 1809, the day he left office as President and less than eighteen months after he established the embargo. However, the problems between France and Britain and their effects on American trade continued to exist. To keep some form of commercial retaliation, Congress passed the Non-Intercourse Act. This prohibited trade with both Britain and France, while allowing it with other countries. It also held out the carrot of restoring trade relations with either of the two belligerent countries if they eliminated their hindrance of trade by neutral countries. Even though the Non--Intercourse Act was also short-lived, it created an unusual situation which led to a financial windfall for John Dabney.

Under the Non-Intercourse Act, "American vessels came pouring into Fayal from the U. S. for the purpose of loading their cargoes to be transhipped to other bottoms to be carried to G. Britain."[3] This created "a prodigious pressure of Commerce" in Horta. He had all therelevant paperwork to deal with, had to carry out the necessary business with the local bureaucracy and, since most shipments were made to his care, he also had to hire many laborers and incur expenses for loading and unloading.[4]

Some of the port expenses of the ships had to be supported by John Dabney against money that would be realized from their cargoes. With the large influx of ships, Dabney's expenses increased greatly, and he had to ask for financial help from Thomas Hickling on São Miguel, who had made his money shipping oranges and other products from that island. The letter requesting the loan also gives an idea of how much John Dabney was making from his business.

"Fayal, April 27th 1809
Thomas Hickling, Esq.

Dear Sir,

I have to request your aid in sending one some money, say Two Thousand dollars, by this cheque, or first opportunity that may be present. I shall send you undoubted bills, or reimburse you in some other manner very soon. Vessels are flocking in from every port in America and their expenses coming so suddenly overwhelm one. We pay no duties on their cargoes in or out, numbers are unloading today. You will endeavor to secure as much of this abundant harvest as possible, which I shall of course expect to divide with you. I hope you will be able to secure full commissions, 2% for landing and 2% for loading in the same or other vessels. They pay me so here, and 4% on vessels or cargoes sold to the Portuguese or British subjects. American vessels, if they chose to take the risk of loading again must not clear for ports forbidden by law. I depend upon your aiding me momentarily." [5]

American ships dealt with the Non-Intercourse Act's control of international trade in a variety of ways. John Dabney described these in a letter to Robert Smith, U. S. Secretary of State.

"Fayal, June 13th 1809

To the Honble. Robt. Smith
Secretary of State, Washington

Sir:

I have the honor to transmit herewith for your information a list of the American vessels arrived at this port since the partial raising of the Embargo to this date, and I enclose at the same time the registers and Mediterranean Passes of five vessels of the above named sold here to Foreigners. Of the others some proceeded on to Lisbon or Madeira, some sold or landed their cargoes here and went back to the U. States. Others after unloading their cargoes and obtaining my certificate of landing have reloaded, and proceeded on, I presume, for British ports, clearing out for: Lisbon, Gottenburg, etc., and lastly a number that had recently arrived here when the news was

received here of the adjustment of our differences with England, sailed direct for England, intending to enter British ports
after the 10th of June. Another vessel the ship "Osage" of New
York, took Portuguese colors here, and the Captain declined
delivering up his register to me." [6]

A high level of shipping activity existed for more than a year
with 160 American ships, and approximately the same number
of foreign ships, entering the port of Horta. At one time there
were fifty large ships loading and unloading in this small port.
All of this activity required John Dabney to work extremely
long hours. However, it also brought him a large amount of
money and provided him with a basis for further expanding his
business.[7] It also helped the economy of Faial in general.

> Although an occupation by foreign forces did not take
> place during this period, it is certain that the complexity of the
> various interests in play, including those of maritime trade,
> did not prevent the placement of the Azores – and particularly
> Faial – in the center of decisions, whether as a function of the
> naval operations intended to give the required security and
> protection to navigation, or through the strength of the rela-
> tionships between the two sides of the Atlantic, above all on
> the United States-United Kingdom axis. The great instability in
> the relationships between these two countries, on the one
> hand, and the latter and France, on the other, during the period
> during which the Napoleonic wars were going on, created a
> situation for which Faial, from 1808 to 1810, would live through
> a period characterized not only by a certain elation caused by
> the relief of unexpected abundance, but principally through
> the fears and unrest in day-to-day life, that the relative dis-
> tance from the theatre of the conflict was not sufficient to di-
> sappear...[8]

While things were going well for John Dabney in the Azores,
the French invaded Portugal for the third time. A French army
of 62,000 men under Masséna entered Portugal in August 1810.
They met 52,000 British and Portuguese troops under the Duke

of Wellington and suffered serious losses at the Battle of Buçaco in late September. Wellington withdrew in front of the French troops, leading them toward the fortifications he had constructed at Torres Vedras. These proved too strong for the French, and the army was too far from its source of supplies to attempt further action. The French retreated part way across Portugal and finally had to give up even this latter position. Wellington chased them across the country, with a major attack near Sabugal in the north, and the French were forced to leave Portugal in May 1811. Following his success in Portugal against Napoleon's troops, the Duke of Wellington continued his pursuit of the French across Spain, France and Belgium to the final defeat of Napoleon at Waterloo.

However, the Portuguese Royal Family still did not return. For many years Portugal remained under the *de facto* control of the British General Beresford. He showed no tolerance for those opposing his jurisdiction and executed many of the dissidents in an attempt to control the emerging liberal movement. During the entire period of occupation by Napoleon's troops, the French, who considered them neutral, had never bothered the Azores. After the French departed the Portuguese in the Azores considered the archipelago to be governed by the Prince Regent in Brazil, not by the governing powers in Lisbon and awaited the return of the Royal Family.

Despite the positive turn in business brought about by the Non-Intercourse Act, John Dabney apparently still considered his stay on Fayal only temporary. To him it was an island far away from the cultural richness of Massachusetts and France and populated mainly by poor farmers and fishermen who lacked much of what he considered to be important. As a consequence, he felt that his children had to be sent elsewhere for their education. Charles was already in America, and in the spring of 1809 he sent ten-year old Roxalina to England for school[9] and then John to Boston about two years later.[10] All of this is pointed out in a letter to Mr. Burnett, his agent in London.

"The want of good society for Mrs. Dabney and myself and total lack of schools for our children are considerations of such magnitude to me that I shall leave the place and probably go to New York whenever my circumstances will enable me to do so."[11]

This is spelled out in more detail in a letter in 1811 from John Dabney to Lemuel Bent, who was his brother-in-law's brother. This letter also gives a good view of life on the island during this period and confirms one of the explanations pointed out previously of why he sought to be the American Consul on Fayal.

The disadvantage of living here is the deficiency of what we call rational society, and the means of educating our children. There is a great deal of conviviality among the people here, and we have balls, cardparties, etc., very frequently, and as strangers are continually coming and going, and by every arrival we receive gazettes and other publications I do not feel any great want of farther society, but my children I am obliged to send to England and America for their education which is painful and very expensive."

"As there are here a sufficient number of persons capable of conducting the commerce of the Island, they are very jealous of strangers coming among them to do business, and combine to cross and vex them in such a manner that they cannot well succeed. The foreign Consuls only are an exception as they know that one from each trading country must reside here. If sent they receive him pretty cordially, and he is immediately received into their commercial community. The only consuls of any consequence here, the British, French, Spanish and American, and they indeed engross a great part of the trade. A great portion of what these people want from abroad, being furnished almost exclusively from the United States, say: boards, staves, timber, wax, rice, whale oil, teas, naval stores, rum, flax, leather, flour and corn (the last two crops having fallen short), and this all passing through my hands, and a greater part imported by myself, enable me to take the lead in commerce in this Island. My exports in 1810 for my own account, and on commission, chiefly in wines and brandies was little short of 90,000 dollars.[12]

After this financially positive period, life on Faial took a turn for the worse, partly as a result of the trade boom that had made it so positive. A number of the farmers had left their farms and taken better paying jobs working with the ships. Consequently, the harvest in 1810 was small, and the island was faced with a famine. To alleviate the suffering of the inhabitants, John Dabney had a supply of grain shipped to the island.[13] This was the first of the charitable acts of for which the Dabney's became well known and respected throughout their years on Faial.

Relations between the United States and Britain continued to deteriorate further with British ships still stopping American ships on the high seas. They confiscated the cargoes and also impressed sailors from the crews to replace British sailors killed by the French or who had deserted because of the bad treatment of sailors on British warships. In 1811, President James Madison prohibited trade with Britain, and the frustration and anger in America toward the British increased to the point where war became inevitable. Once again international trade was hindered.

In late 1811, an example of what was going on occurred when the British ship *Crane* entered the port of Horta and released to John Dabney the ship and sailors it had captured. This is described in a letter to the Secretary of State.

> I have the honour to inform you that a few days since the British Sloop of War Crane, Captain James Stuart, came into this Port & delivered to me seventeen officers and Seamen being the crews of the Ship *Asia* of Boston and Brig *Washington* of Marblehead, captured on their way home from Archangel. These men being in a very destitute situation, I furnished them with a change of clothing & detained the Schooner *Liberty* of New Bedford a few days to take them, being desirous to abridge the expenses of them here by sending them home as promptly as possible. Yesterday the above mentioned ship *Asia* entered this Port, the Sloop of War being still here. Head winds had prevented the *Asia* from reaching St. Johns Newfoundland to which place she had been ordered. As soon as she came to

anchor Capt. Stuart presented himself at my office & after some
preliminary conversation in which he expressed great regret
for having captured the *Asia* and *Washington*, stated that the
object of his visit was to surrender the ship *Asia* and her cargo
to me for account of her owner which proposal I readily
accepted & the ship will tomorrow resume her voyage for
Boston. The Brig it is presumed reached St. Johns. I dismissed
the schooner with a small gratuity for her detention & trouble the Capt. Had as the *Asia* will carry home the crew of the
Washington at her expense to the U. States.[14]

In the midst of the turbulence in the rest of the world during these years, the Dabney family managed to maintain a degree
of normality. Three more children joined the clan – James Madison,
born June 7, 1808, Frederick, born August 2, 1809, and Emmeline,
born August 13, 1811. In addition, Charles had returned to Faial
in 1810 because Mr. Wheaton had found him unmanageable
and no longer wanted to take the responsibility for him.[15]

Nothing gives a better idea of life in the Dabney family during this period than a description in a letter from Mr. Noah Jones,
a distant relative of the Dabney's, to a Miss Kingman in Providence, Rhode Island.

I enjoy a little paradise in the family of John B. Dabney, the
American Consul for the Western Islands. It is one of those
happy families where order, harmony and social intercourse
continually preside. No jarring interests, no discordant passions,
no petty differences, ever disturb its tranquility. The head of
the family has a mild, moderate disposition; his manners are
easy and unaffected and his conversation lively, interesting and
frequently instructive. He has seen much of the world and
drawn his knowledge from personal observation. Having resided
for several years in different parts of Europe his opinions are
free from bias and prejudice, which cannot be always said of
those who have never travelled. In fine Mr. Dabney governs
his house with a mildness and decision truly admirable. Mrs.
Dabney is of a very different order of beings, she is possessed
of much sense, warm feelings and the most graceful and pol-

ished manners; although approaching the age of forty, her person is elegant and handsome and there is a vivacity and intelligence in her eye, which conveys her meaning in the most impressive manner. She is uniformly polite, particularly attentive to strangers, insinuating with women, and almost too captivating for the peace of lordly man. Though calculated to shine in the gayest circles of fashionable life, she is perfectly domestic, making the care of her little nursery the chief object of her attention. Her children manifest the highest degree of affection toward her and vie with each other in endeavours to please. Living in the bosom of such a family how is it possible to be otherwise than happy?[16]

John Dabney's stay on Faial wasn't as temporary as he had originally intended when he first settled on the island because in 1811 he began construction on a home. The home, and also to serve as the American Consulate, was to be the largest and most magnificent on the island and was given the name Bagatelle. It was the family's only residence until the number of children increased, and they had to move into other homes in Horta. Perhaps John Dabney realized that his family's life on Faial described by Mr. Jones outweighed the social and cultural advantages of a big city in America.

Notes:

[1] Francis L. Dabney, *Sketch of John Bass Dabney by his son William Henry Dabney of Boston,* *1887,* comp., n. p.: The Author, 1971, p. 45-47; Roxana Lewis Dabney, *Annals of the Dabney Family in Fayal,* comp., n. p.: The Author, 1900, p. 20-22.

[2] Roxana Lewis Dabney, *Annals,* p. 31.

[3] Francis L. Dabney, *Sketch,* p. 49.

[4] Francis L. Dabney, *Sketch,* p. 62; Roxana Lewis Dabney, *Annals,* p. 36.

[5] Francis L. Dabney, *Sketch,* p. 49.

[6] Francis L. Dabney, *Sketch,* p. 50.

[7] Francis L. Dabney, *Sketch,* p. 54.

[8] Ricardo Manuel Madruga da Costa, "Faial 1808-1810, Um tempo memorável", *Boletim do Núcleo Cultural da Horta,* Vol. XI, p. 138, 1993-95.

[9] Francis L. Dabney, *Sketch,* p. 65.

[10] Francis L. Dabney, *Sketch,* p. 51.

[11] Francis L. Dabney, *Sketch*, p. 51.

[12] Francis L. Dabney, *Sketch*, p. 61-62; Roxana Lewis Dabney, *Annals*, p. 35-36.

[13] Francis L. Dabney, *Sketch*, p. 54.

[14] Document 13, United States Archives, Microfilm T203, Roll 1, March 4, 1795-November 28, 1832.; Francis L. Dabney, *Sketch*, p 66-67.

[15] Francis L. Dabney, *Sketch*, p. 70.

[16] Roxana Lewis Dabney, *Annals*, p. 40-41.

Figure 2

Roxa Dabney (from portrait by Vanderin)

John Bass Dabney

4 – WAR

As the years of war with Napoleon went on and on, the British fleet found it more difficult to find and keep sailors for the crews of its warships. The desertion rate was enormous due to the poor conditions on board and the equally poor treatment of the men by the officers. Many seamen ended up deserting from the British Navy and going home or sailing on ships of other countries.

To keep the crews of their warships at an adequate operating level, the British stopped any ship they found on the high seas looking for deserters from their Navy. Sometimes they went further and impressed men who were not British citizens, a large proportion of whom were Americans. Estimates place the number of Americans "pressed" into the British Navy at around 10,000 men.

Despite the complaints and actions by the U. S. government and negative public opinion, the British navy continued to impress American seamen. Event piled onto event and built up to the point where President James Madison asked Congress to declare war against Britain. Congress cooperated and on June 18, 1812, war was declared.

Trans-Atlantic shipping all but ceased because of the war, and only a very few ships in transit stopped in the Azores. On the island of Faial, the wine harvests failed during the period of the war. This continued the string of failures that had begun two years earlier and resulted in even greater hardships on the residents. It wouldn't have mattered if the harvest had been successful because there was no way to ship the wine from the islands. The isolation of the island is expressed in a letter from John Dabney to James Lovett in February 1813.

> The present convulsed state of the world has not only sus-
> pended all communication regarding commercial affairs, but

has shut the door to almost all modes of communication between this Island and other countries.[1]

Some of the small number of the ships that stopped at Faial were British dropping off American seamen from ships they had captured. These men usually had nothing more than the clothes on their backs, and their maintenance and well-being became the responsibility of the Consulate. Because of the impossibility of direct contact with America, John Dabney had to pay for their upkeep out of his own pocket. Every now and then he was able to send some of the seamen to Lisbon or the U. S., again at his own expense. Reimbursement for these expenses had to wait until 1818 when Congress passed a bill to repay the debt of almost $4,500, a considerable sum at the time, along with other incidental expenses.[2]

The only good thing to happen to the Dabneys during this period was the completion of Bagatelle where the family took up residence in early 1814. It was located down the hill to the southeast of the house at Santo António. Charles Dabney wrote to his brother John about it in June of 1812.

> Our House ('Bagatelle') goes on famously, it will when completed, be the largest and most pleasant one in Fayal. I believe you do not know where it is situated so I will inform you; you recollect the second hill from our house, going to town, there was a considerable space of open land, say about two or three acres of ground, which is at present our garden, and our New House is located in the middle of it.[3]

The house was located in the center of 2-3 acres of garden with a wide variety of plants, several species of them imported from elsewhere. The laying out of the house and getting the garden planted took up a lot of John Dabney's enforced leisure brought about by the elimination of his commercial activities because of the war.

> Although John Bass Dabney still intended to return eventually to the United States, he decided in 1811 to build himself

a comfortable house. He had several carpenters from Massachusetts come out to Fayal and when the house, in 1814, was
finished it was pronounced a great success. It was situated in
the upper part of the town, with a commanding view of Pico
and surrounded by much land which was later turned into a
fine garden. It was of Colonial type, and spacious, and was
built partly with a view to entertaining, having one huge room
leading off from the main hall, suitable for dancing and the-
atricals. The house was named Bagatelle in memory of the
Bagatelle outside of Paris with which Mr. and Mrs. Dabney
had happy association.[4]

The Parc de Bagatelle and its chateau are on the edge of the
Bois de Boulogne in Paris, near where John Dabney lived in
the mid-1790's. These were built by the Comte d'Artois in 1777
as the result of a bet he made with his sister-in-law Marie Antoinette and the gardens are known for their beauty and layout.
   Bagatelle was the Dabney family's pride and joy, and it became the place to visit for all Americans and many of the foreigners who stopped in Faial over the years. Visitors were
received with all the hospitality that the Dabneys could offer
and many glowing descriptions of visits to Bagatelle were written by appreciative visitors. Bagatelle also served as the American Consulate, and, only a few months after being completed it welcomed a visitor who was involved in an incident on
Faial that was to have an effect on the history of the United
States.[5]
   At about one p.m. on Monday, September 26, 1814, the American privateer *General Armstrong* entered the Bay of Horta. It anchored, and its commander, Captain Samuel Chester Reid, went
on shore to get permission to resupply his ship with food and
water. Since Portugal was a neutral country, both sides were allowed this privilege, and the *General Armstrong* was given 24 hours
to complete its resupplying.
   The *General Armstrong* had run the British blockade of the
Port of New York on September 9. It was a 246-ton ship and carried a crew of 90 and it had nine guns, including the 42-pounder
known as "Long Tom". This cannon had been captured from the

French by the British in 1798, bought along with several others by the U. S. government, but not used because of damage to its muzzle. The private citizen who bought the cannon repaired the damage and put it on a ship that attacked the French in Haiti. It was then retired until the War of 1812 when it was put it back into action.

Captain Reid was 31 years old and had gone to sea when he was eleven. His experiences included capture and imprisonment by the French, as well as service in both America's naval and merchant fleets. He was commander of the *General Armstrong* throughout the War of 1812.

While his ship was in Horta, Captain Reid was invited to join the Dabneys at Bagatelle for dinner. After the meal, John Dabney accompanied Captain Reid back to his ship, which was in the process of being resupplied. About sundown, a British ship came around the point of the bay. There was no concern because the commanders of the two British warships patrolling the Azores, the sloop *Thais* and the brig *Calypso*, were considered "prudent men" and wouldn't violate the neutrality of the port. However, it took only a minute to realize that it was a different British warship, the 18-gun brig *Carnation*, Captain Bentham in command. The *Carnation* was soon followed by the 44-gun frigate *Rota*, Captain Sommerville, and the 74-gun ship-of-the-line *Plantagenet*, Captain Robert Lloyd.

The three ships were under the overall command of Captain Lloyd who had acquired the nickname of "Mad Lloyd." This was "a distinction bestowed on him by his own countrymen"[6] because of some of his ideas and actions, including a senseless attack on Craney Island downriver from Portsmouth and Norfolk. Even Captain Mein of the *Thais* considered Lloyd a "savage madman".

Captain Lloyd knew of Portugal's neutrality and had, in fact, taken advantage of the privilege of resupplying his own ships in Horta some three weeks earlier. At that time the crew of the *Rota* had put on several plays and, as their ship entered the Bay of Horta once again, they were rehearsing another play to perform on this visit.[7]

Captain Reid thought about trying to flee from the bay, but the wind had died down, and there was no way to escape. As a result, Captain Reid had no choice but to count on the good faith of the British. By this time John Dabney and other visitors to the *General Armstrong* had returned to shore.

The British ships exchanged signals, and small boats were sent from the *Carnation* to the *Plantagenet*. It was becoming clear that the British were up to something. Captain Reid cleared the decks of his ship in preparation for a possible assault. John Dabney, recognizing that there would be trouble, sent his 21-year old son Charles on board the *General Armstrong* with a message "to recommend Capt. Reid to slip his cable and warp his vessel close-in under the guns of the castle."[8] As Charles Dabney returned to shore, Captain Reid carried out the suggestion.

At around 8:00 p.m., under a full moon, four boats approached the *General Armstrong*. They contained about 120 British sailors and marines. As they got close, Captain Reid yelled a warning for them to stay away. The British boats pressed on. Reid repeated his warning several times without effect. When the boats reached the ship, and their crews were preparing to board, Captain Reid ordered his crew to open fire into the boats, although the first shots may have come from the British boats. The British returned fire, and the *Armstrong's* first Lieutenant was wounded and a seaman killed. The firing stopped after a short battle, and the boats fled back to the British ships with their dead and wounded.

The British later claimed that they were only investigating who the ship was and that their intent was peaceful. However, the pilot-boat had informed the British of the *General Armstrong's* identity when they had first entered.[9]

In addition, in 1853 Charles Dabney wrote a letter to Secretary of State William Marcy saying he had proof that the British Vice-Consul on the island Pico had sent a letter on board the *Plantagenet*. In it he advised them of the identity of the American ship anchored in the Bay of Horta.[10] Even those British observers on shore criticized the action by their country's navy in Horta.

After the attack, Captain Lloyd sent a letter to the Governor of the island saying that his boats had "without the least provocation, been fired into", which resulted in two of his men being killed and seven wounded. He complained about the *General Armstrong* "breaking the neutrality" of the port and threatened that "in consequence of the above outrage I am determined to take possession of her."[11]

Activity on the British ships and the launching of more boats made it obvious that a new attack was being prepared. In anticipation, Captain Reid moved his ship even closer to the fortress for better protection.

About 9:00 p.m. John Dabney sent his son Charles with a letter to the Governor requesting that he complain to Lloyd about the British attack. He also requested permission to send 32 American seamen, who had been stranded in Faial, on board the *General Armstrong* to help in its defense.

Around an hour later the Governor responded to the two letters. The Governor demanded that Lloyd recognize the port's neutrality and not take any action against the privateer. He also refused John Dabney's request to send more Americans on board the besieged ship to help in its defense.

Lloyd's response to this request left no doubt about his intentions. He informed the Governor "that he was determined to destroy the vessel, at the expense of all Fayal; and should any protection be given her by the port, he would not leave a house standing in the village".[12] Since the fortress overlooking the bay was already over 300-years old and had only a half dozen or so old cannons, the town was in no way able to protect itself, let alone protect the *General Armstrong*.

Captain Bentham, whose ship *Carnation* led the attack, describes his actions leading up to the attack on the *General Armstrong*. His letter reports his

> (…) proceedings from the time I received your orders (which to the best of my knowledge was about 8 o'clock p.m.) to get H.M.'s Sloop under my command alongside the American Privateer "General Armstrong", and destroy her, with the boats of the *Plantagenet* and *Rota* under my command, to assist in towing or anything else circumstances might require, together with my reasons why the sloop could not be got alongside the Privateer before the boats made the attack…

the moment I received your orders, the Schooner was reported under weigh, and considerably in shore of us. The Cable of
H.M.'s Sloop was immediately cut, and all sail made. Lieut.
Zanssek who brought the orders was at this time alongside of
us, and had repeatedly asked me if he should shove off, and
other Boats were coming to support him. I consented, and
sent my Gig as a further protection, imagining the Schooner
intended pushing out, and that they would be the means of
retarding her until we got alongside,... before we could gather
sufficient way, to go about, the Enemy had got well in shore,
light baffling winds and a strong S.W. current, prevented our
closing with them although every exertion was made, before
all the boats rendezvous'd round us; I then, seeing the Schooner
close in under the Portuguese Battery, sent my First Lieut. to you
for instructions relative to the attack, and should the Batteries
interfere on his return with orders to bring her out, Lieut Matter-
face senior Lieut. in the Boats brought alongside of us a Boat
with a letter from the Portuguese Governor with which I sent
him to you; on his return he was proceeding to join the Boats
which had collected in shore, when I hailed him, asking what
orders, he replied, we are to bring her out Sir, and immediately
joined the Boats and commenced the attack; it was my opinion,
as well as the officers about me, that it was impossible to take
a proper position in the night, without extreme risk of getting
on the Rocks, and endangering the loss of H.M.'s Sloop. I therefore did not judge it prudent to attempt being towed in, in the
boats. I conceived eleven boats fully adequate to her capture
and attribute the failure to the Enemy's being so to the Rocks,
that the boats could not succeed in getting inside of her.[13]

On shore everyone in Horta, including the Governor and
John and Charles Dabney, was on the walls, along the shore or
hanging out their windows to ensure a good view of the expected battle in the bright moonlight. Their wait ended about midnight when Captain Bentham moved his ship, along with the
accompanying boats, toward the *General Armstrong.*
When the boats, carrying 300-400 men, pulled within shoot-
ing distance, the *General Armstrong* opened fire with its cannons

and received return fire from the boats. The discharge from "Long-Tom staggered them", but they soon continued their approach cheering in high spirits. It wasn't long before the boats had reached their target, and the order to board was shouted out.

> On shore Charles Dabney was learning a lesson in prudence which he was always to remember. ...in his eagerness to see, he kept continually raising himself to look over the breastworks; at last a man near him (an American sea Captain) pulled him down saying, 'You can see just as well with only the top of your head exposed, as with the whole of your chest a target for bullets' which were continually whistling over their heads.[14]

The British boats were too close for cannons to be useful, and the *General Armstrong's* crew used swords, pikes, axes, pistols and muskets to keep the attackers away. They beat the British off as they climbed up the side of the ship urged on by the shouts of "no quarter" from their officers. The Americans fired down into the boats killing a large number of the British. Some of the British seamen and marines reached the deck defended by the Americans using their close-quarter weapons.

The first lieutenant of the *General Armstrong,* who was leading the defense at the prow, was killed and the third lieutenant badly wounded. Captain Reid, who was left-handed, was in the stern of the ship along with several men fighting with his sword in his left hand and a pistol in his right. Hearing of the weakening defense in the prow, Reid "instantly rallied the whole of our after division, and now had succeeded in beating the boats off the quarters. They gave a shout, rushed forward, opened a fresh fire, and soon decided the conflict... ".[15] The crew fired directly into the British boats and tossed bombs into them creating terror among those still there and causing them to pull the boats back.[16] Those British who couldn't get back to their boats jumped into the water and swam to shore. The American seamen continued firing at the fleeing enemy with devastating effect.

When the last shots had died away, the extent of the damage could be seen. Captain Reid discovered that only one of his men had been killed and seven wounded during the approximately 40-minute battle. The British losses, on the other hand, were tremendous. Bodies were washed up on shore, some of the boats were floating about filled with corpses and others with a few survivors made their way back to the ships. The British admitted to having 120 men killed and 130 wounded, but some eyewitnesses considered this an underestimate. Among the British dead were some of the senior officers of each of the ships.

The battle wasn't over yet, however. Captain Lloyd let the Governor know that he would not quit and intended to capture the *General Armstrong*. The American crew, expecting further problems, began to work right after the battle and cleared the decks of their ship and made ready for battle by 3:00 a.m.

In the meanwhile, at around 2:00 a.m., John Dabney sent his son Charles with a letter to Captain Reid. In it he said,

> You have performed a most brilliant action in beating off fourteen [note: all other reports give the number as twelve] boats of the British ships in this wad. They say they will carry the brig cost what it will and that the English brig will hand close in to attack you at the same time the boats do. My dear fellow, do not uselessly expose yourself, if again attacked by an overwhelming force, but scuttle the brig near the beach and come on the shore with your brave crew.[17]

In his report of the incident, Reid describes a visit to the Consulate before the final assault.

> At about 5 a.m. I received a message from the American consul, requesting to see me on shore, where he informed me that the governor had sent a note to captain Lloyd begging him to desist from further hostilities. To which captain Lloyd sent for answer, that he was determined to have the privateer at the risk of knocking down the whole town; and that if the governor suffered the Americans to injure the privateer in any manner, he should consider the place an enemy's port, and treat it accordingly. Finding this to be the case, I considered all hopes of saving our vessel to be at an end. I therefore went on

board, and ordered all our wounded and dead to be taken on shore, and the crew to save their effects as fast as possible.[18]

At daybreak the final attack by the British commenced. The *Carnation* moved in and fired several broadsides. The American crew returned the fire with great effect. "After several broadsides [the *Carnation*] hauled-off, having received a shot in her hull, her rigging much cut, and her fore-top mast wounded."

The *Carnation* came back in again and anchored close to the *General Armstrong*. Reid "then ordered the *Armstrong* to be scuttled, to prevent the enemy from getting her off. She was soon after boarded by the enemy's boats, and set on fire, which soon completed her destruction."[19]

While the ship was burning...

> ...the boatswain declared they should not have the bust of General Armstrong; and he swam off, cut off the figure-head and brought it back ashore. The figurehead was placed over the gate leading into the back garden at Bagatelle, and was regarded by the gardener and servants as the American Saint, and it was always a great circumstance among us children erecting an arbor of hydrangeas and other flowers over it on the 4th of July.[20]

After many years in Faial's humid climate, the wood of the figurehead began to show signs of decay and was sent in 1867 by Charles Dabney to the Museum of the Navy Yard at Charlestown, Massachusetts. Today it is on display in the Naval Historical Center in Washington, D. C., along with Long Tom, which was returned to the United States by Portugal for the Chicago Exposition of 1893.

In April 1867, Charles Dabney gave a complete description of this heroic boatswain's deed in a letter he sent to the Boston Naval Library and Institute after they elected him an Honorary Member.

> Having in my possession an object of Historic interest, connected with an event that shed some lustre upon our Country,

it affords me very great pleasure to place it in the custody of the Faculty of the Boston Naval Library and Institute. It is the Bust, the Figure Head of the "Gen. Armstrong!" The morning after the extraordinary victory of Capt. Reid and his officers and crew of that vessel, over the thirteen boats, manned from the "Plantagenet," "Rota," and "Carnation," they having landed al their baggage and stores, a nine pounder was discharged down the Brig's main hatchway and she was abandoned. The water was so shallow that all above main deck was out of water. The "Carnation," Brig of war, had been brought in close and was firing grape shot at her, when the Boatswain of the G.A. (I regret that his name is not to be found where I expected), a Herculean figure, deliberately walked down, with a mate, opposite to beach where the vessel was, and declared that they (the then enemies) should not have the Figure Head. He came provided with a hatchet, swam off to the vessel about fifteen feet, gone on board, cut off the head and brought it ashore. During that time the mate waited on the beach (somewhat protected by the upper works of the vessel); on their return when running along the beach to where I was with many others protected by an angle of the Fort, the mate was seen to fall, as if mortally wounded; I immediately sent two men to take him to the Hospital, where on examination it appeared that a grape shot had cut through the muscular part of one of his arms and one had carried away a part of the calf of one of his legs; both severe but not dangerous.[21]

After they had sacked and completed the destruction of the *General Armstrong*, the British withdrew from the burning hulk. The *Carnation* moved out toward its companions and dropped anchor. The statement of a British eyewitness on shore published in Cobbett's Register in London probably expresses what many of those involved in the attack were feeling at this point. "We may well say 'God deliver us from our enemies' if this is the way the Americans fight."[22]

Many buildings in the town of Horta near the area of the battle had been damaged. There were also several residents wounded, some severely. One of them was a woman with five children who had been gravely wounded and was not expected to live.

The Governor of Faial thought, "it is certain that the British boats were the first to attack the American Schooner."[23] Despite this, he still wanted to maintain the neutrality of the port in order to avoid further injury and damage to the town. He sent troops to collect the weapons from the crew of the *General Armstrong* after they had come on shore and sent American seamen who were breaking up the British boats that landed on the beach back to their ships. When the British wanted to come on shore, he allowed only a limited number and these without weapons.

Someone who agreed with the Governor of Faial about who had fired the first shot was a British visitor, on Horta in 1814, and only published his recollection of the battle in an article as late as 1850 about the *General Armstrong* affair. He said that the British...

> ...were in the act of boarding, before any defence was made from the privateer... there were 14 boats in the second attack with 400 men. Many houses received much injury on shore from the guns of the *Carnation*. A woman, sitting in the fourth story of her house, had her thigh shot off, and a boy had his arm broken. The American Consul here has made a demand on the Portuguese for a hundred thousand dollars for the privateer, which our Consul, Mr. Parkin, thinks in justice, will be paid, and that they will claim on England. Mr. Parkin, Mr. Edward Bayley, and other English gentlemen disapprove of the outrage and depredation committed by our vessels on this occasion. The vessel that was dispatched to England with the wounded was not permitted to take a single letter from any person.[24]

The crew of the *General Armstrong*, still fearing a continuation of the British assault, sought refuge outside the town. Captain Lloyd sent a message to the Governor saying that there were several British subjects among the *General Armstrong's* crew "and that two of them in particular, formerly belonging to H.M.'s ship 'Gussière' when [he] had the honour to command her." He asked that they be given up to him as "Traitors to their King and Country".

The Governor asked the civil authorities to help in taking the Americans prisoner so British officers could examine them. The Americans were brought into town, but John Dabney and Captain Reid refused to participate in the process so as not "to sanction by [their] presence any such proceedings". None of the seamen could be identified as a deserter, and all were released. John Dabney sent a note saying that one of the men accused of being British and taken forcibly onto the British ships was from Philadelphia and a crewmember of the *General Armstrong*.[25]

At 2:00 p.m. on September 27, a band and 60 men came ashore from the British warships for a funeral for those killed in the battle. The Governor had the Portuguese flag, which he had ordered taken down to show Captain Lloyd his displeasure about the attack, raised in respect. In addition, he sent a force of 40 men to keep all the Americans away from the funeral. Despite these efforts, two American seamen yelled insults and gave cheers for America as the British were leaving the funeral. The incident was quickly ended by their arrest.

However, not all the feelings between the Americans and British were negative.

> The next day some officers from the British fleet came to the American Consul's house and enquired for Capt. Reid and declared their high sense of this gallant action. They asked to see the Captain that they might have the honour of shaking hands with him.[26]

Funerals were held during the next two days for the British sailors and marines whose bodies had washed up on shore and for those who had died of their wounds. On September 30, the British ships *Thais* and *Calypso*, which were the regular patrol ships in the area, entered the Bay of Horta. Captain Lloyd appropriated them to take his wounded men back to England, and the two ships departed the first week in October, each carrying 25 badly wounded men. However, Lloyd did not allow either ship to take any letters back with them.

Meanwhile, Captain Lloyd was demanding that the remains of the *General Armstrong* be given to him, or he would take them by force. In order to avoid additional bloodshed, the local judge wanted to let him have them. John Dabney expressed his opinion that the few remains should be surrendered to Lloyd to lay a basis for a claim against the British government for the losses. The British Consul, Mr. Parkin, who along with Captain Mein of the *Thais* considered Captain Lloyd a "savage madman", talked to John Dabney, and they made a suggestion to sell what was left and use the funds to pay for repairing the damaged buildings. The judge agreed with this position, the Governor went along with it, and even Captain Lloyd was convinced of the wisdom of this idea.[27]

Throughout all the negotiations and discussions during and after the battle, Captain Lloyd never came to shore. The excuse he gave was that he had been injured. Captain Reid did not believe this.

> Captain Lloyd, I am told by the British Consul, is badly wounded in the leg; a jury of surgeons had been held, who gave it as their opinion, that amputation would be necessary to insure his life. 'Tis said, however, that the wound was occasioned by an ox treading on him.[28]

The battle in the Bay of Horta was over, but its effects extended far beyond a simple naval confrontation. When Captain Reid and his crew returned to America, they were surprised by their welcome as heroes of the last naval battle between Britain and America. Captain Reid later received recognition as the designer in 1818 of the present form of the American flag with 13 stripes and a star for each state. A flag made by Mrs. Reid to this design was raised over the Capital eight days after Congress accepted the proposed design.

The consequences for the British were not so fortunate. They had been trying to capture the territory of the Louisiana Purchase up the Mississippi river. The British fleet had earlier made a feint at attacking Washington, D. C., but instead of going to Halifax as they had indicated, they quietly sailed to Jamaica to await rein-forcements. Captain Lloyd and his ships, however, arrived ten days late with some 200 men less than he should have had. Because of this the fleet commander reproached him.

Lloyd's delay caused the British fleet to depart later than planned for New Orleans and arrived there on December 6, four days after Andrew Jackson had captured the city. As a result, Jackson was successfully able to hold New Orleans against the British assault during the famous battle on January 8.

Captain Lloyd's late arrival prevented the British from arriv-ing in New Orleans a week earlier as they had planned. If they had arrived before Jackson, they would have captured the city, held it and had possession of it when the Treaty of Ghent, end-ing the War of 1812, was signed on December 24, 1814. There-fore, the last naval battle between the British and Americans also had a direct effect on the outcome of the last land battle between the two countries, as well as the westward development of the United States.

The legal repercussions of the battle in the Bay of Horta con-tinued for years beyond the war. After the ship owners failed to get Britain to pay for sinking the *General Armstrong*, as well as reparations for Captain Reid and the crew, they asked for help from the U.S. government.

Britain not being willing to pay the reparations, the United States turned to Portugal to pay the claim for sinking of the *General Armstrong* based on an accusation that Portugal had not defended the neutrality of the port, which seems a curious point of view. Portugal countered that its military resources in Horta would not have allowed this and that any action would have resulted in the destruction of the town. In addition, they claimed that the American vessel had fired first, despite the Gov-ernor's statement, and, therefore, Portugal had not been respon-sible for both the attack and sinking.

After 36 years of on-and-off negotiations, the situation was still unresolved, and in 1849-50 the negotiations reached a perilous stage. President Zachary Taylor, under whom Captain Reid's son served as an army officer in Mexico, finally ordered the U. S. Ambassador in Portugal to present an ultimatum to the Portuguese government for payment of various claims, which included the *General Armstrong*. In order to keep the British from attacking in a neutral port, the U. S. felt that Portugal should have opened fire on the British from the Santa Cruz fortress, which, considering the fortresses age and lack of effective weaponry, would have been futile.

After months of correspondence between the American Ambassador, Mr. James Brown Clay (son of Henry Clay), and the Portuguese Minister of Foreign Affairs, the Count of Tojal, the Portuguese eventually agreed to pay all the claims except the one for the *General Armstrong*, which they suggested be submitted to international arbitration with the King of Sweden, or any other friendly head of state, to make the decision regarding the claim. Mr. Clay turned this down.

In July 1850, the U. S. warships *Independence*, flagship of the Mediterranean fleet, and *Mississippi* entered the Port of Lisbon for 20 days with their cannons aimed at the city. They brought orders for Ambassador Clay to give a final ultimatum and, if that were refused, to ask for his passport and for him to leave the country. This threat at gunpoint greatly angered the Portuguese and was condemned by both Parliament and the press.

During this period the Portuguese government made a formal request for Britain to intervene militarily, based on the mutual defense provisions of the Treaty of Windsor signed between the two countries in 1386. However, the British response came only after the situation had been resolved and, in any event, was negative because of Portugal's negative treatment of British ships in Mozambique.

With Portugal unwilling to back down from its position of insisting on international arbitration, Mr. Clay packed his bags, demanded the return of his passport from the Ministry of Foreign Affairs and boarded the *Independence*, thereby breaking diplomatic relations with Portugal on July 19, 1850.

However, Zachary Taylor had died 10 days earlier and Millard Fillmore had become President and selected Daniel Webster as his Secretary of State, replacing John M. Clayton. Webster continued negotiations begun by his predecessor with J. C. de Figanière e Morão, the Portuguese representative to the United States.

The letters the two men exchanged are masterpieces that demonstrate the exceptional political skills of the two men. In August Daniel Webster reversed the American position and agreed to submit the claim for the *General Armstrong* for international arbitration, and a treaty was signed to this end in early 1851 (which interestingly can be found folded up in a letter book in the archives of the Portuguese Ministry of Foreign Affairs).

In August 1851, diplomatic relations were reestablished between Portugal and the United States and Charles B. Haddock, Webster's nephew, was appointed Chargé d'Affaires in Lisbon. The arbitrator selected to make the judgment on the disagreement between the U. S. and Portugal was Emperor Louis Napoleon III. In 1853, Napoleon decided in favor of Portugal against the United States, basing his decision on the fact that the Americans had fired the first shot. If Louis Napoleon had had access to the information described earlier in this chapter, where the island's Governor and a British visitor said that the British fired first, there is a distinct possibility that the decision might have been different.

Charles Dabney, who was then American Consul on Faial, wrote a letter to U. S. Secretary of State Mr. William Marcy complaining about the decision and, since he was fluent in French, offered to go to France to speak to Napoleon, but nothing came of this. He felt that the inherent pride created and the self-respect of Americans resulting from the sinking of the *General Armstrong* was tarnished by the claim for reimbursement for the ship, using a rationale that demanded a neutral power should defend its neutrality through the application of force.[29]

> Charles W. Dabney to W. L. Marcy, Secretary of State, 21 May 1853
>
> Sir
> The award of His Majesty Napoleon 3rd in the case of the *Genl. Armstrong* having just met my eye, I feel impelled by a regard for out National honor as well as justice to the actors in the unparalleled affair, to disavow on their part the slightest infringement of the neutrality of the Port. The pecuniary amount

is of no consequence to us, but I cannot allow the brilliancy of that action to be tarnished or the slightest stain to rest on our National escutcheon. When I heard that His Majesty was to be the arbitrator I felt assured that the case would be thoroughly investigated & that there would not be any doubt, as to the result, and I confess that I was sadly disappointed to find that from some cause or other, the case had not been rightly understood by His Majesty.

In the summer of 1814 the British Sloop of War *Thais* & *Brig Calypso* were cruising on this station their Commanders were prudent men; when the Brig of War "Carnation" hove in sight, it was supposed to be the *Calypso* and no apprehensions were entertained, as we felt assured that the Commander would not attempt to violate the neutrality of the Port; but when we were informed that a Frigate & a larger Vessel were in company, we concluded that it must be the Razeè *Plantagenet*, Frigate *Rota* & Brig *Carnation* under the Command of Mad Lloyd (the same that made the senseless attack on Craney Island) who had been here three weeks before & and had boasted that he had boats built expressly for cutting out Amn. Privateers & that he would destroy them whenever he found them.

Knowing what we had to expect I (being then in my 21st year) was sent by my Father (Consul of the United States) to recommend Capt. Reid to slip his cable & warp his vessel close in under the guns of the Castle. While I was on board, the Carnation anchored within Pistol shot of the *Armstrong*, the Frigate about half a mile and the Razeè about a mile distant, yet under sail, it being nearly calm, & boats were passing between the English Vessels – Capt. Reid immediately gave orders to carry into effect the advice that I had communicated to him & I came on shore; just as I was landing (10 minutes after I left the *Armstrong*) I heard the report of musketry and soon after a Capt. Smith who had cone on board to see Capt. Reid came on shore with a message from the latter informing us that while in the act of warping in, he had been approached by four boats containing by estimate one hundred & twenty men, that they were warned repeatedly not to approach or that he would fire into them, which instead of heeding only seemed to stimulate their exertions and as there could be no mistake of their intention to take them by surprise, not attention being paid to the warning, ha had order'd his men to fire which was immediately returned from the boats killing one man & wounding the first Lieut. But having found their reception too warm they sued for quarter which was immediately granted (they were then nearly alongside of the *Armstrong*). Capt. S. was deputed by Capt. R. to request my Father to take the necessary steps for his protection & I was sent in quest of the Govr. Whom I found at Judge Arriaga's a mile from town. I was commissioned to request him to remonstrate with Capt. Lloyd (the force under his Command being wholly inadequate to cope with that of the British Squadron) and to allow us to sent thirty-two American Seamen that we had here to assist in defending the Armstrong, should she again be attacked. The latter request the Govr. Said he could not grant as it would be an infringement of the Neutrality on his part, but he accompanied me forthwith to Town & no time was lost in dispatching one of his aides with an official remonstrance. Capt. Lloyd returned a verbal answer, indicative of his intention & three hours after, the grand attack was made on the *Armstrong* then within forty yards of the Castle. These simple facts require no comment as they admit of no doubt. If there could be any doubt, the character of the Commander is a circumstance of the greatest importance in forming a correct opinion of the case.

I send a plan of the Harbor, showing the relative position of the *Armstrong* during the first & second engagement.

I trust that my motive in addressing you on this occasion will be appreciated & with the highest consideration and respect have to honor to be, Sir,

> Your most Obedt. Servt.
> Chas. W. Dabney

I am conversant with the French language and if necessary would willingly go to Paris to afford any explanation that may be required.

> Dabney

I can prove that the British Vice Consul who was then residing on the opposite shore of Pico, sent a letter on board of the Commander's vessel two hours before they anchored, consequently there was no necessity for reconnoitering with four boats full of armed men.[30]

In spite of this, the Reid family and others with connections to the ship, having failed with all other parties, turned to the U.S. Congress to pay their claim. After almost 30 years of negotiations, in 1879 Congress finally authorized payment to the heirs of Captain Reid and other claimants of $70,739, although only $54,342 was ever actually paid out. Thus the events relating to one of the little known, but important, heroic military battles in American history came to a close.

Notes:

[1] Francis L. Dabney, *Sketch of John Bass Dabney by his son William Henry Dabney of Boston, 1887,* comp., n. p.: The Author, 1971, p. 70.

[2] ["Repayment of John Bass Dabney's debt"], United States House of Representatives Resolution 85, February 15, 1818.

[3] Roxana Lewis Dabney, *Annals of the Dabney Family in Fayal,* comp., n. p.: The Author, 1900, p. 44.

[4] Roxana Lewis Dabney, *Annals,* p. 11-12.

[5] The story of the General Armstrong has been put together from descriptions contained in the following documents:

Annals of the Dabney Family in Fayal

Anais do Município da Horta

The General Armstrong

História de Quatro Ilhas

Revista da Marinha, Ano XXVII, Nº 490, 31/1/64, p27-32

Sketch of John Bass Dabney by his son William Henry Dabney of Boston, 1887, comp., n. p.: The Author, 1971,

United States Archives Microfilm of Official Consular Documents from Faial

Official Letters of the Military and Naval Officers during the War with Great Britain

Massachusetts Historical Society documents on the Dabney family

Ministério dos Negócios Estrangeiros documents in the Torre do Tombo (Portuguese National Archives)

Miscellaneous Newspaper Clippings, Massachusetts Historical Society Microfilm, Roll 2

[6] Document 17, United States Archives, Microfilm T203, Roll 4, January 6, 1851 – December 31, 1857.

[7] Roxana Lewis Dabney, *Annals*, p. 57

[8] Document 17, United States Archives, Microfilm T203, Roll 4, January 6, 1851 – December 31, 1857.

[9] "A collection of sundry publications and other documents in relation to the attack made during the late war upon the private armed Brig General Armstrong", New York, 1833, p. 8-13.

[10] Document 17, United States Archives, Microfilm T203, Roll 4, January 6, 1851 – December 31, 1857.

[11] Roxana Lewis Dabney, *Annals*, p. 48; Ministério de Negócios Estrangeiros, extract, p. 3, first letter.

[12] Miscellaneous Newspaper Clippings, Nº 3, Massachusetts Historical Society Microfilm, Roll 2.

[13] Ministério de Negócios Estrangeiros, extract, p. 3, last letter.

[14] Roxana Lewis Dabney, *Annals*, p. 57.

[15] [Captain Reid defending the forecastle and beating the British], Official Letters... p. 447.

[16] António Lourenço da Silveira Maçedo, "Notícia do combate de uma esquadrilha inglesa com uma escuna Americana na bahia da Horta extrahida do archivo da secretaria do governo millitar," *História das Quatro Ilhas que Formam o Distrito da Horta, Vol. I*, Direcção Regional dos Assuntos Culturais, Região Autónoma dos Açores, Angra do Heroísmo, Terceira Island, 1981, p. 559, footnote c.

[17] Marcelino Lima, "Um Combate Naval na Horta," *Anais do Município da Horta (História da Ilha do Faial)*, 3rd Edition, Oficinas Gráficas "Minerva", Vila Nova de Famalicão, 1981, p. 672, footnote 5.

[18] [Captain Reid visits the Consulate in the early a.m.], *Official Letters of the Military and Naval Officers during the War with Great Britain*, p. 448.

[19] [Scuttling and burning the *General Armstrong*], *Official Letters of the Military and Naval Officers during the War with Great Britain*, p. 448.

[20] Roxana Lewis Dabney, *Annals*, p. 57.

[21] Roxana Lewis Dabney, *Annals*, p. 1288-89.

[22] Roxana Lewis Dabney, *Annals*, p. 55.

[23] Roxana Lewis Dabney, *Annals*, p. 48.

[24] Miscellaneous Newspaper clippings Nº 3, Massachusetts Historical Society Microfilm, Roll 2.

[25] Document 12, Massachusetts Historical Society Microfilm, Roll 1.

[26] Francis Boardman Crowninshield, *Cleopatra's Barge*, n. p.: The Author, Boston, 1913, p. 53.

27 Marcelino Lima, p. 678; António Lourenço da Silveira Maçedo, p. 565; Document 10, Massachusetts Historical Society Microfilm, Roll 1.

28 [Captain Lloyd's wound and Captain Reid's disbelief], *Official Letters of the Military and Naval Officers during the War with Great Britain* p. 448

29 Information on the claim for the General Armstrong and the resulting diplomatic problems were taken from a large number of documents from American, Portuguese and British National archives.

30 Roxana Lewis Dabney, *Annals,* p. 63.

5 – PEACE AND NORMALITY

With the signing of the Treaty of Ghent, news of which took over two months to reach Faial, life in the Atlantic returned to normal. Ships once again began to carry their cargoes unhindered between continents. As a result, John Dabney's business began to improve. His happiness with his business was increased by the joy of another child in the family with the birth of Olivia on March 16, 1815.

Even though John Dabney was relieved that peace had arrived, he was not optimistic about it continuing very long, as he indicated in a letter to Mr. Burnett, the Dabney representative in England who had arranged for the care of his son George.

> I hope the peace may be of long continuance, but I fear the reverse if Europe remains in a ferment for any time, for your Navy is so despotic, and apparently beyond the control of your government that I am never without apprehension of our being embroiled again from that fruitful source.[1]

In early 1815 John Dabney sent the ship *Dona Maria Thereza*, with Captain Cushing in command, to St. Petersburg. Accompanying the ship as supercargo was his son Charles. Pico wine was a favorite in the Czar's household and shipments of it to Russia by the Dabneys became routine. Later, the Russians visited Faial and and one visit even resulted in a marriage between a young woman of the island and a Russian nobleman.[2]

While in Russia, Charles was greatly impressed by the palaces and the Czar's bodyguard made up of giants. He also heard an unusual horn orchestra in which each instrument played only one note and depended on each musician playing his note at the precise moment required.[3]

On the return voyage Charles Dabney stopped in Washington, D. C. There were two main reasons for the visit. One of them was to try to get reimbursement for John Dabney's expenses in taking care of American sailors during the recent war. The normal number of sailors stranded on Faial because of problems with their ships was increased greatly by those captured by British ships and being dropped off there. Because of the war, sending them elsewhere was difficult and their care on Faial fell on the resources of the Consul.

The second reason was to deliver a request to President James Madison to be named Vice-Consul for the Azores. John Dabney was planning an extended trip to America, the first since his arrival on Faial. He could have asked permission to...

> ...grant me a leave of absence, on leaving a responsible Vice-Consul, named by myself in my stead. Yet it would be on all accounts more desirable, that the appointment should be made by you, as the person would be much more respected, and be more acceptable to the constituted authorities of these Islands than an agent of [his] would be.[4]

Besides the Consular activities, John Bass Dabney was concerned with the "Establishment" he had formed "on a large and permanent scale, highly satisfactory to all ranks and descriptions of our fellow citizens, who visit this Island." Since American Consuls at this time could also have their own businesses, there was bound to be some overlap in activities, and he needed someone who was familiar with both everything he did. He had brought Charles into his office to learn the work and John Dabney was hoping that Charles would "obtain the preference as my successor, over any other candidate that might offer".[5] This is more proof that not only had John Dabney decided he was remaining on Faial permanently, but that he was also committing his heirs to remain there.

John Dabney's request was greeted favorably, although it took months for the appointment to be made. Charles, in the meantime, was enjoying his trip immensely. Throughout his

life he recounted his experiences and told of all the distinguished persons that he came into contact with while in Washington.[6]

Despite receiving the appointment as Vice-Consul, Charles
was not legally able to assume the position because of the problems of having to be accepted by the Portuguese monarch,
who was still living in Brazil. Queen Maria I had died in March
1816 after 24 years of insanity and the Prince-Regent had now
become King João VI. He ruled over Portugal and Brazil which
had become a unified kingdom at the end of 1815 when Brazil
was converted from a colony into a kingdom. His refusal to return to heal his country's wounds, and the appointment of the
British General Beresford as head of the Army led to much discontent. Some people felt that after fighting to free themselves
from French domination they, had been defeated by the British
without a fight and were now under British control.[7]

Following the final expulsion of the French from Portugal in
1811, a liberal movement opposed to the absolutism of the monarchy gained strength. General Beresford supported the Royalists
and used severe measures against the liberals. In 1817, the liberal
leader and many of his supporters were executed in Lisbon.
Also during this year, a republican uprising lasting almost three
months took place in Pernambuco, Brazil. As a result, Charles
Dabney's documents could not be sent there. John Dabney had
hopes, however, that the head of the Government in the Azores,
located in Angra on the island Terceira, would approve the
appointment until the papers could be sent to the crown for
action.

During this period, the Dabney business continued to expand, and they had three or four ships at their disposal carrying
trade to England, America and Russia and even as far as India.
After several years of poor grape harvests, the vintage had finally improved in both quality and quantity. To store the wine
he had produced or bought from other producers, John Dabney
rented a wing of the Jesuit Monastery from the local government. The monastery had become vacant after the Prime Minister, the Marquês de Pombal, had expelled the Jesuit order from
Portugal in 1759 and was taken over by the local government.
The monastery building could be heated to the 44.5° C (112° F)

necessary for the maturing of wines produced from grapes on Pico, as well as those on Madeira.

In addition to wine, there were large shipments of several other products carried by their ships in both directions.[8] Besides shipping, the Dabneys had also established a shipyard providing supplies and even making repairs on ships that had encountered problems on the Atlantic crossing. This was to become a major part of their business as more and more whaling ships began to stop off in Horta on their long voyages.

The Dabney family itself also expanded with the birth of William Henry on May 25, 1817. He was the last of the eleven Dabney children born to John Bass and Roxa Dabney and was 23 years younger than his oldest brother Charles.[9]

Two days before William Henry was born, George Crowninshield, Jr., arrived in the Bay of Horta from Salem, Massachusetts, in his yacht *Cleopatra's Barge*. "It was the first American yacht of any size yet built, the first American yacht to cross the ocean, and one of the finest yet built anywhere."[10] It had been built purely for pleasure and foreshadowed Faial's importance today as one of the main stopping-off points in the North Atlantic for pleasure yachts and sailboats.

Crowninshield and a few friends and relatives were on a pleasure trip in luxurious style to the Mediterranean, a visit which he described in the journal and log kept on the voyage. American newspapers had written about the yacht and its voyage and covered the departure from Salem. As a result, the residents of Faial were expecting the yacht's arrival and were ready to welcome it. "The American Consul and several gentlemen belonging to the place" went out to the yacht to greet it when it anchored in the Bay of Horta.[11] John Dabney took Captain Crowninshield up to Bagatelle where he received "a most hospitable reception."

The Crowninshield's were a prominent Salem, Massachusetts, family. Jacob Crowninshield, who was a U. S. representative from Massachusetts from 1803-1808 was one of the men who provided personal support to the State Department for the appointment of John Bass Dabney as Consul. His younger brother Benjamin William Crowninshield was Secretary of the Navy just after the War of 1812.

The yachtsmen had dinner with the Dabneys and then they took a tour of this "elegant mansion which is two stories high, each of them being sixteen feet in height. The rooms are large... all of them finished and furnished in superb style".[12] The house was in the center of about three acres and surrounded by a high wall. "All around are superb gardens in the laying out and arrangement of which, more taste is discovered than I have ever before witnessed in the art of gardening." The description of the trees and plants in the garden shows that it was designed with an eye not only to beauty, but also to its functionality. The annual produce of their garden made the family almost self-sufficient.

Crowninshield's description of the rest of the island and its inhabitants, however, was not quite so flattering. "Fayal itself is a small town, the streets narrow, the houses in general mean, and the populace ragged. The streets are not so dirty as those of Lisbon, nor the beggars so numerous".[13] As far as the upper classes were concerned, "The manners of this place are stiff and unsocial. The ladies, who embellish all genteel society, have here no inducement to display their charms".[14]

This last comment provides an insight into life on an island and the customs of the age relative to what is expected of women, as well as some of their problems. "They [the ladies] are born to a cruel fate. The island is already overstocked with inhabitants, and very inch of cultivated soil is in possession of some rich landholder".[15] As an example, the daughters of the French Consul were not able to marry and forbidden "to receive the address of any young man without fortune." If a suitor was unable to support his wife, then it would fall on her father to support the two of them, something few fathers could, or were willing, to do. "How inestimably better is the condition in America where we have an extent of country sufficient for our dependents to the thousandth generation. American ladies are, therefore, ready to display all the charms of female excellence." Unfortunately, this was not true in "a country of crowded population. [The women] must waste their lives in single blessedness, in a nunnery, or wither! Wither! Under their parental roof".[16]

The second night on the island, Crowninshield and party were treated to a "splendid ball" at Bagatelle. All the important members of island society attended. The main entertainment was dancing to the accompaniment of a piano and "[t]he English ladies, and the French Consul's daughters, each in turn, sang us their songs. Good humour and hilarity prevailed."[17] At about one a.m., the party broke up, the group from *Cleopatra's Barge* had a "light refreshment" with the Dabneys and returned to their boat.

The next day, those who had gone to the party the evening before visited *Cleopatra's Barge*. Unfortunately, the sea was rough and "it became necessary to put [the ladies] on shore," but they were caught in a downpour before they reached shore. "The gentlemen remained on board, charmed with our accommodations and fascinated with our wine. They poured their libations to Bacchus, and at dark left us in good humour."[18] After the revelries on Faial, *Cleopatra's Barge* set sail toward the island of São Miguel and the rest of their voyage.

Sadly *Cleopatra's Barge* made only one voyage before George Crowninshield died on board. After taking off all the fancy furnishings, the ship was sold and served as a trading vessel before finally being sold to the Hawaiian royal family. It was wrecked on the island of Kauai in 1824.

During this time, Charles Dabney was in America on business and while there met his future bride. One Sunday in the Unitarian King's Chapel in Boston, where he regularly attended services, he saw Frances Alsop Pomeroy. It was love at first sight. His aunt Stackpole, his mother's sister with whom he was staying, knew the young woman's family and offered to make introductions. The next day Charles and his aunt went to the Pomeroy home in Brighton, a trip that became familiar to Charles over the next few weeks. Having only six weeks left until his departure, the courtship was of necessity very short and ended with the couple's engagement.[19]

Frances' father was "a gentleman farmer on his large estate on Brighton hill" that overlooked Cambridge.[20] The family lived and entertained well. In addition, Mr. Pomeroy had traveled west and in 1804 bought property on the Ohio River from Elbridge Gerry, later Governor of Massachusetts and Vice-president under James Madison. Mr. Pomeroy founded the town of Pomeroy, Ohio, and pursued the development of coal mines in the area.

This was an excellent time to be getting into the coal business since the use of steamboats was on the verge of becoming a feasible reality for ocean travel.[21]

Charles Dabney was back in Faial toward the end of 1817 with his appointment as Vice-Consul having been accepted. In Spring 1818, John and Roxa Dabney and some of their older children went to America. The 25-day voyage was not without excitement because their ship sprang a leak after hitting another vessel. As a result they had to land at Nantucket where they spent some time before completing their voyage to Boston.[22]

A child's-eye view of the incident was given by ten-year old James in a letter to his brother Charles.

> It was at eleven o'clock at night, when I was sound asleep, and my sister Nancy came and woke me up and told me that there was a great hole in our vessel, and I was very much frightened indeed on hearing this. I got up and in a hurry, because I thought every minute that the vessel was going to sink, and I came out of my little room that I slept in and I could find but one of my shoes, so I got another pair and put them on; then I went on deck and saw the vessel close by, and our sailors were pumping, and they found that the vessel did not leak any; then we were happy. The other vessel tore all the rigging off the foremast of our vessel and made a great hole in the forepart; and it did not hurt the other vessel any.[23]

The seriousness of the accident is shown by Charles' comment, "I forbear making any comment on the accident you met with, it makes me shudder when I reflect upon your narrow escape".[24]

While in America, the Dabneys and Pomeroys got to know each other and began a long, happy relationship between the two families. Nancy, age 15, said, "I have seen Miss Pomeroy very frequently and I assure you the more I see of her, the more I admire and esteem her. I love her already as a sister and I long for the time when I may in reality call her by that endearing appellation.[25] "She is sensible, amiable and handsome".[26] The Dabneys also visited the Hicklings and Prescotts who were related to the family of Vice-Consul Hickling on São Miguel.

The Dabneys travelled north as far as Salem and south as far as Washington." They also visited Philadelphia, New York and family in Virginia and Connecticut, among other places. "As we were not absent from home more than five months, you may imagine that we did not remain long in any one place".[27] John Dabney and family returned to Faial in late 1818. This was a much shorter stay than the two to three years he had indicated in his letter to President Madison.[28]

In Spring 1819, Charles Dabney went to America where he was to pick up his bride. His absence as a bachelor on Faial was felt by the local young women who "had given up all hopes of Charles".[29] Charles was one of the favorites in Horta society and was known for entering into all the local activities. During Carnival he went about "with an enormous squirt he had made for the purpose of carrying water to the second story... Great battles he would have with the Misses Parkin ...They would have the furniture removed from the lower rooms, which were generally flooded with water at the end of the afternoon".[30] He was also "a beautiful dancer" and used "to dance his hornpipe steps, up to his last years". "He was somewhat of a dandy in his youthful days".

Charles arrived in America in late Spring, and he and Frances Alsop Pomeroy were married on June 10, 1819. After traveling around and seeing friends during the Summer, they departed for Faial to live. For Frances this was a major change in her life. She was leaving a large circle of friends and family in Massachusetts and Connecticut and moving to live with another family in an isolated area far from home where most people spoke a language she didn't know. To relieve somewhat her mother's sense of loss for her daughter, Frances left her a portrait she had painted by the artist Gilbert Stuart, the most famous portrait painter at this time.

Even though she was very well liked and welcomed as a sister by the Dabney family, it took time to adjust, but adjust she did and had "one of the happiest of married lives. They were indeed a united couple."[31]

On April 2, 1820 Clara Dabney, first child of Charles and Frances, and the first grandchild among the Azores Dabneys, was born.

She was only three years younger than John and Roxa Dabney's youngest child, William Henry.

In the same month as his grandchild was born, John Dabney wrote a letter of advice to his eldest son. Reproduced it in its entirety, it reveals John Dabney as an individual whose advice would still have relevance today and shows he would probably be as successful in the early 21st century as he was in the early 19th.

> Dear Charles,
>
> A sketch of my life may be useful to you if you could or would follow my example. Then there are no human obstacles that will or can prevent your going comfortably and respectably through the world. Industry, system, resolution and perseverance were my landmarks. By a steady adherence to them I have frequently overcome the most tremendous frowns of fortune, which would otherwise have been appalling and insurmountable. The true enjoyment of a domestic life (without which this world would be a perfect blank) are infinitely lightened by following those four leading rules, and whoever disregards them will sink into effeminacy, and all energy of mind and body will insensibly depart, and consequently those resources, so necessary to acquire wealth, but infinitely more so to recover from any severe reverse of fortune, is voluntarily surrendered. Industry in business without system is often idle bustle and fatigue. Carley for instance is an industrious man, but want of system paralyzes all his efforts. I presume that no man ever had a more ardent affection for his wife and family than myself, which thank God continues unabated to the present hour. From the day I was married, I rose early and divided my hours regularly to business, attention to my friends, and my duties to society, and to domestic endearments, and thus avoided the rock that many a man's happiness is split on, satiety, and consequent coldness and indifference.
>
> I generally devoted a half hour every evening to a review of the business of the past day, and made notes of what had been unavoidably left unfinished, or in arrears, as well as any new business that the following day would bring with it, etc. At six next morning (having previously classed my business

for particularly hours in the day) I set forth thus systematically, and daily accomplished more than any of my neighbors. Strict regularity in rising, in meals, and even in amusements, made my house a little paradise. I have always noticed that little absences, and those continually repeated, but not too much protracted, gave a rest to domestic pleasures. To be too much about those we love is somewhat like the passengers in a ship who altho' the best friends, get tired of seeing each other and separate with precipitancy the moment the vessel arrives in port.

Your situation in life fortunately does not require the incessant fatigue of body and mind that I was subjected to in first setting out in life. More time may be allowed to you for amusements. This however does not exempt you from a rigid adherence to the above rules for you will otherwise let your amusements destroy your business. A transaction which requires a few hours to bring to a close should be settled at once. A partial attention to it from day to day consumes your time unnecessarily and is a serious loss. A few hours attention to a business which is quite recent, and every circumstance fresh in the memory will do more than days of fatigue and vexation, when the object is almost lost sight of.

For the last time I ever shall revert to this subject, I must beseech you to rise at seven in the morning at the latest. For twenty years I rose at 4, 5 and 6, but certainly to lie in bed beyond seven is undermining your health and prosperity. The one hour before breakfast will enable you to look after your workmen and see that their day is commenced as it ought to be. This will save you in the course of years, thousands of dollars. Or the hour may at times be employed in filing and examining your papers and letters and in making notes and arranging in due order the business of the day. Or again you might make many appointments to speak to people who want to see you from seven to eight o'clock and thus save the time these same people would take up in the more busy and active part of the day. These preparatory steps would enable you to get through the day's business pleasantly, and give you more hours for recreation. You can have no pretensions to be called a man of resolution if you cannot rise at any hour you think proper. 'Prenez garde a la molesse,' sooner or later it will destroy health and prosperity.

Your talents and acquirements and amiable manners have placed you in the foremost rank among the first people in this Island and the influence it gives you in society is very great, and continually increasing. This influence properly managed, will be of great importance to yourself and all your family.

Your purchases and sales are made to greater extent, and more advantage by keeping up a kind of intimacy with the leading people here; by contributing to their pleasures by a thousand little kindnesses and attentions, you get their good will, and in many cases they will deal with you in preference. Thus far interest dictates a due attention to this object, but besides this there is a secret pleasure in being looked up to, as the first man of your age in this society. It adds a name and dignity to your character through life. Do not lightly relinquish this hold on the affections, esteem and respect of these people among whom you are to live, and on whom your peace happiness and prosperity depends, as long as you live in this place.

These few observations which God grant may be useful to you are thrown together in haste by one who has your future prosperity and happiness more at heart than anyone else can possibly have.

Your affectionate father,
J. B. Dabney[32]

Notes:

[1] Francis L. Dabney, *Sketch of John Bass Dabney by his son William Henry Dabney of Boston, 1887*, comp., n. p.: The Author, 1971, p. 88.

[2] César Gabriel Barreira, *Um Olhar Sobre a Cidade da Horta*, Núcleo Cultural da Horta, Horta, 1995, p. 37.

[3] Roxana Lewis Dabney, *Annals*, p. 68; Francis L. Dabney, *Sketch*, p. 87-88.

[4] Roxana Lewis Dabney, *Annals*, p. 69; Francis L. Dabney, *Sketch*, p. 89.

[5] Roxana Lewis Dabney, *Annals*, p. 69; Francis L. Dabney, *Sketch*, p. 89.

[6] Roxana Lewis Dabney, *Annals*, p. 69.

[7] António Lourenço da Silveira Maçedo, "Revolução pacifica na villa da Horta; aclamação e juramento da constituição politica de 24 d'agosto de 1820; festejos por essa causa; nomeação da junta governativa e seus actos-1821," *História das Quatro Ilhas que Formam o Distrito da Horta*, Vol. *II*, Direcção Regional dos Assuntos Culturais, Região Autónoma dos Açores, Angra do Heroísmo, Terceira Island, 1981, p. 3.

[8] Francis L. Dabney, *Sketch*, p. 90-91.

[9] Roxana Lewis Dabney, *Annals*, p. 91.

[10] Francis L. Dabney, *Sketch*, p. 91.

[11] Francis Boardman Crowninshield, *Cleopatra's Barge*, n. p.: The Author, Boston, 1913, p. 52.

[12] Francis Boardman Crowninshield, *Cleopatra's Barge*,. 59.

[13] Francis Boardman Crowninshield, *Cleopatra's Barge*,. 55.

[14] Francis Boardman Crowninshield, *Cleopatra's Barge*,. 57.

[15] Francis Boardman Crowninshield, *Cleopatra's Barge*,. 57.

[16] Francis Boardman Crowninshield, *Cleopatra's Barge*,. 58.

[17] Francis Boardman Crowninshield, *Cleopatra's Barge*,. 56.

[18] Francis Boardman Crowninshield, *Cleopatra's Barge*,. 57.

[19] Roxana Lewis Dabney, *Annals*, p. 75.

[20] Roxana Lewis Dabney, *Annals*, p. 169.

[21] Francis L. Dabney, *Sketch*, p. 93; Roxana Lewis Dabney, *Annals*, p. 103-104; "Early History of Pomeroy", http//www.Genealogy.org/~baf/misc/howe/pomeroy.html.

[22] Francis L. Dabney, *Sketch*, p. 92.

[23] Roxana Lewis Dabney, *Annals*, p. 73.

[24] Francis L. Dabney, *Sketch*, p. 93.

[25] Roxana Lewis Dabney, *Annals*, p.74.

[26] Roxana Lewis Dabney, *Annals*, p. 79.

[27] Roxana Lewis Dabney, *Annals*, p. 79.

[28] Francis L. Dabney, *Sketch*, p. 89.

[29] Francis L. Dabney, *Sketch*, p. 80.

[30] Roxana Lewis Dabney, *Annals*, p. 77.

[31] Francis L. Dabney, *Sketch*, p. 93.

[32] Francis L. Dabney, *Sketch*, p. 95-97.

6 – THE END OF AN ERA

As 1820 drew to a close, Portugal found itself facing a revolution. King João VI was still refusing to return to Portugal from Brazil. This disturbed many people who were waiting for him to "cure the wounds of his people, that still bled."[1] To them it seemed that the king had forgotten his people and wanted to stay in the calm opulence and prosperity of Brazil.[2] The liberal movement took advantage of the popular feeling and began to spread their influence.

Royal control was difficult over such a long distance and the powers of the British General Beresford, who had been appointed head of the Portuguese Army, continued to grow. Consequently, he, in effect, was the regent and ran the country. He was not popular and continued to use severe and repressive measures against the liberals. People of all social classes were discontent with an absent monarch and British domination, especially with the military whose senior officers were also all British. The feeling that they had only traded the French masters of Napoleon for the British masters of Beresford was still strong and infuriating.

On August 24 a revolution started in Oporto and spread to Lisbon where a provisional government was formed. One of its first actions was to prepare for the convening of the *cortes*, the assembly of the three estates – nobility, clergy and commoners – that had provided consultation to Portuguese monarch since the mid-13th century. The difference this time was that the "*cortes*" was a body selected by the people and not representatives of the estates selected by the monarch.

João VI learned of the uprisings in October, but instead of returning or sending his son Pedro back, he pardoned the rebels and permitted the convening of the *cortes*. This didn't put an end to the unrest and, as 1821 began, the revolution spread to Brazil.

The liberal government held its first assembly on January 24, 1821. Their principal task was the development of a constitution that would be agreeable to the various factions. This was not an easy task to carry out. One of the things the members of the *cortes* agreed to was the establishment of a parliament with a single house. They also adopted an anti-clerical stance and, among other things, eliminated the Holy Inquisition, which had been established in the 16ᵗʰ century, although less active in recent years. Clearly, the Church reacted with great antagonism to the liberal movement.

The revolutionaries in Portugal demanded that João VI return to Portugal, swear to the constitution and form a liberal government. He did finally decide to return, leaving his oldest son Pedro as regent in Brazil. King João VI arrived in Portugal on July 3, 1821, three days after the proposed constitution had been adopted and 14 years after the Royal Family had fled Napoleon's troops. The day after he arrived, he took an oath to the basic concepts of the Constitution.

Meanwhile, back in the Azores, the revolution arrived in March 1821 with a liberal uprising on the island of São Miguel, where the senior military officer, Colonel Arriaga, was an absolutist and opposed to the liberal movement. In addition, the Governor General of the Azores, Mr. Stockler, had been trying to prevent the spread of the revolution through threats and repression. He refused to obey orders from the central government and even refused to allow any communication with ships arriving from Lisbon.

On April 1 the liberal uprising spread to Angra on the island of Terceira where ex-General Araújo led supporters of the liberal movement along with some troops, whom he had secretly bribed, in support of the new government and constitution. The next day a provisional government was appointed, and Stockler, who had fled to a nearby village, was deposed. Two days later Stockler returned to Angra and resigned.

Despite his apparent acceptance of the situation, Stockler was plotting a counter-revolution. He got the rebellious troops to go back to the absolutist side he supported because they had not received the money that Araújo promised them.[3] On April 5 they

struck, firing cannons into the house where the provisional government was meeting. Araújo went to the window to see what was
happening and was killed by grape shot from a cannon. The
others present were able to escape out the back. Stockler then
began a reign of terror on the island, annulling all the liberal
actions, demanding an oath to the King and arresting the liberals.

Stockler's actions at Angra caused the liberals on Faial to
hesitate in implementing their action. However, two war ships
from Lisbon anchor in the Bay of Horta just over a month later,
on May 12. The Military Governor followed Stockler's orders and
refused to allow them to land. However, under pressure from the
island's leading citizens, the Governor allowed the commanders
to come on shore where a large group of islanders met and
accompanied them to the Governor's headquarters. They were
warmly received by the citizens who presented their demands
to the government to adopt the liberal system that even the Governor supported. This was not just because of the Faialenses
philosophical belief in the system, but also due to their desire to
be independent from the government on Terceira[4] and to become
"the Capital of the lower islands".[5] As a result, the Governor
quickly agreed to the demands. Cheering started in the chamber,
spread to the crowd in the streets and was joined by artillery
salvos from the fort and ships, and by the tolling of church bells.

The crowd then accompanied the ship's officers and Governor
to the town hall where the council agreed to the action and
elected a governing junta. Everyone wanted to sign the oath to
the new constitution, the King and the *cortes*. Celebrations went
on until late at night and started early the next day, which was
also the King's birthday, and continued with fancy dress balls
in the evening.

The same day that Faial declared support for the liberal government and constitution and a provisional government was
formed, the citizens on the island of Pico followed suit. Like their
compatriots on Faial, they also wanted to be independent and
elect their own representative to the *cortes*, wanting to escape
Faial's control the same as Faial wanted to escape Terceira's.
This naturally upset those in power on Faial, and Pico did not
achieve its aim.

Faial was not able to achieve independence easily because its representative had not gone to Lisbon immediately. He took a long time to get there as he had waited to go with the warships and arrived only one day before the king. Consequently, Faial's voice was almost lost in the multitude of other considerations.[6] Nevertheless, Faial's request to the Cortes for greater autonomy was eventually acted on positively. In early 1822, the king elevated Horta from the classification of town to city and made it the governmental seat for Pico and the two western islands, Flores and Corvo, thereby making it independent of Terceira. The event was understandably greeted with anger on Terceira.[7]

None of the revolutionary activities appears to have affected the Dabneys to any great extent, and they managed to stay out of the conflict. Other than an official letter in May 1821 to Secretary of State John Quincy Adams describing what was going on, the revolutionary activities in the Azores were only mentioned incidentally in letters to family and friends.

However, within the family there had also been a movement toward liberty. John Lewis Dabney, the third child and second eldest son, decided to seek his fortune elsewhere. John was the first to make this move that was almost a necessity given the small number of persons who could be involved in the family business on Faial and the limited possibilities to do anything else on the island.

In 1819 John Lewis, after a long trip that had taken him to India, went to America, "on the shore you have so long and so ardently wished to revisit for which you entertain so much love and esteem...".[8] In the summer of 1820 his sister Nancy wrote a letter.

> I hear there is a probability of your being in Boston, but I fear that it is only a probability, as I think you would not voluntarily venture so near home, or rather you would not trust yourself where there is so much communication with our Island, lest you should be under the unpleasant necessity of coming out to pass the winter in a place, which I believe has but few charms for you; greatly as it would rejoice us all to have you with us, I think we could be disinterested enough not to

wish for that gratification, while we felt assured that you were in a place so much more congenial to your taste as is America.[9]

John eventually did return for a visit to Faial in the autumn of 1820, but he didn't stay long. In the spring of the next year he departed to live in Rio de Janeiro where he was able to go into business and live happily, despite the revolutionary atmosphere. On the other hand, maybe he was just following in his father's footsteps by taking advantage of the opportunities that arose in situations of political instability.

The year 1822 opened with another marriage in the Dabney family. Roxalina, the second oldest, married her cousin Charles Cunningham, son of Roxa Dabney's sister Mollie, whose family's company represented the Dabney business in Boston, and he became their principal agent there in later years. Although Mrs. Dabney "had a strong prejudice against marriages between cousins and with foreigners",[10] all of John and Roxa's children who married, except Charles, ended up marrying a cousin or a foreigner. However, this may have been one of the reasons John Lewis left, or was sent from, Faial when he took a strong interest in his cousin Mary Ann Young, daughter of John Bass Dabney's sister Mary, although it is more likely his mother opposed the marriage because "of his delicate health."[11]

Roxalina's marriage took place in Mrs. Dabney's bedroom in the presence of the family and a few English friends. John Bass Dabney performed the ceremony, a power granted to American Consuls at that time. Perhaps because of this, John Dabney "was so agitated, that he could only with difficulty articulate, indeed I [Nancy] think we were all much more affected than persons usually are on such occasions".[12] On the other hand, the bride, Roxa, "acquitted herself with perfect self possession".[13] The evening after the wedding there was "a ball and supper at which there was more merriment and less ceremony than at almost any party I was ever at in this place".[14] Soon after the wedding, the couple left for Boston where they were to live.

Once again John Dabney took the opportunity to write a letter of advice. The advice he gave his daughter, however, was quite different from that given to his sons.

Your departure occasioned a great void in our family, but for dear little Olivia, who perpetually reminds me of you, I should feel the weight much greater. She looks so much like you, and is just such a reasonable gay girl as you were at her age, that my affection for her seems to be increased since we parted with you.

You must hereafter, my dear Roxalina, expect to derive your chief source of happiness from your own domestic circle, and you must, by a cheerful demeanor, endeavor to make all around you comfortable and happy. As our lives are chequered with good and ill, we cannot at all times command our own with good and ill, we cannot at all times command our own tempers, and they will get ruffled but they can be conquered in a great degree with good sense and resolution. Let me impress upon you one thing, and that is: amidst all your crosses and vexations, from which none are exempt, that you always meet your best friend with a smile when he returns home, fatigued with the labors of the day. This is the consolation that a fond husband seeks and deserves, and I trust that he will never seek in vain for this cheering antidote to all the real and substantial ills of life that he has daily to encounter in his intercourse with the world.[15]

On July 1, 1822, the ship *Strong* sailed into the Bay of Horta with a most unusual group of passengers. On board were 37 freed slaves and 18 Africans whom the U.S. Navy had captured from a slave ship. The American Colonization Society was sending them, "under the superintendence of a Mr. Ashmun,"[16] to the newly founded village of Monrovia at Cape Montserrado on the west coast of Africa in what was to become the country of Liberia.

The American Colonization Society was founded on December 21, 1816, and began plans to establish a colony for freed slaves in Africa. The project had the backing of the Federal and State Governments, including solid support from President Monroe, and raised its funds from private sources.

The freed slaves were looking forward to going to a land where they could feel completely free. Even though many loved America, they felt they could not share equally in the liberties it proclaimed.[17] On the other hand, slaveholders in the South, and much of white society in the North, didn't want freed slaves around. The North saw them as competitors in the labor market and the South saw them as a source for creating discontent among those who still were slaves and potentially weakening the slave owners' hold on them.[18]

On February 6, 1820, the *Elizabeth* with the first group of former slaves sent by the Colonization Society had sailed for Africa. They arrived there on March 9, but it took until April 1822, after surviving diseases, hostility from local tribes and lack of support from the Colonization Society, before the emigrants under the direction of Reverend Lott Cary finally founded the small village, later to be named Monrovia after President Monroe, at Cape Montserrado.

On May 20, 1822, the *Strong*, the third of the ships on its way to Africa with its passengers seeking freedom, had departed from Baltimore. It was an old ship that didn't sail well and met contrary winds and stormy weather. The heavy seas had displaced the cargo, and the delay in crossing had depleted their supplies so that they were happy to arrive back on solid land in Faial.

They spent a week in Horta and the "greater number of them came up here [to Bagatelle] to walk in the garden. It was I assure you a very interesting sight; they all seemed so light-hearted and full of pleasant anticipations."[19] The visitors must have created quite a stir among the Portuguese, many of whom had never seen a black person before.

Jehudi Ashmun, the Colonization Society representative, and his wife spent the week at Bagatelle. The Dabneys found him "a young man of such amiable and agreeable manners and disposition; he was a great favourite with us *all*, and you know it is not *every one*, who succeeds in pleasing my father [John Bass Dabney]."[20] Mrs. Ashmun kept herself busy teaching the female passengers to read the catechism, as well as other subjects while her husband took charge of the male passengers. Their students were "so grateful to their instructors."[21]

On July 9 they set sail and arrived at Cape Montserrado on August 9 where the settlers welcomed them. It wasn't long, however, before Ashmun made himself unwelcome. He had plans for "building a lucrative commercial empire in Africa, where he could become wealthy and pay off the heavy debts which he had found impossible to pay while in the United States."[22] The opinion of him in Africa was quite different from that of the Dabneys. "He, in fact, cared little or nothing about the emigrants and recaptured Africans... except that they might prove of some advantage to himself, and to his imagined commercial operations in Africa."[23] Whatever the truth about Jehudi Ashmun's true aims, he did take over the colony and set about trying to expand its territory, for which he was prepared to use force, and obtain agreements with the local kings. His activities resulted in strife between himself and the other settlers until his death from a fever in 1828.

News arrived that the Dabney's son George had died in April. He had been in an institution in England for 13 years because of the effects of a fall from his sister Roxalina's back. Mr. Burnett who had arranged for his care and watched after him wrote that, "the dear little sufferer without any increase to his pains, yielded up his breath."[24] Although his death was not unexpected, Mrs. Dabney "was shocked and afflicted to hear the distressing tidings." Nancy was sad also, but felt it was "a merciful disposition of Providence, as his existence was painful and useless to himself and of the same nature to those interested in him."[25]

Also about this time, Mary Ann Parkin, one of the daughters of the British Consul, Mr. Parkin, married a Mr. Lane and left to live in Scotland. Her mother had opposed the marriage, "But Mr. P. was too much pleased with getting one of his daughters respectably settled to let this prevent it."[26] As pointed out by George Crowninshield on his visit, finding a good marriage match on the island was virtually impossible for young women, and fathers would grab almost any opportunity to marry off their daughters. Fortunately, Mr. Lane was "well spoken of; for more than five years he has been an admirer of Miss Ann, and only waited to get an establishment before he declared his intentions, or I should say wishes."[27]

In the Summer of 1822, John Bass Dabney was developing a property to be used by his business. "It is as complete for a commercial establishment as my House & Garden are for the residence of a family. It is called here the Arsenal."[28] Among the family it was known as the *Relva* (lawn) or Yard. The buildings were on two acres of land opposite the fortress of Santa Cruz and had a large, two and a half story warehouse. In addition there was a wine-storage area and three *estufas*. These latter are structures that can be heated to the high temperatures necessary for the maturing of Pico and Madeira wines. There was also a cool storage area for oil, salted provisions and naval supplies, a loft to store *bacalhau*, the pungent, dried, salted cod which is an important part of the Portuguese diet, as well as a lumber yard. This was next to land where he grew alfalfa for animal feed and vegetables for both family use and for sale to ships wanting fresh provisions. The company offices were also located here.

The costs of transporting provisions to and from the port area were less than in his previous location in the former Jesuit monastery. It also eliminated the rent of that building and having to negotiate the fees with the town council, which owned it. He likewise wanted to take advantage of the dock that was to be built next to the fortress. This location established a strong presence for the Dabney business in the commercial center of Horta.

The peace after João VI, who had become king after his mother Maria I died in 1816, returned and accepted the liberal constitution didn't last as long as anticipated. Fearing that Brazil would declare itself independent with Prince Pedro's support, the Portuguese government ordered the Prince to return in September 1821. On the other hand, the Brazilian people and government wanted him to stay and he agreed. Pedro sent the Portuguese troops in Brazil home and refused to allow others sent from Portugal to land.

The parliament once again ordered Pedro to return. When he received this demand on the banks of the Ipirango River in São Paulo Province on September 7, 1822, he responded, "*Independência ou morte*!" (Independence or Death). On October 13, the Brazilians proclaimed him Emperor of Brazil.

João VI had no better luck with the rest of his family. In October he took an oath to the text of the constitution. However, his wife Carlota Joaquina, sister of King Ferdinand VII of Spain, was an ardent believer in the absolute power of a monarch and refused to agree to the constitution. João VI banished her from the country, but, because of her poor health, she was allowed to stay near Sintra, about 20 km west of Lisbon.

In May 1823 some of the military at Vila Franca da Xira near Lisbon revolted against the liberals and were joined by some of the Lisbon garrison. João's 21-year old son Miguel, who had the support of his mother, Queen Carlota Joaquina and the nobility, arrived to lead the troops. João VI went there and received the submission of the troops and appointed Miguel their Commander-in-Chief.

The radical actions by the liberal *Cortes*, now functioning as a parliament, had antagonized too many important people. The *Cortes* lost the king's support and this resulted in their collapse in mid-1823. King João VI now appointed moderate ministers, as well as a committee to look at the future direction of the regime. Nevertheless, the committee produced no results during the rest of the king's reign.

This move away from liberalism surprised the Horta town council, but it sent the king congratulations. They also gave the power back to those who were in office before the liberal revolt and cancelled all documents the liberal regime had required them to produce.[29]

Evidence of problems in Brazil arrived with part of the Portuguese naval fleet and its support ships. On board were Portuguese citizens who had fought for their rights against the Brazilians and were forced to flee the country. There had been 13 warships and 32 troop carriers and supply ships that left Bahia that had been chased from Bahia by the Brazilian navy.[30] The Brazilian navy captured some of the ships and scattered many of the remainder. Only 14 ships arrived in the Bay of Horta. They stayed "in this harbour several days recruiting."[31]

When the ships arrived they were flying the colors of the liberal government and were unaware that the constitution had been revoked. As a result, the Governor refused to allow them to resupply or even land until they had sworn allegiance to the king.[32]

With the arrival of the Brazilians,

> Fayal did not look like itself, every thing so gay and lively,
> the streets filled with officers, and ladies, dressed very hand-

somely; the bay filled with beautiful large ships, and boats plying about in every direction, presented such an unusual and pleasing spectacle that it will long be remembered by the inhabitants. This being the time of the Vintage nearly all the families are over at Pico, the strangers have therefore been more at our house [Bagatelle] than they probably would have been had there been more people to invite them to their houses.[33]

The upper levels of society on Faial, including the Dabney's, found some positive aspects to this change in government. Because of the persecution of the inhabitants on Terceira, "great numbers of them have fled to the different Islands, mostly to St. George, some to this place; several officers of distinction have been exiled to these Islands from Portugal. A Brigadier General sent to this place is much liked by the inhabitants, and is a great acquisition to society here."[34]

Every move that King João VI took to resolve problems seemed to create more. In April 1824, Prince Miguel, supported by the Absolutists opposed even to King João's moderate government, attempted to seize power alleging a plot against the royal family. Some of the government ministers fled to ships in the harbor, the king was isolated in the Palace of Bemposta in Lisbon and Queen Carlota Joaquina returned to Lisbon to support her son. Miguel's action dismayed the diplomatic corps. To show their displeasure they went en masse to the palace and escorted the king to the British ship Windsor Castle in the harbor. King João had summoned Prince Miguel there, had him arrested and sent him out of the country. He eventually settled in Vienna, and the Queen returned to her palace of exile.

Negotiations between Brazil and Portugal continued with the mediation of George Canning, British Minister of Foreign Affairs. Despite all the back and forth negotiations, the situation remained unresolved, with Brazil exerting itself even more. The United States recognized the independence of Brazil on May 27, 1824.

Throughout this period of political unrest, the Dabney family continued to prosper and grow. By 1824, John Bass and Roxa had two children get married and four grandchildren were born. Even John Bass got married again, at least as a proxy in a ceremony performed by Mr. Parkin for a groom who wanted to marry but was unable to come to Faial.[35]

Domestic tranquility, however, was shattered in the spring of 1824. One day while Nancy, the fifth Dabney child was riding horseback, José Maria d'Avelar Brotero, a Portuguese lawyer saw her and immediately fell in love with her. He set about courting her and caught her. "She was the best Portuguese scholar, and Mr. Brotero, who was a very well read man, used to lend her books and slip little billets-doux between the pages,"[36] He had wanted to be a judge in Portugal, but the political situation caused him to go to Faial to practice law.[37]

That Nancy would fall in love with a Portuguese man was an event that had never been anticipated. It was especially surprising considering he was Catholic and the comments she had made to her brother John a couple of years earlier.

> I hope no little Brazilian will captivate your heart and render your present, a permanent abode... I must confess, however, that I would prefer you should give me an English or American sister-in-law.[38]

In fact, with the lone exception of Nancy, all of the Dabney children did marry someone American or British and who was a Protestant.

Nancy was first baptized as a Catholic, a major step for someone from an old New England Protestant family. They were married on May 10, 1824, at the house of the Magistrate. The ceremony was very private. John Bass attended, but Nancy's mother Roxa stayed at home.[39] There was probably also a religious ceremony since the Catholic Church requires it, and, in a letter to her brother John, Nancy refers to "the ceremony I went through in the chapel."[40]

Despite not attending the wedding, and her disagreement with Nancy marrying a Catholic, Mrs. Roxa Dabney didn't try to impose her opinion on the rest of the family. In a letter to her son John Lewis in Rio de Janeiro she says,

I flatter myself when you are acquainted with him you will approve of her choice. She had engaged to marry him before I had any suspicion that she had an idea of the kind. He speaks English quite well, and has a finished education, he intends going to Pernambuco to reside, so I hope you will go and visit her when she arrives there.[41]

It wasn't long after the wedding that José Brotero developed an extreme jealousy of Nancy's friends and family, even though they were living in Bagatelle. He became so jealous of her affections for her family that Nancy became unhappy and moved out of Bagatelle to live at the Magistrate's. Brotero "became so reckless at this that he threw himself out of the back entry window and dislocated his ankle, and she was persuaded to come back and nurse him."[42] Even with the family's acquaintances on São Miguel, where most of the family went shortly after the wedding, "her husband did not like her to shake hands" with her male friends.[43]

The Brotero's planned to go to Brazil for their permanent residence, but the unsettled conditions there delayed their departure. José felt that Nancy could help him get himself established as a businessman. As a single man he had been in "a state of apathy" and his ambition "was very limited." In Nancy he saw a person "who would excite my industry, restrain my passions, comfort me in my troubles, and make me look forward to what might be the consequences of my actions."[44] The future activities of this branch of the family bore out his foresight.

For José Brotero, "Fayal or any of these Islands can only offer a slow and tiresome career."[45] His approach to business was along the lines of the ideas of John Bass and John Lewis Dabney as shown in a letter he wrote to John Bass Dabney.

A great writer on the French Revolution says, 'the greater the confusion the more favourable the opportunity for the venturesome; and that great dangers to the bold, who are willing to sacrifice to fortune, are the wreaths with which they weave the crowns of their success'; and I am persuaded that without exposing myself to risk, I can never obtain the situation I desire, which is to put myself and my dear wife in a state of Independence, that we may never burthensome to any one; to have the means of gratifying our desires, and that my wife may not find only affection from me , but also the comfort she was accustomed to enjoy in her Father's house.[46]

After the visit to São Miguel, the newlywed couple went to Terceira where there were better opportunities for them than on Faial. They stayed there for almost a year waiting for the right time to go to Brazil. Before the Broteros left for Brazil, Roxa Dabney went to visit them on Terceira. Nancy wrote her brother John that he would have been "surprised at my Mother making so great an effort to come and see me; much as I wished it, I could hardly flatter myself that it would ever take place."[47] Since Nancy had just lost a baby boy, Mrs. Dabney's visit was not surprising.[48]

José and Nancy Brotero finally set off for Brazil where they arrived in early November of 1825. They did not have to wait long for the resolution of Brazil's status. In May 1825, King João VI was heir to the two thrones and chose to give up his throne in Brazil, conceding the sovereignty of Brazil to Pedro. A treaty was drawn up recognizing Brazil's independence, declaring friendship between the two countries, providing a disclaimer for any interest by Brazil in Portuguese Africa and giving King João VI the honorary title of Emperor. It was signed in Rio de Janeiro on August 29, 1825, and then was sent to Lisbon for approval. Brazil became an independent country in November 1825.[49]

Nancy was never to leave Brazil, and the only members of her family she ever saw again were her brother John and her nephew John (Charles' son).[50] The Brotero family, through its abilities, and the arrangement of some good marriages, became one of the most respected families in São Paulo and all over Brazil.[51]

John Bass and Roxa Dabney along with their two youngest children, Olivia and William, began a visit to the United States in the spring of 1825.[52] They spent the summer in and around Boston where they visited friends and family where all had the whooping cough at the same time.

They decided to spend the winter in Philadelphia because the weather was milder than Boston. During the trip from Boston they stopped and visited more family along the way. Since this was in the days before the railroad, it was a long trip by stagecoach, carriage and steamboat. William, who was eight years old at the time, was much impressed by the trip and his "first steamboat experience; indeed steamboats were new to everybody in those days."[53] They also visited Washington, D. C., and William remembered well "all the incidents of this journey, how we forded several rivers and my fright in doing so."[54] They returned to Boston when the weather warmed, and by the end of June 1826, they were back in Faial.

Mr. Parkin, the British Vice-consul, died in early fall of 1825. He had been one of John Dabney's staunchest friends since his arrival on Faial. Mr. Parkin's family would have been in a very difficult situation if three of his four daughters hadn't been married. Mr. Walker replaced him as Britain's representative on Faial.[55]

During the absence of his parents and two siblings, Charles William Dabney had begun construction on a residence for his family "at the bottom of the Bagatelle garden", that became known as the "new house."[56] It was originally a storage area and granary over stores, but he remodeled it and added another story to the building, as well as a one-story kitchen. However, when his father died later in the year, he halted construction and continued to live in Bagatelle.

In 1835, when his brother Frederick got married and moved his wife into Bagatelle, Charles' family needed more room and moved into another residence, which was called Fredonia, on a lane in the center of Horta called Canada de Beliago, today a main street renamed Rua Consul Dabney. In 1851, William Dabney finally completed the "new house" at the bottom of the Bagatelle property and moved into it.[57]

In addition to adding a house to the family, Charles and Frances had their fourth child. On January 6, 1826, Samuel Wyllys Dabney was born. He was destined to be the third Dabney to be appointed American Consul in the Azores.[58]

It was now the middle of the 1820's, and Portugal had been going through years of unrest. After the recognition of Brazil, it seemed as if the country was finally going to settle down, but on March 4 the king became seriously ill. Too sick to rule, he appointed his daughter Princess Isabel Maria as regent. King João VI died on March 10, 1826, and a conflict over succession to the Portuguese throne began that resulted in another long period of unrest and civil war.

In this same year, the Dabney family also suffered a serious loss when Consul John Bass Dabney died. After his return from the United States, John Dabney returned to work immediately and Charles Dabney went to stay on Pico to prepare for the grape harvest. On September 1, James Dabney sent his brother Charles a note about 1:00 p.m.:

> Dear Father is very ill indeed. He came up from the counting house very well and got a bunch of grapes and in a minute after called to mother for a glass of wine and water and in another minute after that could not articulate a word, and still continues so. Mother is very much distressed and wishes you to come over immediately.[59]

John Dabney was moved from the dining room and put to bed. He never spoke again and remained unconscious until he died in the early afternoon of the next day, September 2, 1826. On the same day and at the same hour, Roxa and Charles Cunningham's 18-month old son Francis died in Boston.[60]

John Bass Dabney was 60-years old and had been United States Consul in the Azores for 20 years. It was the family's belief that his death had been brought about by the misadventures of his nephew Frederick Spaulding. He had sold the ship *Albert* and its cargo, which had been entrusted to him, for less than half its worth. John Dabney's concern was not the financial loss, but the feeling he had been betrayed by a relative and was concerned that his name might be disgraced if the new owners inappropriately used the ship. Frederick was never heard from again.[61]

The obituary of John Bass Dabney from the Boston Paladium of October 24, 1826, shows how well thought of he was far beyond the confines of little Faial.

> Died in Fayal on the 2nd of September of apoplexy, John B. Dabney, Esq., Consul General of the United States for the Azores
>
> He was a native of Boston and son of Dr. Dabney, who removed to Connecticut at the commencement of the Revolutionary war.
>
> Mr. Dabney had resided with his family at Fayal upwards of 20 years. It is well known that this Island possesses the most accessible harbor of any in the Azores and is the constant resort of shipping in want of supplies, in distress, and often mere wrecks. Perhaps no spot on the globe affords greater scope for the display of active benevolence and hospitality towards those "whose march in on the mountain wave," and is believed that no person could have been found whose natural propensities would stimulate more to the exercise of those virtues than Mr. Dabney. The extent can be fully appreciated only by those who have experienced his beneficence. And it may be safely affirmed that no Consular flag ever reflected more credit on its Country by the marked hospitalities which have been received under it by the subjects of most of the maritime powers of Europe.
>
> Though a foreigner and a Protestant, no man was ever more beloved by the People of Fayal. His charities to the poor were extensive and the following fact, related by a native, is worthy of recording. The failure of the harvest, a number of years ago, induced fears that the supply of Indian corn which is the principal food of the laboring classes, and the indigent, was so short that a famine might ensue. Mr. Dabney very promptly imported from the U. S. some cargoes with his own funds and instead of taking advantage of the necessities of such a community, he sold the corn at a price that he supposed would only cover the cost and charges, but on making up the account sales, a surplus appeared. This he paid over to the proper authorities for the use of the poor in the hospital.[62]

John Dabney was buried in the upper garden of Bagatelle until a tomb could be built in the same area. His epitaph was: "By industry, integrity and perseverance he rose superior to the over-whelming frowns of fortune which thrice assailed him during his sojourn on earth."[63]

Notes:

[1] António Lourenço da Silveira Maçedo, "Revolução pacifica na villa da Horta; aclamação e juramento da constituição politica de 24 d'agosto de 1820; festejos por essa causa; no-meação da junta governativa e seus actos-1821," *História das Quatro Ilhas que Formam o Distrito da Horta, Vol. II,* Direcção Regional dos Assuntos Culturais, Região Autónoma dos Açores, Angra do Heroísmo, Terceira Island, 1981, p. 3.

[2] António Lourenço da Silveira Maçedo, p. 3.

[3] Document 24, United States Archives, Microfilm T203, Roll 1, March 4,1795-November 28, 1832.

[4] Document 24, United States Archives, Microfilm T203, Roll 1, March 4,1795-November 28, 1832

[5] Roxana Lewis Dabney, *Annals of the Dabney Family in Fayal,* comp., n. p.: The Author, 1900, p. 107.

[6] Roxana Lewis Dabney, *Annals,* p. 107.

[7] Roxana Lewis Dabney, *Annals,* p. 121.

[8] Roxana Lewis Dabney, *Annals,* p. 79.

[9] Roxana Lewis Dabney, *Annals,* p. 93.

[10] Roxana Lewis Dabney, *Annals,* p. 322.

[11] Roxana Lewis Dabney, *Annals,* p. 322.

[12] Roxana Lewis Dabney, *Annals,* p. 119.

[13] Roxana Lewis Dabney, *Annals,* p. 119.

[14] Roxana Lewis Dabney, *Annals,* p. 119.

[15] Francis L. Dabney, *Sketch,* p. 99-100.

[16] Roxana Lewis Dabney, *Annals,* p. 130.

[17] James Wesley Smith, *Sojourners in Search of Freedom: The Settlement of Liberia by Black Americans,* Lanham, MD, 1987, p. 1.

[18] James Wesley Smith, *Soujourners,* p. 2.

[19] Roxana Lewis Dabney, *Annals,* p. 130.

[20] Roxana Lewis Dabney, *Annals,* p. 130.

[21] Roxana Lewis Dabney, *Annals,* p. 131.

[22] James Wesley Smith, *Soujourners,* p. 26.

[23] James Wesley Smith, *Soujourners,* p. 26.

[24] Roxana Lewis Dabney, *Annals*, p. 131.

[25] Roxana Lewis Dabney, *Annals*, p. 131.

[26] Roxana Lewis Dabney, *Annals*, p. 131.

[27] Roxana Lewis Dabney, *Annals*, p. 132.

[28] Roxana Lewis Dabney, *Annals*, p. 145-6.

[29] Marcelino Lima, "Constitucionalismo, Miguelismo e Liberalismo, " *Anais do Município da Horta (História da Ilha do Faial)*, 3rd Edition, Oficinas Gráficas "Minerva", Vila Nova de Famalicão, 1981, p. 318.

[30] António Lourenço da Silveira Maçedo, "Reestablicimento do governo absoluto, chegada da esquadra portugueza ao Fayal, e d'uma companhia de caçadores 5... 1824-25," *História das Quatro Ilhas que Formam o Distrito da Horta, Vol. II*, Direcção Regional dos Assuntos Culturais, Região Autónoma dos Açores, Angra do Heroísmo, Terceira Island, 1981, p. 24.

[31] Roxana Lewis Dabney, *Annals*, p. 156.

[32] António Lourenço da Silveira Maçedo, *História*, p. 25.

[33] Roxana Lewis Dabney, *Annals*, p. 156.

[34] Roxana Lewis Dabney, *Annals*, p. 155-6.

[35] Roxana Lewis Dabney, *Annals*, p. 167.

[36] Roxana Lewis Dabney, *Annals*, p. 172.

[37] Roxana Lewis Dabney, *Annals*, p. 196.

[38] Roxana Lewis Dabney, *Annals*, p. 143.

[39] Francis L. Dabney, *Sketch*, p. 104.

[40] Roxana Lewis Dabney, *Annals*, p. 176.

[41] Roxana Lewis Dabney, *Annals*, p. 170.

[42] Francis L. Dabney, *Sketch*, p. 104.

[43] Roxana Lewis Dabney, *Annals*, p. 172.

[44] Roxana Lewis Dabney, *Annals*, p. 180.

[45] Roxana Lewis Dabney, *Annals*, p. 180.

[46] Roxana Lewis Dabney, *Annals*, p. 179-180.

[47] Roxana Lewis Dabney, *Annals*, p. 191.

[48] Nancy loses baby, Annals - p. 194

[49] H. V. Livermore, *A New History of Portugal*, Cambridge University Press, London, 1965, p. 267.

[50] Roxana Lewis Dabney, *Annals*, p. 177.

[51] Frederico de Barros Brotero, *Descendentes do Conselheiro José Maria de Avelar Brotero*, São Paulo, 1961, p. 3.

[52] Francis L. Dabney, *Sketch*, p. 106-7.

[53] Francis L. Dabney, *Sketch*, p. 106.

[54] Francis L. Dabney, *Sketch*, p. 107.

[55] Roxana Lewis Dabney, *Annals*, p. 175.

[56] Francis L. Dabney, *Sketch*, p. 108.

[57] Francis L. Dabney, *Sketch*, p. 108.

[58] Francis L. Dabney, *Sketch*, p. 111.

[59] Roxana Lewis Dabney, *Annals*, p. 205.; Francis L. Dabney, *Sketch*, p. 112.

[60] Roxana Lewis Dabney, *Annals*, p. 211.

[61] Roxana Lewis Dabney, *Annals*, p. 206; Francis L. Dabney, *Sketch*, p. 113.

[62] Francis L. Dabney, *Sketch*, p. 114.

[63] Francis L. Dabney, *Sketch*, p. 115.

Figure 3
Bagatelle

7 – THE RELIGIOUS EXPERIENCE

When John Bass Dabney was buried, his tomb was located at the top of the property of Bagatelle. This wasn't just because it was the family's property and they wanted him to be close to them. Portugal was, and still is, a Catholic country with strong religious traditions.

At the time John Dabney died, the Portuguese primarily buried their dead in churches and there were no Protestant cemeteries on Faial. As this was the situation throughout most of Portugal, Protestants could not be buried in the country except below the high tide line on the beach or at sea. In Lisbon, the oldest cemetery is the British Protestant Cemetery whose land was given to the British merchants living in Lisbon by a trade treaty in 1654. The cemetery was not built until 1717, but is still in use, providing a history in stone of the British Community in Lisbon. A similar cemetery has existed in Ponta Delgada on São Miguel since the 1790's. In 1844 the Portuguese government adopted sanitary regulations that forbade the burial of dead in churches. As the result of this action the Maria da Fonte Revolution, named after a legendary figure from Fonte da Arcada, began in northern Portugal among the very traditional rural populace and the conservative nobility in that part of Portugal. However, it was not until 1862 that there was a protestant cemetery established on Faial.

The importance of religion among John Bass Dabney's ancestors wasn't restricted to the Huguenot Dabney side. On his mother's side were Samuel and Hannah Bass who disembarked in Massachusetts not too long after the *Mayflower* had arrived. Their son John married Ruth Alden, daughter of John Alden and Priscilla Mullins, and the first child born in the Plymouth Colony. John Bass IV, grandfather of John Bass Dabney, was a physician who decided to give up this profession and went to become a minister in Ashford, Connecticut.[1]

John Bass IV was dismissed from his position because his religious views were considered too advanced and liberal. Upon his dismissal on June 5, 1751, he wrote in the Church Records:

> I was dismissed from my pastoral relations to the Church and People of Ashford, for dissenting from the Calvinistic sense of the Quinquarticular points, which I ignorantly subscribed to, before my ordination; for which and all other mistakes, I beg the pardon of Almighty God.[2]

From there he went to become the pastor of the First Congregational Church of Providence. After a few years he retired from the ministry and again took up the practice of medicine, which he continued until he died in 1762 at the age of 46.[3]

Religious views among the Congregational Churches in New England were more liberal than the Calvinist churches of the early settlers and gradually became even more liberal. One of the results of this was the development of Unitarianism, which began to compete with the Congregationalists. In 1805, Harvard needed to fill the vacant divinity chair and the Unitarian religious liberals were successful in appointing Henry Ware. The more conservative Congregationalists left and founded Andover University, thereby completing the split between Unitarians and Congregationalists. A number of churches in Massachusetts became Unitarian, including the Anglican King's Chapel in Boston which converted to Unitarian in 1783.

On their visits to Boston, the Dabneys were known to attend services at King's Chapel. It was here that Charles William Dabney saw, and decided to court, his future wife Frances Alsop Pomeroy.

The lack of Protestant churches on Faial is not surprising considering the strength of the Catholic church in Portugal and the continued existence of the Holy Inquisition in the country until 1821. As a result, Protestants were often dependent on visiting chaplains and ministers for certain religious functions. In 1815, the chaplain of the British warship *Chatam*, which had just arrived in Horta, christened the four Dabney children who had not yet been baptized: John Lewis, James, Frederick and

Emmeline. Henrietta Parkin, the British Consul's wife, was their Godmother, and the ship's commander, David Lloyd, the God-father.[4]

Protestants also carried out their own religious activities within the privacy of their own homes. Dabney, Rose, Samuel Wyllys Dabney's daughter, describes their services:

> My Grandmother [Frances Alsop Pomeroy Dabney], and after her death my mother [Harriet Webster Dabney], conducted the Service at ten o'clock each Sunday morning when the members of the family assembled in the library. The services consisted of the reading of a prayer (all standing), followed by selections from the Psalms and the New Testament, and ending with a sermon by some eminent preacher such as William Ellery Channing, Edward Everett Hale, James Freeman Clarke, or Phillips Brooks.[5]

Not everyone agreed that this type of religious service was appropriate for "true" Christians, as noted in this description by Roxana Lewis Dabney of a visit by Emmeline's Scottish sister-in-law.

> Jessie Paterson was here this summer, making her sister--in-law, Aunt Emmie, a visit at Bagatelle; she had come out with Capt. Savage, who had been on a voyage to Liverpool. She was several years older than I, but she took me in hand to read history, etc. At that time she was a very rigid Presbyte-rian, and it shocked me terribly that she should think that our beloved little Fanny could not be *saved* if she died then. It was the first time I had heard of such doctrines, for although my mother [Frances Alsop Pomeroy Dabney] always read parts of the Bible to us, and had every Sunday reading of the Scrip-tures and a sermon and hymns, she never tried to give us any particular bias; she herself with her family, the Pomeroys, had been worshippers at King's Chapel, and had gone over with Dr. Freeman to Unitarianism, and yet she was always attached to the Church services. But she was so wise![6]

This attitude of a strict Presbyterian is understandable be-cause the preachers mentioned are linked to Unitarianism and the Transcendentalist Literary movement and, incidentally, acquaintances of the Dabneys. The Dabneys were long-time followers of these philosophies and beliefs. A large portion of their friends in Boston were also followers of this movement, as were the tutors they chose such as Samuel Longfellow and Harriet Beecher Stowe.

The dominance of religion in Portuguese life, whether in the Azores or on the continent, was noted by visitors. Descriptions of Portugal by foreigners in the 18th and 19th centuries remark on the large number of priests, monks and nuns. Many of them begged in the streets or sold indulgences, and the people were said to be "beguiled" by the Church. William Dabney remarked on "the Mendicant friars of St. Francisco with their brown robes and rope girdles and sandaled feet and bare heads. And one in particular – old Padre Aneceto – who used to pay periodical visits at Bagatelle, bringing us children each time a big *catuxo conifettos.*"[7] However, the power of the religious communities began to wane in the 1820's when the Liberal political movement supported a decrease in the power of the Church.

Not all the priests and nuns were poor. Charles Dabney describes one who was particularly well off:

> In 1832 Father Bernardo António de Bettancourt, a Roman Catholic Priest who had accumulated about 40,000 dollars died and left his property to the Hospital of the Island. At the time of his decease, he had 20,000 dollars in specie deposited in my hands. When he found that his malady was likely to terminate mortally, he expressed his regret that being a heretic, I could not act as his executor, and requested me to suggest some person in whom I had confidence.[8]

The padre was a native of Faial and had lived in Brazil for several years. The money was believed to have come from the trade in slaves while he was there. As stated above, most of the funds went to the hospital and supported it for years.

> One of the bequests of the Revd. Gentleman was provision for a certain number of masses to be said for the benefit of

his soul, for the souls of his Father and Mother; and after removing them from Purgatory, the remainder was to be applied for the benefit of the souls of his deceased slaves.[9]

Because of the hazardous situation created by the civil war (Padre Bernardo was a supporter of Miguel and the Absolutists), there was a great need for money on Faial. As a result, Charles Dabney advised the Padre to keep secret the full extent of his cash assets since the government might seize them. This concern with the Padre's assets turned out to be well founded because the government did in fact request the assets he had reported. Charles Dabney successfully refused the government's request and prevented any confiscation of the Padre's assets. Charles Dabney felt that Padre Bernard's trust in him was "one of the most gratifying events of my life; and one that to me is truly amazing when the strong religious prejudices of such a man are considered."[10]

The monks and nuns, whom visitors to Faial considered a "tourist attraction", are described in a letter written by Mr. Noah Jones, a visitor to Faial in 1811:

> Nothing attracts the attention of foreigners more, upon their arrival in Fayal, that the Convents and Nunneries; there are six of the former and two of the latter. Strangers are admitted into the antechambers of the 'Glória' and the 'St. John's' where they can converse with the Nuns through a grating. They offer you for sale, wreaths of artificial flowers and bouquets made of feathers, and a variety of cakes and sweets of their own manufacture. They are fond of conversing with those who approach the grating and are evidently pleased with being noticed. I have seen several of these recluses, who are young and handsome, they have fine, intelligent black eyes, regular and white teeth, and very small hands and feet, but their complexions are by no means good, being of a sallow, sickly cast, etc.[11]

Some of the sweets mentioned above as being made in the convents are still a delicious part of Portuguese cuisine. Many of these were based on a combination of egg yolks and sugar, plus spices and other ingredients, with the egg whites having been used to stiffen the nuns' headware. In their early years on Faial, Roxa Dabney followed the local custom "in having a Nun in one of the Convents, St. John's or Glória to whom she would send her orders for cakes, or confectionery, and to whom she would take strangers who always wished to see the Nuns."[12]

> There were two convents* in those days, as I have said before, S. João and the Gloria, and they played quite an important part in the early days of the Dabney settlement. Grandmother Dabney had her nun in each of the convents, who attended to the making of all the cakes and confectionery that she might require; and there were visits made to both convents, quite a ceremony. The visitors would send to ask leave and were received by the nuns behind a double grating; they usually insisted upon shaking hands, or at least touching hands across the space between the two gratings. Cakes and sweetmeats would be handed out through the revolving half barrel.[13]

Another viewpoint of these visits to convents is given in a letter from Mrs. Temple Bowdoin, one of the original owners of Naushon Island in Massachusetts:

> At ten we went to the convent of St. António and heard Mass, after to see the nuns of St. John's convent. I spoke to them at the grate, but 'no entende' was all the answer I could get, not a syllable of any language do they speak but Portuguese. However they seem desirous to oblige and let us hear the Organ. Several of them played with great taste and expression; generally speaking they are really ugly.[14]

Most of the convents and monasteries had been built in the 17th century and were in poor physical condition. The largest

---

* In Portuguese, the distinction between convent and monastery is different than in English. Whereas the distinction in English is by the gender of the residents, in Portuguese, convents are within city boundaries and monasteries outside. This creates a good deal of confusion for tourists.

of these buildings had belonged to the Jesuits until the Marquês de Pombal had the order expelled from Portugal in 1759. It became the possession of the municipal government, and John Dabney rented part of it for wine storage. A description of this imposing building is given in Mr. Noah Jones' letter:

> There was formerly a college of Jesuits in this place, they were banished on account of their arts and intrigues. Their College is the largest and handsomest building on the Island, and has never been opened since their banishment. The building is six hundred feet in length. I obtained permission from the Governor to examine this singular Church. It contains a great variety of apartments; besides a magnificent Chapel in the centre; there are private confessionals for each brother in the order, a large room used as a library, a refectory and a long suite of apartments which no stranger was suffered to enter. Beneath the left wing of the building there is a large, damp, unwholesome vault or dungeon, with only one small entrance, through the floor; it is supposed that this vault was used as a prison.[15]

George Crowninshield also described this building when he stopped there on his trans-Atlantic voyage in 1817:

> One of the largest buildings in the place is the Jesuits' College. At present it is used as a cooperage and wine depot, by the American and British Consuls. What a reverse! The nunnery is in decadence. An order has been received to permit no more nuns to take the black veil, without an order from the Prince Regent of Portugal. The nunnery is at present of some use as a college for the education of young ladies.[16]

Residents of the convents and monasteries included a great number more than those who had chosen this life because of a religious calling. Many were the sons and daughters, beyond the first-born, of families who could not afford to support them at home, regardless of their position in society. Many of these men and women forced into the religious life were unhappy with the lifestyle.

One of these nuns was named Delfina. She was young and attractive and had been forced to enter the convent by her father, an event which created an uproar when the daughter publicly refused this treatment. One of the people Mrs. Dabney took to visit Delfina was a Colonel Boyd who was quite taken with her and sent her an engraved cup. One day an English merchant captain arrived, fell in love with her and persuaded her to run away with him. She climbed to the roof of the convent parlor, changed into a dress he had brought, and climbed down a rope ladder.

The captain refused to let the Church authorities search his ship. The Abbess marched through the convent corridors holding Delfina's habit and intoning, "Cursed be the one to whom these garments belonged." Delfina sailed off to England where she was married. In later years she wrote that "she was haunted by the thought that she had broke her vows."

She had left behind all her belongings, including the engraved cup given to her by Captain Boyd. John Bass bought the cup and gave it to his granddaughter Clara. She kept it in the family, eventually passing it on to her brother Samuel.[17]

Another nun eloped with a British Naval Officer. When she was getting ready to leave, she took another nun into her confidence who begged to go with her. Unfortunately, the second nun was too heavy for the escape rope and it broke. She had to be left behind with a broken leg and the prospect of continued life in the convent. There were stories that she was "walled up" or died soon after the event, but nothing certain was known about her fate.[18]

Some nuns seemed to be habitual escapees.

D. Margarida Graham always escaped from the convent when she could, hence one of her notes is dated Mt. De Guia, where I suppose she used to come for baths. Some other notes were written from S. João Mosteiro.[19]

The rebellious nature of nuns sometimes spread to a number of those within the convent. An example of this is contained in a letter from João Brotero to his uncle Charles William Dabney.

He tells his uncle of an amusing revolt among the nuns in a convent just opposite the Brotero's. It seems the nuns thought that they were behind the age in some things, and proceeded to supply themselves with pianos, light literature, and other mundane matters, which so scandalized the Bishop, when he made his periodical visit, that he immediately ordered all the books to be burnt and the pianos sent off; whereupon some of the nuns left the convent and hired a large house, where they could live a retired life, and at the same time indulge themselves in the midst of their vigils with their pianos, etc. John Brotero writes that the Bishop thought the "end of the world" was at hand, but for his part he considered it merely, "A Cloistered Republic".[20]

Other stories such as these date back to the early days of the settlement of Faial and went on till the convents were closed in 1834.[21] The apparent unhappiness of being in a convent went beyond the just the rare elopement. Nancy Dabney describes the nuns' reaction to the absence of changes being brought about by the liberal revolution in a letter to her brother John. "The Nuns are the only persons who regret the new order of things as they had their hearts upon being liberated from their convents and had gone to great expense in dresses, etc. Many of them have appeared lately at the grates with the Constitutional colours (white and blue) cockades, pinned on their shoulders."[22]

The unhappy nuns had to wait until the liberals finally won the war over the absolutist forces. To eliminate the strength of the church, which had opposed the liberals, the religious orders were disbanded in 1834 by the liberal forces after the civil war between Kings Pedro IV and Miguel ended. As a result, the convents and monasteries emptied, although the residents were allowed to stay until they wanted to leave or died. The government took over many of these religious buildings. Others were sold to private individuals in an attempt to raise funds to cover the tremendous deficit incurred as a result of the civil war. This attempt was nowhere near as successful as had been anticipated and may have been outweighed by the animosity it created with the Church. This was foreseen in a letter from

Charles Dabney to Secretary of State John Forsyth in 1836 relating a rumor that the exiled King Miguel was returning to attack the Azores.

Sir

The only circumstance worth recording since I last had the honor of addressing you is the panic produced on the inhabitants of these Islands by the report that D. Miguel had left Geneva with a small squadron. As his destination was unknown it was immediately apprehended that a descent on these Islands was meditated. The alarm has been allayed in part by the appearance of a large corvette sent from Lisbon to protect the Islands.

As you, Sir, have more authentic information respecting his movements, I shall not repeat the rumours that are in circulation here but merely confirm what you have doubtless heard from other quarters. That the neglect and contempt with which the Dominant part has treated the clergy has materially weakened its influence over the minds of the middle and lower classes and the abuse of liberty will reconcile the majority of the natives to the exercise of arbitrary power.[23]

Notes:

[1] Frederico de Barros Brotero, *Descendentes do Conselheiro José Maria de Avelar Brotero*, São Paulo, 1961, p. 86.

[2] Roxana Lewis Dabney, *Annals of the Dabney Family in Fayal*, comp., n. p.: The Author, 1900, p. 1.

[3] Francis L. Dabney, *Sketch, Sketch of John Bass Dabney by his son William Henry Dabney of Boston, 1887*, comp., n. p.: The Author, 1971, p. 2

[4] Francis L. Dabney, *Sketch*, p. 86-7.

[5] Dabney, Rose Forbes, *Fayal Dabneys*, n.p.: The Author, 1931, p. 114.

[6] Roxana Lewis Dabney, *Annals*, p. 456.

[7] Sally Dabney Parker, *William Henry Dabney, Reminiscences, 1820-1853*, n.p.: The Author, 1981, p. 3.

[8] Roxana Lewis Dabney, *Annals*, p. 319.

[9] Roxana Lewis Dabney, *Annals*, p. 320.

[10] Roxana Lewis Dabney, *Annals*, p. 320.

[11] Roxana Lewis Dabney, *Annals*, p. 39-40.

[12] Roxana Lewis Dabney, *Annals*, p. 27.

[13] Roxana Lewis Dabney, *Annals*, p. 703-4.

[14] Roxana Lewis Dabney, *Annals*, p. 26.

[15] Roxana Lewis Dabney, *Annals*, p. 40.

[16] Francis Boardman Crowninshield, *Cleopatra's Barge*, n.p.: The Author, Boston, 1913, p. 59.

[17] Roxana Lewis Dabney, *Annals*, p. 27-8.

[18] Roxana Lewis Dabney, *Annals*, p. 28-9.

[19] Roxana Lewis Dabney, *Annals*, p. 703.

[20] Roxana Lewis Dabney, *Annals*, p. 701.

[21] Marcelino Lima, "Na Clausura", *Anais do Município da Horta (História da Ilha do Faial)*, 3rd Edition, Oficinas Gráficas "Minerva", Vila Nova de Famalicão, 1981, p. 457-464.

[22] Roxana Lewis Dabney, *Annals*, p. 155.

[23] Document 32, United States Archives Microfilm, T203, Roll 2, July 26, 1833 – December 4, 1841.

8 – A NEW BEGINNING

As Vice-Consul, Charles William Dabney took over the responsibilities of the Consulate after his father's death. His first official letter was on September 11, 1826, to Secretary of State Henry Clay:

> Sir:
> With feelings of deepest anguish, I have to announce to you the death of John B. Dabney, My Beloved Father & best Friend.
>
> He returned from an excursion to the United States on the 28th June. On the 1st September was attacked with apoplexy and on the 2nd of Sept. he terminated his Earthly career. He was a foreigner, yet during the last Twenty Years, no man has so generally respected; he held the Situation of the Consul of the U. States for the Azores upwards of Twenty years, was of a very enterprising spirit and found an Establishment here, that is a source of gratification to all our Countrymen who visit the Island, as some who are worthy are neglected.
>
> I have submitted to the President of the United States the appointment of Consul for the Azores and herewith take the liberty of requesting you to countenance my pretension on the assurances that my utmost exertions shall be used to display the duties thereof in a proper manner and afford you satisfaction. I pray you to excuse this recommending myself of your favorable consideration.[1]

Considering the slow speed at which sailing ships and government moved, Henry Clay's confirmation of Charles Dabney as U. S. Consul in the Azores on November 3 was extraordinarily quick. In a letter about Charles' appointment, his father-in-law, Samuel W. Pomeroy, states,

I must be allowed to congratulate you on its very rapid consummation, your application to the President being dated 10th Sept. and forwarded by the circuitous route of St. Michael's and Bath. I received advices from Washington under date of 8th Nov. that the appointment was concluded on, and your commission made out, the whole being effected within 60 days! And publicly announced the 13th![2]

This was a significant tribute to both the manner in which the Faial consulate functioned and to the man who had held the position for so many years.

In 1827, John Lewis Dabney returned to Faial from Brazil and took over the role of Vice-Consul on Faial. He brought back news about his sister and her family and their activities in Brazil. He reported that the Brotero's continued to do well in Rio de Janeiro and that Nancy had a second baby, John Dabney Brotero, who died in 1830. The Brotero's had moved to São Paulo, and José Maria de Avelar Botero had been given permission to open a law school there by Emperor Pedro.[3] In 1832, Nancy had another son named John who survived into adulthood.

Things did not move so quickly in Portugal. Thomas Ludwell Lee Brent, the U.S. Chargé d'Affaires in Lisbon, submitted Charles Dabney's commission for acceptance to the Portuguese Court in March 1828.[4] Its approval took significantly longer than the U. S. appointment and was not granted until 1837.[5]

This was due to the turbulence associated with the succession the throne of Portugal.

> From the year 1826, the year of [John Bass Dabney's] death, up to the period of Dom Pedro's return to Portugal in 1832, the Azores were the centre, as it were, of the conflict that was carried on between the Miguelites and Pedroites; (or Constitutionalists, as they were often called.[6]

The struggle for succession between Emperor Pedro and his brother Prince Miguel led to a civil war in which Charles Dabney became embroiled both personally and professionally.

C. W. D., of course, from his position took no sides, but tried to befriend either side which was in trouble. Bagatelle was the refuge on various occasions, some times of the Pedroites, and others of Miguelites, according to whichever party got the command.[7]

News of the death of King João VI was followed by three days of mourning in Horta. After this, there was three days of celebration for King Pedro IV. However, there were some people who questioned the right of Emperor Pedro I of Brazil to be the legitimate heir to the throne of Portugal since he was already the ruler of Brazil, now a separate country.

Regardless of the legitimacy of his claim, at the end of September 1826, Pedro abdicated the throne of Portugal in favor of his five-year old daughter Maria da Glória, who would become Queen Maria II. She was to marry her uncle Miguel, an occurrence not unique in the Portuguese royal family. In addition, Miguel had to accept the constitutional charter and, when he turned 25 in October 1827, he was to serve as regent until Maria reached legal age. Until that time Pedro's sister Isabel Maria would continue as regent. Miguel agreed to the conditions. In Vienna, on 31 July 1826, swore to the charter and was betrothed to his niece. However, Miguel did not want to return to Portugal until he was of age to be regent.

Notice of the transfer of power was received in Faial and August 28, 1826 was selected as the date when the populace would swear to abide by the constitutional charter. The day opened with rockets and the tolling of the church bells. The city council and those associated with it gathered in the council chambers to take their oath while the governor gathered the troops to do the same. This was followed by *vivas* to the charter, Queen Maria II, Pedro, the princess regent and the Catholic religion. Salvos were fired. Bells tolled. A Te Deum mass was held. This went on for three days accompanied by parties, balls and processions.[8]

In February 1828, Miguel returned to Portugal, was made regent and swore allegiance to Maria II and Pedro IV as the legitimate sovereigns. News of this was greeted by celebrations in Horta. Despite this apparent acceptance of the situation, Miguel began to appoint members of the government who were not Liberal and who supported an absolute monarch. He also dissolved the new "cortes", alleging irregularities in their selection, and reappointed the original "cortes", which were strictly advisory to the king. On June 3, Miguel renounced his marriage to Maria. On June 24, he convened the new cortes with their Absolutist majority and on July 7 Miguel was proclaimed King.

None of the foreign diplomats in Lisbon would have anything to do with Miguel's government. One of the few countries that did acknowledge his regime was the United States, which recognized the new government on October 1. This policy was based on the Monroe Doctrine, which tolerated no European interests in the Americas and the fact that having separate monarchs in Brazil and Portugal definitely established the separation of Brazil from Portugal. The only two other countries to recognize the government of King Miguel were Spain, whose King was Miguel's uncle, and the Vatican.

The Azores was the only part of Portugal that remained loyal to Pedro and Maria since the Liberals in continental Portugal had been defeated and fled, many to the Azores. After news of Miguel's action arrived, the 5th Battalion on the island of Terceira refused to swear allegiance to Miguel and in July revolted in Angra. They acclaimed Maria as Queen, accepted the constitution and established a provisional government, which the population of Terceira supported.

The Absolutist naval forces, with their headquarters on São Miguel, tried to prevent any trade with the island of Terceira and established a blockade. Some American ships were taken prisoner by the Portuguese blockading forces and forcibly taken to São Miguel where they were held. Thomas Hickling, Charles Dabney's Vice-Consul on São Miguel had much work in dealing with the situation in order to get the ships released.[9]

On the other side, some American ships that were able to reach Angra had problems with the Liberal forces. An example being the ship *Gallego*, one of the Dabney ships, which had arrived at Horta after being damaged by a storm. The market on Horta had an adequate supply of the articles in the *Gallego's* cargo, so Captain Savage decided to go to Terceira. Since Absolutist supporters of Miguel controlled Faial at the time, Charles Dabney advised the captain not to let anyone know he was going there. However, before setting sail he had to take on some crew members from Faial to make up for those who had been injured in the storm.

When they arrived at Angra, "The Captain went on shore himself, and his boat's crew were taken up to the Government House, where they underwent a strict interrogatory, and were allowed to go about their business."[10] Since the ship was not allowed by law to export money from Terceira, the captain decided to go to São Miguel. He "carried out the usual formalities" and started out to the ship with his crew. They were stopped by a call from the fort of Santo António saying the order to allow them to pass hadn't been received. After a wait, they decided to return to shore where the ship's crew was taken into custody again and released two hours later.

The next morning, the crew was again arrested. "Application was made by Mr. Riggs [the U. S. Vice-Consul on Terceira] and Capt. Savage to the Government, but to no purpose; they were treated with indignity and no attention whatever paid to their remonstrances, and no reason assigned for their procedure".[11] The Harbor Master had orders to take the captain outside the port and leave him so his ship could get him and sail with the reduced crew, a dangerous situation.

Charles Dabney was angered by the news.

> Immediately on receiving information of the foregoing, I resolved for the honour of the Flag, although my property was not insured, to send the Vessel directly back to reclaim the part of her crew, who had been so unjustifiably detained, and accordingly had five fresh men engaged in lieu of the four men detained; those who remained in the Brig were completely exhausted.[12] ...the sailors were detained upon the suspicion that the object of the Brig's visit to Terceira was for the purpose of ascertaining the political state of the Island, but I do most solemnly declare that the object was exclusively a mercantile one.[13]

Although there is no indication of the final resolution of the incident, Charles Dabney describes the steps he took in presenting the side of the captain and crew of the *Gallego* to General Cabrera, who was the Governor General. He then goes on to complain about the behaviour of the government in Portugal, regardless of who was in control. His statement about this is also a premonition of the troubles that were to face him in the future.

> The absence of virtue in the People and Government, requires the manifestation of interest on the part of foreign Governments, and one instance of oppression unnoticed in such insignificant places as these Islands, opens a source of infinite mortification and disgust. Within the range of my personal influence I have hitherto been very fortunate, and it is not likely to be curtailed, unless some political intrigue should cause my conduct to be misconstrued. In commotions such as we are now witnessing, it is difficult to escape aspersions, and as I have invariably been on good terms with the reigning authorities, without regard to their political sentiments, many lose sight of the fact that my intercourse with them is divested of party considerations. The people are in such a feverish state that I fear some terrible convulsion will shortly manifest itself.[14]

He further defends his conduct in relation to whichever group was controlling Portugal.

> I have observed the most complete neutrality; so much has this been the case, that persons of both parties have sought the asylum of my house, in some cases at the same time, and not one case can be cited in which I have acted against the interests of H. Imperial Majesty, how much less then could I have compromitted myself in a plot, which involved so many witnesses.[15]

The response to Charles Dabney's petitions is contained in a note from General Cabrera, who told him that Charles had no need to explain his political feelings or public actions.

> Since, 'he says', I am perfectly convinced of your integrity; nor of a member of the Great Republic, which forms the United

States could it be in justice supposed that he would be wanting in what is proper to a man of Liberal views. I have presented your despatches to the 'Junta Provisória', etc.

The Junta replies that in their capacity of maintaining the
legitimate authority of the Queen, Sra. D. Maria 2da, they have
to say that the four sailors of the crew of the brig *Gallego* de-
tained by them, it is found, are not citizens of the United States,
but subjects of the Kingdom of Portugal, and therefore to be
used by the Junta as may seem best.[16]

No more is mentioned about this incident, which was not
the only of its kind during the years of conflict.

Shipping in the Azores faced more than the problems created by the clashes between the Absolutists and Liberals. During
the late 1820's and early 1830's, pirates attacked several ships
in the area, although it is not surprising that pirates would
choose Azorean waters for hunting. A large part of the trans-
-Atlantic trading ships made a stop at one of the islands in the
archipelago, usually Faial. That pirate activities never became
as notorious as they were in the Caribbean is probably due to
the weather and the smaller number of islands, which made
hiding more difficult.

While Charles Dabney wrote several reports on the incidents,
his letter of July 31, 1828, to Secretary of State Henry Clay gives
an overview of the types of activity that were going on.

Sir

I have the honor to inform you that about the 6th inst. A Piratical Schooner armed with a Pivot Gun & six carriage guns
& manned with about fifty men appeared off this Island &
robbed an American Whaling Ship the name of which I have
not been able to ascertain altho' the Capt. Landed at Pico the
following day to procure fresh supply of vegetables. I am informed that one of the officers of the Schooner left her and
went on board of the Whaler in consequence of some disagreement. This person is represented to be a Spaniard. He stated that the Schooner sailed from Thomas W. I. with the intention of proceeding to the Coast of Africa for Slaves, that after

leaving the Port they concluded to depredate on all Vessels indiscriminately, this he assigned as the cause of his leaving the Schooner. Accounts from Terceira state that a Schooner answering to the description of the above has robbed an English Schooner and a Portuguese Brig.

On the morning of the 27th inst. A two topsail schooner appeared close in to the anchorage, having an American ensign at her main gaff & a pennant at her maintop gallant masthead. She was full of men & a pivot gun was discerned, a boat was sent off but she made sail & stood to the southward.

A fine Baltimore built Brig appeared the same afternoon in the Port with French colors flying – she hove too & received a boat on board – she was armed with a pivot gun and eight carriage guns & manned with eighty or ninety men; the commander is a native of St. Michael's & is a notorious character. He states that he acts under a Buenos Ayres Commission. He made sail to the northward.

Yesterday the 30th July a Portuguese schooner arrived here with the crew of a Spanish Slave Brig consisting of forty-eight persons who were captured four days since by a Buenos Ayres Brig, the crew of which robbed the crew of the Portuguese schooner of this island.[17]

Another incident shows the pirates in a somewhat different light. In a letter to Charles Dabney dated August 20, 1828, José Brotero says, "I received your last letter of Feb. 24th, which came by the *Urania*, which vessel was robbed and I lost everything, excepting the letters which the Corsair did me the favour of sending to me after having opened them."[18]

During the ups and downs of their political power, the two opposing sides on Faial took turns celebrating whenever there seemed to be some kind of victory over the other. The principal families supported the Liberal cause, but they couldn't support a counter-revolution against the military, which supported the Absolutists.

In September 1828, the Absolutists made a move to gain full control on Horta, during which they created a local tale. One of the people who fled when news of the Absolutist revolt arrived

was the military governor Ruxeleben, a well-liked and very cul-
tured man. In a letter of September 28, 1928, Charles Dabney
states:

> Our worthy Governor Diogo Thomaz Ruxeleben recog-
> nized the 'Governo Provisório' (they having arrested the Gov.
> Gen. Tovar) and thereby compromitted himself with the actual
> Govt. of Portugal. Hearing that a squadron had left Lisbon for
> Madeira and the Islands, he became alarmed for his safety
> and he and Major Luna embarked for London on the night of
> the 3d inst.[19]

Everyone knew that Ruxeleben was romantically involved
with Sister Margarida Graham, daughter of the deceased English Consul. After Ruxeleben had left and nothing more was
heard from him, Sister Margarida contacted Rome to get permission to break her vows. There was no response, so she withdrew to her cell and meditated on Ruxeleben, growing sadder
and sadder until she died.[20]

The military took advantage of Ruxeleben's departure and
proclaimed Miguel King. As was the custom, the Absolutists
celebrated their victory with fireworks and bells. Soldiers began
to go through the streets night and day singing songs, shouting
insults and threatening the Liberals. Their insults and threats
became worse when news arrived that Queen Maria II, instead
of going to Portugal, had gone to Britain in September 1828,
where she was received as the Queen of Portugal. In addition,
they put cannons in the streets and at the entrance to the fortress.

These activities incensed rather than intimidated the people,
and a counter-revolution was planned. Regardless of his intent
to remain neutral in his politics and actions, Charles Dabney
was drawn into this incident.

> The principal inhabitants of the Island are in favour of the
> Constitutional Party, now identified as the Pedroites, and have
> been living in constraint since the 3d Sept. when a conspiracy
> manifested itself among the Militia of the Island, and Dom Mi-
> guel was proclaimed Absolute King.[21]

On October 28, 1828, "the Brazilian Fregate [sic] *Isabella* commanded by the Count de Beaurepaire anchored in the Bay of Horta. On November 3, the Brazilian Vice-Consul on Horta raised and lowered the Brazilian flag with a white flag beneath it several times. About 3 or 4 p. m., three long boats came to shore. A little later a group of "about twenty respectable young men and one or two others, shoemakers, masons, coopers, etc.,"[22] gathered with illegal weapons, some of which were gathered from the Dabney's business at Relva, and attacked the fortress.

The Liberal rebels easily won and broke into cheers for Maria and Pedro and the constitution. The Absolutist soldiers fled, leaving all their supplies and weapons. They gathered in the village of Feteira, about 3 miles away on Faial's south coast. However, the Liberals were very disorganized and thought they'd done all that was necessary and didn't take advantage of the Absolutist troops' mistake.

Shortly after the attack, the weather got worse, and the Brazilian ship had to leave taking several Liberals who had anticipated the situation would deteriorate. The Absolutists saw what was happening and took advantage of the situation

> This inspired the Officers and soldiers acting for Dom Miguel, with fresh courage and they rallied with a few soldiers that could be found, at first not exceeding 30, and cut off all communication with the fortress and during the night and part of the following morning succeeded in conveying two field pieces to an elevation that commands the Castle. Those in the Fort were much disgusted on the departure of the Fregate and during the night most of them made their escape. In the morning no Fregate appearing, the panic spread rapidly when about noon they saw the field pieces ready to open fire upon them. At this they fired into the air, and beckoned to their adversaries to descend, which they did, took possession of the Fort and about 30 prisoners. This fracas cost about a dozen lives and has precipitated the Island into an abyss of misery.[23]

None of the influential people on the island "engaged in the conspiracy which was conducted without any system."[24] The

Isabella returned on November 10, and "the inhabitants were in a state of great alarm on the appearance",[25] and fled to the countryside. The Governor of the island was determined to resist, and the government contacted Charles Dabney for assistance, as he reported in a letter to the Secretary of State.

> I have the honor to inform you that in conjunction with the British Consul for this Island I officiated as mediator between the Governor of this Island & Count Beaurepaire commander of the Brazilian Frigate the *Isabella* respecting a 'Fracas' that occurred here in which the Brazilian Consul was implicated & I have great pleasure to add that our interference produced the desired effect.[26]

The hatred and tormenting by the Absolutists increased. They developed a list of enemies that included Charles Dabney because he was "part of the heretics"[27] for his alleged assistance to the Liberals. Reports of this incident were apparently sent to Lisbon and created problems for him with the Portuguese government two years later.

In August, 1830, Mr. Brent, the U. S. Chargé d'Affaires in Lisbon sent a letter to Charles Dabney.

> Sir,
>
> I have to state to you that the minister of Foreign Affairs of Portugal has informed me, that his Government has declined granting the Exequator upon your Commission, that there exist some charges against you of being implicated in a conspiracy against this government, which would be sent to Washington.
>
> I do not furnish you with the documents relating to them, since I have them not, nor require of you any explanations, since it is to our Government that this subject is to be submitted.[28]

On September 3, Charles Dabney sent a note to Governor António Isidoro de Morães Ancora to request "of him the favor of certifying to his impartial conduct throughout the unhappy period" [29] and asking for a report about the event in relation to the guns that had been taken from the Dabney premises. The Governor

> ...replied with a very flattering letter, certifying that C. W. D. had invariably observed the most scrupulous impartiality, and that he himself felt under great obligations for the services which C. W. D. voluntarily rendered in going on board of the Brazilian Frigate on the tenth of September, and stating to the Commander his (the Governor's) view and the injury the presence of the Frigate in that port was doing the inhabitants.[30]

The next day, September 4, Charles Dabney sent letters to President Andrew Jackson and Secretary of State Martin Van Buren. In his letter to President Jackson he described the incident and his actions to resolve the situation.

> I have a very large establishment consisting of Wine Stores and merchandize of various kinds about a mile from my residence, which is intrusted to two superintendents. On the 3rd or 4th of November 1828, an assault was made on the principal fort of this Island by some of the inhabitants. My establishment being situated very near this fort some of the assaulters aided by my head cooper rushed into the premises and seized seven or nine old broken muskets that had been landed from the Brig *Gallego* as useless about a year previous. This appears to have given rise to the present suspicion. At the time I adopted such measures as I thought necessary to place the affair in the proper light by immediately taking the person who had charge of the premises at the time to the Governor's presence to explain how it occurred. He being well aware of the manner in which I have invariably conducted, declined questioning him assuring me that he was perfectly satisfied that it was as I represented. About a year since a commissioner was appointed to investigate the affair of the Fort and because it is stated that arms were taken from my premises a suspicion rests upon me as it is not known that days pass without my visiting that establishment and that I do not tarry there an

hour a day upon an average as I have my office near my house. To prevent, if possible, you being troubled with any communication and this subject I have resolved to proceed tomorrow in the Lisbon Packet. I leave the office in Charge of my brother John L. Dabney who is at least as well qualified as I am to perform the duties thereof.

I pray you sir to grant me a little time and I engage to forfeit my life if I do not prove myself perfectly innocent.[31]

He hurried "forthwith to the fountain head [Lisbon], there to demonstrate how scrupulously circumspect I have been at every stage of the Political effervescence to which this Kingdom has been prey since 1820."[32]

The first week of October he informed Martin Van Buren...

that the false impression which has been assumed by this Govt. relative to my conduct has been removed & that matters are now placed on their former footing. The misconception of the Govt. has been of serious injury to me in a pecuniary point of view (having left an extensive commercial establishment without any previous arrangement) but also attended with a great sacrifice of personal comfort & it presses peculiarly hard upon one who has been so very guarded in his conduct.[33]

Mr. Brent thought it impossible to resolve the problem in the two weeks that Charles Dabney anticipated, but he met his deadline. Mr. Brent "attributed this in part to his splendid new uniform" that Consular officers then wore on official occasions.

The coat was very heavily and elegantly embroidered round the lappets, pockets, collar, and cuffs, with a vine of bay leaves and berries in gold thread; white kersimere trousers with gold stripes down the sides, sword, epaulettes and cocked hat! No doubt he looked like some ambassador, for although not very tall (5 feet 10) he had a very *distingué* bearing, and I have heard him say that as soon as he presented himself the doors would be thrown open. He never wore the uniform, of course, excepting when upon official business or at a ball.[34]

A summary of this whole event with the benefit of hindsight is continued in a letter Charles Dabney wrote in 1835 to John Forsyth, Secretary of State.

> Dear Sir,
>
> As I have the honor of addressing you on the present question respecting myself, I crave your indulgence Sir, for trespassing on your valuable time, & shall be as brief as possible.
>
> In December of 1827 I received my Commission of Consul of the United States for the Azores. I lost no time in forwarding it to our Diplomatic Agent at the Court of Lisbon who very kindly interested himself to obtain the Royal Exequatur. The Political disturbances of that period retarded the accomplishment of my object. Soon after the Viscount of Santarem took charge of the Portfeuille for Foreign Affairs he stated to Brent that he had found an Alvará prohibiting the establishment of Consuls in the Colonies of H.M.F. Majesty & that his present Majesty (then Sr. Mr. Dom Miguel) had not come to any definitive conclusion on that subject. This occurred at a time when no Portuguese territory of any importance was without Foreign Consuls – After a protracted correspondence to our own Govt., Mr. Brent succeeded in removing the objections & when he was expecting to receive the Exequatur, it was intimated to him by the Viscount of Santarem that it could not be granted as I was implicated in a conspiracy against the Govt. Mr. Brent communicated the circumstance to me by a mail packet which arrived at Fayal on the 4th of Sept. of 1830 and as my conduct had always been scrupulously circumspect, I resolved to proceed at once to the Capital to remove so erroneous an impression. I accordingly embarked within twenty four hours from the receipt of Mr. Brent's letter, having my commercial establishment exposed to the inconveniences of so abrupt a departure. I was in Lisbon eighteen days and Mr. Brent, our worthy Charge at that time to whom I am under immense obligations spontaneously disclosed that in all his intercourse with the Govt. he had never known so much accomplished in so short a time,* but as not a shadow of even connivance could be brought to bear upon me, I was enabled

to urge the Ministers to relieve me from the inconvenience I was exposed to by the inefficiency of the Commission charged with the investigation of the political disturbance in question, and as they were perfectly satisfied of my innocence they did not demur to afford me the reparation which was within their power for the sacrifice of personal comfort & pecuniary advantage which I had made to remove their impressions.

As I had not the utmost confidence in the stability of the then existing Govt., I desired Mr. Brent not to urge the Govt. respecting my Exequatur and in case of a change of sovereign it would spare me the trouble of a second application. As soon as the affairs of Dona Maria II assumed a permanent appearance I wrote to Mr. Brent on the subject of my Exequatur, that Gentleman kindly assured me that as soon as he received his credentials it should have his undivided attention, he remained a considerable time at Lisbon expecting to be reinstated and from delicacy I did not procure any other medium; on learning that Mr. Kavanagh had reached Lisbon I immediately addressed him on the subject, he applied to the Govt. & after some time was informed that a search had been made in the different offices & that my Commission could not be found. Mr. Kavanagh's letter is subjoined to show the actual state of this affair. I have endeavored to explain this business that it may be evident that nothing on my part has been wanting to ensure the regularity of the proceeding and I now Sir, solicit your kind offices to lay my case before our distinguished chief & request that a new commission may be granted to me.

I trust kind Sir, that my zeal & fidelity are not wholly unknown to you & assuring you that your kind attention to my request will leave the most grateful impression.

Charles W. Dabney

Since the death of my predecessor in Sept. 1826 the duties of the office have been performed by me without any inconvenience, in consequence of my holding the appointment under him of Vice Consul since the year 1817 and as my appointment to the office of Consul in 1826 was known here I have engaged all the advantages to which I should have been entitled by the Royal Exequatur.[35]

*This remark is not intended to arrogate any merit to myself, but to prove their strong conviction of my innocence.

Enclosed with this letter was a copy of a letter to Charles Dabney from Edward Kavanagh, the U. S. representative in Lisbon and grandson of President Andrew Jackson. Kavanagh's letter states that Charles Dabney's commission as Consul could not be found and had probably been lost during the war, although the objection had been dropped.

> Sir,
>
> After I had the honor to receive your letter of the month ulto., measures were taken to ascertain, by a new search in the Department of Foreign Affairs and elsewhere, whether your commission as Consul of the United States for the Azores could be found, and I regret to say that the attempt had has been unsuccessful. There can be no doubt that it has been either destroyed or so mixed up with other papers in the confusion attending the late troubles as to render its recovery altogether hopeless. Permit me therefore to advise you to apply to the Secretary of State at Washington for a new one, to the granting of which I can foresee no objection. The records of this legation bear witness to the difficulties which were encountered in the time of my predecessor in repeated and ineffectual attempts to procure your Exequatur, although an objection appeared to have been removed.
>
> Edward Kavanagh[36]

In 1836 a new Consular commission was received in Lisbon and acted on by the Crown – ten years after Charles Dabney had taken his position as Consul upon his father's death.[37] This whole situation had been the result of the government of King Miguel attempting to take revenge for Charles Dabney's supposed hostility toward the Absolutists. Charles Dabney specifically blamed it on

> João Bettencourt, Major of Militia, who had been the chief promoter of the overthrow of the Constitutional Government

in Fayal. C. W. D. had incurred his enmity by refusing to lend his best horse for J. B. to ride in some cavalcade, such as often formed one of the amusements of the Azoreans, in one of which C. W. D had already had a horse injured.[38]

A little over 25 years later, in 1856, Charles Dabney's honor was attacked in the newspapers in São Miguel and in Lisbon by "Estacio Manuel"

> ...but it was well known that the real assailant was the lawyer, João Bettancourt Correa de Vasconcellos. He was the son of that José Bettancourt, who was a Miguelite, and therefore, one of the sufferers in 1828, at the time the Constitutionalists took possession of the Fort. It was he who sent forward the false accusation against C. W. D. which obliged him, in 1830, to go to Lisbon to clear himself. His enmity was supposed to have been incurred by a refusal to lend a horse on occasion of one of their "Cavalhadas." Upon a previous occasion when a horse had been lent to him, he was much injured. Mrs. C. W. D. sacrificed some of her ribbons to braid the horse's tail on that occasion.
>
> It was after the episode of 1830 that C. W. D. befriended the family in assisting them to embark for Lisbon; and some time after José Bettancourt wrote, begging C. W. D. to use his influence to have him allowed to return to live in Fayal, but he ended his days in Portugal.[39]

Another situation that Charles Dabney had to deal with in Lisbon at this time was a challenge to the validity of Thomas Hickling's appointment. A letter had been sent to Thomas Brent by the Viscount of Santarém, the Portuguese Minister of Foreign Affairs, saying Hickling had never been "duly confirmed by the Government" and asking for information about why he was serving as Vice-Consul.[40] Brent contacted Charles Dabney and, in a letter to Mr. Brent dated the day before his letter to President Jackson, Charles Dabney explains that Hickling had been Vice-Consul so long that he was "ignorant of the origin of his appointment." He thought that his father "may have deemed it unnecessary to reappoint him." Charles Dabney also stated that "as the functions of the Vice-Consuls are limited to these Islands, the confirmation by the local Government is all that has hitherto been required".[41]

In 1829, the Liberals took a step toward victory in the civil war on the island of Terceira. A large fleet was prepared in Lisbon and sailed to attack the Azores. In the meantime, the Liberals on Terceira were able to land more troops, including the Count of Vila Flor, despite the blockade set up by the Duke of Wellington who was a supporter of King Miguel. The Absolutist fleet arrived and was badly defeated at the town of Praia, later known as Praia da Vitória (Victory Beach). The Absolutists lost approximately 1,000 dead on the beach compared to a loss of only 116 for the Liberals. A note from the Portuguese Ministry of Foreign Affairs at the top of Brent's letter forwarding Charles Dabney's letter said that the appointment "being recognized by the local authority is not sufficient, it is necessary that it be the sovereign authority."[42] Like the charges against Charles Dabney, the government of King Miguel was most likely motivated by revenge for Thomas Hickling's letters regarding the American ships that ran the blockade of Terceira.

On his way home from Lisbon, Charles Dabney stopped at São Miguel. There he learned "the news of his brother James' death in that island, whither he had resorted on account of his health. I have not the full particulars, but am well aware that Uncle James received every attention and kindness possible from Mr. Hickling's family."[43] James was 22 at the time of his death from "consumption".[44] Charles' wife Frances says of him, "Almost every day brings to my remembrance, some trait of the good and kind feelings of his heart."[45]

In the midst of all the political turmoil, the potato crop on Faial failed, and the population was again faced with a famine. Charles Dabney offered "to import a thousand barrels of Flour to be sold at cost and expenses, which seemed a benefit to the whole population."[46] This was done because of "the debt of gratitude I was under to the Municipality."[47]

Another example of Dabney benevolence was brought about by the arrival of 114 victims of the shipwreck of the ship *Robert Fulton* in 1830, which had been run into by a British Bark. The

British ship *Mary Catherine* passed by and refused to take anyone but three cabin passengers on board despite the desperate situation.[48] The *Fulton* was barely able to land at the island of Flores eight days after the accident. Fortunately, "All the lives were saved, amounting to one hundred and fourteen, I think, five cabin passengers and upwards of ninety in the steerage, men, women and children (of the latter twenty!). They are principally Scotch and Irish emigrants, returning home, destitute of course."[49]

Mr. Borges, the American Vice-Consul on Flores, arranged for three boats and got the passengers to Faial, some with "no more than the clothes they had on. The next year the incident was published in a book, "Fowler's Tour in the State of New York, and shipwreck at the Western Islands." The author describes the Dabney family, saying, "it was never my lot to be introduced to a more interesting and agreeable family circle, than that of the Dabneys, one in which a stranger would or ought sooner to feel at home".[50] The author called Bagatelle "Fredonia House," a name whose origin is unknown and which created some confusion among later visitors, such as Captain Vidal who included it on a map he made of Horta. However it eventually became the name of the house Charles Dabney built and moved into in 1836.[51]

On the Liberal side, Queen Maria II returned to Brazil at the end of 1829 and the staunch Absolutist Queen Mother Carlota Joaquina died in January 1830. However, the Absolutists still continued their persecution of the Liberals on Faial and in Angra, the Marquis of Palmella, José António Guerneiro and the Count of Vila Flor formed a regency council for the Queen. On Terceira, the Count of Vila Flor prepared troops and ships to capture the other islands in the archipelago.

On April 7, 1831, Pedro abdicated the throne of Brazil in favor of his son Pedro de Alcântara. Charles Dabney was near the island of Terceira on March 13 and

...received advices of the arrival of Dom Pedro de Bragança and suite at Terceira in the Frigate *Rainha de Portugal* of 44 guns & that the Frigate *Dona Maria da Glória* of 42 guns & two transports had also reached that Island preparatory to the contemplated Expedition against Portugal which it was expected was to be ready to sail about the first of May. It may be interesting for you to know that the officers and crews of the Frigate are English, those officers who hold commissions in the British Navy act under assumed names.[52]

The Count of Vila Flor set sail with his ships and troops and landed on the island of Pico on April 21. They took the three main towns and were received triumphantly by the population, which swore allegiance to Queen Maria II. Then he captured the island of São Jorge and sent a ship to Faial to inform them of the recent actions and suggest that the island surrender rather than lose lives. The leaders on Faial disagreed with each other significantly about what action to take.

On May 30, 1831, the English ship *La Volage* entered the Bay of Horta with King Pedro IV on board. The British Consul confirmed this to those on shore. The king gave the master of the launch that went out to the ship four gold pieces and a note saying, "He who speaks to you and gives you these four pieces is the father of your Queen. To arms, to arms against the usurption. To arms, to arms, that the Count of Vila Flor is on Pico – Pedro".[53] Following his stops in the Azores, Pedro went to Brest in France to raise support for recovering the throne of Portugal for his daughter Maria. After the king's stop at Horta, the leadership on Faial decided to stand together with the Liberals and send a message to the Count of Vila Flor on São Jorge announcing the submission of the island.

The Count of Vila Flor sent a personal letter to Charles Dabney on June 8. In it he describes the situation from his point of view and asks Charles Dabney's help in getting his message through.

The knowledge I have of the uprightness of character and honourable sentiments which characterize you leads me to address this letter and papers to you by the vessel *Princeza da Victória*, which put into this port and goes consigned to you.

On the 6th of this month, when I was awaiting a tolerable wind to effect a landing on your Island Major D. José Maria

Carlos de Noronha arrived at this Town with a cartel sent by the Governor of that Island with propositions for the submission of that Island to the Government of D. Maria Segunda. I answered immediately with an ultimatum which you will find enclosed in despatch no. 1, under an open seal and despatched it yesterday with the aforementioned Parlamentário in a Chalupa, the weather not allowing him to go in the boat which brought him. As without any previous warning the Chalupa was fired upon by a Portuguese vessel of war, at anchor in that port, the Sloop returned to this Town brining the Messenger. Today as the weather allows I send him in the boat, with the despatch which you will find under no. 2, he also is the bearer of a letter from me to the Commander of the war vessel, the duplicate of which I send under the cover no. 3.

As the Messenger seems fearful of being ill received or not admitted (which is certainly very strange and difficult to believe) and reflecting that no one may suppose that he was delayed, and also that these duplicate despatches should reach their destination, I take the liberty of sending them to you, so that in case of the failure of the "Parlamentário" you should make the use of them which your prudence, and recognized character and sentiments should dictate, authorized as you are to deliver them to their proper addresses as well as to communicate the contents of the present letter.[54]

Vila Flor's forces gathered on Pico in preparation to go to Faial. These preparations could be seen from Faial and were described by Charles Dabney's sister Roxana.

One beautiful summer afternoon the inmates of Bagatelle spent the whole afternoon on the balcony (as it then was, before Uncle Frederick made the upper veranda), watching the little fleet at anchor off Areia Larga, Pico. They soon saw them get under way, bent upon coming over to Horta. Then a panic overcame the Miguelites and the hurried off, seizing upon the *Harbinger* and some other vessels lying in port to take them to St. Michael's. It was in the act of leaving the fort and going down the quay to embark, that one of the soldiers raised his gun and shot James Searle (a nephew of the musical Searle) through the heart. He was standing with a friend in the balcony of Mr. Guerra's house (which was where Walter Ben Saude's house now stands).

The wind failed and the fleet could not get over. After dark, Aunt R. said, they were startled by the sound of fifes and drums coming over the Lomba. The Conde de Vila Flor had landed at Praya with his detachment and come over the ridge. They took possession of the town and fort.[55]

The Absolutists on Faial had tried to get away on two merchant ships. However, only one of these was to escape, with the men on the ship other being taken prisoner and sent to the fortress. The next day the young soldier who had shot James Searle was condemned to death and killed by firing squad in the same place where he had killed the youth. He declared his repentance for his actions so strongly that many people were sickened by the execution. A sad note in the middle of the general jubilation.[56]

Charles Dabney's official report of the capture of Faial is contained in a letter to the Secretary of State dated June 30, 1831.

I have the honor to inform you that on the 28th inst. This Island was taken possession of by a detachment of 800 men, under the command of Count Villa Flor sent from Terceira, & Dona Maria II immediately proclaimed Queen of Portugal, which change was affected without any fighting, the Royal forces having previously evacuated & left the Place in a defenceless situation. The Islands of Pico & St. George's had already fallen: at the latter some slight resistance was made. The garrison that left this, were embarked onboard a Portuguese Corvette & an English Schooner; the American Brig Harbinger was also taken for a transport; but the Constitutionalists entering before she could get out of Port, the troops onboard were made prisoners; the two former vessels are supposed to have gone to the Island of Saint Michael's which is likewise threatened with an invasion.

The English Frigate *Galatea* has been stationed here during the disturbances, to protect British & property. The new

Authorities have been quietly installed, & affairs assume a peaceful aspect.

A short time since H.B.M.'s *Volage* called here for refreshments bound to Brest having onboard the Ex-Emperor and Empress of Brasil & suite. We have just learnt that France has declared war against Portugal & a Portuguese Sloop of War has recently been captured by a French Government Brig in the vicinity of these Islands.[57]

There were the usual celebrations with bells, salvos, balls, dinners and masses. The next day oaths were taken to Queen Maria II. On July 1, The Count of Vila Flor once again wrote to Charles Dabney, this time from Angra:

> As it is of great importance to effect as soon as possible the chartering of two vessels of three masts for the transport of troops, the Regency in name of the Queen deemed that no one better than you could aid them in this object, frequent as are your communications with the whaling ships of your Nation, and relying fully upon your character and good will, they have charged me to write to you, and ask this service, which from its importance will in due time be acknowledged in the name of the Queen.
>
> The vessels should be here by the middle of this month and if two cannot be obtained let there be one. The time agreed upon will be for one month and as to the terms, you must act as seems just and proper, not allowing the price, if not exorbitant to be a motive to break the agreement. This letter will be delivered to you by my aide de camp D. António de Mello, who is aware of its object, which must be kept secret if possible from all others.[58]

The Count was right that around this time the Dabney business was becoming heavily involved with the many American whaling ships that were stopping at Horta, and some could possibly have been available. Nevertheless, Charles Dabney had to tell the Count that he could not provide the ships requested since the only ships coming through were whalers that wouldn't change their orders. He went on to ensure the Count that this request would remain secret.[59]

By the end of July, the seven central and western islands were controlled by the Queen's forces and by the end of August 1831, the principal island of São Miguel, as well as Santa Maria had joined the fold so that the entire archipelago supported the Liberals.

Throughout all of this turbulence, Charles Dabney maintained that he was impartial regarding who would eventually win the civil war, a claim not especially credible because Dabney clearly would have supported a republican form of government over a monarchy. While he may not have taken an obviously active role in the dispute, his personal feelings appear more in sympathy with the Liberal forces of King Pedro IV and Queen Maria II.

Notes:

[1] Document 34, United States Archives, Microfilm T203, Roll 1, March 4, 1795-November 28, 1832.

[2] Roxana Lewis Dabney, *Annals of the Dabney Family in Fayal*, comp., n. p.: The Author, 1900,.p 213.

[3] Roxana Lewis Dabney, *Annals*, p. 217 & p. 282.

[4] "Letter from Thomas Brent submitting Charles W. Dabney's commission to the Portuguese Court, Torre do Tombo (Portuguese National Archives), Minstério de Negócios Estrangeiros (MNE), Correspondência das Legações Estrangeiras em Lisboa, Estados Unidos da América, 1820-1833, Cx (Box) 412.

[5] Document 38, United States Archives, Microfilm T203, Roll 2, July 26, 1833-December 4, 1841.

[6] Roxana Lewis Dabney, *Annals*, p. 211.

[7] Roxana Lewis Dabney, *Annals*, p. 225.

[8] António Lourenço da Silveira Maçedo, "Reestablicimento do governo absoluto, chegada da esquadra portugueza ao Fayal, e d'uma companhia de caçadores 5... 1824-25," *História das Quatro Ilhas que Formam o Distrito da Horta, Vol. II*, Direcção Regional dos Assuntos Culturais, Região Autónoma dos Açores, Angra do Heroísmo, Terceira Island, 1981, Ch. 4.

[9] Document 51, United States Archives, Microfilm T203, Roll 1, March 4, 1795-November 28, 1832.

[10] Roxana Lewis Dabney, *Annals*, p. 238.

[11] Roxana Lewis Dabney, *Annals*, p. 238.

[12] Roxana Lewis Dabney, *Annals*, p. 239.

[13] Roxana Lewis Dabney, *Annals*, p. 240.

[14] Roxana Lewis Dabney, *Annals*, p. 239-40.

[15] Roxana Lewis Dabney, *Annals*, p. 240.

[16] Roxana Lewis Dabney, *Annals*, p. 240-41.

[17] Document 44, United States Archives, Microfilm T203, Roll 1, March 4, 1795-November 28, 1832.

[18] Roxana Lewis Dabney, *Annals*, p. 233.

[19] Roxana Lewis Dabney, *Annals*, p. 234.

[20] Marcelino Lima, "Constitucionalismo, Miguelismo e Liberalismo," *Anais do Município da Horta (História da Ilha do Faial)*, 3rd Edition, Oficinas Gráficas "Minerva", Vila Nova de Famalicão, 1981, p. 320.

[21] Roxana Lewis Dabney, *Annals*, p. 246.

[22] Roxana Lewis Dabney, *Annals*, p. 246.

[23] Roxana Lewis Dabney, *Annals*, p. 247.

[24] Roxana Lewis Dabney, *Annals*, p. 247.

[25] Roxana Lewis Dabney, *Annals*, p. 247.

[26] Document 48, United States Archives, Microfilm T203, Roll 1, March 4, 1795-November 28, 1832.

[27] Roxana Lewis Dabney, *Annals*, p. 323.

[28] Roxana Lewis Dabney, *Annals*, p. 248.

[29] Roxana Lewis Dabney, *Annals*, p. 248.

[30] Roxana Lewis Dabney, *Annals*, p. 248.

[31] Document 55, United States Archives, Microfilm T203, Roll 1, March 4, 1795-November 28, 1832.

[32] Document 56, United States Archives, Microfilm T203, Roll 1, March 4, 1795-November 28, 1832.

[33] Document 57, United States Archives, Microfilm T203, Roll 1, March 4, 1795-November 28, 1832.

[34] Roxana Lewis Dabney, *Annals*, p. 250.

[35] Document 25, United States Archives, Microfilm T203, Roll 2, July 26, 1833 – December 4, 1841.

[36] Document 25, United States Archives, Microfilm T203, Roll 2, July 26, 1833 – December 4, 1841.

[37] Document 28, United States Archives, Microfilm T203, Roll 2, July 26, 1833 – December 4, 1841.

[38] Roxana Lewis Dabney, *Annals*, p. 251.

[39] Roxana Lewis Dabney, *Annals*, p. 802-3.

40 "Letter questionning of Hickling's appointment", Torre do Tombo, Ministério de Negócios Estrangeiros (MNE), Correspondência para as Legações Estrangeiras, Estados Unidos da América, 1822-1841, liv.(book) 157.

41 "Letter to Brent about Hickling's appointment", Torre do Tombo, Ministério de Negócios Estrangeiros (MNE), Correspondência das Legações Estrangeiras em Lisboa, Estados Unidos da América, 1820-1833, Cx. (Box) 412

42 "MNE's note on letter about Hickling", Torre do Tombo, Ministério de Negócios Estrangeiros (MNE), Correspondência das Legações Estrangeiras em Lisboa, Estados Unidos da América, 1820-1833, Cx. (Box) 412

43 Roxana Lewis Dabney, Annals, p. 251.

44 Sally Dabney Parker, William Henry Dabney, Reminiscences, 1820-1853, n. p.: The Author, 1981, p. 9.

45 Roxana Lewis Dabney, Annals, p. 260.

46 Roxana Lewis Dabney, Annals, p. 252.

47 Roxana Lewis Dabney, Annals, p. 252.

48 Roxana Lewis Dabney, Annals, p. 255.

49 Roxana Lewis Dabney, Annals, p. 260-6.1

50 Roxana Lewis Dabney, Annals, p. 257.

51 Roxana Lewis Dabney, Annals, p. 258.

52 Document 66, United States Archives, Microfilm T203, Roll1, March 4, 1795-November 28, 1832.

53 Marcelino Lima, p. 330.

54 Roxana Lewis Dabney, Annals, p. 268.

55 Roxana Lewis Dabney, Annals, p. 269-70.

56 António Lourenço da Silveira Macedo, p. 100.

57 Document 63, United States Archives, Microfilm T203, Roll 1, March 4, 1795-November 28, 1832.

58 Roxana Lewis Dabney, Annals, p. 268-69.

59 Roxana Lewis Dabney, Annals, p. 269.

Figure 4
Charles William and Frances Alsop Pomeroy Dabney

9 – ROYAL VISITORS

With the Azores fully supporting Queen Maria II, the provisional government in many parts of Portugal began preparations for the invasion of continental Portugal. Local militias were formed on the islands to replace the regular troops who would be sent off to Portugal, and ships and supplies were being made ready. In early 1832, Maria's father King Pedro IV returned from France with a fleet he had gathered there. Upon arriving in Terceira he formed a government made up of those who had been part of the provisional government of Maria II.

On Faial news of the king's arrival was greeted with celebrations. The local supporters of the king decided to build an arsenal to prepare ships for the expedition to Portugal. They knew that Horta was the logical choice for this since it had the best port and most skillful ship workers. José Sebastião Carreira donated a piece of property as a shipyard, and all the supplies necessary were obtained from the Dabneys. Financial support was provided by a spontaneous public subscription, each according to his means. Those without money donated a day of work.

In the spring of 1832, Charles and Frances Dabney, along with their children Clara and Charles, Jr., sailed to Trinidad and then to New Orleans. From there they traveled by steamboat up the Mississippi and Ohio rivers to Cincinnati. This was about 150 miles down river from where Frances' parents, the Pomeroys, were getting established at the future site of Pomeroy, Ohio

Samuel Pomeroy's coal project was proceeding better than expected, and he believed that "the reputation of our coal over any other that can be brought here, I consider as established beyond all questions."[1] Pomeroy also had great plans for further development, which in future years would actively involve several members of the Pomeroy and Dabney families, as he indicated in a letter to Charles Dabney.

So soon as all the coal lots can be purchased that will be necessary, it is my intention to have that part of Salisbury where our domain is, incorporated into a Burough by the name of Pomeroy, and Mr. Fry is the very man for Intendant or Mayor. Our coal is already denominated Pomeroy coal and I shall be mistaken in my views if you do not before 2 years hear of Pomeroy salt, Fire brick &c.[2]

The Dabneys left their 12-year old daughter Clara with her Pomeroy grandparents in Cincinnati where she was put into school and became quite a good student. They then continued east and dropped off their 11-year old son Charles, Jr., at Mr. Stephen Weld's school in Jamaica Plain, New York, and their 13-year old son John was transferred there from Mr. Ripley's school in Waltham, Massachusetts. They then picked up Charles, Sr.'s 15-year old brother William, who had finished his schooling at Mr. Ingraham's, and returned to Faial in October 1832.[3]

Because of his trip to the United States, Charles Dabney missed the visit of Emperor Pedro to Faial. However his brother John, who was acting as Consul, served as host in his place. His 21-year old sister Emmeline maintained a chronicle of the royal visit.

On the evening of Friday, April 6, 1832, the corvette *Juno*, the frigate *Rainha de Portugal* and two French transport ships arrived in the Bay of Horta with news that the king was on his way. At about 1:00 p.m. the next day, a ship came around the point into the bay. It attracted much attention not only because it was carrying the king, but it was also the first steam-powered ship to visit Horta.

It must be remembered that steamers were then very rudimentary (no steamer had crossed the Atlantic) and perhaps this one attached to Don Pedro's Expedition was the first one which had ventured out so far from Europe.[4]

When it first appeared in Terceira, they thought it was on fire, and were on the point of sending off to save the crew.[5]

The two-mast, sidewheel steamer *Superb* anchored, the royal colors were hoisted on the *Rainha de Portugal* and a salvo was fired which the cannons at the fortress echoed. A launch went out to the ship with the island's officials. At about 3:00 p.m. King Pedro came to shore followed by "the Count of Villa Flor and then came a crowd of grandees."[6] Huge, wildly cheering crowds greeted them to the accompaniment of cannon salvos, fireworks and church bells. The town council welcomed him and mayor Ávila, who was the youngest member of the council, made a short speech, the first public speech he had ever made. After Pedro's response, the procession and crowd set off towards the house of the Morgado Terra Brum who was the "Capitão Mor", Commander of the Militia, on Faial and a strong political supporter of Liberalism to which he gave much financial assistance. Along the way elegantly dressed women leaned out their windows decorated with silk cloth and waved handkerchiefs and threw flowers. The crowd was so large and noisy that the chanting of the Te Deum in front of the main church could not be heard.

That evening there was to be a ball for the King with all the important families in Horta invited.

> On our way home we encountered José Sebastião Jr., who told us he was commissioned by His Majesty and Mr. Terra to invite all the friends of the young ladies (the Terra girls) and as we were included in that number we were invited to go to their house this evening. We answered that we should be happy to do so.[7]

One of the visitors interested the Dabneys in particular. This was the grandson of the American Revolutionary War hero Lafayette. It was decided "between Ma [Roxa Dabney, who had been a young girl at the time of the American Revolution] and Brother John to invite him up to the house to stay".[8] He was "a very modest, unassuming young gentleman, but very ambitious to distinguish himself. His Mother was Lafayette's daughter, his Father is Count Lasteyrie, but he signs his name Lasteyrie Lafayette"[9] and he served as his grandfather's aide.[10] Conversations with the young Count were mainly in French because he spoke very little English, but he was "very agreeable and seems to be well informed. He is very young, tall and light-complexioned, quite lively and talkative."[11]

In her chronicle Emmeline says, "I must not forget to tell you that when we sent upstairs to tell the Count we were ready (as he had desired that we would) Frederick found him busily writing, he said he was writing to his Grandpapa, giving the old gentleman a description of *this place*. Ahem! What an honour!"[12]

Roxa Dabney accompanied her daughters to the ball for the king at the home of Morgado Terra Brum. This was her first social outing since John Dabney had died.[13] The principal families on the island were all there, and Mr. Terra took the Emperor "round and introduced every lady in the room separately."[14] After the introductions, the dance began and Pedro danced first with Francisca Terra and Emmeline danced with the Marquis of Loulé, "a very handsome man."[15] "We all danced until twelve when the Emperor disappeared and the company soon broke up... It was generally understood on leaving the room, that the same company were to meet the next evening again; on Monday they are invited to come here to this house [Bagatelle] in the evening."[16] The general population was not left out of the festivities. They gathered outside the house to hear the music and sounds and to have the feeling that they were also participating.

On the following days Pedro met with all the civil, military and religious authorities from the islands of Faial and Pico and performed all the official functions expected of a monarch. He visited the arsenal where the ships for his fleet were being prepared, thanked all involved and watched the local military go through its maneuvers. The Emperor "had our new Horse and Count of Villa Flor had St. George, all the time they were here, that is whenever they were on horseback."[17] However, as Roxana wrote to her sister-in-law Frances, "the honours the horses have received by having such great personages ride them, has not agreed with them, they go every day to Monte Carneiro for their health; they are much better."[18]

Each night there was a ball in the Emperor's honor. On the second night he once again opened the dancing with Francisca Terra. Emmeline reported on the honor that was accorded her at the ball,

When they struck up for the third dance, His Majesty did me the supreme honour of asking me to dance with him, of course I accepted, and stood up with him; he recollected giving the passport or whatever it was to Mr. Brotero to go to St. Paul [São Paulo, Brazil]; or at least he remembered there was such a man, only think what a gracious memory to remember all that! The dance was soon over, we walked up and down the room for some time; I had forgotten to find out whether it was according to etiquette for me to make the motion to be seated, or whether I must walk until His Majesty chose to be tired; however, I chose the latter and he asked me if I were tired, I said 'a little,' and I at the same moment espied a seat, asked his leave, and seated myself.[19]

In her descriptions of the parties she attended, Emmeline comes across with a mixture of innocence and allure. Her sister Roxana described Emmeline as a young woman with...

...such grace and a natural coquettishness that never generated into hoydenism. She could not help coquetting, but it was perfectly spontaneous and natural. The others would say to her sometimes 'Why Emmie, how could you lead so and so on as you did?' 'Why, what did I do? I cannot see that I did anything; he wanted to talk and so we talked. What did I do?' I have never seen anyone with such charm of manner.[20]

On Monday night, April 9, the Dabneys held the ball at Bagatelle. Emmeline's chronicle describes the Royal Ball as it happened that memorable night at Bagatelle.

The Emperor came about nine o'clock, came round by the verandah. We had some good music, two flutes, two violins, and a bass viol, with Brother John's piano, as the other did not agree with the instruments. Ma would not listen to having the great piano moved from the other room.

The Emperor danced with me first, I did not consider this any compliment as he had visited at the House; he afterwards invited me to gallopade with him. It was too bad he neither

invited Roxana nor Livy to dance with him, I think he might,
perhaps he was on his guard not to dance too much with
English for fear of jealousy. I was very sorry, for I know Roxana
was a little disappointed, though she did not say much about it.
The Emperor regulated the dances, Fred asked the musicians to
play some thing, they told him they could not for H.M. had told
them not to play anything but when he told them." "You must
know that although H.M. is so very fond of music, we have had
very little at these parties; it is a constant succession of Quadrilles,
one or two waltzes and Gallopades, in the course of the evening.
It would amuse you to see with what spirit the Emperor dances
the Gallopade." "The Emperor staid until after two o'clock,
unusually late for him; the only person who went with him was
Almeida, all the rest remained much later; it was four o'clock
before all had gone. They never bid good night, when they are
tired, slip off unobserved; the Emperor does so and all his staff.[21]

On the night before he left, the ball was at Mr. Lane's house,
and Pedro once again danced with Emmeline.[22] During the evening, Dona Joaquina Terra, the oldest daughter of the Capitão
Mor, presented Pedro with a silk flag that had been embroidered with the coat-of-arms of Queen Maria II by the women
of Faial. He was also presented with an enormous table of sweets
made by the nuns of the Convent of Glória, including 32 sweet-
meat hearts each with the initials of one of the 32 nuns.

On April 12, Pedro and his entourage set sail, promising that
he would return. On the same day, the Faial battalion left to
cheers and tears to join the troops assembling for the expedition
to Portugal. Very few of these men were ever to return.

Even after Pedro sailed, there were still several ships in the Bay
of Horta being prepared for the Expeditionary Force and others
returned to wait their turn. On one of these was British Admiral
Sartorius and his secretary Captain Boid. The Admiral "had been
struck out of the navy lists" because he had volunteered for Pedro's
expedition. He was later reinstated in the British Navy.[23]

Admiral Sartorius and Captain Boid spent a lot of time with
the Dabney family and a strong relationship developed. In his
book, "Azores or Western Islands", Captain Boid reports, "Our

stay at Horta, whilst performing the various services of the expedition, was rendered extremely agreeable by the kindness and hospitality, not only of our own countrymen, but especially of the amiable family of the American Consul, Mr. Dabney."[24]

Tuesday, May 23, was Dona Joaquina Terra's birthday. Emmeline describes an unusual custom of the Terras.

> We hear there are preparations made to receive company, though as yet not an invitation has come. We youngsters had formed the determination not to go, unless absolutely obliged to, for you know that according to the usual custom there is always some 'faux pas,' in fact I do not believe there ever was a party in that house, without some blunder. Mr. Terra expects that all strangers are to know and fall into the customs of a place directly; not even the Governor is invited.[25]

However, the ball took a surprising turn when King Pedro kept his word about returning, although it was sooner than anyone had anticipated. He knew that May 22 was the birthday of Dona Joaquina Terra, and her father, Morgado Terra Brum, would be having a large party. King Pedro wanted to arrive as a surprise to demonstrate his appreciation for the hospitality extended him on his first visit.[26] The Emperor landed on the dock at about 10 p.m. and made his way to the Terra Brum's.

> He did not stop any where, came directly up to Mr. Terra's in boots and a great coat, came into the ball-room in that trim. The only person he met, whom he knew, was Mr. Sergio, whom he stopped and spoke to; the poor old gentleman was very much frightened, and asked, 'what do you want with me?' however directly afterwards recognized him and exclaimed? Oh! Hé! Sua Majestade!' The Emperor told me the anecdote himself, and seemed to enjoy it so much, they say he is fond of surprising people in that kind of manner.[27]

Pedro entered the house and handed his hat and coat to the startled servants. He quickly climbed the two flights of stairs and entered the room where the party was going strong and created a major surprise. According to Emmeline, the ball had begun, and, after a dance she was walking up and down the room with her partner when

> there was a slight bustle in the ante-room, I involuntarily looked around and saw – Don Pedro!!! I was thunderstruck, every lady seemed to be struck dumb, at last recollecting themselves, they rushed forward with one consent; H. M. enjoyed the scene very much.[28]

Some guests had already left and there were others who had not been invited, but "about an hour afterwards, they came pouring in. Mr. Assiz looked as if he had just jumped out of bed...We had a good laugh at them all for being obliged to rout out at that hour of the night".[29] Once again Emmeline was Pedro's first partner.

> As soon as the Emperor arrived, after the compliments had passed, he told them to strike up a dance; Dona Clementina had to play; to my surprise the Emperor came up to me; after making an excuse for his dress, he asked if I would dance with him.[30]

The next morning the King inspected the arsenal along with local officials. "The object of the Emperor's second visit to this Island was to hasten the vessels which were here preparing, and repairing."[31] His day of inspecting was followed by another ball at the Terra's. Emmeline tells us she "had the honour of dancing again with him, for the seventh and last time!! Francisca Terra is the only girl here who has exceeded me; you cannot deny it is something to boast of, notwithstanding our republican principles."[32] She remedies her apparent lack of modesty by telling Frances that she was sure that she would have danced less with Pedro if Frances had been there. The King also invited the Dabneys and some others in Horta to take what was probably their first ride on a steamboat.

> The Terras, Ribeiros and we were invited by his Majesty to go on board of the Steamboat tomorrow morning, and sail a

short distance, so we went this morning and had a pleasant time of it.[33]

At dawn on May 24, Pedro departed to lead the Expedition to Portugal. Before leaving, he addressed the young mayor with some affectionate remarks about Faial, "the friendly island, the rose-bud of the Azorean bouquet."[34]

In order to maintain secrecy about the Expedition, orders were received for an embargo on any ships arriving in the port. This was a great hardship on the American whalers that were starting to arrive in large numbers. Finally, on June 27, 1832, the Expeditionary Squadron sailed and the embargo ended.

John Dabney wrote a brief summary of this whole period to his father Charles Dabney.

> (...) We have had a very busy time, two visits from Dom Pedro, several ships of War, and Transports have fitted. This house has witnessed one continual scene of entertaining visitors, by day and by night, ever since you departed. At length however there is a general clear out, thank God! And we suppose the Expedition consisting of 60 sail, 10,000 men are this day about leaving St. Michael's. The Emperor and his suite were delighted with the hospitality of Fayal.[35]

When the ships were free to leave, John Dabney decided to sail on one to England because "he did not feel as well as he did some time ago and wished to consult a physician,"[36] and ended up spending the winter there. It is reported that he had a long--term health problem that caused great concern to his family, although what it was is never specified. The Consulate was left without its two senior members, and in a letter to Charles, John says, "I assure you I should not have departed from Fayal, during your absence had it not been Imperiously, I may say vitally necessary for me to do so."[37]

To cut a long war short, Pedro left the Azores with his expeditionary force and captured Oporto in July 1832 and Lisbon in July 1833. Then King Pedro IV restored the constitution in the name of his daughter Maria da Glória. King Miguel's forces were

ON THE EDGE OF HISTORY   170

finally defeated in 1834 and he was sent to Genoa and finally ended up back in Austria. It was now the Liberal's turn to take action against the Absolutists and their ideas. All the supporters of Miguel were dismissed from government offices. In addition, Pedro ordered the abolition of all monasteries and convents, and the State took over their property and possessions, with pensions being paid to those dispossessed until they could care for themselves.

During the entire period from the death of King João VI in 1826 to the final victory of the Liberals in 1834, the only part of Portugal that had remained consistently behind the Liberals were the Azores, particularly the central group where Faial is located. King Pedro was grateful for this support and granted special favors among the islands. Angra, because of its heroic refusal to submit to the Absolutists, was given the name of Angra do Heroismo. The town of Horta was also upgraded in the Portuguese municipal hierarchy and, as described by Charles' youngest sister Olivia, was

> (...) changed to a City which has of course, altered its appearance *amazingly*. Dr. Ávila, no longer the Philosopher, but the Sub-Prefeito of Fayal has been to Oporto where he obtained several privileges for this Island. There is to be a new Market, where the Glória Convent is. The few nuns left in it are to go to Terceira. The streets are to be lighted, of course what would a City be without the streets lighted! The roads are to be repaired all over the Island and the "Bicas" water is to be brought to the City. The College is undergoing a thorough repair and looks very nice indeed.[38]

King Pedro IV survived his victory by only three months, dying on September 24, 1834 at the age of thirty-six. His daughter Maria da Glória was declared of age and ascended the throne of Portugal as Queen Maria II at the age of fifteen. She married Prince August of Leuchtenberg, brother of her father's second wife, but he died shortly after arriving in Lisbon. In 1836, she married Ferdinand of Saxe-Coburg-Gotha, cousin of Albert of Saxe--Coburg-Gotha, future husband of Queen Victoria of England.

The year 1834 also saw another royal visitor arrive in Horta, the Prince of Joinville, the 16-year old third son of King Louis-Phillipe of France. Charles Dabney describes the Prince's arrival and the role he had as host to the Prince.

> When the Prince de Joinville visited this Island, he preserved an incognito, but I called upon the Count d'Oysonville, the Commander of the *Sirène* at the French Consul's. Mr. Sérgio Pereira Ribeiro [the French Consul] was an elderly gentleman, and was passing the summer in Pico; his son with whom I was on familiar terms held an office in the Custom House. I took an opportunity to tell him that my resources were at his service to do the honours of the Island in a suitable manner; he thanked me, remarking that his family were mostly at Pico, and he could do but little. I asked him if it would be agreeable for me to volunteer? 'de tout mon coeur, c'est la plus grande faveur, que tu puisses me faire.' ['with all my heart it is the biggest favor that you could do me.'] I immediately explained the state of things to the Frenchmen and invited them to repair to my house. Upon arriving there, they expressed their sense of kindness, and introduced the Prince, saying that with one, who had thus treated them there could be no concealment.[39]

The 16-year old Prince and his retinue were taken on trips around the island, given excellent meals and treated to a ball at Bagatelle, experiencing the complete round of Dabney hospitality. Roxana, then seven, says that she could "remember showing the Prince, on one occasion, the way down to the billiard room, and thinking his voice was squeaky; nevertheless he was a great hero in our young eyes."[40] Charles' brother William remembers "that bashful young Prince sitting much of the time in the corner and not dancing."[41] He stayed from September 22 to 28 and, before leaving, presented the Dabney's daughter Roxana with an accordion, then new in Europe, his son Samuel Wyllys a box with a gold watch chain, seal and key and Charles and his son Frank a basket of six boxes of chocolate cakes.[42]

Charles Dabney had received a live American eagle from Thomas Hickling a short time before. He gave this to the Prince, along with enough live fowl to feed it on the voyage. The note with the gift said:

> The undersigned Consul of the United States of America for the Azores has the honor of presenting his respects to his Highness the Prince of Joinville and offering to him an American Eagle, exceptionally pleased for the opportunity to present the magnificent emblem of his country the Prince of a nation that has assisted so much the spreading of the wings of Liberty and Independence.[43]

> ...the gift that most delighted the Prince de Joinville was a sea-unicorn's horn, which some captain had given to C. W. D. as something quite rare. The Prince was overjoyed when it was presented to him and departed from Bagatelle bearing it in triumph in his hand.[44]

He also sent several cases of Malmsey to the King and Queen of France. The Eagle ended up in the Jardin des Plantes in Paris.

In addition, Charles Dabney may also have aided the United States in obtaining funds that France owed America in the "French Claims."

> M. Verneaux [the Captain of the Ship], as I before mentioned, is a member of the Chamber; in our first conversation he acknowledged that he was opposed to the treaty of indemnity, but previous to his departure, he confessed that he had been convinced of the justice of our claims, and that I might depend on his vote, and that of those over whom he had influence.[45]

In 1836, the Queen of France sent the Dabneys a small tea set of Sèvres porcelain. Since U. S. Consuls were not allowed to accept gifts from foreign governments, Charles Dabney wrote to Congress to ask for an exception to keep the gift. In 1843, Caleb Cushing, U.S. envoy to China, was in Horta and informed Charles Dabney that he had been "one of the committee that decided that C. W. D should retain the gift, but that nothing should be said about it, that it might not serve as a precedent."[46] In keeping with this fear of a precedent, the State Department did not send official written permission to Charles Dabney.

After the end of the civil war in 1834, Portugal entered a period of relative peace. Although there was no lack of political posturing by the various groups to attain predominance in the government, there was no outright fighting. This was the first time that there had been peace and stability since the French invasions approximately 30 years earlier.

This long period of political and social unrest had covered virtually the entire period that the Dabneys had been American Consuls in the Azores. It was now possible for them to focus on aspects of their life in the Azores without significant interference from major European or American political machinations.

As a result, the Dabney businesses began to progress with the improvement in conditions. At this time, although U.S. Consuls could still operate their own businesses, questions began to be raised about the appropriateness of this activity. Obviously, Charles Dabney was in favor of continuing with the *status quo* and sent his opinion in 1834 to Louis McLane, Secretary of State.

> The influence of persons admitting that they are equal in point of honor, courtesy & being in proportion to the money which they expend in entertainments and the number of persons they employ in the prosecution of their business, there are many cases in which the influence of a Consul would be diminished were he to relinquish his commercial establishment & retire on the largest salary that could be allowed, persons thus situated would prefer holding the commission without salary & be permitted to attend to their business; and in such cases, in fact of their not accepting the salary which, were they not actuated by a strict sense of honor they might do, and conduct their business clandestinely, would afford a strong security for the propriety of their conduct in regard to those engaged in similar pursuits.[47]

Negotiations were begun in 1835 for a trade treaty between the United States and Portugal led by the U. S. representative to Portugal, Edward Kavanagh, who was President Andrew Jackson's grandson. However, the Portuguese did not want to lose British favor and put off action on the treaty with the Americans while Portugal was negotiating a new trade treaty with Britain. In 1839, the British parliament passed the Palmerston bill, which aimed at suppressing Portuguese slave traffic because Portugal had refused to sign a treaty with Britain to abolish slavery. The Portuguese condemned the bill and accused the British "of masking mercantile interests with philanthropy and calling law and justice that which was only despotism and ambition." In this anti-British climate and with a change in the Portuguese government, Almeida Garrett, a famous Portuguese author in addition to being an eminent politician, was appointed to conduct the treaty negotiations with the U. S. that were brought to fruition in 1840. It contained a "most-favored" nation clause, as well as the concepts of freedom of trade and reciprocity. In Britain, the Conservatives replaced the Liberals and, in face of the trade treaty with the U. S., negotiations were reopened with Portugal for the British trade treaty of 1842 that contained the same concepts as the treaty with the U. S. As a result, Portugal agreed to sign a modified treaty for the abolition of slavery.[48]

In the early 1840's, the Dabneys got into a new business that was completely different from any of their previous businesses – the production of silk. Charles Dabney ordered 2,000 mulberry trees from the United States to plant on Faial to feed the silkworms. In addition, this labor-intensive business also "seemed such a delightful occupation for women, whose employments were so limited."

One of the reasons for this new project was the loss of orange trees due to infection with *coccus hesperidum* in 1842. This blight virtually destroyed the citrus growing and exporting business on Faial, which was known for the quality of its oranges, baskets of which were a common gift from the Dabneys to friends in America.

Silk production was also a business that was started in Portugal after the disastrous earthquake of 1755 and made Portugal a major producer of silk for several years. In fact parts of Lisbon still bear the name of the mulberry tree, *Amoreira*, which produces the leaves that the silkworm eats.

Charles Dabney imported silkworm eggs from Italy and the U. S., but when all came together there were problems:

> C. W. D imported silkworm eggs from Italy and the United States, and at first the enterprise seemed to promise very well. One difficulty was the trees putting out too early and being blighted, and this happening several times in a season, as occurred some years, the leaves finally would be wanting in proper nourishment, or the worms would come out before a second crop of leaves was grown; this could be obviated by keeping the eggs in an ice house, which C. W. D had constructed, importing the ice from the United States.

The project was developed on the Bagatelle grounds, but unfortunately it did not turn out well.

> The upper part of the house below Bagatelle, which was being built for C. W. D. at the time of his father's death was fitted up with slight partitions and shelves, into which the trays with the worms could be placed. It was arranged to accommodate seven hundred and fifty thousand worms. He sent for reels, and Bernarda, Luiza, Joaquina, and others were employed in reeling. The silk was pronounced very fine. Samuel W. Dabney had the principal charge of this enterprise entrusted to him, and I am sure he was very zealous, some nights, when the worms were fully grown, staying up there to see that they were properly fed; but he has said in later years that he was too young and inexperienced. The worms after a time became diseased, it is thought now from overcrowding and overfeeding. Much money must have been spent and the failure was a great disappointment to many. C. W. D. distributed fifteen thousand plants of *morus multicaulis* [mulberry trees] among his friends.[49]

In 1845, Charles Dabney, Jr., wrote his brother Samuel and told him that, "the three crops of silk-worms were total failures,

Garcia, the assistant succeeded in his first crop very well, but failed in his last.[50] Among the many businesses the Dabneys entered into, this was one of the few that failed.

Notes:

[1] Roxana Lewis Dabney, *Annals of the Dabney Family in Fayal*, comp., n. p.: The Author, 1900, p. 326.

[2] Roxana Lewis Dabney, *Annals*, p. 327.

[3] Sally Dabney Parker, *William Henry Dabney, Reminiscences, 1820-1853*, n. p.: The Author, 1981, p. 10.

[4] Sally Dabney Parker, *Reminiscences*, p. 11.

[5] Roxana Lewis Dabney, *Annals*, p. 286.

[6] Roxana Lewis Dabney, *Annals*, p. 290.

[7] Roxana Lewis Dabney, *Annals*, p. 290.

[8] Roxana Lewis Dabney, *Annals*, p. 290.

[9] Roxana Lewis Dabney, *Annals*, p. 314.

[10] Roxana Lewis Dabney, *Annals*, p. 292.

[11] Roxana Lewis Dabney, *Annals*, p. 292.

[12] Roxana Lewis Dabney, *Annals*, p. 292.

[13] Roxana Lewis Dabney, *Annals*, p. 290.

[14] Roxana Lewis Dabney, *Annals*, p. 291.

[15] Roxana Lewis Dabney, *Annals*, p. 291.

[16] Roxana Lewis Dabney, *Annals*, p. 291.

[17] Roxana Lewis Dabney, *Annals*, p. 293.

[18] Roxana Lewis Dabney, *Annals*, p. 287.

[19] Roxana Lewis Dabney, *Annals*, p. 292-3.

[20] Roxana Lewis Dabney, *Annals*, p. 270.

[21] Roxana Lewis Dabney, *Annals*, p. 293-4.

[22] Roxana Lewis Dabney, *Annals*, p. 295.

[23] Roxana Lewis Dabney, *Annals*, p. 300.

[24] Captain Boid, *A Description of the Azores or Western Islands*, London, 1834, p. 270.

[25] Roxana Lewis Dabney, *Annals*, p. 303.

[26] José Bettencourt Brum, Coisas da Nossa Terra: Crónicas, Câmara Municipal da Horta, Horta, 1994, p. 46.

[27] Roxana Lewis Dabney, *Annals*, p. 304.

[28] Roxana Lewis Dabney, *Annals*, p. 303-4.

[29] Roxana Lewis Dabney, *Annals*, p. 304.

[30] Roxana Lewis Dabney, *Annals*, p. 304.

31 Roxana Lewis Dabney, *Annals*, p. 305.

32 Roxana Lewis Dabney, *Annals*, p. 305.

33 Roxana Lewis Dabney, *Annals*, p. 305.

34 Marcelino Lima, "Constitucionalismo, Miguelismo e Liberalismo," *Anais do Município da Horta (História da Ilha do Faial)*, 3rd Edition, Oficinas Gráficas "Minerva", Vila Nova de Famalicão, 1981, p. 344.

35 Roxana Lewis Dabney, *Annals*, p. 315.

36 Roxana Lewis Dabney, *Annals*, p. 311.

37 Roxana Lewis Dabney, *Annals*, p. 316.

38 Roxana Lewis Dabney, *Annals*, p. 337.

39 Roxana Lewis Dabney, *Annals*, p. 353.

40 Roxana Lewis Dabney, *Annals*, p. 354.

41 Sally Dabney Parker, p. 14.

42 Roxana Lewis Dabney, *Annals*, p. 357; *Reminiscences*, p E9

43 Roxana Lewis Dabney, *Annals*, p. 354-5.

44 Roxana Lewis Dabney, *Annals*, p. 355.

45 Roxana Lewis Dabney, *Annals*, p. 356.

46 Roxana Lewis Dabney, *Annals*, p. 363 and p. 455.

47 Document 25, United States Archives, Microfilm T203, Roll 2, July 26, 1833 – December 4, 1841.

48 José Calvet de Magalhães, *Breve História Diplomática de Portugal*, Publicações Europa-América, Mem Martins, 1990, p. 136-141.

49 Roxana Lewis Dabney, *Annals*, p. 424, 434-5.

50 Roxana Lewis Dabney, *Annals*, p. 525.

10 – GROWING UP IN PARADISE

During the 1830's the youngest of John Bass Dabney's children were becoming adults and joining their older brothers and
sisters in getting married and raising their own families. At the
end of May 1835, Frederick Dabney, John Dabney's eighth child,
and now a Harvard graduate, wrote home from London to
announce his marriage. The only member of the family present
was his youngest sister Olivia. His bride was Roxana Stackpole,
daughter of his mother's younger sister Nancy. The young couple
had been engaged 1-2 years before they announced their plans,
with Frederick's sister Emmeline being the only one who knew.

Frederick's marriage led to a major change in the family's
living arrangements. Charles Dabney, who had seven children,
had been building another house for his own family at the bottom of Bagatelle, but stopped construction when his father died
and stayed with his mother at Bagatelle. Now a move into a new
home was necessary. Charles purchased another house almost
in the center of Horta, just above the Dabney place of business
and near a garden he had previously bought.

> In 1835 Charles W. Dabney bought Mr. Goulart's unfinished
> house and after altering moved into it with his family, leaving Ba-
> gatelle to his brother [Frederick] who was married in that year.
> Sometime later Captain Vidal of the H. M. S. "Styx" when survey-
> ing the Islands, wrote "Fredonia" into the chart of Fayal to indi-
> cate C. W. D.'s house, and this name it has borne ever since. Up
> to this date no one has discovered what the name means.[1]

The name originated when Mr. Fowler, who, as described
earlier, had arrived on Faial after his ship had sunk in 1830 and
had to stay in Faial, wrote a popular book about his adventure.
For some unexplained reason he used the name Fredonia to

apply to Bagatelle, a fact unknown to Captain Vidal. Because the Consulate had also moved, he confused the properties when he was making his excellent maps of Faial and Horta. Like Bagatelle, Fredonia was known for its gardens. A short description of them is given in a letter from Samuel Longfellow to his mother, when he was there as tutor for the children in 1842-3.

> The gardens are full of trees and shrubs and shady walks and nooks; but what strikes you most is the lavish abundance of the flowers, and their luxuriant growth. Walking out in the morning, you would think it rained flowers all night. It was some time before I could learn to pick choice flowers with as little compunction or ceremony as if they were dandelions or buttercups, sure that to-morrow would repair the loss of today.[2]

Charles Dabney and his family took up residence in Fredonia, where he lived until his death. However, he did not let having a separate residence affect his close relationship with his mother.

> The bond between C. W. D. and his mother was a very close one, and so we all continued at Bagatelle, until the end of the year 1835, or rather the beginning of 1836, for the boys and Mr. Brooks [the children's tutor] remained at Bagatelle for several months after their arrival.[3]

Marriages continued in Horta with Emmeline announcing "her engagement to Mr. Adam Paterson of Edinburgh. He stopped here in the "Waverly," a packet ship, which put in for repairs, and was here nearly two months".[4] In late 1836 Emmeline's wedding took place with her father performing the ceremony.

> Mr. Paterson came out that autumn (1836), and the marriage ceremony was performed by C. W. D., as in those days the United States consuls were allowed to perform the marriage ceremony. A ball was given at Bagatelle in honor of the occasion. I was very fond of Uncle Paterson, we had many a romp together. The bridal pair went to Scotland where Aunt Emmie was exceedingly admired by his family, as they have themselves told me.[5]

The young couple moved to Canada where life started off well, and within three years they had added two more children to the large Dabney clan. Unfortunately, their happiness there was short lived. In 1839, shortly after their second child was born, their house burned and they lost almost everything they owned.

> C. W. D and wife went to Canada to see them. They were living in a sort of barn, in a most uncomfortable manner, but mother often said it was truly wonderful to see the equanimity with which this young mother, with her two boys, Andrew and James, bore their reverses, doing honors of their barn with the same sweetness and grace as when surrounded by the indulgences and comforts of Bagatelle. The result of this visit was that the Patersons should return with us to Fayal.[6]

A year later, in 1840, after Adam Paterson had returned from a visit to his family in Scotland, he took his wife and oldest child and left Faial on the Dabney ship *Harbinger*. They were on their way to Pomeroy, Ohio, where the mining and other businesses of Charles Dabney's father-in-law, Samuel Pomeroy, were located. Adam hoped to find work there, but their voyage ended in tragedy. Little Andrew wasn't feeling well when they left and gradually got worse until "he died very quietly at the last."[7] It was thought that he died of "brain fever", most often interpreted as meningitis or encephalitis. His body along with a letter from Emmeline were returned to Faial on a passing whale ship and buried in the family plot at Bagatelle. Andrew's death took place not long after the death of Frederick Dabney's one-year old son Frederick, the second of his children with this name to die.

In early 1841, Adam Paterson himself died, and Emmeline returned to Faial with Charles' wife Frances Pomeroy Dabney who was returning from Pomeroy, Ohio, where her father had recently died. As a result of Samuel Pomeroy's death, Charles Dabney inherited a part of the business and had to commit more time to the concerns of the coal business in Pomeroy, including making long trips to Ohio.

Schooling had always been a major concern for the Dabneys. As indicated in the previous chapter, John Bass Dabney sent his children to America and England to school, and some went to university at Harvard. When the Dabney family arrived on Faial, "young Charles was placed to board with Dr. Roque for the purpose of learning the Portuguese language."[8] He had already attained fluency in French during the family's stay in France. In 1809, at the age of 15, Charles was sent as a counting-room apprentice to Mr. Wheaton in the U. S.

> I put him under your charge and hope you will make a clever fellow of him, but I earnestly request you to be very strict with him. He has I believe no vices, and if he is kept from improper company, he may arrive at maturity without any. By changing from French to American and Portuguese masters, he has lost his handwriting, and I have no other alternative but to request you to procure him a good writing master of whom he can take lessons every day, until he writes well. I trust he will soon write a useful hand and as commerce is eternally finding out new channels, if yours should bye and bye lead you into speculations with French, Portuguese or Spaniards, Charles may become very useful to you in speaking and interpreting now, and with a little application in winter evenings may soon write all these languages. I cannot consent that your friendship for me should cause Charles to be a pecuniary charge upon you. It is my earnest desire, and that of his mother, if not too inconvenient, that he should live in your family, that his morals may be watched over, and the he may profit of the counsel of yourself and Mrs. Wheaton, but in all cases, I wish you to state to me a certain sum per annum that will remunerate you for the expense of his living. As to his dress and pocket expenses, I wish you to use your judgment and discretion but would recommend that he be dressed plain and neat, and be very moderate in the latter article.[9]

He didn't stay there very long and returned to Faial because,

> He proved to be somewhat unmanageable and Mr. Wheaton not caring for the responsibility sent him back to Fayal, when

or how e do not know, but it was probably some time during 1810. He seems to have remained at home all through 1811 and 1812 as we find him in his father's counting room late in the latter years as we have seen above for in November 1812 he is mentioned in a letter of his father's as being then with him.[10]

Unlike Charles, his younger sister Roxalina was sent to school in England at the age of 10 in 1809. She went with Mr. Burnett, who was John Dabney's agent there, and his family. In London she joined two of Mr. Hickling's daughters in school there. Roxalina apparently did quite well in school as shown in this response by John Dabney to a letter from Mr. Burnett.

> My mind turns with pleasure to the accounts you give me of my daughter's (Roxalina) improvement and good conduct. She always was a child of great promise.[11]

Roxalina returned to Fayal in the spring of 1813 during the time of war between the US and Britain. As for the younger children, they were all sent away to school as they came of age. In the autumn of 1817, 9-year old James and 8-year old Frederick "are gone to school at Mr. Knapp's at Brighton."[12] The boys apparently did very well because their father wrote in a letter to his son Charles' father-in-law, "Yours and Mr. Knapp's eulogiums on the boys were highly flattering and I hope they will continue to deserve them."[13]

For the children who were too young to be sent away, in 1821 John Bass Dabney's niece Mary Ann Young "came to reside permanently with him and to teach his younger children, Emmeline, (but she must have gone next year to America to go to school), Olivia, and myself [William Henry]. She was then 24 years of age, very pretty and fascinating to gentlemen. In other words, a flirt, and a dreadfully tight lacer."[14]

It was this not very strait-laced young lady that apparently caught the eye of John Lewis Dabney, who was interested in developing a relationship with her. William Dabney says that this was the reason John "was sent away to Brazil in 1822 to break this up."[15] As a result, John's relationship with his family suffered and even when he returned to Faial he lived separate from the rest of the family and never married.

At this time, James and Frederick were attending Mr. Knapp's school in Jamaica plain. Emmeline was at Mrs. McKedges' school, but after the quarter was to go to Boston to her sister Roxa's and attend school in Boston.[16] However, just a year later, 15-year old James returned from school and went to work in the counting room of the Dabney business.

In 1825, the two youngest of John Bass Dabney's children, Olivia (age 10) and William (age 8) were sent away to school. "Olivia was placed at school at Mr. Wm. B. Fowle's school and I went to Miss Newman's next door to Sister Roxa´s where we resided. Emmeline was at Mr. Emerson's school right behind in Chestnut Street."[17] Shortly after this, "Emmeline was placed at Madame Grilland's French boarding school to learn French, etc. She had previously been at school at Mr. George B. Emerson's school while living with her sister Roxa. This school was right behind sister Roxa's house in Chestnut Street."[18]

William, who had suffered a serious bout of scarlet fever, was taken back to Faial for recovery. However, "Olivia was left in Boston and Frederick also, then at Harvard College, in his sophomore year. (He graduated in 1828)."[19] William returned to Massachusetts to school after his father's death in 1826 and his recovery from his illness.

> My mother intended that I go to the Round Hill Academy at Northampton, Mass. Under the charge of Messrs. Cogswell (afterwards Librarian of the National Library at Washington) and Mr. Bancroft (afterwards the great historian). But Sister Roxa thought differently owing to my puny weakly appearance and she put me at Waltham under the charge of Rev. Samuel and Mrs. Ripley who took six or eight boys into their family to educate.[20]

William was very happy in this school where he stayed from 1828 to 1831 when he transferred to "Mr. Ingraham's private school in Tremont St."[21] and lived with his sister Roxa.

Finally, William was 15-years old he returned to Fayal and started to work in the counting room of the family business.[22] In the
meantime, his sister Olivia had returned to Faial in 1829 and the
education of John Bass Dabney's children was accomplished.

Charles Dabney agreed with his father's opinion of the importance of schooling and continued the custom of school away
from Faial. In 1834, he and his wife took a trip to America with
three of their children, 14-year old Clara, 13-year old John and
11-year old Charles, Jr.

> They ascended the Mississippi to Cincinnati and left Clara
> there [...]. After visiting Pomeroy, Ohio, Boston & other places
> they embarked in Oct. 1832, only C. W. D. & Wife. Charles
> was left at Mr. Stephen Weld's school in Jamaica Plain where
> John and António Garcia had been transferred from Mr. Rip-
> ley's in Waltham. I [C. W. D.'s 15-year old brother William]
> accompanied them (to Fayal) having finished my schooling at
> Mr. Ingraham's.[23]

Clara attended several schools in Ohio, and, in 1834 she
was put into a school with "the Misses Catherine and Harriet
Beecher, afterwards Mrs. Stowe, [20 years before she wrote
"Uncle Tom's Cabin"], daughters of Rev.d Lyman Beecher and
sisters to Henry Ward Beecher who kept a popular school in
that city,"[24] Her aunt Mary wrote to Frances that Clara's

> (...) reading and composition exercises are under the di-
> rection of Miss Harriet Beecher, who has a most admirable
> plan I think for conducting them; she goes through a course
> of reading to them, selections from the standard English writers
> both in prose and poetry, makes observations herself upon the
> style, sentiments &. And calls upon her pupils for their opinion;
> she has a happy faculty of doing this in an easy familiar manner
> which will lead them to examine and compare what they read,
> without the danger of falling into a formal pedantic manner.
> She requires them also to express their own thought, in writing
> composition and in their own language, and tells them if they will
> only do it grammatically she cares not how simply it is done.[25]

Around 1835, the Dabneys decided to take a different approach to their children's education as pointed out in a letter to Frances Alsop Dabney from her sister Mary in Cincinnati.

> I am truly delighted with your plan for the boys; I have felt much for you on their account; it seems as if this would unite advantages of the most important nature. If you are only fortunate in the selection of a Tutor, I am satisfied you will have no reason to regret recalling them. I was speaking of this to Mr. Perkins yesterday, and he said nothing would delight him more than to go out there and pass a few years (...).[26]

With the change to having a tutor on the island, John and Charles, Jr., returned from Mr. Weld's school in Jamaica Plain In October of 1835. Their new tutor, Mr. Eben S. Brooks, a Harvard graduate, arrived with them on the same ship.

> We are very sorry to part with the boys, but return them to you, I hope, improved by their residence with us. I think Mr. Brooks will find, that they have been carefully and critically instructed, as far as they have proceeded in their studies. They are very good boys and have studied very well of late. I congratulate you on being able to have them with you again, and think you have chosen the most judicious course. The loss of the society of their children is to parents a most trying sacrifice. Mr. Brooks, whom you have engaged as a teacher is a very fine man and perfectly qualified in every respect to have charge of their studies.[27]

A year later Clara completed her studies in Cincinnati and returned home to Faial accompanied by her Uncle William. Over the next few years, there were a number of tutors who came to Faial. However, in between the various tutors that came to Faial, Clara, Charles Dabney's oldest daughter, took over the teaching activities.

The "school" at the Dabney house wasn't limited to just their own children, but included one or more of the local children. One of the activities of Mr. Brooks and the three boys was to carry out a survey of the Bay of Horta in preparation for a plan for the construction of a dock.[28]

In addition to the older boys who had returned from America, some of the younger children began their schooling with the tutor. As can be expected, children like 11-year old Samuel Wyllys, 10-year old Roxana and 7-year old Frank who had never been in a formal school, didn't know exactly how to conduct themselves in a classroom with rigid rules.

In the spring of 1839, Charles Dabney followed the advice of a Mr. Guthnick and sent his sons John, Charles, Jr., and Sam to school in Geneva accompanied by Mr. Brooks. The boys were put into M. Briquet's school, and Mr. Brooks went to Paris to study medicine, where Charles, Jr later joined him.

> Poor Charles had a very dreary recollection of his life in Paris, fitting himself for entering Harvard. The principal diversion he seems to have had was going to Gen. Cass's, our then minister to France, who was very kind to Charles and often played billiards with him. It was difficult for my brothers Charles and Sam to do justice to Mr. Brooks, he certainly towards them was wanting in judgment, if not justice, at times.[29]

A year later they left Switzerland and returned to Faial with their new tutor Mr. Deyhle, who proved to be unsatisfactory. Mr. Brooks' comments on what was expected of Mr. Deyhle while their Uncle William indicates that his stay wasn't very long and that better tutors followed him to Faial.

> Deyhle did not expect to teach mathematics! He knew very well they were required, I asked him in London, when urging him to give Sam some instruction, if he did not expect to teach mathematics? And his reply was, "Certainly, I shall teach all that is ordinarily taught in schools." Guthnick was instructed to procure a man, not a fool.[30]

> The boys – John, Charles & Samuel – returned this year [1840] from Geneva with Mr. Deyhle, as German tutor. He proved to be totally inefficient and was soon despatched back to

Geneva. Soon after, Mr. Edward Clarke came out as tutor to them – and remained, I think two years. He was followed by Samuel Longfellow, brother of the Poet, who remained I think about as long and completed fitting Frank for Harvard.[31]

Not all the problems with Mr. Deyhle may have been his fault, as pointed out by Roxana Lewis, 13-years old at the time.

Mr. Deyhle, our French teacher, did not prove satisfactory. I think some of us were rather rebellious at first, at having to recite our lessons in French; and he really had no control over us. I am mortified now to think how, with our propensity to laugh, we almost drove the poor man wild. I can see him striding up and down the school-room, brushing up his bushy red hair, and exclaiming, "Oh, mon Dieu, qu'est ce que je ferais!" [Oh, my God, what will I do!] Just before he left S. W. D. took him up to the Caldeira and all he said was, "C'est affreux!" [It is dreadful!][32]

Even their ex-tutor Mr. Brooks knew that the Dabney children could be difficult students, as he states in this letter to his former student Frank.

Clara is again your teacher you say, but not what books you are studying. What did you do to Mons. D? Either you or Fanny, sadly ill used him, and as F. is rather too small for such an offense all the blame lies at your door. Did you learn all he could teach, or did you try to teach him?[33]

The next teacher, Edward H. Clarke, was recommended by Josiah Quincy, President of Harvard University and son of the Revolutionary War patriot who along with John Adams, acted as defense lawyers for the British soldiers involved in the Boston massacre.

My dear Sir, – The bearer Edward H. Clarke is a member of our senior class. The brightest student in it, in all branches. He has been threatened with a pulmonary affection, and has been advised to get a residence, for a few years in a warm climate. I part with him with regret from the College, for he is excellent in all his attainments and dispositions.

I advise you to engage him for Mr. Dabney; he cannot do better. Indeed an opportunity to obtain a young man of such high qualifications and so thorough a scholar, and excellent disposition is rare.

Yours Respectfully
Josiah Quincy[34]

Clarke worked out better than the previous tutors – "When Mr. Clarke took hold, we soon recognized that we were in good hands".[35] However, he only stayed two years and was replaced by Samuel Longfellow, youngest brother of Henry Wadsworth Longfellow.

Our much prized tutor, Edward H. Clarke, left us to go and study medicine in Europe; and Mr. Samuel Longfellow came to us.[36]

You are also aware that Edward H. Clarke came to be one of Boston's renowned physicians. His daughter married Dr. Fitz, who now occupies a front rank in this same city.[37]

At first Roxana Dabney was not happy with the change in teacher, but it did not take long before she changed her mind.

I confess to feeling some antagonism at first towards Mr. Longfellow, for I was very much attached to our former tutor, Mr. Clarke, as indeed we all were.[38]

Who could help liking Mr. Samuel Longfellow, and I became, from the first, when he started me with Italian, so charmed that I sorely regretted that I was to lose his tuition, when it was decided that I was to accompany my grandmother and Aunt Annie to the United States to go to school, either in Boston or Philadelphia.[39]

As she noted, Roxa did not stay a student of Samuel Longfellow's for very long because she went to Boston in early autumn
where

> They tried to get me into Mr. George Emerson's school, but
> there was no vacancy, so I went to Dr. Folsom's. Mr. Emerson,
> father of Mrs. Judge Lowell (Lucy Emerson), always chose to
> regard me as a pupil, and was ever kind and delightful.[40]

While Roxana was in Boston staying with her aunt Roxana,
the Dabney family took up their annual stay on the island of
Pico where, in addition to lessons, they "got up a newspaper,
'A Voice from the Priory', I believe, was the title; Mr. Longfellow
editor".[41] Samuel Longfellow describes this period in a letter to
his friend Edward Everett Hale.

> ...I might tell you of the delightful October which we spent
> at Pico; how we lived at "The Priory," æ which was a real priory
> or had been; how we slept in monks' cells and dined in the
> refectory; how we jumped rope and danced Scotch reels;
> how I read Lamb (your Lamb) and Bremer to the ladies and
> edited their newspapers; how we bathed in the surf in the
> morning, and took long strolls in the afternoon, and virtuously
> read Portuguese in the evening; how in short, we enjoyed our-
> selves as only people on the seashore can enjoy themselves.[42]

In the same letter he describes his daily life as a teacher to
the Dabney children.

> This winter is only a cool summer. I find myself in some-
> what improved health; teach the three R's and such higher
> branches as are needed to docile pupils; study Portuguese with
> a young padre in the Franciscan convent; attend Catholic mum-
> meries with poetic faith; read the literature of the day, and
> enjoy the rest in the bosom of the best family in the world.[43]

From the letters Samuel Longfellow wrote, as well as those he
received, it appears that one of his reasons for his accepting a

teaching position on Faial was to give him time for reflection on
what he wanted to do with his life. In a letter dated January 12,
1844, his older brother Henry Wadsworth gives him some advice.

> I am publishing a book, a collection of translations from
> various European languages, to the number of 10, the translations
> by various hands – and a few by my own. If you have found
> anything pretty in the Portuguese, pray let me have it. Have you
> translated any thing yet? Don't neglect this opportunity of learn-
> ing the language thoroughly. You ought to speak it muito bem
> [very well] by this time. How much longer shall you stay in Fayal?
> I want you to go to Europe before you return home, to fit your-
> self for that Professorship you have sometimes thought about.
> Pray write me about this by the next Harbinger, and let me
> know you plans and wishes and how I can assist you in them.[44]

In his response to this letter, Samuel says, "as to the Professor-
ship I have given up the idea."[45] Samuel Longfellow left Faial
in the autumn of 1844 on the Dabney ship *Harbinger*. On its
return voyage it brought Charles Dabney, Sr. and Jr. along with
several members of the family and friends from Charles, Jr.'s
graduating class from Harvard.

In 1840 Charles, Jr., had reached the point of going to University and went to Cambridge at the end of summer of that year,
passed his entrance examinations and entered as a freshman.
Charles followed his uncle Frederick who had gone there and was
one of a number of Dabneys to attend Harvard. In 1842, he asked
to visit Faial for a "season," and Josiah Quincy sent a letter back
with Charles in order to tell his father how well he was doing.

> You have great reason to be gratified, and none of dis-
> satisfaction. It gives me great pleasure to be able thus to write
> concerning him, and that my praise has nothing in it of exag-
> geration.[46]

Not much is heard about Charles Dabney, Jr.'s time at Harvard
until his senior year in 1844. In April of that year he wrote a
letter to his father.

I am happy to inform you, dear father, that I have got a part which places me amongst the first twelve or thirteen of my class, thus verifying my supposition; I trust I shall be well contented with my rank, and trust you will be; I only wish that I could feel that I had made a better use of my time and advantages than I have done.[47]

The "part" he refers to was a speaking part in Harvard's Spring Exhibition. It appears that he was quite active and well--liked at Harvard. Although the following letter to his brother Samuel is quite long, it gives a good picture of Charles, Jr., the Harvard Senior, as well as campus life at the time. Following this is another letter to Samuel Dabney from his cousin Frederick Cunningham, a junior at Harvard, describing the same event:

I am happy to say that I got through with my Part at Exhibition quite as well as I expected, and had a "devil of a blow out" after it, which only cost about $125 between Henry and myself; this, however, obviates all necessity of giving one at Commencement, which is a great relief to Father and Mother. In four weeks more the term will be out and after writing my commencement Part I shall be free – Hurrah! – four years is quite enough of College life. It seems pretty much determined that I am to return in the autumn with Father and Mother, and to take charge of Frank and Fanny for the next year; which to me is quite a pleasant idea. I think I shall occupy one of the rooms in the house at the corner of the garden, as my own; inasmuch as it will be very convenient, and at the same time more quiet than the large house. What good times we shall have when we all get together again. I am delighted to hear that the silk business is coming on so well; I only trust that it will continue to prosper. Quite a wonderful thing for Cambridge – I have something to tell you which I think may be interesting. It was an affair in which I took quite a conspicuous part; but I shall give you a faithful account of the whole affair notwithstanding.

In the first place then, there was in the Law School a man by the name of Miles from Maryland – a gaunt looking fellow

of about 23 or 4, standing about 6 feet 1 inch – with a disagree-
ably ugly mug – and ridiculous from his stiff and pompous
manner of carrying himself. There is also in our class a weak,
sickly looking fellow by the name of Wheelwright, accounted
the feeblest fellow in the Class. Now it appears that some weeks
since Stewart, another law-student from Mississippi – a rascally
scamp – had felt himself aggrieved by this poor inoffensive
Wheelwright, and Miles had gone with him to that individual's
room to see the affair settled. Wheelwright was out, and Stewart
afterwards arranged the affair of himself.

Miles, in passing Wheelwright, a few days after, thought
that the latter looked at him as if he recognized him; although
Miles himself says in a statement made before a committee
appointed by the Law-School to examine into the affair, the
he cannot say which of the two stared first; at this his southern
honour felt itself touched, and he expressed himself in an oath
and a contemptuous expression. Wheelwright, who is a non-
-resistant member of the Church &c. &c. contrived to avoid
him for about a fortnight, but came upon him suddenly one
day, and as Miles thought, stared at him again; the latter then
stopped him and told him if he ever looked at him again, he
would break his damned skull for him, and then, as if to vent
a little of his spleen, tapped Wheelwright on the shoulder with
his cane. Wheelwright declares that he did not know Miles and
had not the slightest intention of staring at him. A day or two
after this occurrence, as Wheelwright was going to dinner,
Miles passed him and imagining that he again stared, dropped
his umbrella and struck Wheelwright, with his open hand in
the face, and then with his fist behind the ear, knocking him
down flat.

Wheelwright was taken up apparently senseless and carried
into the nearest house, and Miles passed on. The affair was told
to us as we were going to dinner, and after dinner we went
up to see Wheelwright, who seemed quite unwell. There were
about a dozen seniors, all very much exasperated, but not seeming to know exactly what to do. I perceived from their talk
that they would do nothing, and I asked Stone, if he would
go with me and see Miles – as I wanted some one to see fair

plan – and I knew that he was "good grit," being moreover one of my particular friends. We then started off in quest of Miles, with the plan, that I was "to dip" into Miles first, and if I got thrashed, as the scamp had been taking boxing lessons, he was to try his luck.

We found Miles standing upon the platform before the Lyceum, a brick building with a stone portico in front, upon the large square by the President's house. There were several undergraduates and Law Students round, but I was wrathy, as you may suppose, and ran across the street and up to the steps to where Miles was standing, and without stopping to think what I said, I asked him by what right he knocked down Henry Wheelwright of my class) he said he would show me, and began pulling off his gloves, handing them and his hat to one of his friends. I did the same with mine. Some one then proposed that we should go to some less public place, to which proposition I willingly acceded – have no desire to fight there. I took my hat and ran down two or three steps, but Miles stood on the platform, and said he would see me about it the next day. I told him I would settle it then and would go any-where with him – to his room if he chose – this was a little too much for him and he struck me over the shoulder with his umbrella, – this was a little too much for me, and it did not take long for me to rush up the steps, pick him up by his leg and waist, throw him head and shoulders upon the stone platform, and pummel with him all my might for a minute or two. I could have held him there and pummeled him to a jelly, but altho' it was fair, I did not like to strike a man when down, and moreover there were many about who attempted to inter-fere. After Miles got up he fastened both hands into my hair, and all I could do was to attempt to do the same; we swung about there for some time, and I am quite sure the dirty toad meant to gouge my eyes, for I took his fingers away from them four or five times, and there were little notches of skin taken off all round them by his nails, and all noticed the peculiar appearance of my eyes when we got through.

This is the sum and substance of a round, unvarnished tale of the whole affair. I went up to Mr. Quincy's, being sent for, and related the whole affair, the fact seemed to please him the most, being that of the overthrow of Miles.

Then followed some Faculty proceedings with regard to Miles which would be of little interest to you. After prayers the Class gave me nine cheers, and Miles as he was passing through the yard three groans, which led to a fight between Dexter of the Junior class and Graves of the Sophomore, the former from Boston, the latter from Mississippi. Dexter struck the most blows, but was unfortunate enough to trip in the grass and fell twice. The southerners now seemed to take it up as a sectional affair, and there was a good deal of excitement here for about ten days; meetings were held and committees appointed to enquire into the affair, but it seems now to have blown over. Stewart was expelled from the Law School for drawing a dirk during mine and Dexter's affrays. Graves was sent off for wearing one; and Miles was obliged to depart in haste, a few days afterwards at ten o'clock at night, as Wheelwright's father had a writ out against him. You will readily perceive the reasons, which induced me to take up Wheelwright's cause. Miles had perpetrated a most insulting outrage upon the community, upon the Class, and upon a weak and inoffensive object; and from the knowledge I had from experience, of the College Government's proceedings in such cases, I felt pretty certain that Miles would get off without punishment, if some individual did not take the affair into his own hands – and I considered this case as coming within my jurisdiction.[48]

Your "beloved brudder" has been distinguishing himself of late, and in a manner different from the usual mode of acquiring College distinction. He has become the Hero of his Class, by avenging the insult offered to its honor – vis, a Law Student (Southerner) knocked one of the Class down, for staring at him, as he said; he was senseless for some time, having been hit just under the ear. Charles met his Law-Student after dinner and after some words the fellow struck Charles with his umbrella, whereupon Charles "pitched into him," knocked him down and pounded him tremendously. The fellow tried to gouge C.'s eyes out, and pulled his hair out by the handfuls

– a very manly way of defending himself, hey? I wish I had seen it but I was in recitation when it happened. The Class were very much pleased at it, and after prayers gave 9 cheers for "Dabney, an honor to his Class." It was great, I assure you, I never heard such cheers – everybody yelled, and every cheer seemed to come from the right place. I think I hear you say "I wish I had been there." It would have made you thrill all over to have been present at the whole affair.[49]

Charles, Jr.'s sister Roxana points out one other occurrence at Harvard during this period.

It was while Charles was at Harvard that the Oxford cap and gown were adopted; and, in consequence, there arose some encounters with that class of people in this *free country* of ours always ready to resent any innovations of that sort. It was soon discontinued, and as you know, probably, is only worn now (1893) by the graduating class on Class Day.[50]

His parents, brother Frank and sister Roxana all attended graduation.

Charles's part was upon "The Inhabitants of the Mountainous Regions of Europe". I particularly remember that his bearing upon the stage struck me as very distingué, but I think I could not have heard much.[51]

All of the family went to Faial in 1844 on the *Harbinger* which had returned Samuel Longfellow to Massachusetts. Accompanying them was Charles' classmate Leverett Saltonstall, of the famous Massachusetts political family, who spent the winter at Fredonia.[52] His father, a former Congressman, wrote a letter to Charles, Sr., about the visit. He also adds some interesting notes about US politics at the time.

Your several favors have been duly received and are gratefully acknowledged. We are gratefully acknowledged. We are delighted to hear of the good health of our Son, and of his happiness in your beautiful Island, and in your kind family. I hope that his residence at Fayal will be of lasting benefit to his health, and beneficial to him in every respect; and I trust that he and his friend Charles have kept their good resolutions as to reading, for which they must have much time, and they know that every acquisition of knowledge now made, will be valuable to them through life.

Leverett will inform you, and perhaps to your surprise, that we have consented to his visiting Europe, before his return. You will learn with more surprise, that I have concluded to join him in Europe... Perhaps Leverett may go with your son John; I do not know when he will leave or for what place. I must ask of you the arbou to introduce him to your Agent in London, as if he goes alone he will need advice as to lodgings etc. in London... You see the result of your kindness to us is to rely on it for further favors.

As before, the Harbinger will be bearer of no good news to you. Before, she carried out tidings of the defeat of Mr. Clay – now you will learn by her, that the House has passed resolutions for the annexation of Texas!! This was unexpected to most; I feared it, as I knew the zeal of the slave States, and the servility of Northern partisans. It must make trouble, if not now, for those who are to come after us. I fear the Senate will concur. It is the most important question, which has come before Congress these twenty years, if not, since the formation of our Government. May the result be different from my fears. My trust in Providence still remains strong – that kind & gracious Providence, which has always protected us & our fathers.

I thank you for the box of oranges; it came to hand in good order, & they are excellent. I hope the barrel of apples, which I have ordered, will be received in good condition.

It will give all my family the greatest pleasure to have frequent opportunities of seeing you & your family, and I hope that it will be in our power to make some return for your great kindness to Leverett.[53]

As pointed out in the long letters, Charles, Jr., took over as tutor for his younger brothers and sisters.

C. W. D. Jr., besides teaching Frank and Fanny, superintend-
ed my [Roxana's] studies and carried on his own at the same
time; that, he always contrived to do wherever he might be;
never was there a being more zealous to improve himself.[54]

Samuel Dabney also continued his education through correspondence with Samuel Longfellow over a number of years. They
shared opinions, gave and accepted advice from the other, and
maintained a close friendship over the vast distance between
them.

Of course, all work and no play does not fulfill the day. As a
result, the Dabneys participated in a variety of leisure-time activities. As has been mentioned a number of times, the Azores
were isolated from what was going on in the rest of the world
and depended on outside sources for the latest, cultural information and knowing what was in fashion. When ships arrived,
they usually brought packets of letters from family and friends,
newspapers from different parts of the world, as well as the latest
books and music. This is in addition to family and friends, as
well as visitors who became friends. However, on a day-to-day
basis the Dabneys were left to their own ends to occupy and
entertain themselves, when not working or studying of course.
    Perhaps the most popular activity, especially among the
Dabney women, was visiting. This was not an activity limited to
the Azores, nor to just the Dabneys. Whenever they visited America, they routinely dropped in on relatives and friends for a
visit. Since this was before the telephone, people were used to
others appearing at their door and were ready to welcome
them. In her *Annals* Roxa included a typical couple of days of
visits in Faial.

I find the account of this day, Sept. 12th, quite amusing and
will copy it, as it gives an exact account of the rushes we sometimes had: – "Began with the basket men as soon as I arose
from the breakfast table and it was one rush, Barca Feitor's wife,
Mrs. Aurelio, the Adelsteins, Marianne, Carrie Oliver, Mrs. Burke,
the Allens and just as Edie and I were trying to escape to Ba-

gatelle, the Davieses – but we went. The thing became so ludicrous that I was neither tired nor *cross,* only worried when I could not change

Miss Wellman's gold. [Harriet *never* got cross over anything].

The little visit to Bagatelle was very refreshing. That afternoon I went down with Edie to Porto Pim; the Adelsteins had dined there and gone sailing in the 'Bayadere'. Fan came down on a donkey with an extra one for me, and we went to see Miss Nash, found Mrs. Burke there. As usual Miss N. made me feel sad. Was glad to go to bed that night, no time even to darn stocking". It has been somewhat of a worry about getting Bab and Frisk married; I suppose they will be married on Thursday; everything seems to have come at once. Father and I started to take the Allens over to Pico Sept. 15 in the 'Bayadere', but found there was too much surf, so sailed round to Porto Pim and went into the cave in a fishing boat. Went ashore and lunched on the verandah. All the family down there had gone in the 'Ripple' down the coast. We came home on foot, all the party saying they had had a nice time.[55]

Another activity that everyone participated in, whether day or night, was reading books aloud to each other. These could be either secular or religious and arrived as gifts or were purchased at the request of one or the other member of the family; books were shared in the family and sometimes sent on to friends. Considering that there were among their friends in Boston some of the intellectual elite of the 19th century, including several in the Transcendentalist movement, they were always well-advised as to what was best and most popular to read among this group and they, in turn, forwarded their opinions to their friends who read the same genre of book. Sometimes their reading sessions developed into conversations or debates about the content of the books. While one of the family read, the others were frequently involved with other activities, such as repairing clothes or working on handicrafts. The Dabneys taught some of handicrafts to the local residents and the items they created were sent to the U. S. on the Dabney shipsand sold to provide an additional source of income for the people on Faial.

In addition, some of the family members were fluent in different languages, and they could translate German, French and Portuguese into English for the rest of the family. Besides this, Roxana translated English texts into Portuguese, the most famous into English being *"Fidalgos de Casa Mourisca"* by Júlio Dinis, which was published and is in the National Library in Lisbon.

There always seemed to be a reason for a ball on Faial. When either civilian or military American ships, or those from other countries with famous personalities as passengers stopped in Horta, the captain, officers and sometimes the passengers were invited to a ball at the Dabneys. Of course, friends in Horta and officers of foreign ships were always invited. Furthermore, when other members of high society in Horta had balls, the Dabneys were almost always included on the guest list.

The balls went on to the early morning hours and the music was of the latest fashion because of the trips by the Dabneys and upper class Portuguese to America and Europe. This demanded, of course, someone who could teach the newest dance steps. The first dance instructor to make an appearance was the Italian Signor Carlos in 1824 that taught John Bass Dabney's youngest children. When the next generation was ready to learn, another teacher was brought in to show them the steps in vogue at that time.

> Your grandfather [John Bass Dabney] attached great importance to dancing lessons from a master, who was a good *drilling* one, as regarded carriage and the free use of the muscles of the ankles, and he was much pleased at the advent that winter of 1838 and 1839 of Pedro Serrati, a Spaniard, who came with a company of acrobats and dancers. He gave us lessons in dancing, taught me the cachucha, and the boys and myself, the minuet, gavotte, hornpipe, etc. Theresa Oliveira and one or two others used to come to "Fredonia", where the lessons were always given.[56]

In addition to the formal dances they learned for balls and parties, they also learned some of the dances of the rural population, which they sometimes demonstrated for their friends in Boston. In addition, groups from the countryside or the servants performed dances on special occasions for the Dabneys and their guests, such as at Christmas when the servants and their families wanted to thank the Dabneys for their generosity towards them.

Obviously, if dance was so important to the Dabneys, music also had to be important. In fact, some of the Dabneys were accomplished musicians. Roxana was known for her skill in accompanying dances on the piano, something she began just before the Dancing Master Pedro Serrotti arrived. In addition, Samuel played several wind instruments, others played instruments such as guitar and wind instruments and, if we count voice as an instrument, some of them sang, the most outstanding singer being Sarah Webster Dabney, wife of John Pomeroy Dabney.

There were a number of bands on Faial that were used for religious and lay celebrations, and sometimes Samuel Dabney played with certain of them. These bands were not just in Horta, and most of the larger rural villages could put together a band from its citizens. At times, such as for arrivals of Charles Dabney or other special visitors, the bands competed with each other for the attention of the people.

At this time, most large military naval vessels carried a band with them. They played upon entering and leaving ports, at times put on concerts on the ships for the local residents and sometimes played at the balls to which their officers were invited. The Russian ship on which Prince Merchersky sailed played during the celebration after his wedding to Carolina Curry. Roxana describes one ship's concert.

> I shall always remember this evening, it was a 'succés' this evening on board of the "St. Louis", and how pretty she looked with all her lanterns. We had songs and dances from the "St. Louis Minstrels". There was quite a long programme, "Twinkling Stars", "Uncle True", "Shells of the Ocean", "Champion Dance", &c, &c. The Officers were all so kindly and pleasant – Americans forever![57]

There was also theater on Faial, both from local groups, as well as from visiting professional theater companies. The earliest theaters on Faial date back to the early 19th century, some located in private mansions of the Faial nobility. In a letter to her brother, Nancy Dabney describes the first theater in Horta, which opened in 1817 in the house of Mr. Terra. It was called the "Teatro Tália", named after the Muse of the theater.

> I suppose you will be quite astonished to hear we have a *Theatre* in Fayal. Mr. Terra has put himself to considerable expense to have a room fitted up as a stage, adjoining his large ball-room which accommodates easily two hundred spectators. There have been several plays represented to the great gratification of the spectators; the scenes were painted by a *Padre*, and they were produced a very pretty effect I assure you, although the painting was none of the most beautiful. Sig. Gamboa was the principal performer, and possesses considerable talent as a comic actor; I hear he once took a character in Comedy, on the Lisbon stage, in which he succeeded very well.[58]

Unfortunately, the theater in Mr. Terra's residence lasted only five years. Nancy also describes the closing of the theater to her brother John who had described the theater, which he attended where he was at the time.

> (...) ours (not that I wish by any means to compare it with yours) has just been taken to pieces, the owner said he could not consent any longer to have his largest parlor encumbered with what rendered it unfit for any other purpose.[59]

The very first regular theater in the Azores was opened in 1856 in Faial and called *Teatro União Faialense*, however it eventually became too small and was replaced in 1916.[60] Over the years local and visiting groups put on numerous plays there, and several theater groups were formed on Faial and in villages around the island.[61] Even some ships had theater groups and as mentioned in the chapter about the battle with the *General Armstrong*, the British ship *Rota* had put some plays on during an earlier visit and were rehearsing another when they entered the bay and found themselves facing a battle.

Of course, the Dabneys put on their own shows. Some of them were standard pieces, but some of their best productions were created from scratch by whichever members of the family group were going to put it on. Some of their productions made fun of the characteristics or actions of the other family members. Regardless of the subject matter, they were able to put on entertaining plays while ensuring that all the production details were handled with skill.

Besides all the more formal activities described above, the Dabneys enjoyed a variety of games and activities. Some were outside games such as bowling and croquet, others were card games or numerous other games and amusements that were popular in the 19th century, such as Speculation, Blind Man's Bluff, Snap, Dragon, Pool, etc.

Of course, no place could say that it had a complete range of entertainment without a passing circus. This was a very rare event for islands in the middle of the Atlantic, but with the large number of people and ships going to California, it so happened that one carrying a circus in order to entertain the residents, prospectors and miners in California and Brazil made a stop in Horta.

> The winter of 1847-48 was also an eventful one. There was much excitement for us young folks in the arrival of an American circus, a branch of Sands & Co., on its way to Brazil and California. The California fever had been felt here, several vessels had touched here on their way out with "gold seekers". How well I remember that vessel with the circus, sailing in one bright morning, all decked out with flags, sweeping along in front of the town, the band playing on the deck. What could it be?
>
> C. W. D. allowed the circus company the use of the "Field" which had just come into his possession, having been purchased from Dona Francisca Paula Terra. It had not yet been regularly laid out, as you have known it, and the great tent was erected close to the gate leading into the "Relva". The horses

were kept in the large store under the office. From our verandah we could see much that was going on and hear the band, and of course attended all the shows, excepting those on Sunday afternoon.[62]

Notes:

[1] Dabney, Rose Forbes, *Fayal Dabneys*, n. p.: The Author, 1931, p. 59-60.

[2] Joseph May, Editor, *Samuel Longfellow, Vol. 1, Memoir and Letters*, Boston & New York, 1894, Houghton Mifflin & Co., p. 45.

[3] Roxana Lewis Dabney, *Annals, Annals of the Dabney Family in Fayal*, comp., n. p.: The Author, 1900, p. 369.

[4] Roxana Lewis Dabney, *Annals*, p. 381, 383

[5] Roxana Lewis Dabney, *Annals*, p. 383.

[6] Roxana Lewis Dabney, *Annals*, p. 403-4.

[7] Roxana Lewis Dabney, *Annals*, p. 414.

[8] Francis L. Dabney, *Sketch, Sketch of John Bass Dabney by his son William Henry Dabney of Boston, 1887*, comp., n. p.: The Author, 1971, p. 8.

[9] Francis L. Dabney, *Sketch*, p. 44.

[10] Francis L. Dabney, *Sketch,*, p. 70.

[11] Francis L. Dabney, *Sketch*, p. 55.

[12] Francis L. Dabney, *Sketch*, p. 93.

[13] Francis L. Dabney, *Sketch*, p. 94.

[14] Francis L. Dabney, *Sketch*, p. 97.

[15] Francis L. Dabney, *Sketch*, p. 98.

[16] Francis L. Dabney, *Sketch*, p. 102.

[17] Sally Dabney Parker, *William Henry Dabney, Reminiscences, 1820-1853*, n.p.: The Author, 1981, p. 4.

[18] Francis L. Dabney, *Sketch*, p. 106-7.

[19] Francis L. Dabney, *Sketch*, p. 111.

[20] Sally Dabney Parker, *Reminiscences*, p. 7.

[21] Sally Dabney Parker, *Reminiscences*, p. 8.

[22] Sally Dabney Parker, *Reminiscences*, p. 8.

[23] Sally Dabney Parker, *Reminiscences*, p. 10.

[24] Sally Dabney Parker, *Reminiscences*, p. 10.

[25] Roxana Lewis Dabney, *Annals*, p. 349.

[26] Roxana Lewis Dabney, *Annals*, p. 349.

[27] Roxana Lewis Dabney, *Annals*, p. 366.

[28] Roxana Lewis Dabney, *Annals*, p. 398.

[29] Roxana Lewis Dabney, *Annals*, p. 422.

[30] Roxana Lewis Dabney, *Annals*, p. 430.

[31] Sally Dabney Parker, *Reminiscences*, p. 21.

[32] Roxana Lewis Dabney, *Annals*, p. 429.

[33] Roxana Lewis Dabney, *Annals*, p. 429.

[34] Roxana Lewis Dabney, *Annals*, p. 431.

[35] Roxana Lewis Dabney, *Annals*, p. 431.

[36] Roxana Lewis Dabney, *Annals*, p. 446.

[37] Roxana Lewis Dabney, *Annals*, p. 456.

[38] Roxana Lewis Dabney, *Annals*, p. 455-6.

[39] Roxana Lewis Dabney, *Annals*, p. 456.

[40] Roxana Lewis Dabney, *Annals*, p. 467.

[41] Roxana Lewis Dabney, *Annals*, p. 467.

[42] Joseph May, *Samuel Longfellow,*, p. 39-40.

[43] Joseph May, *Samuel Longfellow,*, p. 40.

[44] Andrew R. Hilen, Editor, *The Letters of Henry Wadsworth Longfellow*, Harvard University Press, Cambridge, M A, 1966, p. 21-22

[45] Andrew R. Hilen, *The Letters of Henry Wadsworth Longfellow*, p. 23, f. n. 7.

[46] Roxana Lewis Dabney, *Annals*, p. 442.

[47] Roxana Lewis Dabney, *Annals*, p. 481.

[48] Roxana Lewis Dabney, *Annals*, p. 482-85.

[49] Roxana Lewis Dabney, *Annals*, p. 486.

[50] Roxana Lewis Dabney, *Annals*, p. 487.

[51] Roxana Lewis Dabney, *Annals*, p. 488.

[52] Roxana Lewis Dabney, *Annals*, p. 489.

[53] Roxana Lewis Dabney, *Annals*, p. 493.

[54] Roxana Lewis Dabney, *Annals*, p. 491.

[55] Roxana Lewis Dabney, *Annals*, p. 1359-60.

[56] Roxana Lewis Dabney, *Annals*, p. 399

[57] Roxana Lewis Dabney, *Annals*, p. 1133.

[58] Roxana Lewis Dabney, *Annals*, p. 94.

[59] Roxana Lewis Dabney, *Annals*, p. 149.

[60] César Gabriel Barreira, *Um Olhar Sobre a Cidade da Horta*, Núcleo Cultural da Horta, Horta, 1995, p. 98.

[61] José Bettencourt Brum, Coisas da Nossa Terra: Crónicas, Câmara Municipal da Horta, Horta, 1994, p. 70.

[62] Roxana Lewis Dabney, *Annals*, p. 597.

Figure 5
The Dabney Family Musicians
L to R: Hester, Rose, Alice, Charles, Jr., Roxana Lewis, Ralph Pomery

11 – WHALING

Being in the middle of the north Atlantic, the Azores are located on the superhighway used by whales and porpoises between the north and south Atlantic. Today whale and porpoise watching is a major tourist attraction in the islands. Traveling by boat between the islands of Faial and São Jorge in certain seasons, one can have the spectacular sight of large groups of porpoises as far as the eye can see, frequently with more than ten jumping into the air together. As a result of the large number of whales that traveled this route in the 19th century, this was one of the major hunting grounds for sperm whales, as well as some other types of whales.

The Basques are credited with the development of modern whaling starting in the 12th century, sending their boats out into the Bay of Biscay and the North Atlantic. Their contribution is recalled by some of the words used in Portuguese for whaling and whales, such as *cachalote* for sperm whale. During the 17th century, the Dutch and English became the whaling powers, with England carrying the industry to its colonies in the New World, particularly the United States. Whaling continued as an important business until petroleum oil, the first American discovery being in Pennsylvania in 1859, became a competitive replacement for whale oil resulting in a tremendous decrease in its price. At its height, whale oil was selling for $40 per barrel, but with the advent of petroleum, its price dropped to as low as $14 per barrel.

In the Azores hunting whales from boats launched from shore is an important part of Azorean culture, and there probably had been a low level of whaling from the shore from early in their history. However, it never became very important because they produced olive oil that was used for lighting and cooking and was much easier to obtain. Nevertheless, whaling in small boats from the shore remained an integral part of Azorean life and culture until the international ban on whaling came into effect not so many years ago. According to oral tradition, the first offshore whale boats came into use in 1832, but the business was not profitable. In the early 1850's, it started up once again and became a major source of income. Many of these later whalers were men who had been forced into it because of the *phylloxera* blight that killed the grapes in 1853 and all but destroyed the wine industry.[1]

The original boats for offshore whaling, known as *canoas*, were brought from America. Contemporary authors and oral tradition give the Dabneys credit for the introduction of these boats to the islands.[2] These boats continued to be brought from the U. S. until 1894 when a Pico island whale man named Machado built the first local *canoa.*[3] Most of the offshore whaling took place on the island of Pico, which suffered the most from the destruction of the vineyards. In fact most of the offshore whalers on other islands in the archipelago were also from the island of Pico, arrangements with the local authorities having been made by the Pico whalers.

When offshore whaling took off in the 1850's, the Dabneys soon had competition from the Bensaúde family, which also started up its own business. This was a family of Jews from Morocco who had come to the Azores in the early 19th century. Beginning with the importation and sale of cloth on São Miguel, they became very successful on some of the islands. Elias Bensaúde opened a maritime supply company on Faial that competed with the Dabney businesses. Although they were competitors in business, the Dabneys and Bensaúdes were both generous in their financial support of the needs of Horta, sometimes joining forces.

Whaling ships from the English colonies in America, specifically New England, were hunting whales in Azorean waters by the second half of the 18th century.[4] In the second quarter of the 19th century, the arrival of whale ships at Horta increased significantly, and the number of American whalers visiting the Port of Faial reached its high point around the middle of the 19th century. In 1827, six American whalers arrived in Horta, and, by 1841, this had grown to 180. Whaling decreased, however, during the U. S. Civil War due to attacks by Confederate raiders.

Credit for the increasing the use of the port of Horta by whalers "is due principally to Charles William Dabney, at that time American Consul in the Azores and one of the most respected members of the distinguished Dabney family that remained in Faial about a century, promoting the growth and prosperity of the island, along with his own business and fortune."[5] American whaling ships continued to visit the Azores until 1921, when the last whaler made its visit.[6]

Faial was the most important port of call for whalers in the North Atlantic. Not only was it on the route traveled by whales, but it also had the best port in the archipelago. Nevertheless, some ships stopped at other islands in the archipelago to take on supplies. As a point of interest, one of the ships that stopped at Flores was the "Essex", the whaling ship that was later attacked and sunk by a Sperm whale in the Pacific and became the basis for Herman Melville's "Moby Dick".

On Faial, ships were able to take a break from the long voyage and restock their fresh water supplies and buy vegetables, fruit, meat and wine produced by the islanders. As would be expected, the Dabneys were in the middle of the provision business, and their shipyards were able to repair damage suffered on the voyage to reach the archipelago. Furthermore, the Dabney try works processed whales already caught and shipped the oil back to the U. S. along with already processed oil that whale ships had dropped off on Faial. In addition, if needed, Charles Dabney's official U. S. government representation could be called upon for assistance in commercial or other problems of ships.

In the early days of the Dabney presence on Faial, any ship's arrival was a cause for celebration, and this was one of the side benefits of the arrival of a whaling ship for the Dabneys. As the number of whaling ships increased, the novelty lost some of its thrill, but the ships were still welcome sources of news and, of course, business for the Dabneys. Whenever merchant or whaling ships arrived in Horta, the officers were always invited to dine at the Consulate and, not infrequently, to take part in a Dabney-sponsored ball. This was especially true when American warships arrived. Sometimes there were several ships in the Bay of Horta at once. Emmeline found that "some of the captains are really very entertaining with their accounts of their adventures; others again are rather shy, but they generally improve as they hear the bolder ones go on."[7]

Some of the whale ship captains took their wives along on the voyage. Roxana Dabney reports that one captain's wife who visited in 1832 suffered greatly from seasickness, and her husband asked if she could stay in Faial while he continued the voyage. Since the first hotel in Horta was not opened until 10 years later in a small cottage at the top of the Bagatelle gardens[8], she stayed in the Bagatelle house. Three months later the captain returned and when his wife had packed to leave she said, "'Now, Mrs Dabney, there only remains my account to settle with you.' Grandmother was astounded and did not at first comprehend what was meant. When it was explained that there was no boarding house, poor Mrs. P. felt extremely mortified, of course." It also happened on occasions "when we had several captains to dinner that some of them would ask how much the dinner was." The Dabneys were always ready to extend their hospitality and were "paid" by the presence of interesting company. Living on an island with few other resident foreigners they would have been completely isolated from the world without the whalers and other visitors arriving by ship. "This mode of living had the advantage of our seeing various sides of life and deriving much information we could not perhaps have acquired in other ways."[9]

While the Dabneys received the captains and officers of visiting ships, their crews, besides not being invited to dine and dance at the Dabney's, were not always welcome visitors to the city. The sailors came from a variety of backgrounds: professional sailors/whalers, runaways, adventure seekers (including a number of well-to-do young men), plus those who were "Shanghaied."

Faial was generally the first landfall for the ships and their crews, and they took part in the usual sailors' pleasures. It was not infrequent that drunken sailors were seen staggering through the streets of Horta and getting into fights or creating other problems. The *"Monte das Moças"* (Mount of the Girls), now site of the Prince Alfred of Monaco observatory, would have been a popular spot with the word *"moça"* being a slang term at the time for prostitutes.

Figure 6
*View of House at Porto Pim (on right) and
Whaling Station. Pico in the background*

The ships also dropped off crewmembers that were sick or injured or were troublemakers, and others jumped ship after discovering that the harsh life at sea on a whaler was not to their liking. Many of the seamen left on Faial had no money and only the clothes on their back. As a result, they became the responsibility of the U. S. Consul who had his hands full providing food and clothing and keeping them out of trouble.

In 1890, Samuel Dabney reported to the State Department some of his ideas about the "causes of desertions from American vessels," most of which were from whaling ships since few merchant vessels stopped in the Azores (at least at that time).

> The main cause is the dislike to the life engendered by various features thereof, two of which are the great length of the voyage and the small remuneration.(...) It is my opinion that men are seldom cruelly treated onboard our whaleships, or at least sufficiently so to warrant discharge in conformity with our Consular Regulations... I would say: that undoubtedly the number of desertions is increased by the knowledge held by the men that they can claim protection; for among many reckless ones there are some that would not run the risk of deserting in a foreign land to be left entirely on their own resources.[10]

Despite Samuel Dabney's comment, there are a number of documents and books that indicate that the life of seamen on whaling ships was notoriously bad. Their living and working conditions were poor, and the captain and officers often mistreated them – Captain Bligh was not a unique example. A number of laws had been passed that aimed at protecting the seaman, but they were difficult to enforce on a ship at sea for two to three years. The implementation of many of these laws fell to the U. S. Consul in the whaler's ports-of-call.

In November 1832, Charles Dabney sent a letter in which he describes his view of the situation in the Azores and on whaling ships to Edward Livingston, Secretary of State.

> I have had the honor to represent to your predecessors that almost all the whaling ships that leave the U States from

the first of April to the 30th of August stop at these Islands to receive vegetables for their voyage. As no precaution is taken to examine the crews when they leave home, numbers of the men are found diseased. I soon perceived that, if I required three months advance [wages], few of the men would be left as the commanders of the vessels conceive that they have been imposed upon by them and are unwilling to submit to any expense on their account and thus many unfortunate men would become victims, either terminating their lives during the course of the voyage or reach home with their constitutions sapped, thenceforth to be a burden to their country.

The course I have hitherto pursued has been to have the men examined. If their indisposition was slight, instructions were furnished as to the necessary treatment and they have proceeded on their voyage. When the malady has been of a serious nature they have been received by me free of charge to the ship.

By this mode of proceeding I feel confident that I have served my country more than I could do in any other manner – averting certain misery from one class of our citizens & achieving others from an encumbrance, and I must acknowledge that it has been highly gratifying to me to find that my conduct has been approved, inasmuch as the expense has from time to time been regularly reimbursed. (…)

While on this subject, permit me to remark that the construction of the law requiring three months advance wages for sick seamen landed from our vessels in foreign ports is truly lamentable. It does not even produce a saving of expense to Govt. while it unquestionably entails misery on a most useful class of our citizens – their disorders become deeply seated by the neglect which they are sure of experiencing under the present application of the law & when they reach home it costs our country more money to restore them to an inferior state of health than it would to a more perfect state, had they been landed in a foreign place at an earlier stage of their disorder. This observation applies to cases generally but more forcibly to our whaling ships which far removed from medical advice for periods of ten & twelve months. Few of our countrymen are aware of the extent of this and I am sure the attention of Congress to the subject long ere this have been solicited.[11]

In early 1834, he amplified his remarks on caring for the seamen in another letter, this time to Secretary of State Louis McLane.

> The management of seamen has occasioned me great perplexity as the communications which I have had the honor to address to your Department will testify. I had made such arrangements respecting Sick Seamen landed from ships employed in the whale fishery as I conceived were satisfactory to Government, to the owners of the ships and to the seamen when at the commencement of the summer the ship *Swift*, Tobay Master called here for refreshments and proposed landing two of his crew on account of ill health stating at the same time that their Parents were affluent, and as they had not derived the expected benefit from the voyage from America to this Island he thought he had better leave them here to be sent home. This case cast a new light on the subject, and it occurred to me that a distinction might be made which would secure the advantages formerly suggested to your Department and prevent persons from undertaking voyages for the improvement of their health at the expense of Government: and after deliberating some time, I concluded to draw the line between chronic and acute disorders, for the former, I required three months advance, the latter were received free of expense to the ship, conceiving in the former case that the owners rendered themselves liable by some degree of negligence in not ascertaining the state of the men previous to sailing or that they were suffered to come for the benefit of their health by those concerned in the voyage.
>
> It may be proper to remark that in most cases of chronic affections that subjects were on their first voyage.
>
> The payment of three months advance for sick men is considered by many an unwarrantable exaction and is never submitted to without disgust. (...) The Act relative to seamen wherein it is provided that vessels over one hundred and fifty

tons measurement shall be furnished with a medicine chest which shall from time to time be replenished &c and that in the event of negligence in the particular the vessel shall be liable for payment of the medical advice and medicines which may be requisite for any of the crew, would seem to warrant a favorable inference with reference to those who do conform to the law, and it admits of such a construction in the mind of the Attorney General a most desirable object will be accomplished.[12]

Taking care of the ill and injured was not the only concern and, as mentioned, many of the seamen were put ashore with only the clothes on their back and not much else. It sometimes could be months before seamen could be put on another whale ship or sent back to the United States. Giving them money for clothes or food was not a viable solution either since they frequently chose to spend it elsewhere, as can be seen in this letter to Secretary of State, John Forsyth, in 1836.

The hospital of this Island is located in a building formerly occupied by the Franciscan friars and affords ample accommodations, but at present it is impossible to afford the patients the benefit of exercise in the open air without allowing them to go into the street. Whoever has any knowledge of the habits of sailors must be aware that few and perhaps it would not be going too far to asset that none can withstand the temptation of liquor, by indulgence, they retard their recovery which of course increases the expenses of their cure and they are frequently so riotous that it has required all my influence to prevail on the managers not to exclude them entirely.[13]

Charles Dabney then goes on to request funds to build a passageway into an adjoining yard where they could walk and "obviate all the difficulties arising from their having access to spirituous liquors." These kinds of, among others, with seamen put ashore in Horta continued to plague Charles Dabney and his successor Samuel Dabney throughout their period as Consuls, resulting in their having to spend their own money and exert their political and social influence on Horta to correct the problems created.

One of the people most concerned about the treatment of seamen was Richard Henry Dana. He put some of the blame for the poor treatment on the government and, more specifically, the American consuls. His book "Two Years Before the Mast", published in 1840, graphically describes his life on a ship traveling from Boston around Cape Horn to California and resulted in tremendous public concern about the poor treatment of seamen by officers on ships. It also pointed out how ship owners and public officialdom acted in ignoring the seriousness of this situation.

Richard Dana contacted Charles Dabney and expressed his opinion that Consuls were not helping the seamen and in many cases causing more harm than good. Charles Dabney presented his own ideas on the problems of seamen to the U. S. Attorney General in a letter from Boston in 1852.

> Sir
>
> I have the honor to inform you of my arrival here and that I have been applied to by Mr. Richard H. Dana who has expressed his intention to institute a suit in the District Court to test the right of Consuls to make any deduction from the two months advance to seamen on their being discharged at a foreign Port on account of expenses incurred for their support and also whether the course adopted by me of [illegible] the promulgation of the act of July 1849 of receiving thirty six dollars for account of the Gov. of the United States in the discharge of seamen, bans the right of seamen to receive two thirds of that amount free from all deductions – as there are questions affecting the interest of Gov, I have deemed it my duty to communicate them to you in order that I have receive instructions how to act.
>
> I have the honor to be with the highest consideration & respect.
>
> [He asked that the response be sent care of Dabney & Cunningham in Boston][14]
>
> Dept. of State to J. J. Crittenden, U. S. Attorney General – 2 June 1852

Sir

I have the honor to enclose, herewith, copies of three letters addressed by S. G. Thomas and Frederic W. Sawyer to the Department, and also a copy of a letter in reply to the first communication of Mr. Sawyer in relation to a claim preferred by certain seamen for the two months extra pay, which was placed in the hands of the United States Consulate Fayal, at the time of their discharge, respectively, from American vessels.

It appears that some seamen were discharged at Fayal, and in accordance with the law of Feb. 28th 1803, for the protection of American seamen, three months extra wages, in each instance was paid into the hands of the Consul; that they remained at Fayal for a considerable time, at the expense of the United States; that they were afterwards shipped at high rates, as passengers, by the Consul, to the United States. Notwithstanding the expenses to which the Government was subjected, much exceeded the amount for extra wages, paid in each case, into the Consul's hands, a claim is preferred to two months extra wages, by the Consul for the seamen.

It has heretofore, been the practise of the 5th Auditor, (and approved by this Department) to consider no seaman destitute who is in possession of two months extra pay; and also, to defray any expenses which the Government may have incurred for medical attendance, board or the passage to the United States of any Seamen, from the money in the possession of the Consul arising from the three months wages deposited at the time of discharge of such seamen.

This construction of the law is denied to be the correct one, and it is contended, that the two months pay shall be paid into the hands of the seaman, when he embarked for home, altho' he may have been in the meantime, a charge upon the Consulate.

The Department will be pleased to receive your opinion as to the proper construction to be given to the law in cases of this nature, which are now of frequent occurrence.

Hon Dan'l Webster, U. S. Secy of State
Boston Dec. 18, 1851

The response was not exactly what Charles Dabney was hoping for when he wrote his letter and sent off another providing further details.

> Sir
>
> We recd your letter in reply to our requesting the 2 months pay of certain seamen discharged at Fayal.
>
> We applied under the act of 28 Feb. 1803, art. 3. That seems to us to provide as expressly & without reserve, that the two months pay shall be paid into the hands of the seamen when he embarks for home, as the Consul shall reserve the other one months wages to meet the expenses that you name. Your construction of the act is new to us. We have not been able to find any act, supplemental to that act, giving the power to the consul that you name, viz. to pay his passage & expenses out of his two months wages, nor can we see how it can be fairly deduced from the act in question.
>
> No such authority is given the Consul in terms. So far from it, the act expressly provides that he shall pay into the hands of the seaman 2 of his 3 mo wages when he embarks – without one word of qualification or reservation. It expressly provides that the other 1/3 shall be retained by the Consul to raise a fund to meet the very expenses you name.
>
> We have looked at the act of July 20, 1840, and do not perceive that that act can be construed to grant this power you seem to suppose.
>
> We enclose herewith a statement of such seamen as happen to be at hand, giving the names of those discharged on account of sickness, the time of their stay at Fayal & the place & price of boarding and the character of the passage home.
>
> We submit the whole matter to your for such action of the department as shall be due to the petitioners. It is plain that unless they obtain redress through your department they are left without remedy.
>
> Frederic W. Sawyer

There were also three other letters that gave a list of seaman, how long they were in Horta, the amount they paid for board (some did come close to the $24) and their shipment back to the U. S., all saying that C. W. D refused to give them their two months pay.[15]

In addition to those sailors put on shore by their captains, some sailors just decided they did not want to continue their voyage. These were mostly persons forced into signing on as crew or young adventure-seekers who found that the fun had run out during the trip to Faial and were not willing to face the months or years left on the voyage. Others fled for an assortment of reasons, including: the job was not what they expected it to be; the adventure was non-existent; they wanted to be with their families; and, bad treatment at the hands of their officers. Although cruel captains were rare, they did exist. However, it should also be noted that many of the sailors were longtime agitators who wanted to avoid continual onboard punishment. Some of the men were even sent to prison on Faial by their Captain until they could be returned to America for trial in the company of an officer (creating another drain on the number of crewmembers).

The sailors who jumped ship created major problems on Faial. For the Dabneys, it was that they became the responsibility of the Consulate. This was due to the fact that sailors coming off ships were also very poor and lacked clothes except those on their backs, which were in very poor condition. After their ships departed, the majority of the men put ashore legally sought support and clothing from the Consulate, and the money available to support them was limited.

In addition, while some of the men who created problems were cooperative once they were off their ship, others who had been involved in onboard problems continued as troublemakers on Faial. After weeks at sea with no women and little or no alcohol, they tried to quench their appetites as quickly as possible in their first landfall, Horta. Needless to say, not a few found themselves in trouble with the local law enforcement authorities. A final group of seamen were too ill to continue their voyage and were treated or hospitalized until they were well. Some sailors who had come on shore illegally hid in the hills until the ships left and then they came out and made the same demands for support as those who were entitled to them legally.

The Consulate returned those sailors who were well enough to America when it could find a ship that had space and was willing to accept the price the government paid. Fortunately, there were others who voluntarily joined the crew on other ships that had stopped in Horta, hoping this voyage would be more to their liking. Finding ships that were available to take these kinds of men took much time for the Dabneys, and it was not always possible to find a ship that went directly to America, especially in the winter months. Sometimes it took months for an appropriate ship to arrive, other times they sent the men via another country or the Dabneys had to use their own funds to pay for the passage, without assurance that the government would reimburse them within a reasonable period, or at all.

Despite all the aggravation and hassle from a number of the men, who sometimes could be numerous, many of those left in Horta in the Consul's care respected him a great deal and thought that he was treating them fairly. That they would do almost anything for him is demonstrated by the torchlight procession they provided for Prince Luís during his visit in 1853 (see chapter 16).

However, there was another problem from ships having to leave part of their crew behind. Some ships were not able to find a sufficient number of Americans, or sailors of other, non-Portuguese, nationalities to man their ships fully. Consequently, it was not unreasonable from their standpoint, to seek additional crew from among the island's inhabitants. However, the Portuguese Crown did not allow emigration of its citizens without permission, in part because of the eight-year requirement for young men to serve in the military, from which many did not return to the islands. Despite the law prohibiting emigration, the high level of poverty and lack of employment opportunities meant there was no lack of local men willing to sign on as crew of whaling ships. They secretly rowed boats out from the villages along the rural coastline on other parts of Faial in the middle of the night to meet the ships that had sailed from the bay of Horta. These young men were attracted mainly by the money, which was far more than anything they could get from their subsistence life on Faial.

Thus began a mass migration of Portuguese young men, some later followed by family, to America, particularly to those areas linked to fishing and whaling. In particular, large communities formed in the areas of New Bedford, Massachusetts, Nantucket, Rhode Island, the San Francisco Bay area and the Hawaiian Islands. The immigrants from the Azores represented almost 80% of the total Portuguese immigration to America.[16] This type of emigration continued to be an important loss of population for the Azores as long as foreign whaling continued to be important. This migration has been the subject of several studies and books, and their descendants have formed associations to preserve their historical and cultural heritage.

Notes:

[1] Robert Henry Clarke, *Open Boat Whaling in the Azores*, v. XXVI in the series *Discovery Reports*, Cambridge University Press, London, 1954, p. 298.

[2] Robert Henry Clarke, p. 289, p 298; Marcelino Lima, "Indústria," *Anais do Município da Horta (História da Ilha do Faial)*, 3rd Edition, Oficinas Gráficas "Minerva", Vila Nova de Famalicão, 1981, p. 391-392.

[3] Trevor Housby, *The Hand of God: Whaling in the Azores*, Abelard-Schumann, London, 1971, p. 16.

[4] Trevor Housby, p. 14-15.

[5] *Boletim do Núcleo Cultural da Horta*, Vol. 1, Nº 3, 1958, p. 144.

[6] Samuel Eliot Morison, *The European Discovery of America: The Northern Voyages AD 500--1600*, Oxford University Press, New York, 1971.

[7] Roxana Lewis Dabney, *Annals of the Dabney Family in Fayal*, comp., n. p.: The Author, 1900, p. 311.

[8] Roxana Lewis Dabney, *Annals*, p. 441.

[9] Roxana Lewis Dabney, *Annals*, p. 322-23.

[10] Document 50, United States Archives, Microfilm T203, Roll 10, January 2, 1889 – December 30, 1893.

[11] Document 67, United States Archives, Microfilm T203, Roll 1, March 4, 1795-November 28, 1832.

[12] Document 7, United States Archives, Microfilm T203, Roll 2, July 26, 1833 – December 4, 1841.

[13] Document 34, United States Archives, Microfilm T203, Roll 2, July 26, 1833 – December 4, 1841.

[14] Document 11, United States Archives, Microfilm T203, Roll 4, January 6, 1851 – December 31, 1857.

[15] Document 12, United States Archives, Microfilm T203, Roll 4, January 6, 1851 – December 31, 1857.

[16] Lionel Holmes and Joseph D'Alessandro, Portuguese pioneers of the Sacramento Area, Portuguese Historical and Cultural Society, Sacramento, C A, 1990.

12 –THE WORLD DROPS BY

The same decade of 1835 to 1845, during which the schooling of the Dabney young was so active, there were a series of interesting visitors to Faial. A number of these were persons who were in the Azores on scientific expeditions.

One of the early visitors during this period was the Count de Vargas Bedemar, who was Chamberlain to the King of Denmark. He was in the Azores during the spring of 1836 with a research ship doing geological surveys of the archipelago. He was invited by C. W. Dabney to stay at Fredonia and attended a ball there in his full regalia as a Knight of Malta from under which his Chamberlain's key appeared. He was over seventy, had a bullet lodged in his leg from some battle and had the formal attitudes of European nobility.

The count was a true courtier, – somewhat of a chameleon, as it turned out. He had in conversation with C. W. D. always expressed very liberal, not to say republican sentiments; and C. W. D. had formed the notion that he did not regard rank as all important, but on one occasion when he went round the island, father had borrowed for his use Mr. Silva's (father of Thomas da Silva) house at Praya de Norte. Mr. Silva himself entertained the count during his stay out there, and the old gentleman was so much pleased with him that he proposed to call upon him in town and accompanied by C. W. D. he paid the call. In descending the stairs, the door at the foot happened to be open into the pharmacy (Mr. Silva being an apothecary), whereupon the count almost fell over in a fit, and struck his head "Ou sommes nous? Un apothecaire! Mon Dieu, est il possible, un apothecaire!" [Where are we? An apothecary! My God, is it possible, an apothecary!] Although C. W. D. could make allowances for his training and education, he could not quite feel the same after towards the count.[1]

The count spent six months in the Azores collecting plants and geological specimens in various parts of Faial and the western islands of Flores and Corvo. Despite his age and leg injury, he also climbed the over 8,000 foot volcanic peak on the island of Pico.

From Fayal he corresponded at every opportunity with the great Alexander Humboldt, "that Aristotle of modern times," as the Baron of Marajó called him in the excellent book "The Amazon," whose fame was already universal since his voyages of exploration to the American continent.

> This correspondence dealt with investigations that the Count de Vargas carried out concerning the existence referred to by some writers of a statue set on the island of Corvo, overlooking the sea on a high promontory and indicating the west with its right finger, perhaps to announce the existence of a continent in that direction to the European navigators. This notion being true and before 1492 would rob Christopher Columbus of the glory of the discovery of America.
>
> Along with this there was also the investigation relative to the finding of a portion of Carthaginian and Cyrenian coins on the same island in 1749. They had been sent to Madrid to a Padre Flores who gave them to M. Podolyn.[2]

After an extensive tour of the Azores, he went on to Madeira and then to the Canaries before returning to Lisbon and then Denmark.

In the summer of 1838, three more scientists, this time Swiss naturalists, showed up in Faial. Their interest was in collecting plants and fish from the Archipelago. Charles. Dabney's youngest sister, Olivia, showed her interest in scientific pursuits through her own collecting activities, helping to provide the team with a large collection of fish. These were sent to Mr. Louis Agassiz, the Swiss geologist and palaeontologist who became an important figure at Harvard University. Some of the specimens sent by Olivia are on display at Harvard to this day.

Charles Dabney himself was active in sending specimens of different types to various organizations in the United States. In April of 1836, he was elected an Honorary Member of the

Massachusetts Horticultural Society because of the samples of Azorean plants he had provided them. He gave Harvard University a collection of rare corals that he had collected over a period of 30 years from fishermen who found them while dredging around the island. As a result the "President and Fellows of Harvard College" sent him a letter of thanks.[3]

Among Dabney's other scientific interests was the design of a dock for the Bay of Faial. He attempted to convince the engineer Sir John Rennie, who had surveyed for the proposed dock at São Miguel, to come to Faial. However, Sir John did not go to Faial because of the "jealousy of the inhabitants of Saint Michaels prevented him from accepting the invitation as he was preparing to do."[4] This did not stop Dabney, however.

> ...I resolved to have a plan made to show the advantages this locality possessed over all others of this Archipelago, and I made all the arrangements for a survey, which was made by E. S. Brooks (Tutor to my children) and my three eldest sons. It was well executed and I had it lithographed, one hundred or more copies made; the most of which were sent to Mr. José Curry da Camara Cabral, at that time Deputy from this District to the Cortes at Lisbon, for him to distribute. The times which followed were not propitious for such undertakings.[5]

The Horta City Council also sent these plans to Queen Maria II. It is obvious that the interest of Charles Dabney went beyond the scientific since Faial would lose its status as the best port in the archipelago if São Miguel could build a dock. Regardless of the efforts, it was still many years before a dock was to be built in Horta. A copy of the plans for the dock is in the Collection of the Portuguese Geographical Society in Lisbon.

When Charles Dabney moved the Consulate to Fredonia, the hospitality of the Dabneys remained as it always had been. This is documented by the welcome given to the US Navy ship "*Cyane*" and its passengers and crew. Roxana Dabney recalls the visit.

> In July of 1838 the United States Sloop of war "Cyane" was here. Her commander, John Percival, was known in the navy

as "Mad Jack". Almost every other word was an oath. He had two passengers, – Mr. Thomas Carr, who was going out to Tangier as United States Consul, and his friend, Dr. Mayo, who afterwards wrote "Kaloolah" and "The Berber". C. W. D. mistook Dr. Mayo for the surgeon of the "Cyane". "What!" said Capt. P., "you don't think that is our surgeon? We have a d – d sight handsomer man than he is." These two gentlemen were C. W. D.'s guests the few days the "Cyane" was here, and Dr. Davies who arrived at that time was also staying with us for a time. I well remember the exciting times those were for us children. There was a great ball given at "Fredonia," and as the custom always was to keep open house at the time of any of our naval vessels being in port, the officers were always going and coming. Either at that time or perhaps a little later on, there was a Mr. Blackler consul to the Sandwich Islands, who arrived in a whaler, also staying with us.[6]

There were visits by other American warships with famous names in American history. In 1843, the *U.S.S. Missouri* arrived with Mr. Caleb Cushing, the first US Envoy to China on board. During the ship's two-day visit, Mr. Cushing, an old acquaintance of the Dabney's, was a guest at Fredonia and, as was customary, the Dabneys hosted a ball for the visitors. The mayor of Horta, Senhor Almeida, who was a "very rotund little man, with a broad blue belt with large gilt letters, '*Administrador de Concelho da Horta*'" also attended, and some of the ship's officers asked if he was the head gardener since the word "*horta*" means garden in Portuguese (the actual origin of the city's name was derived from the name of one of the first Captains of the island of Faial, Joss van Huerta).

The remainder of the Missouri's voyage was cut short. The ship "was burnt up at Gibraltar, and poor Mr. Cushing... lost his effects," including a signed first edition of a book loaned him by Mrs. Dabney, "which she never ceased to regret."[7]

The other ship with a famous name to visit was the *Constitution*. "Old Ironsides" was built in 1794 and, after being extensively repaired several times, had set sail in March 1844 on an around-the-world cruise that would last $2^1/_2$ years.

While C. W. D. was absent from Fayal that summer [1844], the United States Frigate 'Constitution,' commanded by Capt. John Percival, visited the Island on the way to Brazil, whither she was taking our minister Hon. Henry A. Wise and family.[8]

The Wise family stayed at Bagatelle except for the eldest daughter, Mary, who stayed at Fredonia as guest of Charles Dabney's sons, Charles Pomeroy and Samuel Wyllys, in the absence of their parents. The boys carried out the Dabney tradition and gave a ball for the Wise's and the ship's officers before they continued on their voyage.

In 1843, two interesting visitors arrived from Europe. One was Charles de Savigny who was Secretary of the Prussian Legation in Portugal. He was acquainted with Frank Cunningham, a cousin of the Dabneys who was studying theology in Berlin. Savigny's father was the Baron de Savigny, a jurist who had been given the responsibility of revising Prussian law during the 1840's. The Baron's sister-in-law was Bettina von Arnim who had published a book of letters she had exchanged with Goethe when she was young. In later life she supported German liberalism and radicalism and counted among her friends the brothers Grimm, Heinrich Heine and Karl Marx.

Charles de Savigny visited other islands in the Azores and was so impressed that, in a letter to Charles Dabney, his father said it *"touche aux tableaux de la fable."* The letter had been sent to thank Charles Dabney for the wine and "productions maritimes" he had sent the Baron.[9]

Accompanying Charles Savigny was the French lawyer Dr. Guenoux, who was a "follower of Mesmer", the 18th-century physician who had developed a healing principle based on hypnotic induction involving "animal magnetism".

They visited Fredonia frequently and Dr. Guenoux exercised his power upon mother one evening in the parlor. She was a good deal affected by it, as were your Aunt Clara and Aunt Mollie, although some distance from the mesmerizer.[10]

Charles Dabney was extremely interested in this. In fact, he tried his hand at it when his daughter Frances, known as Fan, was very ill later that year.

> She had severe brain fever, it was thought to be caused by exposure to the sun. She was delirious, and as usual in such cases (not suffering those they love best to approach them), she could not bear her father near her. Her head was shaven and cooling applications made, but without any effect in producing calm sleep, until at last C. W. D. determined to try and mesmerize her. At first his patient was most obstreperous, but she gradually calmed down and this seemed the turning point of her malady.[11]

> Even Roxana Lewis Dabney tried her had at mesmerizing a couple of years later when Dr. Davies was very ill with brain fever. She "succeeded in quieting him and he even dozed a short time".[12]

During the winter of 1844, Leverett Saltonstall arrived for a prolonged visit to Fredonia, which was apparently for his health like many visitors to the archipelago. He was a classmate of Charles Dabney, Jr., at Harvard and was the son of Massachusetts Congressman Leverett Saltonstall and the grandfather of Massachusetts Senator Leverett Saltonstall.

In a letter from the Congressman to Charles Dabney, he thanks him for a box of oranges he had sent and says a barrel of apples was on the way back. In addition, he mentions a trip to Europe for the father and son Leverett after his son's visit to Faial and asks for the an introduction to the Dabney's English Agent to help them while there. The Congressman's letter contains an interesting comment about his political concerns at the time.

> As before, the Harbinger will be bearer of no good news to you. Before, she carried out tidings of the defeat of Mr. Clay – now you will learn by her that the House has passed resolutions for the annexation of Texas!! This was unexpected to most; I feared it, as I knew the zeal of the slave States, and the servility of Northern partisans. It must make trouble,

Figure 7
Fredonia
Charlie on "Zuma"

if not now, for those who are to come after us. I fear the Senate will concur. It is the most important question, which has come before Congress these twenty years, if not, since the formation of our Government. May the result be different from my fears. My trust in Providence still remains strong – that kind & and gracious Providence, which has always protected us & our fathers.[13]

Almost all of the people who have been mentioned in this chapter were guests of the Dabneys at either Bagatelle or Fredonia. However, there were a number of people who arrived at Faial and had to take care of their own arrangements for lodging and eating. Before 1842, this meant finding an available room in a private home, a standard procedure for travelers in many places at this time. Some of them could be quite spectacular, such as that used by John Bass Dabney on his first visit to Faial in 1804-5 (see Chapter 1), and others a room with just the bare necessities.

In 1842, the first hotel opened in Horta in a cottage at the top of the Bagatelle gardens. This cottage replaced an earlier structure used in the garden.

It was about this time that the first hotel was started. C. W. D. had always considered it a very important matter, but the right persons had not presented themselves to take the management; but now Ann Harper, housekeeper at Bagatelle, since nurse Jane Emerson had left, married the waiter, José Maria Silva.

When Thomas Aurelio brought out his bride, Lucy Goodwin, they lived in an old house at the top of our garden [at Bagatelle]. I only wish I had a picture of that old place, for it has ever seemed to me the most romantic, fascinating residence, with a lattice window. I have no doubt, however, that it was very dilapidated. C.W.D. had that all taken down and built the cottage for the Aurelios, you know, at the top of our garden.

Sometimes we could prevail upon Thomas A. to play hide and seek with us. After some years the Aurelios went to live at C. W. D.'s St. Amaro garden.

And then the cottage came to be used by José Maria Silva and bride for the first hotel!

I think among their first guests were Mr. March, United States consul at Madeira, and his friend, Co. –, an Englishman.[14]

Thus the first hotel on the island of Faial was open. However, since it was in a cottage built for a family, it obviously could not accommodate many guests.

At one time the Silvas had as many as seven guests; where they were all accommodated remained a mystery to those who knew the house. Among these was an English family (Luxford) consisting of a mother, two daughters, and son, and a young friend.[15]

As a result it did not take long for the hotel to move to new quarters.

That winter [1844] José Maria Silva and Ann Harper removed their hotel to the Rua do Livramento, the house owned at present by Dr. Simas, and Miss Greene boarded with them, but was every day either at Bagatelle or Fredonia if she chose.[16]

The Dabneys also traveled and visited other places. Most of their personal trips were to the U S to visit family and friends and to go to school. Their voyages on business took them as far afield as India and Russia. A few of these voyages encountered problems, some of which came close to being tragic. One such voyage occurred in 1845 when Charles Dabney's sons John Pomeroy and Samuel Wyllys were on a ship carrying fruit and wine from the Azores to Stettin in Pomerania, today Szczecin in Poland, close to the border with Germany.

After about two weeks of sailing, the night of May 1ˢᵗ became very stormy off Jutland and the ship, despite all efforts, was forced toward the shore and beached. Nothing they tried could get the ship off the shore. At daybreak they began unloading the cargo, and Sam was sent to find out where they were, but found the surrounding area deserted. Soon some fishermen appeared, and they went to get the local officials who were shortly on the scene. Fortunately, as the result of frequent wrecks in this area of the west coast of Denmark, the government had adopted strict regulations to protect wrecks, as well as their cargo, crew and passengers.

The empty ship was finally gotten off the shore and was taken to the nearest port to see if it could be repaired. The fruit was auctioned off and the price "was much better than I expected in such an out of the way place."[17] The boys chartered a ship to come and pick up the wine. After "having passed two of the most tedious and unpleasant months that I ever recollect,"[18] the shipping and bureaucratic details were resolved, and the wine was on its way to Copenhagen. The two boys "had rather a tedious ride across the country in open wagons, sometimes without springs, but arrived safely in Copenhagen without adventure, having stopped half a day at Elsineur."[19]

They had problems finding a buyer for their cargo at an appropriate price in Copenhagen and went on to Stettin, from where they took a trip for a couple of weeks to Berlin. Returning to Stettin they found there was no market for their wine there, so they arranged to sell it in Königsberg (today Kaliningrad). They also planned to go to Riga, Latvia, to arrange for the purchase of flax to be taken to Faial on the return voyage. They then went to Hamburg to wait for the ship to be repaired, and Sam went back to Faial while John Pomeroy remained to wait for the ship and complete the transactions until around the middle of September, almost five months from the time of the shipwreck.

John Pomeroy sailed directly from Europe to America where he went "to seek his bride", Sarah Hickling Webster, another tie to the Hickling family of São Miguel and to the Webster family of Massachusetts. Samuel, who was very happy to just make it back to Faial, would later marry Sarah's sister Harriet Wainwright Webster. Thus ends the harrowing adventure that the two young men (John, 24 years old and Samuel, 19) not only survived, but ended up learning how to handle some very complicated situations with minimal assistance. This demonstrated how well they had learned the business from their father and the confidence he had in his children.

It was at the end of this decade "that a dark cloud came upon the little American Community in Fayal." An unwanted visitor in the form of a new Consul for the Azores arrived. President James K. Polk and his Secretary of State James Buchanan appointed Mr. Samuel Haight from Louisiana in the Fall of 1845 to replace Charles William Dabney as Consul. Correspondence between friends in America and Charles Dabney, along with comments from the family, best tell the story.

A letter from Mr. Abbott Lawrence shows the indignation of a friend, in addition to how far the influence of Charles Dabney in the merchant community of the Northeast had extended:

> Boston, Nov. 1st, 1845
>
> My dear Sir, – The President of the United States in the plenitude of his power, has exercised it, in removing you from Office, very much to the annoyance of those who best know the ability and fidelity with which you have discharged its duties. I entertain this opinion that there does not exist a Consul in the world, whose official Administration has been more satisfactory to the people and Government represented than that of Fayal. I confess that under all the circumstances my judgment dictates some expression of opinion by persons, who have had intercourse with you, as the Consul of our Country to the Senate, when the confirmation of you successor shall come before the body. I think your ability, fidelity, urbanity & noble hospitality not only to our own Countrymen, but to all Nations, and your peculiar adaptations to the situation you hold should be set forth in strong language to the Senators, and from them published to the world. I believe this due to your character as a man and public officer of this great country. I have proposed to Mr. Cunningham [the Dabney agent and cousin in America] to obtain the signatures of the Merchants of New Bedford to such a paper, and cause it to be laid before the Senate. This shall be followed or preceded by letters from myself to the most prominent Whig Senators, many of whom are my personal friends. I do not propose this course, with an expectation of having you restored at present, but as an act of public justice to an able and faithful office and with a view of leaving a testi-

monial that will speak in your favor, when *we* shall again come into power, or even when there shall be a change in the Administration of our Government...[20]

Mr. Charles F. Lester, who was a customs officer in New London, Connecticut, was well aware of the value of a good Consul to merchants.

> Permit me to express my surprise and regret at the change recently made at the Azores in the Consulate. Had my Administration been possessed of the knowledge which I possess, in regard to your position and influence, as the representative of the United States, no change could ever have been effected. Within the scope of my acquaintance, among Merchants and Ship Masters, the new of the change of Consul at the Azores has been much regretted. I say to my friends, that it is a good thing for your more *pecuniary* interest, as you have given away more dinners to American Captains, than the fees of your office amount to. I am not aware of the name of your successor, nor do I know anything of his character even by report, but if he is a poor man and depends on his office for his means of support, the contrast between the future and the past in the U. S. Consulates of the Azores, will be moth marked and mortifiying to the observers...[21]

In response to this letter Charles Dabney reveals how he perceived of and approached his position as Consul and how it related to his business and personal life on Faial. It also reveals how he thought President Polk arrived at his decision. Polk was acting based on his evaluation of the norm among American Consuls, while Dabney was clearly someone special in a unique situation.

> I acknowledge that the announcement of the appointment of Mr. Haight as my successor surprised me, having exerted myself so much to be distinguished for the faithful discharge of my duty and to impress all foreigners most favorably in regard to our Country, and as there never was any cause of complaint

during the whole course of my official career, I deemed the situation perfectly secure; and I feel confident that had Mr. Polk been rightly informed with regard to what are essential requisites, for the satisfactory discharge of the duties of a Consul in these Islands, he would not have displaced me. I have been told that he has expressed the opinion that Consuls should be occasionally recalled that they might have an opportunity of mingling with their fellow citizens and renew their love of country. If Mr. Polk could witness the operation of affairs here for one year his opinion in relation to this subject would undergo a radical change. These Islands are at a sufficient distance from the Metropolis to render the good will and favorable regard of all the local authorities of the greatest consequence to a consul, who is desirous of affording the most prompt relief and protection to his countryman; this feeling must not be expected to emanate from a regard for the United States as a Nation, but must be elicited by personal intercourse with its representatives; consequently the longer any one is established in a country (if he possesses the requisites for his situation) the more extensive his influence ought to be. I challenge any one to produce a man more assiduous in his exertions to cultivate a friendly felling with the inhabitants than I have been, and I am now reaping the advantages of a thirty years practice; my countrymen enjoy all the privileges of my social position; and it afforded me no small gratification to be able to exercise a greater degree of influence whenever an occasion required it than was in the power of any other person in the place.

My revered Father was I may say a pioneer in these Islands. He was a man of great mental resources; he had met with great reverses of fortune and his attention was accidentally directed to the Azores; he obtained the first appointment of U. S. Consul for these Islands from the Immortal Jefferson and established his residence at this Island in 1806. Although he was a man of uncommon activity and suavity of manners, it required many years to ingratiate himself extensively in the good graces of these people, and his Commercial establishment was incomplete at the time of his death, which occurred in 1826; consequently

20 years from the time it was commenced (I mention this to show how slowly such things progress).

I was introduced here in 1807, when only thirteen years of age and with the exception of about five years, I have resided here, consequently have grown up with the community. I was engaged in business with my father at the time of his death and having since carried out a more extensive system of operation I may say that there are not five individuals of any not on the Island, who are not under some obligation to me. My relations with the people are not limited to this Island, but as all of them from their position are liable to have American property cast upon them, I have been careful to have persons of responsibility and character to act as my agents, and I have in some cases laid myself under obligations to me for appointing them. This kind of policy has been pursued in all the branches of my official conduct. Good service to my countrymen and the desire to place my Country above all the others in the estimation of foreigners has been my constant aim.

A Consul for these Islands requires (besides the regard of the people) an establishment capable of succouring in case of need those of his countrymen who may have occasion to revert here in distress. My establishment is the only one in these Islands that can furnish masts of any size, spars, etc. etc. etc. for the repair of shipping. Since I have been in office no sacrifice has ever been made of American property for the equipment or repairs of vessels. When property has been sold here from any extraordinary cause, I have stood forward as the protector of the Underwriters, leaving it optional to receive the property thus purchased by me, in this manner. I can show how thousands of dollars have been saved for them; without the necessary means, such measures could not be adopted...[22]

Secretary of State Buchanan appointed Mr. Samuel Haight as the new Consul to the Azores. A letter from T.C.H. Smith to Charles Dabney's brother-in-law S. Wyllys Pomeroy seems to indicate that there had been attempts to have the government change the appointment, but President Polk was somewhat stubborn. It also shows the support Charles Dabney had from the New England merchants.

> By appearances it will be hardly possible to effect any change at present in the Consulate. Had Mr. Haight not left the country, perhaps the result would have been different. Mr. Buchanan has no personal objections as I understand to him to the removal of Mr. Haight, and reappointment of Mr. Dabney. The thing is entirely in the control and responsibility of the Pres^t., who made the removal without advice and appointed Mr. Haight out of his own mind. The Pres^t. has much inflexibility of character and has not yet been known to alter or revoke any measure however small; at least such is the impression. Mr. Buchanan told me there would be but little hope, but advised me to try; and this I shall do. As I told you in my letter from N. York, the Messrs Cunningham's cousins and his business representatives in Boston] had drawn up a paper, which was signed by all the principal merchants of New Bedford and Nantucket without distinction of party, certifying to Mr. Dabney's fitness for the Office, and unequivocally that no person could make his place good, or give our Commercial and National interests in that quarter equal protection, with that he had given.[23]

The family's reaction to the replacement is described in a letter from Charles Dabney, Jr., to his brother Samuel Wyllys. It also provides a good portrayal of the problems they thought Mr. Haight would, and eventually did, face.

> By some news, however, which we met with a few days since in the papers, William's plan [Charles Dabney was going to appoint his youngest brother William vice-consul on the island of Terceira] is in a measure destroyed, and we somewhat fallen from our 'high estate' in the estimation of many. Father has been superseded and a Mr. Haight of Louisiana appointed in his place! The effect of a thunder-bolt could not have been more sudden or astounding. William in looking over the Presidential nominations, accidentally met with this paragraph.

The justice of this act, it is useless to question, as party leaders nowadays are obliged to sacrifice all other claims to those of the party, but the custom of turning men out of office is no longer desirable or respectable, when it shall have become insecure, as it must be henceforth, unless it return to Father; for no man of honor or spirit will submit to be dependent on the whims of a democratic government. I do not believe Mr. Haight can live in this Island, for he can have nothing to live upon, unless he were a man of property, and in that case he would not probably have come out here to spend it. I think he will either go to one of the other Islands, or finding his expectations so far from being realised return home in disgust. In the latter case, should the office be returned to Father it will be more secure than ever; if not it will be subject to change with every Administration; and the 'Devil may have it' so he do not trouble us. It on many accounts a disagreeable affair, but I care only for Father, who must feel it most; for myself I am philosophical, '*et puis*,' I do not think the shower will be as bad as it threatens, '*en tout cas*' we are Dabneys, and our name even Mr. Polk cannot take from us.[24]

Mr. Haight finally arrived in the autumn of 1845 and took over the position of Consul. With their usual good grace, the Dabneys invited Mr. Haight to stay in their house, which also served as the Consulate. In January after Mr. Haight's arrival. Charles Dabney wrote to President Polk.

Fayal, 10th January, 1846

I feel, Sir, that I am about to address the chief of a mighty nation, whose ardent desire must be to promote the prosperity of its people; I shall therefore attempt to conceal that the appointment of a consul for the Azores was mortifying to me. I am proud of my country and have spared no pains to have it represented here in the best possible manner; of the success of my efforts any one who has been here can testify. My successor has been here some time and what required no sagacity to predict has occurred, his experience having taught him that there is not inducement for anyone to establish himself here. The fees of office are very precarious and very limited in amount, and if I could have realized the value of the property I have here, I should have removed long since, notwithstanding the many inducements that I have to reside here. The office is of little or no value to any one but myself who, from circumstances are obliged to reside here, and as I have a numerous family it is necessary to cover them with the flag of my country. As I have no doubt but that Mr. Haight will be provided for, I only request the favor of being allowed the opportunity to satisfy you, Sir, that in no way can you promote the interests of our fellow citizens more, in this quarter, than by conferring upon me the office of Consul for the U. S. for the Azores. With the highest consideration etc.

Yours most etc.
Charles W. Dabney[25]

Roxana Dabney describes Consul Haight's stay.

Mr. Haight came out that autumn and was our guest. He must have felt completely out of his element, being a society man and having lived in Washington a good deal. His chief recreation was playing cards with any one he could get to play with, 'Boston' being his especial favorite. Many and many a game of *écarté* I played with him for Persian limes! He had always been accustomed to play for stakes (some trifling sum perhaps), a practice entirely forbidden in our family, so he contented himself with the limes. He accommodated himself tolerably well that winter, but *one* was quite enough, and he returned home to exert himself to have C. W. D. restored to his consulate.[26]

In fact Samuel Haight did not even wait to get back to the US to recommend Charles Dabney. On April 29, 1846 he wrote an official letter to James Buchanan.

I have the honor to tender you my resignation as Consul of the United States for the "Azores or Western Islands."

I take this opportunity of stating that the pecuniary value of this situation is so insignificant as to render it entirely unworthy of the consideration of any one except, the late (and present acting) Consul, Charles W. Dabney [*illegible*] to whom – in consequence of his having large interests in these islands – it would be important as a protection. I would therefore most respectfully recommend this gentleman to your consideration for reappointment; as every way qualified to discharge the duties of the office with credit to himself, and to his country – his highly honorable public and private character, not only with the inhabitants, but also with his numerous countrymen who have been compelled by accident or by other causes to seek these islands and to who his appointment would give great satisfaction.[27]

Upon his return to the U. S., Haight continued actively supporting Charles Dabney's reappointment, as shown in a letter to C. W. D. from Mr. Francis Markoe (a clerk in the Diplomatic Bureau of the State Department, corresponding secretary of the National Institute for the Promotion of Science, botany collector and mineralogist who lost to Joseph Henry to be first Secretary of the Smithsonian Board of Regents).

Washington, 2d. June, 1846

My dear Sir, – I have been about to write you for some time past, but delayed, 1ˢᵗ. till your nomination for the Consulate for the Azores should go into the Senate, & 2d. till it should be confirmed. It has come in & will be confirmed as soon as the case comes up. No one is more gratified by this result than myself, but I feel that it is due to our friend Haight, who enjoys the confidence and esteem of the President, to say that he has behaved very handsomely in regard to yourself, and has made the Govt. and the principal men of our country perfectly understand you high character and respectability. Mr. Haight's exertions in this matter have been unremitting. He is still here and will not leave Washington till your commission is made out and sent to you, which must happen in a very short time. Mr. Cushing aided Mr. Haight in every possible way, and manifested by his zealous co-operation to serve you, the high regard & respect he feels (in common with all your numerous friends) for you & your charming family.[28]

Charles W. Dabney was once again appointed as U. S. Consul to the Azores, a position he kept until his death many years later. He then appointed his youngest brother William as his vice-consul on Terceira to replace Mr. Rigg who had died the previous August. This was a position William had sought because he felt that there was not enough to do on Faial and had not had much success with the other ventures he had tried. Despite their love of Faial, the feeling of a lack of opportunity on Faial was shared to varying degrees by other members of the family as it grew even more numerous, but with work opportunities virtually remaining the same.

Samuel Haight had left, but in the short period of time that he was in Faial, he fell under the thrall of Charles Dabney. Several years later, a Dr. Sims in New York approached one of the Dabney cousins Mary Alsop and said, "If ever Charles Dabney of Fayal comes here, I wish you would let me see him, for I never heard one many speak of another as I have heard Samuel Haight speak in praise of Mr. Dabney".

The replacement of Charles Dabney as Consul was not the only trauma in the Dabney family during 1845. On November 7, Charles Dabney's mother, Roxa Lewis Dabney, died at the age of 73. After the death of her husband in 1826, she had continued to live in Bagatelle as the matriarch of the family. She was much loved and respected, and the family always gathered for Sunday dinners and holidays at Bagatelle where she lived. Roxana describes the final scene in the life of her grandmother.

> We were *all* there, the whole family, when the last breath was drawn – just like an expiring light – so solemn, so elevating, a truly patriarchal scene, which made a profound impression upon me! The last few years of her life, grandmother's intellect had been clouded, her memory particularly, owing, Dr. Davies always averred, to her withdrawing so much within herself after her husband's death; but she was always a pre-

sence in the family. I can see her now sitting up so erect in her arm chair in the corner of the upper hall at Bagatelle, just outside of her bedroom door, her clear white muslin hand-kerchief, scrupulously folded and crossed over her fine bust. She was most tenderly nursed in those last years by her devot-ed daughter Olivia, even at the expense of her own health, but she never begrudged that, and was rewarded by the re-covery of it after a change of scene. We can imagine what the severance of his tie was to the eldest born, even though there was much to reconcile him to his mother's leaving.[29]

Notes:

[1] Roxana Lewis Dabney, *Annals of the Dabney Family in Fayal*, comp., n. p.: The Author, 1900, p. 374.

[2] Ernesto do Canto, *Archivo dos Açores*, reedition, 15 vol., Ponta Delgada: Instituto Universitário dos Açores, 1980-1985, p. 49.

[3] Roxana Lewis Dabney, *Annals*, p. 490.

[4] Roxana Lewis Dabney, *Annals*, p. 398.

[5] Roxana Lewis Dabney, *Annals*, p. 398.

[6] Roxana Lewis Dabney, *Annals*, p. 394-5.

[7] Roxana Lewis Dabney, *Annals*, p. 455.

[8] Roxana Lewis Dabney, *Annals*, p. 487.

[9] Roxana Lewis Dabney, *Annals*, p. 450.

[10] Roxana Lewis Dabney, *Annals*, p. 448.

[11] Roxana Lewis Dabney, *Annals*, p. 456.

[12] Roxana Lewis Dabney, *Annals*, p. 582

[13] Roxana Lewis Dabney, *Annals*, p. 493.

[14] Roxana Lewis Dabney, *Annals*, p. 441.

[15] Roxana Lewis Dabney, *Annals*, p. 441.

[16] Roxana Lewis Dabney, *Annals*, p. 442.

[17] Roxana Lewis Dabney, *Annals*, p. 497.

[18] Roxana Lewis Dabney, *Annals*, p. 502.

[19] Roxana Lewis Dabney, *Annals*, p. 502.

[20] Roxana Lewis Dabney, *Annals*, p. 511.

[21] Roxana Lewis Dabney, *Annals*, p. 512.

[22] Roxana Lewis Dabney, *Annals*, p. 512-14.

[23] Roxana Lewis Dabney, *Annals*, p. 515.

[24] Roxana Lewis Dabney, *Annals*, p. 523-24.

[25] Roxana Lewis Dabney, *Annals,* p. 539-540

[26] Roxana Lewis Dabney, *Annals,* p. 530.

[27] Document 43, United States Archives, Microfilm T203, Roll 3, July 26, 1833 – December 4, 1841.

[28] Roxana Lewis Dabney, *Annals,* p. 541.

[29] Roxana Lewis Dabney, *Annals,* p. 529.

13 – THE MID YEARS

In the middle of the 19th century, only a year after the death of Roxa Lewis Dabney, who along with John Bass Dabney comprised the 1st generation of Dabney's on Faial, the fourth generation, and the last to be born on Faial, made its appearance. In 1846, Charles Williams Dabney's eldest son, John Pomeroy Dabney, and his wife Sarah Hickling Webster became the parents of a baby boy, who they named after his grandfather. To avoid confusion with his grandfather and uncle Charles, Jr., he was called Karl. Three years later, Charles Dabney's first grand-daughter, Mary Oliver Alsop, was born, and over the next decade and a half, they were joined by almost 20 cousins. Among the contributors to the increase in the number of grandchildren was Samuel Wyllys Dabney who arrived back in Faial with his bride Harriet Webster Dabney, sister of John Pomeroy's wife Sarah Webster Dabney, who was known for her magnificent singing voice. Samuel and wife moved into Fredonia while his wife's mother and sister Katherine moved into what was known as the Italian residence, located at the bottom of the hill next to the Dabney business offices in the "Relva".

At about the same time a new revolution broke out in Portugal. After the civil war between the Liberals and Absolutists, there were a series of political disturbances and minor revolutions, mostly led by those favoring the Absolutists who lost the 1828-1834 Civil War to the Liberals. The one that was underway in 1846 was among the most interesting and was known as the movement of "*Maria da Fonte*" (Maria of the Fountain or Spring), a mythical figure taken as a symbol by the women in the rural north who were at the forefront of the revolution, which was also supported by the rural nobility and clergy. They were upset with the new government health regulations in 1844 that prohibited burials in churches (cemeteries were not yet in common use). In addition they felt their religious rights were being taken away, a concern that was not unfounded considering the action already taken to abolish the religious orders in 1834.

The back-and-forth progression of the revolution went on for a few years and, as usually happened, this revolution on the continent had an effect in the Azores. England, France and Spain supported Queen Maria II, and warships from the three nations visited the islands in 1847. When the local authorities were deposed, the Civil Governor and Military Commander on Faial were afraid there would be an uprising of the people and took refuge in the Dabney's house. The ship *"Quilha de Ferro"* (Iron Keel) belonging to William and John Pomeroy Dabney was chartered to take them to safety in Gibraltar. Samuel Dabney allayed their fears of being fired on from the fortress and made sure that they got safely on board the ship. A letter of thanks was received from Gibraltar.

Charles Dabney briefly describes his actions during this event.

> On the 28th Ult. The Civil & Military Governors finding their positions untenable, applied to me to mediate between them and the opposition party; everything was arranged and they and those who remained faithful to them departed the same evening, the principal passengers in the Cutter 'Quilha de Ferro' for Gibraltar, and the subalterns & soldiers for Lisbon in the schooner 'Favorita'.
>
> C. W. Dabney[1]

In addition to his function as American Consul, Charles Dabney sometimes also acted as British Vice-consul, and by coincidence, it was while Charles Dabney was serving in this capacity that he provided the description of Faial's government representatives fleeing the revolution mentioned above. Mr. Minchin had gone to England that winter of 1846 and 1847, and Roxana provides the following notes.

To John S. Minchin, Esq., *H. B. Majesty's V. Consul for the Islands of Fayal & Pico.*

FAYAL, 10th Dec. 1846.

My dear Sir, – Having consented to act for you during your contemplated visit to England and being very tenacious of my reputation for non interference in matters not strictly my own, or that my duty to others does not require me to exert my influence over, I have to request of you the favor to state how it happened that you applied to me to manage your affairs, during your absence, and if you will have the goodness to append your statement to this, you will oblige

Your friend & servant
CHARLES W. DABNEY.

BRITISH CONSULATE OF FAYAL & PICO,
Dec. 12th, 1846.

My dear Sir, - I have much pleasure in acceding to your request by declaring that the very high opinion I have ever entertained of your honor and integrity, which I have had such frequent opportunities to test during the last ten years, together with your superior business habits and your unequaled resources, affording you such facilities for the relief of vessels putting in here in distress, induced me to solicit and (if possible) secure your services for the protection of British subjects; with this view I requested you to act for me during my temporary absence. I am happy to have the opportunity thus afforded me to bear testimony to your eminent eligibility to fill a Post of so much trust; with much esteem and regard, believe we, my dear Sir, Ever sincerely yours,

JOHN S. MINCHIN,
H. B. M. V. Consul.[2]

In the mid-1850's, Charles Dabney was once again acting as British Consul on the island of Faial when Mr. Minchin left. The two Minchin daughters had been friends of the Dabney daughters, but Roxa Dabney in the *Annals* comments that she thought the behavior of Mr. Minchin seemed somewhat strange and provides the following illustration.[3]

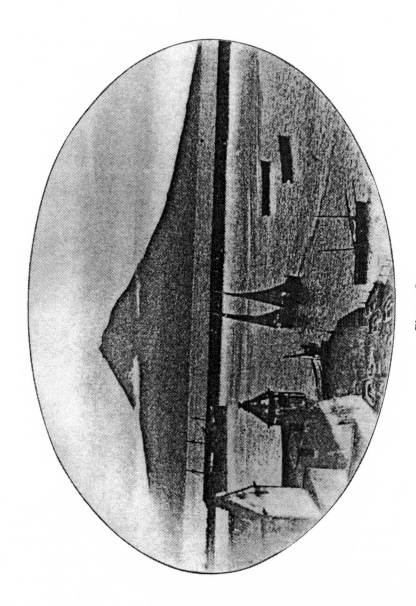

Figure 8
View from the Dabney's Office Window

It was on this occasion that Mr. Minchin uttered his memorable speech to Mrs. Spence, "That Mrs. Minchin would have been happy to call if she had been living." She died about a year previous; the especial joke was that had she been living she never would have come with him.[4]

In addition to Charles Dabney representing the British, other members of the Dabney family were Consuls or Vice-consuls for other countries. Among these was Charles Dabney's youngest brother William, whom he appointed as his American Vice-consul in Angra do Heroísmo, on the island of Terceira, and was later appointed American Consul in the Canary Islands. On Faial, John Pomeroy Dabney represented the country of Prussia for a few years.

As has been stated a number of times, as a Consul and a person, Charles Dabney was well liked by the inhabitants of Faial and by most of those who visited the island on commercial ventures. It was not uncommon for small displays of appreciation, an example being when all the ships in port raised their flags and signals for his birthday in 1846,[5] as well as periodic important demonstrations of appreciation, such as the formal letter from Queen Maria II for his donation to the local "alms house."[6]

However, even those persons who are liked best have their detractors, and Charles Dabney was no exception. One of those who disliked Charles Dabney was Mr. Luiz Sampaio, the Civil Governor, who wrote a series of letters in 1853 to the newspaper "*Açoriano*" on the island of São Miguel. Roxana describes the incident:

Mr. Sampaio, the civil governor, began about this time to publish articles in the "Açoriano," a St. Michaels paper, reflecting upon C.W.D., accusing him of being the greatest monopolist that the world perhaps had ever seen! It was true that C. W. D. had acquired a monopoly in business owing to a combination of peculiar circumstances. When he first came here and for many years after, it was thought to reflect discredit upon the sons of "Morgados" [Nobility] to enter into any kind of business;

but if he did enjoy a monopoly, I am safe in saying there are not many men in the world who would have made a more disinterested use of it, and he certainly did not merit such language as Luiz Sampaio used, who was all along professing a great friendship for C. W. D. He had a perfect mania for writing and expressed himself remarkably well; hardly a day passed that he did not write one or more notes to C. W. D, a cause of great annoyance to my father, who had not the time to be replying.[7]

Finally, Charles Dabney had had enough and responded in a long letter in which he states:

> Yr. Ex. As a Political Economist must know that a monopoly established with exclusive privileges, and an Establishment which furnishes articles for so moderate a price as to disarm competition, are entirely opposed in their nature; but in order that you should have an idea of this business, I will pass in review some branches of commerce, which I exercise today.[8]

He then proceeded to provide the details of how he got into each branch of the many businesses the Dabneys operated in Faial. Some of these were monopolies from the beginning, such as ship repair, but only the Dabneys could afford to bring material to the island and store it for long periods against its possible use. Others were in competition, or sometimes cooperation, with other merchants on the island, virtually all foreigners. As these people retired, decided to go out of business because of increasing costs or decreasing demand, or went bankrupt, Charles Dabney stepped in and continued with his own business in these areas. However, he was careful to point out that his current prices were either the same as those during competition or even somewhat lower, as opposed to the common practice in a monopoly, "and if we have obtained any good results it has been entirely owing to the integrity and assiduity we have always employed in the discharge of our duties".[9]

Over the years there were other critics, but most of these were ship owners who were unhappy with having lost money

when their ship was severely damaged or wrecked and needed someone on whom to take out their anger for having to pay
for salvage and repairs or losing their cargo. The worst example of this was the wreck of the *Ravenswood* in 1856. That it
created exceptional problems for the Dabneys is shown by the
fact that the *Annals* devotes more text to this single event than
to any other incident.

The ship had been dismasted in a storm and arrived off the
island of Pico near the Cães de Mourato. Charles Dabney, Jr.,
and Samuel Dabney went from Faial to Pico in bad weather
and proceeded to the location of the wreck.

> *Caes de Morato,* 15th Jan., 1856.
>
> *Dear Father, – On* arrival here we found the ship to be the
> "Ravenswood," of New York from Havre, bound to New York.
> All the crew were ashore, excepting a French boy, who perish-
> ed in trying to reach the shore, and the Captain, whom we
> found on board in a state of beastly intoxication; we were
> obliged to sling him and pass him down the rope we had,
> to the rocks. The crew would not assist and were forwarded
> to Magdalena to go over in the morning. We have saved but
> little I regret to say as the men on board worked with but
> little zeal. The cargo seems to be principally wine and mer-
> chandise. Tomorrow if she holds together, and it be smooth,
> we shall probably save a good deal. It would be well, I think,
> if you see she is whole in the morning, to send a few tarpau-
> lins, the boxes being so heavy, that some may have to remain
> on the coast over night. Thus far we have brought everything
> up to José da Cunha's, about 100 champagne baskets and a
> few boxes of merchandise. The ship no doubt was lost through
> gross neglect, as there were several spare sails in a house on
> deck. It makes one sad to see such a loss of property through
> the incapacity of those to whom it is intrusted. Charles is
> writing, and between us you will probably get some idea of
> the case. We are staying at a little box belonging to the vicar
> of Bandeiras.
>
> Your affectionate son Samuel W. Dabney.

The brothers worked for twenty days in bad weather and terrible living conditions while having to guard the salvaged goods from local looters, although not completely successfully because some of the guards they used also pilfered the wreck. The road to the main town of Madalena on the island was almost impassible, but they finally got salvaged goods there and sold them for what they considered a fair price.

Unfortunately, the insurance underwriters did not agree and an unpleasant series of letters were sent between the U. S. and Faial regarding the allegations from local sources that the Captain had been drunk and the accident was caused by neglect versus accusations that the Dabneys had not been diligent in protecting the salvaged goods nor completely forthright in their handling of the sale of the ship and its cargo. Needless to say, the Dabneys denied all the accusations and eventually the situation was resolved amicably, but not without bitter feelings on the part of the Dabneys for having been accused of wrongdoing when they considered that they had done their best for the ship owners.

Although Nancy Dabney Brotero never returned to her family's home, her oldest son, João, who had grown up in São Paulo, Brazil, visited his Azorean relatives in the late 1840's. He had received a degree in Law and was sent to visit his family on Faial before going on to America. His parents wanted him to practice English and to learn how to act in American and European society. His father sent a letter saying,

> My son is a young Bachelor of Laws, brought up in the woods and among students, without much society of ladies, and to tell the truth, a young Brazilian Savage, so you must pardon his want of polish, and I must beg the Dabney ladies to act as his Mentors and fashion him into a Gentle-Homem. Nancy looks for this favor from them; in fact, it was for this purpose she desired him to visit Fayal, and these the arguments she used to induce me to consent to this unnecessary voyage, which God grant may turn out well.[10]

However, this was not how the Dabney's saw him.

John Brotero was not the savage his father described, although he was much more frank and unceremonious than Portuguese from Portugal, which we have always found to be the case with Brazilians. He spoke English very well, though with a strong accent and he was remarkably well informed and intelligent. He was, perhaps, a little too sober for us young folks, not caring to learn any games (billiards, etc.) that were not improving, but he took great delight in talking to his Aunt Frances, his Uncle Charles and all his relatives at Bagatelle.[11]

On the other hand, João Dabney Brotero saw his Azorean relatives in a somewhat different manner than they saw him.

I am convinced that among all the torments for which I could be martyred, one of the most vulnerable is "a family evening", you have no idea, me accustomed in São Paulo to spend a night luxuriously reclining in a hammock, in shirt sleeves, among a dozen of the chaps full of friendliness, full of happy craziness, or other times devising intense arrangements in card games or solitaire! All this with the witticisms or a friends joke; to now have to be enveloped with appallingly serious and solemn women, enjoying the simple pleasure of seeing one embroider, another read a sermon, sometimes interrupting the silence with some frivolous question about the number and size of the snakes or characteristics of certain insects in Brazil and other trivialities... *What a horror.*[12]

He also provides probably the most revealing picture of the Dabney family's daily routine.

I went to dinner today at Bagatelle House, where we spoke more than at home [Fredonia], and I will now enter into the activities and customs of our family. Here is how they spend the day. Everyone gets up at 5 and immediately goes to a large metal basin that looks like a hat with a wide brim; the basin contains cold water and they take a general bath with a sponge shaped like a large cap. Then all do gymnastic exercises, men and women, small and large, even my uncle Charles. At 8 a bell rings and all come to breakfast. Some members of the family never touch tea or coffee (as well as never touch vinegar or mustard at dinner) and are content with a glass of spring water, and almost nobody in the family drinks green tea or Hysson, but rather black tea.

Then all the men go to the office where they remain until 2 o'clock, and the ladies go to the library, working with a needle or reading or taking care of other customary activities. Aunt Olivia gives school to all the family children, and so goes the morning. Then dinner hour arrives and after this the ladies go to the salon and play billiards, of course we have a billiard table.

The afternoon is as unerring, it is inevitably a long and extensive walk because the word exercise is always in the mouth of everyone and concerns their attention up to the point of seeming like a mania. At night there is sometimes a little bit of music, and then the evenings that I have already mentioned that appall my poor patience so much. Then we sleep; however, even here there is a peculiarity and it comes from our family thinking it detestable to sleep with the windows closed, and always leave a window open a slit to renew the air. Forgetting, however, all this nonsense, one thing I notice is extremely reasonable; and that is the care that they take that the children always have a lot of activities; in both the houses here we have a "Gymnasium" for the children to do gymnastic exercises, they have a large number of little wagons, ships and small carpentry and cabinetwork tools. All of this seems to be necessary if you Sir had remembered that the children in each house have a certain level of usual activity, and if an "issue" had prepared them, the result would be that Ralph or Frederick would have less pleasure in pursuing the great Iphygenia, and even you Sir, and they are not accustomed to that diabolical and secret pleasure of everything that is prohibited. The little ones here are well-fed, robust and live happily; their education is very religious; I should say that once I said "devil" in front of these young people and this caused a complete scandal in the entire regiment of the "Young cousins".[13]

When João Brotero died in 1859 at his family's home in São Paulo at the young age of 33, he was greatly eulogized by the

Brazilian newspapers. Extracts from newspaper tributes show how great an effect this young man had on a country that was not much older than he was.

Dr. Brotero was born in Rio de Janeiro, December 24th, 1826, and was baptized March, 1827. His birth, which came at a memorable period in our Country's history seemed to have an influence in the development of his political ideas. Breathing the first air of life in a country, which had so lately thrown off its yoke, and was just beginning to feel the effects of liberty, Dr. Brotero was born in the light, which reflected those sacred ideas, and vivified by them, he espoused later the liberal cause – fearing on one had the anarchy, which often arises from political convulsions, and on the other hand, the absolutism, under which the Mother Country had so lately suffered.

That same year [1848] Dr. Brotero was elected Deputy to the Provincial Assembly of San Paulo, in which he associated himself with the party called "Luzias", which proved that he did not owe his appointment of "Promotor" in the Capital, to party interests, but to his own intrinsic merit, as it was after his appointment, that he joined the liberal side.

In 1855 he took his seas as "Supplente" in the Legislative General Assembly, in which he held himself true to his high aims. That same year he was appointed Assistant Professor in the "Faculdade" of Recife, an appointment which highly honors him, as it was made by his political opponents.

It was there that his career as "Professor" began. But the state of his health obliged him to request that he might be transferred to this Capital [São Paulo], this was granted and he returned the following year.

On the 5th of August, 1857, he entered upon the Presidency of Sergipe, which he held until March 7, 1859. He was the only one during the Administration of the last Ministry, who received from all the people of that Province, evidences of gratitude and sincere esteem, whilst others, with administrative ability and long practice had been feeling, not knowing what course to pursue.

Dr. Brotero rigidly pursued a new policy of conciliation and lived among the Sergipenses, as a father in the midst of his children. This is a monument of glory, which will immortalize his name! He returned to San Paulo, April 15th, and was received with universal enthusiasm. He was appointed President of the Province of Parahyba, but he declined it from a presentiment of death, or perhaps because he wished to be near his parents. That he was a good son, you all know, good citizen – good teacher – good friend.[14]

Among other events that involved the Dabneys during this period was a visit to Paris by a few members of the family in 1855.

Uncle Frederick and party were in Paris for some days; very much we enjoyed the beautiful Exposition and other sights of that world-renowned city. Louis Napoleon was in the height of his career, and entertained the Queen of England while we were there. One of the sights that perhaps made the deepest impression was the reviewing of the troops before Queen Victoria.[15]

A sadder event was the death of John Lewis Dabney in 1853 at the age of 52, the first of the second generation of Dabneys born in the Azores that survived beyond their 20's to die. He was the first of his generation to leave Faial, and, as mentioned in Chapter 8, this may have been because his mother opposed his relationship with a young cousin. However, he was ill and considered weak for a large part of his life and apparently suffered greatly, as indicated in a letter from Francis Dabney.

I suppose you will be somewhat prepared for the sad news I have to communicate, for in my last I wrote how ill dear uncle John was; I know how much you will feel this, he was so very fond of you. I have never felt anyone's death so much and it seems as if I ought not to feel so badly, for I am sure he must be so happy to be released from suffering; he told aunt Livy, the day before he died that it would make the stoutest heart quail to go through such suffering; and you know how

seldom he ever spoke of his sufferings. He was the most disinterested person I ever saw, and he was so to the very last.
Yesterday after all was over his countenance looked so com-
posed, it did not seem as if he could have suffered.[16]

Almost exactly a year later another death affected the entire
country, that of Queen Maria II. She had been queen for almost
20 years and was succeeded by her son King Pedro V.

> One circumstance I remember was that everyone was
> dressed in mourning [for the launching of the *Hortense*] for
> the Queen of Portugal, Dona Maria Segunda, news of her death
> having arrived a few days previously. We wore black for a month
> whenever we went out. At a party that winter, at Mr. Sergio
> Augusto's, the Minchins and ourselves were the only people
> not in black.[17]

With disagreement on a national and international level at a
lull, Charles W. Dabney had his own personal altercation in
Horta. The Dabneys were the most respected of the foreign
merchant families on the island, and Sebastião d'Arriaga Brum
da Silveira was from one of the most prominent aristocratic
families in the Azores, who looked down on those who actually
had to earn their living. At one point the two men had a confrontation, which, however, seemed more like two kids fighting it out in the schoolyard. Up till this event, the two families
had been most friendly, and d'Arriaga Brum da Silveira had been
a welcome guest at the Dabneys.

> But he was eaten up with family pride, conceit and vanity,
> and really was at times quite off of his balance; and later showed
> himself to be a very immoral man. The governor had invit-
> ed some of the leading men of the place to take part in a con-
> ference upon agricultural matters. The meeting took place at
> the governor's official rooms at the college. I will mention here
> that a year or so previous to this, Mr. A. had offered C. W. D all
> his property on lease, and it may have been that C. W. D.'s refusal
> to take so indisposed him; be that as it may, in the course of

the proceedings C. W. D advanced some opinion, perhaps in opposition to some hobby of this half crazy Arriaga. After C. W. D. sat down, Arriaga rose to his feet and said, "It is well known that there is no honour among merchants." "That's a lie!" exclaimed C. W. D., striking his fist on the table. The governor was much alarmed and there was general consternation, but order was restored, and the meeting went on to an end. C. W. D. remained after the other gentlemen had all left to say a few words to the governor, and on descending to the entrance hall, there was Arriaga in waiting for him and instantly ran at him head first; C. W. D. being unprepared for such an attack lost his balance a little, but recovered himself in time to give the other a good blow under the eye, the marks of whiche he bore for some time. The sentry, who is always on guard at the college, at once stepped up and arrested them both, but immediately released C. W. D. Mother, C. P. D. [Clara Pomeroy Dabney], and I had just sat down to dinner, when C. W. D. came in and sat down, looking stern, and somewhat agitated; "What is the matter Charles?" asked mother. I have been chastising a rogue." "Oh Charles!" said his wife in an agonized tone.[18]

At this point visitors and messages began to arrive expressing sympathy and support and condemning the actions of Senhor d'Arriaga. "The feeling seemed to be that their national honor was touched".[19] Among the messages was one from Sr. d'Arriaga's mother expressing her respect and esteem for Charles Dabney and denouncing her son.

The importance that Charles W. Dabney gave to this incident is indicated by the fact he made formal reports to Gen. W. Hopkins, the U. S. representative in Lisbon, as well as to the Secretary of State, John M. Clayton.

I have to inform you that on the 22d ult. I was assaulted by Sebastião d'Arriaga Brum da Silveira. I was satisfied with the punishment I bestowed on him and declared that I by no means desired any judicial proceedings; notwithstanding my declaration the judge of the island has taken cognizance of the case. It was a most outrageous affair and the universal manifestation regarding it has been exceedingly gratifying to me. I have never heard of a case that produced such unanimity of feeling, but I shall not trust myself to say anything more in regard to this subject, as you might consider me vain.[20]

I have the honor to inform you that I was assaulted on the 22nd ulto. By Sebastian d'Arriaga Brum da Silveira who has hitherto been considered a Gentleman – I declared that I was perfectly satisfied with the punishment that I bestowed on him, but his conduct was so outrageous, that notwithstanding my declaration the Judge of the island has instituted proceedings against him.[21]

As pointed out in the chapter about the battle with the *General Armstrong*, in 1850 the disagreement between the U.S. and Portugal over who should pay for the sinking of the *General Armstrong* was submitted to international arbitration. However, Charles Dabney was not aware of this until after the decision had been made. Although it may seem strange at first glance that Charles W. Dabney did not know what was going on with such an important event in his life on Faial as the *General Armstrong*, the family's focus was on a drama on the other side of the Atlantic.

The Dabney family was very close to the Webster family who were related to the Hicklings on São Miguel. The Websters made frequent visits to the islands, sometimes stopping in Faial to visit the Dabneys, and, when the Dabneys visited Boston they reciprocated. In 1845 John Pomeroy, Charles Dabney's 2nd oldest child, married Sarah Webster, renowned for her remarkable singing voice, and they provided C. W. D. with his first grandchild. The relationship between the two families is understandable given that Sarah's mother Harriet was the daughter of Thomas Hickling, Sr., who was the U.S. representative on São Miguel before John Bass Dabney arrived in Faial and was later vice-Consul there under both John Bass Dabney and Charles Dabney.

On November 23, 1849, in Cambridge, Massachusetts, the Webster women were preparing to go to a party and waiting for their father, Dr. John Webster, a Harvard chemistry professor to come home from Boston Medical College. At the same time, Dr. George Parkman, a physician, was on his way to Professor Webster's laboratory to collect a long-overdue debt. Apparently they began to argue, and, finally, Dr. Webster lost control and hit Dr. Parkman over the head with a grapevine, killing him. According to trial testimony, the body was dismembered and the clothes and skull burned in a furnace. The rest of the pieces were hidden under a privy and in a tea chest. Ephraim Littlefield, the janitor, who was searching for Parkman's body because he was sure Webster had killed him, later discovered these and called the police.

With the evidence pointing towards Dr. Webster, he was arrested on November 30. His twelve-day trial ended in conviction on April 1, 1850, and he was hanged at the Leverett Street Jail on August 30, 1850.

Virtually every text that deals with this trial calls it "the most celebrated murder trial during the 19th century". It involved two Harvard professors embroiled in a dispute that "gentlemen" should not have had and that had an especially vile result even less in keeping with their social status.

The friends of both the Websters and Parkmans included a large portion of the Cambridge-Boston academic and literary community, including Henry Wadsworth Longfellow and his wife Fanny and Dr. Parkman's brother, the Rev. Parkman, who had baptized the Webster daughters. The entire community was greatly shaken by the events that transcended the social code that governed the behavior of their class, although there had always been rumors that Dr. Webster had a checkered past and was considered financially irresponsible.[22]

With the indictment and trial, the Boston Brahmins behaved according to their rules, which considered that even among family members, the less said about negative events the better.[23]

> This brutal crime paralyzed the community. After the professor's arrest, Mrs. Webster and her daughters immediately went into seclusion. When Mrs. Longfellow called to show support, she "of course was not admitted." During the ensuing months,

Mrs. Webster coped with the unthinkable by rejecting anyone who even questioned her husband's innocence.[24]

As the trial progressed, the community emerged like the Greek chorus who commented on the unfolding tragedy. Henry Wadsworth Longfellow's wife, Fanny, witnessed the community's retreat into a social dumb show: "All gaiety in Boston is stopped by this tragedy – the community is stunned, and cannot easily recover, nor should it..." Other community members were equally as incredulous.[25]

Longfellow wrote to Richard Henry Dana: "I do not dare to touch upon the dreadful Cambridge Tragedy which pollutes the very air around us." The sordid murder turned his world upside down and destroyed those values and traditions that the poet prized.[26]

The trial judge was Lemuel Shaw, Chief Justice of the Supreme Judicial Court of Massachusetts (1830-1860) and who was also Herman Melville's father-in-law. Witnesses testifying as to Webster's character included Dr. Oliver Wendall Holmes who worked in the hospital with Parkman and Jared Sparks, president of Harvard at the time. The prosecution used a very graphic strategy displaying a three-dimensional model of the school, maps of the various locations important to the trial and even placed pieces of a life-size drawing of a skeleton on the positions where they were found. However, there were some who felt that there were other suspects who should be considered, such as Littlefield, who was a

> ...perfect scapegoat. After all, the janitor, a working class bloke, allegedly gambled in Dr. Webster's laboratory and trafficked in corpses. This certainly described the profile of a murderer better than the cherubic faced, intellectual Harvard professor who socialized with Charles Dickens and Henry Wadsworth Longfellow.[27]

In his charge to the jury, Judge Shaw had to address the fact that the legal grounds were shaky since no clear evidence of a single body had been found. He was later criticized because of his "treatment of burden of proof concerning *corpus delicti*, his presentation of the law of circumstantial evidence and the extreme bias of his summation of evidence in his charge to the jury."[28]

After Webster had been convicted and sentenced to death, he wrote a confession saying that he had killed Parkman in a fit of anger, without premeditation. Thus, he was guilty of man-slaughter and not first-degree murder. Despite numerous protestations to the Governor from his friends and people around the country, he was hanged on August 30, 1850.

The murder and trial had effects that extended far beyond those it had on the community of Webster's friends and colleagues. One important legal outcome is that Justice Shaw's charge to the jury is still cited as a precedent on circumstantial evidence (see *Commonwealth v. Webster*, 59 Mass. (5 Cush.) 295 at 303 (1850)).

In addition, it appears to have had some effect on literature, specifically resulting in a new phase in mystery writing. Karen Halttunen asserts that the investigation and trial of Webster makes it impossible to dispel the mystery through the reconstruction of the crime, as well as the unavoidable failure to dispel the moral uncertainty.[29] Herman Melville appears to have used the charge to the jury by his father-in-law Justice Shaw as a basis for statements by Captain Vere in the trial of Billy Budd in his book *Billy Budd*. Similar to the real life event, and despite his questionable guilt, Billy Budd was convicted and hanged.[30]

As far as the Dabneys were concerned, this would obviously have been a traumatic experience. In addition to Webster's wife Harriet being the daughter of Thomas Hickling, Sr., and John Pomeroy Dabney being married to Webster's daughter Sarah, Samuel Wyllys Dabney married Webster's daughter Harriet Wainwright Webster on April 2, 1851, a year and a day after her father's death.

> In the spring of 1851 S. W. D. brought home his bride accom-
> panied by her mother and sister Kate; her sister Mary Ann was
> already here having come out in the "Io". Mrs. Webster and her
> two daughters went to live in the Italian Villa; it is needless

to say how welcome an addition. S.W.D. and his wife, as you know, came to Fredonia to live with us.[31]

The actions of the Dabneys regarding the trial and execution of Dr. Webster were consistent with those of their close friends in Cambridge and Boston and followed their social code of "the less said the better," when it came to questionable events.

> Although the community had closed the door on Webster, it opened it to his family and created a charmed haven against further censure or publicity. Mrs. Nye continued to protect her sister from the secrets that governed Webster's behavior. Mrs. Webster never learned about his alleged youthful indiscretion, the actual amount of his debt, or even the exact time of the execution.[32]

Writing in her journal about events in 1863, Roxana Lewis Dabney makes an even clearer statement about how the Dabney family dealt with the sadness of the period that was just as relevant to the period of the Webster trial.

> There were many sad hours that summer for all of us (how could it have been otherwise?); there are some mentions of these in my journal, but our theory of life is to keep any sadness as much as possible to ourselves; and this was part of our training.[33]

Mrs. Webster died of cholera in Cambridge, Massachusetts, on October 10, 1854.

In late 1850, Thomas Henry Huxley arrived in Faial on the *HMS Rattlesnake* after a four-year exploration voyage in the Pacific and Atlantic. The great British naturalist was an ardent supporter of Darwin and his research culminating in the Theory of Evolution, whose acceptance some have attributed to Huxley's activities in upholding the theory. In addition to visiting the British Ambassador and climbing the 8,000-foot plus peak on the island of Pico, he visited the Dabneys. His comments about them relate to their reactions to the Webster case and show the response of someone outside the Boston-Cambridge social group who did not understand the code of conduct that supported the coherence of the group.

> The American consul, Mr. Datney [sic], was very civil to us. His family was in some affliction as one of his sons had married the favorite daughter of that unhappy man Professor Webster who was hanged the other day. I did not see her, but I am told that she is a clever person of great musical talent, but very apathetic. She seems to care nothing for the horrible catastrophe which has befallen her father. When her husband broke the news of the murder to her, she listened very quietly and when he had done only said "what an unfortunate occurrence". I think that is the sublime of bathos. I should have boxed her ears had I been her husband – I love a snowhouse but not an iceberg.[34]

In the years before Thomas Henry Huxley arrived, there were two other interesting visitors. One was Lord Elgin, of Elgin Marbles fame, who spent a short visit in 1846 and enjoyed the Dabney gardens, and the other was Lord Howden, British Envoy Extraordinary and Minister Plenipotentiary, who stopped in 1848 for a visit and dined with the Dabneys since Frederick Dabney, in the absence of his brother Charles, acted as both American and British Consuls. Howden was on his way back after dealing with diplomatic problems involving European powers and the division between Argentina and Uruguay.

In 1852, the Dabneys had a visit from one of their most prominent Americans of the 19th century, although at the time he was just a child. Charles W. Dabney had become a friend of Junius Morgan, whose 15-year old son John Pierpont had been ill for several months with what may have been inflammatory rheumatism in the hip and knee on one side. He was weak after recovering, and one leg was shorter than the other. He improved rapidly and, although he still could not walk, he was sent to Faial over the winter of 1852-53 for recuperation.

> And now we come to a great event in Pierpont's life in connection with which he made friendships and formed habits

which lasted all his life. This event was nothing less than a voyage on a sailing ship to the far-off island of Fayal in the Azores in order to get back his health.

So the problem raised by the doctor's advice that Pierpont should be sent away to regain his health was delightfully solved. A foreign place in a semitropical climate – Pierpont was certainly a lucky boy![35]

John Pierpont sailed to Horta in November 1852 on the *Io* with Charles Dabney along with other Dabney family members and their friends. He did not get sick the entire voyage, something that he was very proud of, and his health began to improve markedly.

On November 20 they arrived in Horta and

Pierpont took a room at Silva's Hotel and had a wonderful time exploring the town and doing his first shopping. No one ever enjoyed shopping more than he did, at any age, and he always made himself quickly at home wherever he found himself. Foreign people and languages never seemed to bother him in the way they do some people.[36]

He became part of the Dabney family and wrote letters to his parents between November 23 and December 11 in which he includes a good description of Horta in the middle of the 19th century and also gives an insight into the interests of an uncommon 15-year old boy.

The houses in Horta are built principally of stone stuccoed over and all whitewashed. The outside around the windows and doors is painted black and to a stranger has a very queer appearance. There are no docks or wharfs, but the vessels are obliged to lie at anchor in the bay, and are discharged and loaded by what are called lighters. The streets are very narrow and mostly paved although the paving is anything but smooth. There are no wagons of any kind and very few horses or mules. The transportation of merchandise or the inhabitants is done principally on donkeys. Ladies ride very often in what are called sedan chairs which are carried by two men, and the houses are so arranged that they take them in at the doors so when it is rainy there is no chance of getting wet. Nearly all the countries have Consuls here and their residences are usually distinguished by the flag which is raised on a pole in front of the house, and in some cases the coat of arms of the nation is placed on the house, either painted or cared on board. The houses of the consuls are usually the handsomest and best in the place. The people here are very poor indeed and are very lazy. They go around begging and it is very difficult to go through the street without being accosted several times for money and food. Everybody bows to everybody and they consider it an insult if you do not return their bows. They go barefoot and often without any covering to their heads except an hand-kerchief.

The gardens in Fayal are very handsome and are now (Nov. 29) full of flowers, fruit, etc. Japonicas of all sizes, colors and varieties. The bushes are now actually loaded with them. It seems very queer to see flowers in the open air at this time of the year. Orange trees as large as peach trees in America are now loaded with fruit which is now about arriving at per-fection although still a little acid. I shall send you some by this conveyance and then you can judge of their goodness for your self. What I miss most in Fayal in the table line is good water. The well water here is very bad and unfit to drink. The best water that can possibly be obtained here is rain water fil-tered. There are places arranged to catch all the rain possible. There is a large coal depot here where the British West Indies Mail Steamers stop and obtain their coal, when in want, on their to England. When going from England they stop at Madeira.

None of the houses in Fayal are shingled but the roofs are covered with tiles which is half a tube such as is used some-times for drains and the like. Mr. Dabney has a limekiln and Mr. William H. Dabney his brother has just returned from En-gland with engineers, etc. for the erection of a gristmill so as to have good flour. For by the laws of Portugal, Flour is con-

traband and cannot be imported here. So is also soap and tobacco. Those three cakes of Windsor soap I was obliged to
smuggle in my pocket, or it would have been taken from me.
Tobacco they are very particular about indeed, and they keep
tobacco guards on board while a vessel is discharging to see
that no tobacco is there, and when a vessel is discharged then
they do what is called juking the vessel, that is searching it all
over. These officers and also the custom house officers they
are obliged to board on board the vessel and pay them for
staying besides.

Mr. Chas. W. Dabney I find takes the *London News* and the
London Times, so I see them although their arrival is uncertain.
I shall expect on the return of the *Io* a large bundle of letters
and papers. I should like you to save me the *Traveller, Trans-
cript, Witness* and *Courant.* Captain Pillsbury says he will take
care of anything for me that may be sent, and my watch he
will take under his especial care. I should like the nos. of *Har-
pers Magazine.* An English schooner arrived from Liverpool in
17 days this a.m. (Dec. 1) so I saw the *London News* to Nov.
6 two weeks later than those I saw in Boston. [He then discusses the exchange rate of various currencies and which is
the best to use in Fayal.]

I have now been in Fayal three weeks and have got as to
like it pretty well. I don't believe I should live, however, if
Mr. Dabney's family were not here. Tell Dr. Hayward I fully
agree with him that they are some of the best people that ever
lived. They are all *very* kind to me, and do all they can to
amuse and gratify me, not only Mr. Chas. Dabney but his
brothers and sons. I go to Mr. C. W. Dabney's, (as he told me
to) whenever I choose and make myself perfectly at home.
Sometimes I go in and don't see anyone. If not I go into the
library and take a book and amuse myself with that, and
when I get tired if no one makes their appearance, I go back
to the hotel. He has a most delightful garden back of his house,
and I often go there and eat as many oranges as I choose. In
front of his house there is a large open field, leveled off and

a nice walk of red lava around it. This is a good place to take exercise between showers both riding and walking. Mr. Dabney has also several horses and donkeys and he told me whenever I felt like taking a ride to go to the hostler and he would give me an animal. The weather here is rather different from America. Showers come up here when the wind is in certain directions, very suddenly, and as quickly pass over and it is as dry underfoot as ever. Yet should you ever have the misfortune to be caught by one without an umbrella, you would be thoroughly soaked (for the drops are uncommonly large) before you could get under shelter. Mr. Dabney has fruit vessels running continually to England and if you have no objection I should like to go home by that route in the spring. It is only about 7 or 8 days by sailing vessel and the expense would not be much greater and I am so near now it would be a good chance just to get a glimpse of it.[37]

He also provides an idea of his religious preferences and indicates that the religious practices in Bagatelle and Fredonia were somewhat different from his own.

His New England background showed strongly in his Sunday habits. In one of the entries in his journal he explains the fact the he went to church service at Mr. Frederick Dabney's, in preference to going to Mr. C. W. Dabney's, because at Bagatelle it was held punctually at the hour appointed. He notes that at his friend the Consul's house the young ladies attended the service and it was "therefore very irregular." His duty-doing impulse was stronger than his natural longing for the girls' society, and yet he was a healthy, fun-loving boy always fond of the girls, and not a bit of a prig nor sanctimonious. It was just his bringing-up and his innate religious feeling that made him very punctilious about observing Sunday.[38]

He was sick during the winter and could not leave the hotel, and Charles Dabney visited him every day. After a while, he accommodated his life on the island to the coming and going of ships, as did all the island natives, including the Dabneys.

They regulated their lives entirely by the arrival and departure of the ships which kept them in touch with the home-lands. Just as did the Portuguese and English, so the Americans watched eagerly for the topsails that came up over the rim of the ocean. When the vessel was in plain sight and her flag was hoisted, the colors could be recognized; and then there were expectant hearts on shore. As soon as the ship could be signaled from the lookout station and her name sent down to the appropriate consul's office by a native boy, there was glad assurance to one or another of the national groups that there were long-looked-for letters and packets from home.

On February 12, Pierpont noticed that the flags on the signal station on the hill showed that a vessel was being signaled, and to his great delight it proved to be the *Io*. He went around to C. W. Dabney's, and there "found them jumping and dancing around in high glee." Pierpont adds in his diary, "Until it has been experienced I don't think the pleasure can be imagined of a vessel coming into a place like this bringing letters, etc. from your friends when you can only receive them every two or three months."[39]

After three months in Horta, Pierpont began to get tired of visits to ships, walks through the countryside and the island life-style.

> I *do* like the Dabney families very much indeed. I don't think I ever met with more kind people anywhere and although I am in quite a hurry to get home, still I feel very sorry to leave them for I have spent many happy hours here.[40]

His diary shows him to be a very meticulous young man who was interested in much the same kind of things as his father, such as American politics and business and was used to much more regular sources of information. The Dabney young had grown up with information arriving only sporadically, but from and about a much greater variety of places. Because of this he may not have hit it off with the young Dabneys as the *Annals* contain very little about his visit, and that which is included is not very flattering.

The girls used to get rather bored with him, but C. W. D. won his affection and gratitude by his patience and kindly counsels.[41]

In March of 1853, he began preparations to leave and bought a great number of presents that he sent home for his family and friends. On April 15, he sailed on the steamship *Great Western* for Southampton, England. After arriving in England he wrote to Charles Dabney.

Queen's Hotel, Manchester, April 29th, 1853

My dear Sir, – As this steamer (Cambria) will probably arrive in Boston ere the Io with her new rig will be able to depart from there, I take my pen this p.m. to let you know of my arrival in England, safe and sound. We had a most delightful passage of six and a half days and with the exception of one day the sea was as smooth as in Boston Harbor and an open boat could have been out without danger. After I had been in London a few days I received a telegraphic message from Father's agent in Manchester, that I was to come out there that evening, and so I did, and on my arrival at ten and half p.m. who should I meet at the cars but Father who had arrived in the Atlantic from N.Y. the day before.

...I am very much pleased with all that I have yet seen of England, but still I don't see anything to be compared to "Yankee Land." My winter at Fayal was indeed a very pleasant one and the pleasure all caused by the great kindness which I received from you and all friends there. Give my very best respects to Mrs. Dabney and all at your house, "Bagatelle" and "Sunnyside" [Uncle William's house], and that Heaven's richest blessings may ever fall upon you and yours is the earnest and frequent prayer of your ever obliged friend,

J. Pierpont Morgan[42]

As mentioned earlier, Charles W. Dabney thought a great deal of young Pierpont and "always prophesied that J. P. Morgan would make his mark".[43]

In 1861, at age 24, J.P. Morgan was the agent for his father's banking company in New York. In 1864, he became a partner with Charles H. Dabney (a first cousin of Charles W. Dabney) who was the U. S. representative of George Peabody and Co., where Junius Morgan was a partner. The firm that Charles H Dabney and J.P. Morgan established was called Dabney, Morgan and Company In 1871, John Pierpont left the company and became a partner in Drexel, Morgan and Company that became J.P. Morgan and Company in 1895.

In 1906, J.P. Morgan returned to Horta.

> The Commercial Cable Company had just completed laying a transatlantic cable by the southern route. There was a station on the island of Fayal, at Horta, where Mr. Morgan spent the winter of 1852-53. He had never been back there, but had always wanted to revisit the scenes of his first adventurous trip away from home and to see again the houses of his hospitable friends the Dabneys. George Gray Ward, president of the Commercial Cable Company, a passenger on the *Celtic*, had got the White Star line to make Horta a port of call on the way to the Mediterranean, so that he could formally open the cable station there and Mr. Morgan could send the first message to New York... He pointed out the little hotel in which he had lived, the houses of those residents who had been kind to him, and some of the shops where he had bought things. Scarcely anything had changed. As far as he could see, not a single new house had been built in the town, and but few seemed to have been altered in appearance. The shipyard was there, but it was not much of an affair in 1906 compared with what it had been in 1853 because almost all of the ocean freight was now carried in steamers that did not stop at Horta, and anyhow there were no repair shops there for steel vessels and machinery. Mr. Morgan bought oranges and souvenirs for the party and had a good time telling them the story of his experiences in Horta as a boy. He took his party to the little American-English cemetery and, finding the headstones of the graves of the friends of his boyhood, he described them affectionately. "It makes me very sad, but I would miss doing it," he said. "They were all so good to me."[44]

Notes:

[1] Roxana Lewis Dabney, *Annals of the Dabney Family in Fayal*, comp., n. p.: The Author, 1900, p. 590.

[2] Roxana Lewis Dabney, *Annals*, p. 560.

[3] Roxana Lewis Dabney, *Annals*, p. 742.

[4] Roxana Lewis Dabney, *Annals*, p. 702

[5] Roxana Lewis Dabney, *Annals*, p. 538.

[6] Roxana Lewis Dabney, *Annals*, p. 690.

[7] Roxana Lewis Dabney, *Annals*, p. 693.

[8] Roxana Lewis Dabney, *Annals*, p. 694.

[9] Roxana Lewis Dabney, *Annals*, p. 694-699.

[10] Roxana Lewis Dabney, *Annals*, p. 578-579.

[11] Roxana Lewis Dabney, *Annals*, p. 582.

[12] *Descendentes do Conselheiro José Maria de Avelar Brotero*, p 95.

[13] *Descendentes do Conselheiro José Maria de Avelar Brotero*, p 95-96.

[14] Roxana Lewis Dabney, *Annals*, p. 931-33.

[15] Roxana Lewis Dabney, *Annals*, p. 733.

[16] Roxana Lewis Dabney, *Annals*, p. 668-9.

[17] Roxana Lewis Dabney, *Annals*, p. 706.

[18] Roxana Lewis Dabney, *Annals*, p 626.

[19] Roxana Lewis Dabney, *Annals*, p. 626.

[20] Roxana Lewis Dabney, *Annals*, p. 627.

[21] Report to Sect. of State, Microfilm 3-75

[22] Karen Elizabeth Chaney, *The Cambridge Tragedy: The George Parkman Murder Case and a Community in Crisis in Mid-Nineteenth Century*, Boston, p. 13-14.

[23] Karen Elizabeth Chaney, *The Cambridge Tragedy*, p. 13

[24] Karen Elizabeth Chaney, *The Cambridge Tragedy.*, p. 17

[25] Karen Elizabeth Chaney, *The Cambridge Tragedy* p. 18

[26] Karen Elizabeth Chaney, *The Cambridge Tragedy*, p. 19

[27] Karen Elizabeth Chaney, *The Cambridge Tragedy*, p. 18

[28] "Divine Providence and Dr. Parkman's Jawbone: The Cultural Construction of Murder as Mystery", Karen Halttunen, address to the National Humanities Center, p. 9

[29] Ibid., p. 9

[30] *Billy Budd*, Herman Melville, Ch. 21

[31] Roxana Lewis Dabney, *Annals*, p. 642.

[32] *The Cambridge Tragedy...* p. 23

[33] Roxana Lewis Dabney, *Annals*, p. 1131

[34] *A Diary of Thomas Henry Huxley*, p. 339

[35] Herbert L Satterlee, *J. Pierpont Morgan: An Intimate Portrait*, p. 38

[36] Satterlee, *J. Pierpont Morgan* p. 39

[37] Satterlee, *J. Pierpont Morgan*, p. 41-44

[38] Satterlee, *J. Pierpont Morgan*, p. 51

[39] Satterlee, *J. Pierpont Morgan*, p. 52

[40] Satterlee, *J. Pierpont Morgan*, p. 54

[41] Roxana Lewis Dabney, *Annals*, p. 659

[42] Roxana Lewis Dabney, *Annals*, p. 682

[43] Roxana Lewis Dabney, *Annals*, p. 683

[44] Satterlee, *J. Pierpont Morgan*, p. 430-31

14 – MOVING SOUTH AND WEST

From the mid-1840's to the beginning of the Civil War, the focus in America was drawn towards the West and South. In 1848, gold was discovered along the banks of the Sacramento River in California and this caused a "Gold Rush" with a large number of men attracted to the possible riches on the west coast. Many decided to take ships from the east coast, a number of which stopped in Horta on their long voyage around South America to the Pacific and on north to San Francisco. However, some of those on San Francisco bound ships were not seeking gold, but had ideas for businesses and services that the prospectors would pay for.

"Gold Fever" was everywhere, but some people were more infected by it than others. One of the latter was Samuel Longfellow who wrote a letter to Samuel Dabney in which he gives an idea of what was going on in Massachusetts and gives his opinion on California fever.

> I hope you are not going to California. Some 100 persons have gone from here I am told; from New Bedford it is said 1500 & more. The excitement is great, the prospect glittering from afar, but I doubt if many know what they will have to encounter in the way of danger & discomfort, & the lawless & corrupt state of society there; if society it can be called.[1]

Nevertheless, some 40 years later Samuel Dabney eventually did go to California, as did a few other members of the Dabney family after they finally left Faial. Some settled near Santa Barbara, but Samuel Dabney went to San Diego where he lived on the Fayal Ranch where he died in 1893.

For those who were involved in building and provisioning ships on the east coast, the hunt for gold led to other problems because a large number of the ships that went to the west coast stayed there as their crews caught "Gold Fever" and headed inland behind the prospectors. Photographs of San Francisco Bay during the 19th century show a "forest" of masts, made up of the ships that arrived and stayed. The problems that the Dabney representatives in Boston were having is indicated in a later from Frederick Cunningham.

> We send you this time a vessel which does not command our unqualified admiration, but the demand for vessels is far greater than the supply; the late accounts having revived to a certain degree the 'California emigration mania.' The question is beginning to pass from mouth to mouth, 'What is to become of all the vessels sent to San Francisco?' Of course the old ones will lay their bones there, or on the way thither, but so many new ones have gone that there must be a time when they will all return or at least a large proportion; what then will become of ship-owners and ship-builders, who are now reaping a golden harvest?[2]

As the interests of the United States spread across its continent and ships began to call at Latin American ports, American interest in the influence of the "Old Continent" in the "New World" began to grow along with its interest in adding more of the New World to the United States.

> News or report by way of Lisbon that peace had been concluded between Mexico & the U.S. with the cession to the latter of New Mexico and California.
> President Monroe mentioned in one of his speeches to Congress [in 1823], that the United S. should never allow any foreign potentate to interfere in the International affairs of the Western Hemisphere. But the British have recently interfered by taking and making an English Greytown of St. John de Nicaragua.
> Report confirmed that a preliminary Treaty of peace had been settled between Mexico & the U. S., by which Upper California & N.M. are ceded to the U. S., Mexico receiving an indemnity of 15 millions &c. &c.[3]

In 1848, the Dabneys warmly received their friend Mr. Thomas Starr King, who was to become one of the most important figures in California history. He then returned to Boston and became a very respected Unitarian minister at the Hollis Street Church. Later, King decided that California was a challenge he couldn't pass up and went there in 1859. He arrived in the midst of the pro – and anti-slavery arguments going on in California shortly after the assassination of Sen. David C. Broderick, the leader of the anti-slavery faction. King made his anti-slavery position clear and was taken on as the spiritual leader of the Union sympathizers supporting Lincoln. He continued as a minister and had Leland Stanford, who later became governor of California, in his congregation. Through King's activities as an orator and advocate against slavery and his support for patriotic and charitable causes, he became possibly the most influential man in California at the time. Despite this, he continually refused to run for public office. He died in 1864 at the age of 40 from diphtheria and pneumonia. In 1913 California voted him as one of the two California heroes (the other being the Spanish Franciscan, Father Junipero Serra) to represent the state in the Statuary Hall of the U. S. Capital.

As the gold-seekers rushed west and streams of settlers flowed in the same direction in their covered wagons, major projects were undertaken to connect the two coasts by railroad. The Central Pacific railroad company extended its tracks from Sacramento, California, toward the east and the Union Pacific from the Missouri River Bluffs near Omaha, Nebraska, toward the west. The two companies eventually met in May 1869 in Promontory Point, Utah, where a golden spike was driven to commemorate the accomplishment of linking the east and west of the North American continent.

While northern industry continued growing, the plantation owners in the south were not doing as well and not only increased their holdings of black slaves to keep their agricultural interests viable, but they now entered into the business of slave trading. As the United States sought to expand its interests in the new territories annexed by the growing nation, a problem

arose. The southern coalition demanded equality in the spread
of slave and free states, a move not supported by the northern
states. Over the years several compromises, were reached between
the slave and non-slave states; the courts found some of these
compromises illegal while and others were simply ignored.

An excerpt from a letter from former Harvard President
Josiah Quincy to his good friend Charles Dabney in 1856 gives
an idea of the feelings in Boston. The second excerpt from Mr.
Weiss anticipates the war that would begin five years later.

> To a U. S. Consul, I take it for granted the state of things
> in our Union will be most likely to be acceptable and interest-
> ing. In my opinion then, the condition of our country is most
> critical and hazardous. The abrogation of the Missouri Com-
> promise and the subsequent invasion of Kansas by Missou-
> rians, who occupied the ballot boxes and by their votes over-
> powered those, who had intended to make it a free state has
> excited ferment throughout the Union and within Kansas.
> Emigrants from all the free states have rushed to arms and for-
> tifications are prepared and every demonstration hostile to
> the making of Kansas a slave state are under way. Our Admi-
> nistration is apparently determined to support slavery's estab-
> lishment there, and concentrating forces for this object on that
> point. How armed collisions and bloodshed are to be prevent-
> ed, no human eye can foresee; nor, should they occur, how
> separation of the free from the slave states can be prevented,
> is alike impenetrable by human foresight. My own opinion is
> that a way of escape will be found for the present at least. The
> slave power has found ways and means to manage the free
> states and make them submit to their purposes from the days
> of Washington until the present time; and the free states must
> continue to be as they always have been, bitted and bridled
> by Southern jockies.[4]

> Certainly if this Union is to be preserved, and devoted to
> the legitimate objects of a Republic, it shall only be by great
> patriotic unity at the North, that shall swallow up all prejudices
> and partisan issues, and make Freedom the predominating

influences... Our history stretches darkly into the future, and we are about to repeat one of those bitter periods, which we have been accustomed to read about with startled pity and interest. There is nothing new on this earth.[5]

Even during this period of greater instability toward which the United States was moving, life on Faial continued more or less the same, and at the end of the 1850's they had two more interesting visitors, one from each side of the Atlantic.

In 1857, the artist William Morris Hunt, who was a Harvard classmate of Charles Dabney, Jr., and his wife Louisa D. Perkins (nicknamed Loulie), who was a friend of Roxana and Frank Dabney, arrived in Horta. Their son Morris, had recently died and as a result of urging by Roxana, who visited them in Newport, they went to spend the winter on Faial. They were accompanied on the ship by Charles Dabney, Sr., several family members, the new tutor and his family, along with other visitors to the island, as well as a horse, which Roxana Dabney says died because of the "very boisterous passage."[6]

A large crowd of Dabneys and friends met them on their arrival in Horta, and Hunt said it was his first experience "being in the train of a Prince, or Monarch."[7] With so many people gathered in the Dabney household, it was a most active winter for all. W. M. Hunt participated in the fun with an artistic practical joke.

C. W. D. had brought out quite a number of things; among them was a large and beautiful mirror, purchased of Mr. Edmund Dwight (a classmate of C. W. D, Jr.'s), which was placed in its destined position in the drawing room when W.M. Hunt bethought himself of a clever trick, which, with F.O.D.'s connivance, he carried out. With a candle he drew on the mirror what looked like a long crack, and that evening each of us in turn was led up to see the terrible accident, at which we exclaimed in dismay, much to the satisfaction of the perpetrators of the joke. C. W. D. was spared.[8]

From January 16-18, 1858, there was a very severe storm in Faial that resulted in the sinking or destruction of nine ships.

Several lives were lost, some within view of those on shore. There were numerous stories of tragedy and heroism, some of which Hunt captured in sketches. He also turned his hand to painting portraits of Charles Dabney and his wife.

> Later on that winter, Mr. Hunt painted the portraits of C. W. D and wife, but he labored under many disadvantages, in the first place, not having a good atelier. Mother was not very well that winter and could not give many sittings and had not the usual animation in her eyes. C.W.D remarked to Mr. Hunt when he came to see the finished portrait, 'But, Mr. Hunt, my wife has always had such very bright eyes." C. W. D had always felt a repugnance at having his portrait painted, but as we all wished it so much he acquiesced. He had a acquired a habit of clasping his hands and snapping his two fingers, when engaged in thought; we used to like to hear him, because he could make such a loud sound. Mr. Hunt, who was always glad to portray any marked characteristic, immediately seized upon this one, which some regretted, thinking that it took from the dignity, which was one of the distinguishing characteristics of C. W. D. The first charcoal sketch Mr. Hunt made was a speaking likeness. Had I spoken to Mr. Hunt of how much I had often wished I could have had this sketch, I might now have been the possessor of it. It was burnt in the great fire of 1873, which consumed Mr. Hunt's atelier with all its treasures, among so many other buildings.[9]

William Morris and Loulie Hunt continued their visit through the winter. Hunt even went on a hunting trip with a few of the Dabney boys to Capello, one of the Dabney residences in the western part of Faial.

> William M. Hunt did more sketching than shooting, I fancy, but the following note received one morning at the breakfast table amused us very much:
>
> *My dear Mrs. Dabney,* – I send you a few birds that I have just knocked down with my club. I am glad I did not

take my gun as I find that the birds are so thick that there is no use for it.

Love to Loo
Yours truly,
W. M. Hunt[10]

In May 1858, the Hunts returned to the United States. In June after he returned, William Morris Hunt wrote to Mrs. Charles Dabney and told her that her sons, Charles and Fred had seen Mr. Dabney's portrait and seemed to like it. "I am having a frame made for it and shall send it to the Athenaeum. I find that so may persons expect to be pleased with it that I begin to tremble, lest it may not satisfy the general opinion already formed by hearsay."[11]

In December of 1859, he again wrote the Dabneys to present his opinion of his artistic production.

> I have been very busy all summer having been occupied constantly, since the middle of May, in painting portraits. I have painted a full-length portrait of Chief Justice Shaw, for the members of the Essex County bar, to be placed in the Salem Court House. Three half-length portraits and two heads. This for me a pretty good six month's work, and I only hope I may be well enough to do as much for many a 6 months to come.[12]

The friendship between the two families continued for years, and, in 1864, Charles Dabney, Jr., mentioned paintings by Hunt that he had obtained.

> I have just acquired two fascinating pictures by Hunt. They are copies in oil of the pair he painted in pastel of the cottage. One the gate into the garden, and the other the gate into the 'canada' with a portion of the house. I enjoy them immensely.[13]

The most important visitor during 1858 was 18-year old Prince Luís of Portugal, brother of King Pedro V, who later became King of Portugal when his brother died three years after the Prince's visit to Horta. On November 2, two Portuguese warships arrived in the Bay of Horta. When the health and customs officers returned to shore, news that the Prince was on board quickly spread throughout the town. The Prince's arrival was a complete surprise because he had been expected to go to São Miguel first.

> The St. Michaels people were terribly mortified at his giving them the "go-by," as they had made extensive preparations for his entertainment.[14]

Later in the day, the island's officials went on board to greet the Prince and the following morning the various foreign Consuls went out to the ship to visit, and even the island of Pico displayed its best appearance.

> The next morning at sunrise the vapor in the light of the sun behind the mountain showed like a beautiful white plume out of the summit. Soon after breakfast that morning, C. W. D., accompanied by his son, S. W. D., went off to pay his respects to His Royal Highness. C. W. D. signified his desire to give D. Luiz a ball, – the Civil Governor was proposing the same thing, – and it was left to the Prince which should come first; he politely accepted C. W. D's, as having been the first proposed. We were somewhat dismayed, having so short a time to prepare, for there was much to be done before the next evening, but we went bravely on, and fortunately the next day was stormy, and the Prince, as it was left to him, postponed if for the next evening. We were very glad to rest, though we could have been ready, for the whole family took hold and worked with a will, and certainly, although I say it the ball was a very pretty one, and the only one of the four given to him, in which D. Luiz was "upon his dignity."[15]

Although Charles Dabney often felt that the seaman left on the island were a difficult burden for him, many of them felt an obligation to him because he had treated them fairly and paid attention to their problems, so they were ready to lend him a

hand whenever he asked. The Prince's visit gave them an opportunity to perform a unique task for him.

> There were quite a number of the 'Consul's men' (as the
> seamen left by the whaling vessels were called), and C. W. D.
> bethought him of getting them to accompany the sedan chair
> (which he sent for H. R. H.) with lighted torches. Don Luiz was
> highly amused, especially with their hearty cheering, and the
> men thought it 'great fun'.[16]

The Archives of the Azores describe the ball at the Dabney's.

> His Royal Highness entered the American Consulate a lit-
> tle after eight o'clock at night.
> The residence of the respectable Dabney family was deco-
> rated with care and simplicity, the main room having the por-
> trait of King Pedro V surrounded by flowers in the place of
> honor and in several places were linked Portuguese and
> American flags.
> The family of the American Consul awaited the Prince at
> the entryway to the room and were presented to him by their
> head.
> The dignified Prince distinguished the house by dancing
> the first quadrille with Clara Dabney, oldest daughter of the
> American Consul, his opposite number being the commander
> of the military subdivision.
> His Excellency was high spirited throughout the night, re-
> turning on board at three o'clock in the morning.[17]

The Prince stayed on Faial a few days longer and made the
official visits expected of him in addition to participating in other
social activities.

> Col. Creagh talked a great deal to him, being accustomed
> to *high society* in London and he made up two hunting parties
> at S. W. D.'s (or his father's) expense, as they furnished horses
> and provender for both occasions. S. W. D. accompanied, and
> one of the days, when sitting next to the Prince, S. W. D. was

opening a bottle of champagne, the cork flew almost into this Royal neighbor's face, fortunately only *near enough* to raise a laugh. D. Luiz was only eighteen, Commander in the Navy, and seemed to have a foreshadowing that he should some day be King, and required of his to kiss his hand when he came on deck. His brother, Don Pedro, who was a very intelligent, sensible young man, had done away with the ceremony of 'Beija mão' ('kissing of the hand' when introductions were made), but D. Luiz saw fit to have that ceremony at the Military Governor's a day or two after his arrival. None of us were present, and it is not necessary to add that we never kissed his hand. Our house was the only one he honored with a call. He came with his chamberlain, the Count of Linhares; we received him standing, and my impression is that he was not asked to sit down, for he asked to see the garden and to be taken to see the 'Bayadere,' the little yacht. There were parties given by the Civil Governor, the Senate, and the Baron of St. Anna. At the last two he acted like a school-boy on a spree. The Prince's visit formed an epoch in the annals of the little island.[18]

These same years also saw major changes that would affect the Dabney family during the remainder of their stay on Faial. The Christmas of 1857 at Bagatelle, with the Hunt's as guests, was one of those times that can be seen in retrospect as a point where life afterward was forever transformed.

Christmas at Bagatelle was as usual bright and festive. Mrs. Hunt has often said that, take it all in all, it was the most elegant entertainment she was ever at. The honored guest seemed less able to enter into the pleasures than usual, but he evidently enjoyed looking on, and little did we suspect that that Christmas was to close the beautiful ones that we had passed under that roof. On the 29th of December 1857, Uncle Frederick breathed his last at 2:30 in the morning. This event was the beginning of the great changes that have swept over our little community on this spot in mid-ocean. William Davis used to say to me, "This circle of yours is the happiest, most beautiful I have ever known, but I cannot help thinking what it will be when death invades it, as it must sooner or later, isolated as you are from the rest of the world." Of course, next to his own wife, and perhaps to aunt Olivia, the break came the hardest to C. W. D. The fraternal tie is remarkably strong in this family, owing, perhaps, to inheritance, and also to circumstance.[19]

Frederick was the first of John Bass Dabney's children, and Charles Dabney's siblings, that lived to adulthood to die, undoubtedly the reason for the extent of the reaction. To this was added the fact that the six children of Charles Dabney and the numerous children of his siblings were reaching adulthood, and the family business on the island of Faial could only absorb a limited number of them, Faial did not provide an overabundance of other opportunities. As a consequence, some had already left to start their own lives in America, including Charles Dabney, Jr. The breaking up of the first Dabney home on Faial was a forerunner of the gradual movement of the family to America and an indication of what was to come.

Four years later, Frederick's wife Roxana Stackpole Dabney decided to leave Bagatelle and take her sons to America. Two were already attending Harvard, and she was determined that the other two follow in their footsteps in accordance with their father's wishes.

Roxana Stackpole was highly thought of on Faial and was able to accomplish much within her limited means. The effect of her leaving is reflected in the following:

> It was a terrible wrench to her, the leaving Fayal, for she had spent the most of their life there, and she never ceased to think of it with a great "saudade." The Abbess of the Gloria Convent sent word that she wished Aunt Roxana to come and take leave of her, so one festival morning, when there was to be a High Mass at the Chapel, I breakfasted at Bagatelle, and accompanied her to the Church. After the Mass the lower door of the Convent, which was always kept locked, excepting on occasion of some august visitor, was thrown open and the

Abbess in her dress advanced to the threshold and gave Aunt R. a most affectionate embrace, including me in a less fervent one, and bestowed some sweets, etc.[20]

To Aunt Olivia this breaking up of the old home, perhaps, came the hardest, and she had no idea then that she might, in later times return to it. She had her share in the house and grounds.[21]

In April of the 1858, Charles Dabney's youngest son Frank prepared to leave for his own adventures in life. Following the Dabney tradition of seeking out business opportunities, he planned a business trip to Mexico and

On the 25th of April dear Frank left his home. How little we realized that it was for the last time; and yet we had anxious thoughts in connection with Mexico and Havana. He went in the French bark "Laure" to Vera Cruz.[22]

After a 46-day voyage, they arrived in Vera Cruz. On board the ship was a Mlle. Frezini, who Frank describes in one of his letters.

Mlle. Frezini, the second in command, or, I should perhaps say the first, was a lively, chattering, silly little woman, half Italian, half French, – she could tell lies with the most extraordinary facility, and possessed other accomplishments such as tinkling the "Vivandeira," on a guitar, utterly out of tune. She was good natured though in the main, excepting when the other ladies called her hard names, when she became a perfect little tigress. I had twice to assist in holding her down during an "Attaque de nerfs," occasioned by these "émeutes."[23]

For reasons not explained, the mademoiselle was under Frank's protection during the trip on their way to Mexico City. The country was in turmoil with President Benito Juarez leading the Liberals in the Reform War. He made Vera Cruz his capital, and his forces controlled this city and Mexico City.

However, the area between them was not completely under his domination, and the trip was considered dangerous. Stagecoaches were "robbed half the time going up and more frequently going down."[24]. As a result Frank took as little as possible with him. They left at 11:00 p.m., traveling on bad roads and only stopped for meals until the next night. In his Travel Journal[25] Frank gives an excellent description of their trip over mountains, across plains and through the different, spectacular varieties of Mexico's vegetation from desert to forest and past fields of corn and fruits of all kinds. Frank thought it "the greatest country for fruit in the world." Every now and then they stopped in Indian villages for a rest and small purchases. They arrived in Puebla, a city of around 50,000, and from here on they were escorted by troops of between 15 and 25 lancers "according to the supposed danger of the coast."

> Frezini and I who were alone on the back seat, *came the regal*, in bowing to the escort, who, whenever they were relieved, galloped forward and drew up in line at the side of the road – touching their caps as our coach dashed by. It must have had a fine effect. I fancied I looked like Prince Albert, and I suppose Frezini thought she resembled Victoria.[26]

After about four days travel, during which "a pleasant old Spanish gentleman" joined them, they descended into the "magnificent valley of Mexico." Frank considered it one of the most spectacular views he had ever seen with new things to see at every turn.

> I did not know which way to look I can assure you. The Spanish gentleman seemed to fear I should dislocate my neck as I kept my head out of the window and kept turning it constantly.[27]

Once they arrived at their hotel in the city, Frank delivered Frezini to her friend and set about on his own activities. He remained there a week and, although he couldn't get permission to see much "owing to the disturbed state of things, I was yet amply repaid for my journey to and from Vera Cruz." After a round of business, touring and visiting people to whom he had letters of introduction in addition to others he met there, as well as experiencing an earthquake, he decided it was time to return.

In preparation, he bought himself a pair of pistols. When he got to the stagecoach, he found another American with pistols plus a rifle and a shotgun. Along the way they picked up another armed American. Word about their being armed must have preceded them because they got all the way to Vera Cruz without problems – a virtually unknown occurrence for a trip between Vera Cruz and Mexico City.

Frank took passage on a ship and sailed to Havana where Yellow Fever "was raging," stayed one day, and proceeded on to Charleston. The police enforced a Yellow Fever quarantine by not allowing the passengers to remain overnight and put them all on trains and sent them on their way. During his trip Frank visited family and friends between the east coast and Pomeroy, Ohio.

Frank then decided to go on a business trip to Beirut, which was part of Syria at the time. He wrote several letters about his trip and his stay in Beirut, his last letter indicating that he was starting on a trip to Damascus. In February 1859, Charles Dabney, Jr., wrote his family in Faial that his youngest brother had died while living in Beirut. Among the numerous other letters of condolence that the family received, one from the American Vice-consul in Beirut to Charles Dabney describes the circumstances of Frank's final illness.

Dear Sir, – It becomes my sad duty to inform you of the death of your son Mr. Francis. O. Dabney in this place. Yesterday evening at 6 o'clock he breathed his last in the house of Mr. Ayoub Tabet, where he had been staying since his arrival in Syria. He died of Typhus, after an illness of ten or twelve days. It will be gratifying to his family to know that every attention and kindness were shown him by the family of Mr. Tabet, who seemed devotedly attached to him. During his short stay with us, he had secured many warm friendships and it was my privilege to have him thus express himself in relation to those about him when attending his dying bed. He expired without the least apparent pain – saying that he was "happy" and that "Angels are around my pillow."

All the medical skill of the place was exhausted in his be-half, both the American Physicians in this City having been with him, Drs. Vandyke and Smith. He will be buried with proper funeral ceremonies in the American Cemetery in this place...

May I offer you my sympathy and that of his numerous friends in this place, in this heavy bereavement.

Mr. Johnson. U. S. Consul in this place is temporarily absent.

> With highest regard, etc., etc.
> J. Judson Barclay
> U. S. V. Consul at Beirut[28]

The American Consul in Beirut, J. Augustus Johnson wrote a brief description of Frank's funeral in his letter to Charles Dabney.

His funeral which took place on the day following his death, at 4 p.m. was attended by the Americans and Europeans of this place, as well as a large number of natives, who entertained an affectionate respect for the deceased. The funeral procession moved from the house of Mr. Tabet after prayer by Rev. Mr. Ford and on reaching the American Chapel, appropriate remarks were made by Revd. Messrs. VanDyk and Eddy – American Missionaries with whom your son had formed a pleasant acquaintance.[29]

While in Beirut, Frank had been living with Mr. Ayoub Tabet, a wealthy and influential local resident of Syrian heritage, and his family. They were close personal and business friends, and it was reported that he never left Frank's bedside during his last days. Mr. Tabet describes how Frank had made himself welcome in the Beirut expatriate community.

Our hearts are indeed so filled with sorrow that we can give but a rambling account of the circumstances attending

the last illness and hours of our friend; for during the time he
has spend with us he was considered as a member of the
family, and he himself repeatedly assured us that he felt quite
at home; and in his remarkable goodnaturedness and kindness,
at times expressed fears that we were bestowing unnecessary
attention and troubling ourselves too much for his comfort
– of course we assured him to the contrary. We only allude
to this circumstance that you and his friends may believe that
our friend did not die a stranger in this land, but that up to
his last moments was surrounded by friends affectionately
attached to him, whose hearts he had won by his remarkable
affability and extreme kindness – that we share their affliction
and entirely sympathize with them in their sorrows and mourning. In short, he lived with us as a member of the family and
left us as such.[30]

The family, especially his brothers and sisters, grieved a lot
for Frank. The close relationships and feelings among the Dabney siblings is well expressed in a letter from Charles Dabney, Jr.,
to his brother Samuel.

It is a blessed thought that we love each other so strongly,
for I do not know but whichever had gone first, we should have
felt that we loved him or her the best. Really there can be no
best where the bond is in each case the strongest that can
exist.[31]

A little over a year later, Beirut was again in the Dabney family letters, as well as in the American press. A letter from cousin
Frederick Cunningham describes what was going on and gives
an uncanny glimpse, especially in the last sentence, of what
was to come in the next century.

Long before you get this, you will have read the accounts
in the English journals of the awful atrocities in unhappy Syria;
the horrors of Judea again perpetrated, and that within hail and
almost under the very nose of Christian Europe. It makes me
heart sick to read the circumstantial and pathetic letters of the

faithful American missionaries, than whom no more sincere and earnest pioneers of the true faith ever trod the stage of life. Of course we can go over in memory every step of the country so desolated and imagine the actors in the scenes so described, though not the scenes themselves, which are said to beggar description. Our friend Tabet in Beirut is not, we hope, in any danger, unless it should be that these fanatics, made absolutely wild by their bloody prudence, as to fancy they could contend successfully even with European Christians. Ayoub's house is directly upon the road by which they would approach the city and it is quite in the suburbs, but it is probable that his very road would be the point of defence of the marines and sailors landed from the ships in the harbor and therefore the advance of the attacking force would be checked long before they reached his house. I cannot believe that they would ever think of attacking Beirut. One consolation there is that the result must be favorable to the progress of the country, as by the interference of the European powers, a better permanent and more certain trade will be secured. I shall be much interested to visit the place in after years again and note the changes.[32]

As described before famines on the islands were not uncommon, nor was the assistance the Dabneys provided. However the famines of 1858 and 1859 were the worst that struck Faial and Pico in the 8 $1/2$ decades the Dabneys had lived there. Most of the crops were destroyed by disease with the addition of major storms in these two years, and the people had almost nothing to eat. Unlike other efforts by Charles Dabney to provide relief, the famines of 1858-59 stretched his resources to the point where he had to seek outside help.

In 1858, Charles Dabney provided a large amount of grain and received financial assistance from some of the wealthier individuals on island, thereby controlling the famine. For his actions in providing food to the population, Charles Dabney received letters expressing gratitude not only from the Civil Governor of the District, but also from the King of Portugal.

Unfortunately, the next year the harvest was even poorer, and the famine became worse and could not be dealt with by

Charles Dabney, even with the assistance of those on Faial. As a result, he wrote a letter to the people he knew in Boston to ask them to raise money for the purchase of grain, while he would transport it to Faial for free in one of his ships. Below is the letter he sent followed by some comments from Roxana.

FRIENDS AND FELLOW COUNTRYMEN: The time has arrived when great efforts must be made to avert from the inhabitants of this District the horrors of famine, and wishing to promote the good work beyond my own immediate means, where shall I look for aid? To my countrymen! Whose chivalrous benevolence has always been so conspicuous whenever a well founded appeal have been made to their philanthropy. I therefore invoke the assistance of the all potent press of my Country, ever ready to proclaim the distress that requires Public sympathy to relieve it, to announce that the people of this District have for many years had their potato crops destroyed by *the* disease (this alone occasioned very great distress); that for the last four years the "oidium" has ravaged their vineyards, occasioning the ruin of most of the proprietors, and deprived the laborers of employment; that for the last three years the corn crop has been *much* injured, rendering it necessary to import large quantities of corn; and as wine is the only great staple of export, and that having been destroyed for the last four years, the corn that was imported had to be paid for in cash. This has nearly drained the Island of specie and paralyzed almost all operations, so that, in addition to the high price of grain, the laboring class cannot find employment; thousands have hitherto lived independently are now almost penniless, having pledged their property at a ruinous rate of interest, or sold it for a very small proportion of its value. There are thousands, and the number is daily increasing, who sustains life with wild arrowroot, a very acrid, unwholesome kind of food, and some even use the roots of ferns; these resources will soon be exhausted. The Windsor bean ("vivia faba") crop, on which great reliance was placed for a month or six weeks' support, has been destroyed. A northerly gale has prevailed these last three days; at one time so violent as to uproot trees, and causing great damage to the coming crops. These are the causes of the distress that impel me to have recourse to your philanthropy. I am aware that I am going to occasion trouble, but I am reconciled to it by the consideration that it will be only to those who appreciate the luxury of doing good.

With pride I subscribe myself your friend and fellow countryman.
Charles W. Dabney, Consul U. S., Azores

Messrs. Dabney and Cunningham of Boston, Mass., will afford any information or assistance, and will make known any arrangements that may be made. I have not addressed my friends individually, deeming it unnecessary.

Fayal, 17ᵗʰ May, 1859

You cannot imagine anything more repulsive than some of the cakes they made of the fern roots and the blood they collected at the slaughter house. Of course this food engendered much illness. Your grandmother had the thought of sending a specimen of the food made from the "jarro" (wild arrowroot). This was placed in the Boston Exchange, and was a very convincing proof of the suffering, and the idea always remained among the people of how much they owed to her, and they ever called down prayers and blessings upon her.[33]

The letter struck the philanthropic spirit of 20-30 of the influential men who the Dabneys knew, and they formed a committee in June 1859, on which Charles, Jr., participated. The group grew to 279 persons and companies and the amount contributed raised over $10,000 for the purchase of grain to help fight the famine.[34]

Boston, June 29ᵗʰ, 1859
Charles W. Dabney, Esq.,
U. S. Consul for the Azores:
Dear Sir, – At a meeting of Gentlemen held in Boston on the 16ᵗʰ inst. A Committee was appointed to solicit contributions for the suffering inhabitants of the Azores, and to invest and

ship the proceeds. We have shipped on board the barque "Azor", and herewith hand you Bill of lading of ten thousand bushels of corn, purchased with the funds so procured, which we send consigned to you, begging you to use your discretion and good judgment in the management of the distribution of the same. The bags are a part of the contribution and you will dispose of them as you see fit.

Respectfully yr. &c. &c
G. R. Russell, Chairman
James Sturgis, Secretary[35]

After the famine had been controlled, articles describing the extraordinary action initiated by Charles Dabney appeared in Portuguese and American newspapers. There were also numerous personal and official letters expressing appreciation for the action. However, the expression of thanks from the people of Horta was the one that touched Charles Dabney the most. When the ship he was returning from São Miguel on entered the Bay of Horta, he received a surprise welcome.

Slowly we steamed up to Fayal, little imagining what was preparing for us, nor did I suspect when a signal rocket was sent off from one of the boats that it was to announce that father had come. Then came a deputation from the Senate, some of the other authorities, the Currys, &c., &c. The two bands, Philharmonic and Artistas followed, and began to play under the stern. There were three hearty cheers for father and his illustrious consort. The music touched me, even through some discord. As we rowed ashore the bands accompanied us, one on either had , and by the time we reached the quay, which was crowded with people of all classes, I felt quite overcome. Hundreds of rockets were sent off. I never saw father so moved, and, to tell the truth, there were not many dry eyes in that multitude. Mr. Sequeira was kind enough to offer me his arm to lead me out of the crowd, – I scarcely knew how I got out, – there was embracing kissing, crying. There were ladies, too, to meet us, the band playing up on our lawn, and many escorting up to the house. Miss Curry said it was "more glorious than an emperor's entrée, because it was voluntary". The dear little lady had enlisted some little girls to strew the road from the landing with flowers.[36]

Among some papers I found the following, written in C. W. D.'s hand to translate, I presume into Portuguese: –

To the mind of man there is nothing more grateful that the approbation of those whom he esteems and respects; imagine therefore what were my sensations on the 27th July 1859, profoundly impressed as I was by the manner in which I was received. I am most grateful to the Almighty for having in so eminent a degree crowned my efforts on behalf of the Poor! I am grateful to my friends and fellow countrymen of Boston, who so generously granted the relief implored; and to you friends and fellow citizens, I am grateful, for the manner so very gratifying, in which you manifested your approbation of what I had done. Never in my life did I shed so many joyful tears, and while I live the 27th of July 1859 will be the most flattering anniversary to my 'amour propre'.[37]

Charles Dabney himself was faced with a life-threatening crisis in the spring of 1860 when he came down with smallpox, which was "raging at the time in Fayal". He had been inoculated in France as a boy, and, as a result, he was at first diagnosed with "brain fever". Two doctors, "after a careful scrutiny the second or third day discovered a slight eruption on his forehead, whereat there was great rejoicing throughout the place".[38]

On his worst day the Governor ordered that, despite it being a holiday, the cannons not be fired at the fortress since it was so near Fredonia. He was taken care of by his daughter Clara, recognized among the family for her abilities in caring for sick people. The rest of the family did what they could to keep clear of the patient so they would not get sick.

One of his treatments was eating the oranges off the family's trees, and once he had passed through the stage of his "eruption out very fully," he began to improve. Mrs. Dabney describes the reactions to Charles Dabney's illness among the islanders.

This illness has certainly been one of the remarkable experiences of our lives. I believe I have not spoken of the universal interest manifested for dear Father – it is not that I have not been deeply touched by it. The feeling is quite different from that of last summer, now it seems a spontaneous tribute to his Life and Character, that burst from all classes – then it was like an ovation offered for the great result of his good work; I do not think I explain myself exactly, but I feel that you will understand me. You will no doubt hear from others of the unceasing demonstrations of regard and sympathy, which have ben shown throughout. I wish I could give you an idea of the perfect satisfaction expressed by words and in the countenances of some of our humble friends.[39]

About $2^1/_2$ weeks after Charles Dabney became ill, his "nurse" Clara succumbed to illness herself and was "obliged to yield", the doctors thinking that, "there is no doubt that it is variloid", a mild form of smallpox. She had kept Charles Dabney "soothed and relieved" by reading to him and cheering him with "pleasant talk." Not having a full-blown case of smallpox, she recovered quickly, and life returned to normal in Fredonia.

However, not everything that happened to the Dabney family during this period was bad. In November of 1859, Charles Dabney's youngest child Frances Alsop Dabney, known as Fan, married George Stewart Johonnot Oliver after a long engagement.

George Oliver was the son of Francis Johonnot Oliver, who died in 1858. The senior Mr. Oliver was the first president of the American Insurance Company in Boston and then several-time president of the City Bank. He also was a representative in the Massachusetts legislature and the Boston Common Council, as well as a warden at King's Chapel. His first wife was an Alsop, whose daughter Susan Heard Oliver married Charles Dabney Jr., who was her cousin. George Oliver was the son of Francis Oliver's second wife.

Consuls couldn't perform marriage ceremonies as in earlier years, and since there still was no protestant minister on Faial, the couple returned to the U. S. to get married, accompanied by most of the family. However, for the parents "it was *hard* to let the youngest go."

The prospective bride and groom visited Charles, Jr., at his home Stanhurst for a few days and then went on to Boston where they were married in King's Chapel by James Freeman Clarke, a friend of the family, as well as of Samuel Longfellow. After the wedding, the family stayed for a while in Massachusetts and went to visit and stay with various family and friends, while Fan and George went to Providence and then on to their home in Kentucky.

There were two other events that always seemed to be a pleasant part of Dabney life. One was the birth of Samuel Dabney's fifth child, Ralph Pomeroy Dabney. The other was a ball that Roxa Lewis Dabney attended in New York for the Prince of Wales in the fall of 1860.

As usual there were famous visitors. However, among the large number of well-known acquaintances of the Dabneys, not all of them were American. In January of 1861, Charles Dabney received a letter from one of Portugal's most famous men.

> Illmo. Snr. – I was much touched by your letter, not only by the remembrance of my father, which accompanied it, but especially in seeing that you still bore in remembrance a man, who has always had the highest appreciation of you, and done full justice to your shining qualities. Accept my most cordial and sincere thanks for all. For whatever service I can render you do not hesitate to command
>
> Your friend and much obliged servant
> António José d'Avila

Senhor d'Avila had been born in Faial and his father was a shoemaker. "The son very early showed talent, and he always said he owed much to C. W. D.'s encouraging words." He was Prime Minister several times and developed the treaty that led to the marriage of King Luís I and Queen Maria Pia of Savoy, daughter of King Victor Emanuel II of Italy. He was also involved in international activities, mostly in Africa and was made the

Marquis of Bolama (a small island off Guinea Bissau) and returned to be Prime Minister of Portugal again in later life.

António d'Ávila was not the only important political personality to be born in the Azores. The Azores seem to have had a more than a proportional share of Portugal's distinguished politicians, including the elderly Manuel de Arriaga, born on Faial and Portugal's 1st elected President after the fall of the monarchy near the beginning of the 20th century. In fact, President Arriaga paid a visit to the Dabneys years after they had left Bagatelle and caught Roxana Dabney by off guard.

> I was very much astonished one day (...) to have Dr. Manuel d'Arriaga, the foremost Republican of Portugal had come on a visit to his family, one day, walking in our garden, say to me, "I have the greatest admiration for Mrs. Frederick Dabney; how is she" "Why," I said, "I should hardly have though you would have any recollection of her, you left Fayal when you were so young." "Oh!" he said, "I have always looked upon her as a 'Spartan mother' in the truest acceptation of the term.[40]

Notes:

[1] Roxana Lewis Dabney, *Annals of the Dabney Family*, p. 624.

[2] Roxana Lewis Dabney, *Annals*, p. 632.

[3] Roxana Lewis Dabney, *Annals*, p. 598-600.

[4] Roxana Lewis Dabney, *Annals*, p. 790-791.

[5] Roxana Lewis Dabney, *Annals*, p. 795.

[6] Roxana Lewis Dabney, *Annals*, p. 831.

[7] Roxana Lewis Dabney, *Annals*, p. 831.

[8] Roxana Lewis Dabney, *Annals*, p. 836-7.

[9] Roxana Lewis Dabney, *Annals*, p. 844.

[10] Roxana Lewis Dabney, *Annals*, p. 845.

[11] Roxana Lewis Dabney, *Annals*, p. 850.

[12] Roxana Lewis Dabney, *Annals*, p. 930.

[13] Roxana Lewis Dabney, *Annals*, p. 1189.

[14] Roxana Lewis Dabney, *Annals*, p. 881.

[15] Roxana Lewis Dabney, *Annals*, p. 880.

[16] Roxana Lewis Dabney, *Annals*, p. 881.

[17] Canto, Ernesto do, *Archivo dos Açores*, reedition, 15 vol., Ponta Delgada: Instituto Universitário dos Açores, 1980-1985, p. 67.

[18] Roxana Lewis Dabney, *Annals*, p. 880-881.

[19] Roxana Lewis Dabney, *Annals*, p. 837.

[20] Roxana Lewis Dabney, *Annals*, p. 967-8.

[21] Roxana Lewis Dabney, *Annals*, p. 968.

[22] Roxana Lewis Dabney, *Annals*, p. 845.

[23] Roxana Lewis Dabney, *Annals*, p. 852-3.

[24] Roxana Lewis Dabney, *Annals*, p. 854.

[25] Roxana Lewis Dabney, *Annals*, p. 855-866.

[26] Roxana Lewis Dabney, *Annals*, p. 859.

[27] Roxana Lewis Dabney, *Annals*, p. 860.

[28] Roxana Lewis Dabney, *Annals*, p. 886.

[29] Roxana Lewis Dabney, *Annals*, p. 887.

[30] Roxana Lewis Dabney, *Annals*, p. 887.

[31] Roxana Lewis Dabney, *Annals*, p. 893.

[32] Roxana Lewis Dabney, *Annals*, p. 957.

[33] Roxana Lewis Dabney, *Annals*, p. 898-899.

[34] Roxana Lewis Dabney, *Annals*, p. 915.

[35] Roxana Lewis Dabney, *Annals*, p. 903.

[36] Roxana Lewis Dabney, *Annals*, p. 913-4.

[37] Roxana Lewis Dabney, *Annals*, p. 914.

[38] Roxana Lewis Dabney, *Annals*, p. 941.

[39] Roxana Lewis Dabney, *Annals*, p. 944.

[40] Roxana Lewis Dabney, *Annals*, p 967.

Figure 9
View of Cedars

15 – WAR BETWEEN THE STATES

On April 12, 1861, the southern batteries under General Beauregard opened fire on Fort Sumter, South Carolina. These were the first shots leading to the American Civil War. The four-year war had terrible costs in life and property for the United States and even extended its reach into the middle of the Atlantic, having its effect on the Dabney family in Faial.

In a letter to Charles Dabney, Josiah Quincy, the 87-year old former president of Harvard and close friend of the Dabneys, gives an analysis of the Civil War from the viewpoint of one who had been born just before the Revolutionary War.

In the United States we are as the papers have already informed you, in a broken, divided and confused state and how and when our former union will be restored if ever, it is not within the reach of human vision to perceive. Such a state of things has long been anticipated by those, who deeply looked into the construction of our union, and saw the heterogeneous mixture of slavery and freedom, which entered into its composition. Hitherto it has been preserved and kept tumultuously moving, by the simple fact that the slave states had their own way in everything and so managed our affairs as to control and direct the course of the union. But as soon as the result of our election showed that the sceptre had passed into the hands of the free States then they withdrew from an association they could no longer command, and setting up for themselves, are concerting a new union, of which slavery is the cement, and the opening of the slave trade a condition. Of our future, no man can speak or possibly foretell. The labor of the free states will be first, if possible, to recall or reunite the separatists. Should this prove impossible, as it probably will, their next attempt will be, to divide the

Cotton States from the Border States, and keep together the older Union, mutilated as little as possible. What will come of this is as difficult to be foreseen as any other of our future destinies. It is not to be denied that they are in every respect dubious and full of impending dangers; it is impossible not to see and feel this. I acquiesce in these attempts to keep together the whole or as many parts of the old ship as possible, but my own judgment inclines rather to letting the whole body of the slave States drift away if they please. But at the age of ninety, no man ought to have or expect any right to his opinion, which is based upon a conviction that no permanent union between Oligarchies of Slave States and Democracies consisting of free states, can ever be durable. The present state of public affairs is therefore far from being unexpected. I have long seen the elements of political dissolution, active in our union, but had hoped it would live out my day; to all appearances, however, I, who witnessed the formation am destined to witness its close. Pardon the political aspect of this letter and believe me inseparably and without any possibility of dissolution, forever

Yours
Josiah Quincy[1]

Despite the unrest created by the Civil War, life in Faial generally went on as usual, including the continuation of visits to and from the United States. In 1861, Charles Dabney planned a trip to America with a number of family members, including Roxana Stackpole Dabney, widow of Frederick, who was leaving Bagatelle and returning to America with her three sons still in Horta. As Charles Dabney was finishing up some important business prior to leaving, William Ribeiro came up to ask him "in case there were a separation between the North and South, to try to get for him the consulate for the Southern Confederacy".[2] This request must have greatly irritated Charles Dabney because he was a strong supporter of the Union and wanted nothing of the Confederacy in the Azores.

The Dabney's ship had not even arrived in America when

the effects of the war were noticed. At sea, under still winds, they stopped by a fishing boat to buy fresh fish and received news that "There was war! Alexandria had been taken – an Army of 250,000 men raised, larger than *Buonaparte* had ever had! All Southern ports blockaded!"[3] As they entered the port of Boston, the pilot came on board with two newspapers and the latest gossip.

> Coming up the harbor, we passed close by the 'Massachusetts' on her way to Fort Pickens; we waved to them. There were regiments drilling at the Fort. We passed one small Steamer loaded with troops, going down to the Fort, and another took in her live cargo at 'Lewis' Wharf while we were lying off 'Commercial.' A band played as they pushed off 'Auld lang syne' and then struck up 'Yankee Doodle.' It was indeed stirring! Charles [Jr.] came off in a small boat, he had been drilling too. What times! Everything seemed swallowed up in the fact that all the loyal were engaged, heart and soul in the good cause of Freedom and Progress.[4]

While they were in Massachusetts, Charles and Frances Dabney visited their children who had returned to the U.S. and established their lives there, as well as the large number of friends that the family had in Boston and the surrounding area. Roxana Lewis Dabney describes the social whirl of visiting, rambling, visiting, returning, visiting that seemed to go on without end to a seemingly endless number of persons, many of whom were related in multiple ways. And, as would be expected, the major topic of conversation was the Civil War.

Charles Dabney, Jr., had already enlisted in the Army, as had a number of their friends, or sons of friends. However, the general belief was that the length of any war would be limited, with the industrial strength of the north allowing them to win.

> I remember one evening when Mr. James Freeman Clarke, who was a neighbor of C. W. D Jr.'s, was making a visit, he said he thought it take but three months to put an end to the

war. Father said he thought the North entirely underrated the resources and power of the south, he feared it would take nearer three years.[5]

Obviously, Charles Dabney was much more accurate in his estimate of the war's length. Roxana Lewis, along with her mother, sister Clara and Sallie Pomeroy decided to take a trip to Cincinnati and to visit Fan and George Oliver in Dent, Kentucky in July 1861.

> Kentucky being in a shaky state as to whether she should remain in the Union or not, made it particularly anxious as regarded Cincinnati. That day the news of the battle of Bull's Run came; we happened to be in town, and I well remember how cast down all the men seemed, and there was no use in our trying to make them take a more hopeful view; the accounts seemed so very exaggerated to some of us.[6]

Returning from visits one day, they were greeted with the news that Clara had come down with Diphtheria. The family caregiver was sick with a serious illness for second time within a year. Roxana Lewis describes the treatment that Clara received.

> I went up to see the patient, found her sitting in her chair, sewing – a necklace of bacon round her neck, she did not wish me to go into the room, but I have no fears of such things (the truth is I knew very little about contagious diseases at that time) and insisted upon shaking hands with her. I thought her looking remarkably well. She was quite delighted with Dr. Aigen's treatment. George and Fanny have always regarded Dr. A as a *horse* doctor; the other day he was describing to George his mode of treatment of Diphtheria, which seemed so reasonable to G. that he determined to try him in a case, if he ever had occasion, so when they discovered Clara's state, for she did not speak of it for some time, G. went after him. The first thing Dr. A. does is to make a little swab – a rag rolled round a piece of whalebone, puts 5

grains of sulphate of copper into an ounce of water; with the
swab he removes all the with fungi, then the patient is to gargle
with raw whiskey and with sage tea – drink whiskey and
water half and half four times a day and wear a necklace of salt
port which brings out a little white eruption. The first thing that
Clara said was that she was glad now that she had had it, because
she should know how to treat it – How exactly like her.[7]

During the next few weeks, several other members of the
family arrived in Ohio, including Charles Dabney. In late August
they made a trip to Pomeroy, Ohio, founded by Frances Dabney's
father, and where some of her family still lived. In addition,
Charles Dabney still had financial interests in the coal mine
operations there.

> We had the usual most enjoyable times with our dear re-
> latives in Pomeroy. The doubtful state of Kentucky and a pros-
> pect of a convulsed condition of the whole country for some
> time to come, induced C. W. D. to persuade Uncle George to
> come to Fayal and give up his vineyard at Dent. He and aunt
> Fan had been very happy there, and it was a sacrifice to them
> though affording us much happiness.[8]

Charles and Frances Dabney returned to the east in order to
prepare for their return to Faial. Roxana Lewis Dabney stayed
with Fan and George until they could get ready to leave. In
addition, Roxana and her sister Clara got permission from their
parents to travel to Saint Louis accompanying Clara Pope, wife
of General Pope, and accompanied by her father. Roxana kept
a diary of their trip and reported on how greatly impressed she
was by her first view of a prairie and the varieties of flowers
covering it.

One of the couples they met was Mr. And Mrs. Thomas
Yeatman, she being the daughter of General Pope. She was a
decided Abolitionist, but he was

> ...the queerest talking man I ever met with, it was impos-
> sible to make out what his real opinions were. Later he went

over to London, and the worst articles against the North that appeared in the 'London Times' were dictated by him.[9]

In her diary Roxana describes the development of early Civil War military training, weapons and new military fortifications that they saw, as well as her observations on the war. She also tells about the relationship between General Pope and General Fremont, the latter being important in taking California from Mexico. Her opinion of General Fremont was generally negative, an opinion she expresses in several references to the life of Fremont.

> Upon our way down to Carondelet, we alighted from the carriage to see a large fortification, one of the many, which are being thrown up around St. Louis. There is one, each side of the road out to Mrs. Allen's. This one we visited, was superintended by an old veteran, who had served the wars of Prussia. He could scarcely speak any English, though he said he had been in the country fifteen years. One of the grounds of complaint against Fremont is that he is surrounded by foreigners. This old veteran explained as well as he could all about the fortifications; they were beautifully made of turf. Two hundred and sixty men had been at work at one time; there were then one hundred and seventy. He showed us an eight-four pounder – Dahlgren 9 inch bore, would carry three miles, – 10 inch bore means 124 pounder.
>
> The gun-boats were interesting; we were on board of the 'Nathaniel Lion.' Carondelet is quite a place, some very quaint old French houses still remaining.
>
> Just before retiring for the night, Mr. J. Yeatman, showed me some of those photographs on glass that one must look at through a microscope – they are wonderful certainly.
>
> There were several companies of raw recruits drilling; the temporary barracks looked neat. I realized more than ever that we were at war. The state of things in that State seems a little discouraging; I cannot help wishing that Gen. Pope were in Fremont's place, a really military man must know more about these matters. We passed by Fremont's quarters on Monday;

a large house at the top of a long flight of steps – Negro waiters lounging out of the windows, plenty of soldiers about the gate. Fremont drives out with four gray horses. Mrs. Fremont is very ambitious I hear. [Mrs. Fremont was the daughter of the powerful former Senator Thomas Hart Benton][10]

From St. Louis Roxana returned to Cincinnati and then accompanied the Olivers on visits to New York, Middletown and Boston before returning to Faial.

A letter in early 1862 from Eliza Quincy, daughter of the 88-year old Josiah Quincy who was recovering from a broken hip as the result of a fall, describes the viewpoint of the liberal Boston Community, including an indictment of the British attitude towards the war.

Britannia can say like the old lady who took chloroform that 'she has lost her conscientiousness.' The English have been thought to be the friends of the slave, but I fancy it is only a small portion of the nation, as in the U. S., who are in arbou of emancipation. However, it is not a *small* portion of our people now, and the number is constantly increasing, who think the abolition of slavery – must be the cause of the end of this war. Our New England men, who have gone into the Slave States and seen the institution in is its own home, it is said, will all return abolitionists. Officers, who were conservative when they went, have changed their opinions during their campaign in the middle and southern states.[11]

The "traitors" Mason and Slidell attempting to go to Britain in December 1861 prompted the negative remarks about Britain. James M. Mason, Confederate representative to London, and John Slidell, Confederate representative to Paris, were captured at sea near the Bahamas in November 1861 and taken to Boston. Despite the seizure of the men being illegal, it was highly praised by the public and in the House of Representatives. However, the British were angry and wrote a letter demanding their release within seven days. The British Ambassador to the U. S. delayed delivering their note several days, even though he told

Secretary of State Seward about it. Feelings on both sides calmed down, and Seward renounced the action and had the men released, thereby avoiding a possible war with Great Britain.

However, not everyone shared Eliza Quincy's opinion about Britain. Charles Dabney's nephew Frederick Cunningham gives a somewhat different opinion in January 1862 of the two men going to Britain.

> It was altogether the most exciting period of the war yet. – yesterday we received the first intelligence of its having been announced in England that we intended to give them up; but as they had only just got it, we do not hear what kind of reception it would have. I am not among those who believe England desired war, I think there will be a great sense of relief throughout the land, when the cause of all anticipated difficulty is known to be removed and I doubt if anything short of another insult to the Ensign of St. George, will be likely to rouse up the British lion again. I think the episode has had the effect of awakening our own people to the position they would hold, were any such misfortune as war with Great Britain to be inevitable.

Another letter at this time from John Jeffries, one of Charles Dabney's childhood friends whom he had met again after many years, gives the same opinion about Britain, but varies considerably with Charles Dabney's opinion on the length of the war.

> There will be no war with England; the immediate threatening has passed by, and the religious element in the British Nation, declares "There *shall* be no war with America," and this is an element, which most powerfully influences the throne. Next comes the civil war of most gigantic dimensions. Before this reaches you, the strength of this rebellion will be subdued. The insurrectionary Southrons (*sic*) are a doomed people... In their folly the Seceders will not return to their allegiance and resume their rights, but madly rush on to be buried with their wicked institutions. Everything in all quarters[12]

One other letter shows the great difference in the dissemination of major news events between now and then. Nancy Dabney Brotero was isolated in mid-19th century Brazil as people in any modern country would be without a daily dose of TV, radio or newspapers covering international events.

> What a dreadful thing the war in the United States is. As I never read the papers, and as that country is very little known or talked about here, when I first heard of the civil war it seemed to me like a dream. I have seen the 'Illustrated News! Of Dec. and read some interesting articles in it and in the 'Jornal de Commercio'; so that I find that the question is far from being settled and that perhaps a war with England and France may not be impossible; how dreadful must be the consequences! It fills me with horror to think of it.[13]

In the midst of the uproar created by the beginning of the Civil War, two pieces of pleasant news arrived at the family home. The first was William Dabney having been appointed Consul to the Canary Islands. Being the youngest of the first generation, he had always had problems finding something to do in the Dabney businesses and did not have much success in any of his own business ventures. As with many of the Dabneys at this time, he had returned to the U. S. to live and try his luck.

> You will be pleased to hear that I have been appointed Consul to the Canaries much to my surprise at last. I received a telegraphic dispatch on the 10th announcing that the appointment had been made and gone to the Senate for confirmation. I have subsequently received one from Mr. Horton saying that the Senate Committee had reported favorably and no doubt the appointment would be confirmed.[14]

In a letter Charles William Dabney wrote to his cousin Charles Henry Dabney, he comments on William's appointment.

I have faith in William's success, he has experience and now that he will have the stimulus of self reliance, will develop his energies.[15]

Since the Dabneys were devout Protestants. and because Portugal was strongly Catholic, they buried their dead within the boundaries of Bagatelle, despite the fact there was an "English Cemetery" separate from the main cemetery. In 1862, Charles Dabney wrote to the State Department stating that he had applied to the Horta City Council to purchase land for a burial place for his family. The City then applied to the District Council for their concurrence.

The Horta City Council agreed to grant Charles Dabney's request and in recognition of more than half a century of philanthropic activities by the Dabney family, they gave them an area in the upper part of the Municipal Cemetery and indicated their plan to erect a monument on the site. In the northwest corner of the municipal cemetery you can find the grave markers of the Dabneys who died on the island of Faial, including those who had formerly been buried at Bagatelle. However, not until 1884 were all the burials at Bagatelle transferred to the new cemetery, which is in a corner of the main city cemetery and no longer exclusively Protestant.[16]

A year later, the official entities of the government on Faial made their official presentations that guaranteed the use of the cemetery property and erected a monument. In addition, they decided to change the name of the street where Fredonia was located to Rua Consul Dabney, the name it still bears today. Following his character of always wanting to comply with the law, Charles Dabney queried the State Department stating, "I presume that this will not come under the head of receiving presents".[17]

Although the texts are long, it is worth quoting them all to provide the official view of the Dabneys' contributions to the island and the specific events that led to these opinions.

TESTIMONIAL FROM THE SENATE OF HORTA AND OTHER GENTLEMEN; OF FAYAL, TO CHARLES W. DABNEY, ESQ., U. S. CONSUL AT FAYAL.

[Translated from an article by Roxana Dabney in "*O Fayalen-se*" of Nov. 15, 1863.]

The following extract from the records of the Senate of Hor-ta, renders it unnecessary for us to relate what took place on Tuesday last at the Protestant Cemetery of this city. This record expresses in itself more than anything we could possibly write:

TESTIMONIAL relative to the highly important services rendered by CHARLES W. DABNEY, and by his much esteemed family, in the various political crises and periods of distress, which the people of Fayal have experienced.

On the tenth day of November, in the year of our Lord one thousand eight hundred and sixty-three, there being present in the Protestant Cemetery, situated in the suburbs of this city of Horta, the Senate, and all the public functionaries and other gentlemen whose signatures are appended to this testimonial, who were invited by the Senate to be present on this occasion, the Senate ordered this testimonial to be drawn up for the purpose of making especial mention of the most timely and generous services rendered by Charles W. Dabney, Esq., Consul of the United States of North America, in this city, and by his esteemed family, in the various political crises and periods of distress, which the people of Fayal have experienced, which services cannot be too highly estimated.

In acknowledgment of these services, the Senate has pre-sented him with a lot in the aforesaid cemetery, containing about fifteen hundred square feet; and to further perpetuate the gratitude of the people of Fayal, has also caused a monu-ment to be erected in which a copy of this testimonial is to be deposited. Another, copy will be delivered to the aforesaid Charles W. Dabney, Esq., together with – the key of the monu-ment, by a committee of the Senate, in the name of the Senate as representatives of the people of Fayal. This day has been selected, as being the first anniversary of the death of the much esteemed and lamented wife of the said Charles W. Dabney, Esq., Mrs. Frances Dabney, whose loss the people of Fayal can never recall without deep and heartfelt sorrow. We also desire to record hereby the following as some of the most prominent of the services referred to:

In the year 1847, on the occasion of the purchase of the cargo of the American brig "Tally Ho" (which consisted of corn), for the relief of the inhabitants of Fayal, he was obliged to pay the ship owners twelve hundred and fifty dollars, on account of a misunderstanding between them and the owners of the corn, which resulted in the latter refusing to pay freight, said sum being one third part of the freight.

In the year 1857, when the ship "Adrian's" Captain was induced to sell a part of the cargo of corn at this port (to alleviate the distress then existing through scarcity of cereals), he assumed the responsibility of paying the same price therefore, which it would have brought at its port of destination.

In the year 1857, when a portion of the cargo of the American barque "North Sea" amounting to nearly ten thousand bushels of wheat, was sold at this port (for the same reason as the preceding), he assumed in the same way the responsibility of purchasing the wheat at the same price which it would have brought at its port of destination, -being always ready to assume the heaviest responsibilities in performing acts of humanity in periods of distress.

He also, in the year 1858, distributed (at his own expense) wheat and Indian corn to eight hundred of the most indigent inhabitants of Pico, each one receiving daily half a pound, for the period of four months, and he also distributed a like amount to an equal number of the inhabitants of Fayal.

In the year 1859, he made an appeal to the generosity of his friends and countrymen in Boston, the result of which was a subscription, sufficient to purchase ten thousand bushels of corn (the sale of the bags in which the same was transported realizing nearly five hundred dollars). This corn was transported in the barque "Azor" which he owned, free of cost; and he also refused to accept any compensation for the use of his granaries, and landed the corn at his own expense.

In the years 1858 and 1859, he imported over 43,000 bushels of corn, adjusting the rate of sale nearly to that of cost. The brig "Newsboy " happening to arrive here on a Sunday, with nearly tell thousand bushels of corn, at a time when there was not a single grain of corn for sale, it was landed that same day, and immediately, offered for sale in small quantities, at the rate of five hundred and sixty "reis" per "alqueire," the last cargo having been sold at the rate of seven hundred and twenty "reis."

He has always been ready to aid the local authorities by placing his; vessels at their disposal, as was the case in the year 1856, and at other periods of dangerous political dissensions. Always scrupulously and invariably circumspect as regards the politics of this country, in all crises since the year 1826; serving as mediator between the contending parties, and having it in his power, from his position, to alleviate in many instances cases of peculiar suffering.

(Signed) A. J. FERREIRA ROCHA, *President of the Senate.*
JOSÉ PAMPLONA M. CORTE REAL, *Vice President.*
JOAQUIN P. DE LACERDA.
F. P. DE LACERDA COSTA REBFLLO.
JOAO CARVALHO DE MEDEIROS.
ANTONIO JOSÉ VIEIRA SANTA RITA, *Civil Governor.*
ANTONIO DA TERRA PINHEIRO, *Chief Dignitary of the Church.*
MIGUEL STREET D'ARRIAGA, *Secretary General.*
JOSÉ D'ARRAGAO MORAES, *Judge.*
CHRISTIANO F. D'ARRAGAO MORAES, *Deputy Attorney- -General.*
LAUREANO PEREIRA DA SILVA, *Mayor's Substitute.*
DR. MANOEL F. DE MEDEIROS.
MANOEL MARIA DE TERRA BRUM.
FRANCISCO C. DA SILVA RFIS.
MANOEL JOSÉ SEQUEIRA.
BARON OF ST. ANNA [MANOEL GUERRA].
ROBERTO AUGUSTO DE MESQUITA HENRIQUES.
JOAO JOSÉ DA CUNHA.
MANOEL VICTOR DE SEQUFIRA, *Clerk of the Senate.*

Next in order, His Excellency the Governor, A. J. Vieira Santa Rita, deposited a copy of the testimonial in the niche of the monument, after which Senator Francisco Peixote de Lacerda Costa Rebello made the following address:

Gentlemen – The act at which we have assisted, this demonstration of pure gratitude, ought to convince us that by beneficence can we best win the hearts of our fellow-men; that beneficence is always rewarded by the affection, esteem, and respect of those who have been its objects. A generous man is always regarded by society with sentiments of esteem, and his acts of generosity always applauded by all feeling hearts. Such is the lot of the virtuous and much esteemed Dabney family; and if great have been the benefits received by the needy at all times from the generous hearts of this family, certainly the public gratitude awarded them in return, has been equally great. The people of Fayal feel that they do themselves honor on this occasion by acknowledging the obligations of gratitude under which they have been placed; more especially since those bitter days when the population of this island struggled with famine, the severity of which was mitigated by the aid received from the United States of America, through the appeal and influence of the American Consul, C. W. Dabney, and his much esteemed and lamented wife, Mrs. Frances Dabney. These are services, which cannot be sufficiently rewarded in this world, and only in the world to come, can they receive their full and just reward. In the meantime, the Senate of this district, interpreting the sentiments of the people which they represent, have, in order to perpetuate the memory of facts so worthy of honour, testified the gratitude of the people, by bestowing this land upon the Dabney family, as a place of sepulture, and have caused a hasty enumeration of such timely, important and humane services to be inscribed upon their books of record, and have also given to "Beleago Street," which leads to the residence of the much esteemed family, the name of "Consul Dabney Street." In this laudable endeavor, the Senate has been actively assisted by a distinguished and illustrious committee, and by His Ex. A. J. Vieira Santa Rita, who so admirably administers the government of this district, actively striving for the material improvement of the country, as well as for the moral elevation of the people.

Assembled here today in this place, where the highest and the lowest rest side by side in perfect equality; feeling that any day we may be called to rest in a similar place ourselves, we trust that these examples of the most lofty civic virtues, and of the most deserved public gratitude will not be lost upon posterity.

Accept gentlemen, the cordial acknowledgments of the Senate of Horta for your presence, which has contributed so much to the solemnity of this occasion.

At the conclusion of the foregoing address, the committee appointed by the Senate, consisting of its President, Vice-President and Senator Francisco Peixote de Lacerda Costs Rebello, proceeded to the residence of Charles W. Dabney Esq., and delivered into his hands another copy of the testimonial, together with the key of the urn, and were received by that worthy gentleman with the urbanity and extreme politeness, which so highly distinguished him. When the President of the Senate placed in his hands, the copy of the testimonial and the key of the niche, he was so much moved as hardly to be able to express his acknowledgments, but handed to the President a paper of the following tenor: –

Gentlemen, the monument which you have caused to be erected, and the record inscribed in the municipal archives, to commemorate the services, which by the grace of God, I have been able to offer to the people of this district and of the Island of St. George, in periods of distress, are justly appreciated by me and by all the members of my family. The day selected by you for this ceremony, is a proof of the delicacy of your sentiments, and that you know how to appreciate mine. It struck a chord which vibrated at once to my inmost being. There can be nothing more touching to me than so significant a compliment paid to the memory of her, whom it, life I loved most, and whose memory I most fondly cherish. Your proceedings have placed me in a position, of which I can show my appreciation only by saying, – happy the man who finds himself the object of such demonstrations, and who knows bow to appreciate them; adding, also, that I am grateful to God, and eminently indebted to you, worthy representatives of the people of Fayal, for all the evidences you have been pleased to afford me of their consideration and kindness. I pray that God may-grant you happiness.

(Signed) C. W. DABNEY.

And then follow the other signatures given above.

The Senate having returned to the Municipal Chambers, ordered this record to be closed and signed by the President and Senators present, in my presence.

MANOEL VICTOR DE SEQUEIRA, Clerk of the Senate.

PROCLAMATION.
The Municipal Chamber of Horta publishes the following proclamation, received from the Civil Governor of this city:
Whereas, the Senate Chamber of Horta has forwarded to me an official communication, bearing date the 10th Day of this month of October, requesting that the street formerly known as "Beleago Street" may on and after the tenth day of November next, be styled 14 Consul Dabney Street," on account of the very great services rendered by Charles William Dabney and his honored family to the people of this district, in periods of distress:
Now, therefore, I, Antonio Jose' Vieira Santa Rita, Conselheiro, Civil Governor of the District of Horta, in consideration of the commendable sentiments of gratitude, which prompted the Senate of Horta to forward me this petition, and dispensing the power which the law permits me, do hereby declare that "Beleago Street" shall hereafter be styled "Consul Dabney Street". By this proclamation those whose duty it is to see this purpose carried out will be duly notified.
Signed and sealed in this Government office of Horta, on the 22d. day of October in the year of our Lord 1863.

(Signed) ANTONIO JOSÉ VIERA SANTA RITA.

The above proclamation is hereby made public.

Signed and sealed in the Municipal Chamber of Horta on the 26th day of Oct. in the year of our Lord 1863.

JOSÉ PAMPELONA MONIZ CORTE REAL, Acting President.
MANOEL VICTOR DE SEQUEIRA,

Clerk of the Senate.[18]

Charles Dabney sent a letter of thanks in response to the action of the local government.

The Title, which you have been pleased to bestow upon me excites sentiments of profound gratitude. True philanthropy always endeavors to conceal itself from Public knowledge, but we are so constituted that only those who devote themselves entirely to study and meditation, can fail to be moved when their acts are noted and praised publicly. The offering of a place of sepulture for the ashes of myself and family is extremely touching, and I find it difficult to express all I would, to your Excellencies and to the Exmo. Sr. José Vieira Sta. Rita, most worthy Civil Governor of this district, in whose mind arose the idea so cordially adopted by yourselves and the Illmos. Senrs. Members of the District Council, who contributed with their approval. This Title will be always considered by me the most honorable one that could have been conferred upon me; and will have the effect of an incentive to those who come after me, to merit the consideration so kindly manifested toward me on this day.[19]

Even while the laudatory actions were taking place on Faial, the United States Civil War was not far from anyone's thoughts. One reminder arrived around noon on February 23, 1862,

...a Steamer came in with the Confederate flag flying! Father was the first to discover her, and give the alarm. We took her at first for a privateer, but she is a merchantman – propeller – the 'Annie Childes' from Charleston reported, but it is more probable from N. Carolina (from the nature of her cargo), to Liverpool. They wished to consign to the British Consul, but Lloyd's Agent has taken the consignment. Great indignation all round, so Mrs. And Miss Maynard informed us.[20]

The ship remained in Horta for a week. During this period there was a major storm; holes were bored through the bottom of an American ship, but were plugged before it could sink. The passengers of the rebel steamer had dinner with the British Consul, and, the Dabneys had a dinner party at which one of the English Captains invited said that "all the sympathies of the English are with the South."[21] On Sunday, March 2, 1862.

> The Secession steamer left, with the Portuguese flag at her fore and a very large English flag at her main. It was in consequence of this, I suppose that the English Steamer's band played 'Dixie'.[22]

The Civil War remained the big news carried in the letters crossing between the Azores and Massachusetts. However, many of the events that were reported were considered of major importance at the time, but are no longer commonly known due to the vast number of battles that took place over the four years. An example is the capture of Fort Donelson on the Cumberland in Tennessee, which Roxana Lewis felt "was glorious! I wanted to shout Glory Hallelujah,"[23] but is known primarily among Civil War buffs. A letter from Clara Pope discusses two major events.

> The more we hear about Manassas and its wooden guns and inefficient fortifications the more bitter is the feeling of mortification, that for so many months it should have held at bay such an army as that on the Potomac. It is said the soldiers shed tears when they found what the bug-bear really was. I have often thought of what uncle Charles [Dabney] said last summer about the 'Merrimac' and what a terrible engine of destruction she might prove. If it had not bee for the little 'Monitor,' his words would have been realized; it was almost by chance that

the 'Monitor' reached Hampton Roads in time, but the 'Merrimac's' one day of fearful execution will never be forgotten by hundreds of bereaved families. After all, the first trial of iron clad vessels of war has been made in America, a most unenviable distinction. I suppose it will create an entire revolution in the Navies of the world, and I hope it will be a warning to our Government.[24]

As a forerunner of events to come, Charles Dabney had to make a decision about providing coal to Confederate ships that stopped in Horta to take on supplies. His decision was not to provide coal for their steamers, a decision that distressed the Confederacy. In fact, this was used as a basis by Captain Semmes of the Confederate warship Alabama, who wreaked havoc among Union ships in the Azores, to seek out Dabney ships in particular.

> Father after due reflection and consultation with his 'aides' decided not to furnish coal to the 'Stanway' particularly as Sam found they were bound to Nassau (a depot for the South), and they reported for *St. Thomas*. Sam saw the manifest at the Custom House. I never saw Father more tried, of course he runs much risk, for they may come upon Mr. Camroux for thousands of pounds. She went to Terceira.[25]

Complicating the situation was the fact that Mr. Camroux, the Dabney agent in Britain, was taking action that went against Charles Dabney's policy not to supply coal.

> At the beginning of the Civil War, his agent in London, Mr. F.R. Camroux was so imprudent as to agree that C. W. D. would supply coal to two steamers then fitting out in England to run our blockade, the first of the large fleet sent overseas for this purpose. On their arrival at Fayal, C. W. D suspecting their destination, refused to furnish them with the coal, preferring to forfeit the penalty of the breech of contract viz. two hundred pounds, which had been paid by his agent for his account. Besides this he paid to two other Fayalese, holding coal, six

hundred dollars and three hundred dollars, respectively, to keep them from selling to the two steamers and during the continuation of the War he did all in his power to prevent privateers or blockade runners from obtaining coal in Fayal.[26]

Charles Dabney wrote a letter to Mr. Camroux expressing his displeasure in the action taken.

> My appreciation of your unvarying friendship for upwards of thirty years, is a very strong tie; I therefore shall merely remark that I cannot account for this act of yours. I should have thought that an application to supply even one Steamer (unless you were very certain of her being inoffensive) bound to the neighborhood of the Southern States, would have been rejected as it might compromise me.[27]

The year 1862 began as 1861 had ended, with the continuation of the American Civil War, yet normal, everyday life persisted on Faial. However, by the end of the year, Roxana Lewis Dabney referred to it as "this most eventful year in our lives."[28]

Some of the news was happy, such as the action of the American Geographical and Statistical Society at its May 1 meeting.

> At a meeting of the Society held this evening Joseph P. Thompson, V. President in the Chair-
> On the recommendation of the Council, Charles W. Dabney, U. S. Consul to Fayal, was duly constituted and declared to be an Ex-Officio Member of the Society.[29]

Other news was not as good, such as that concerning the war. One of the items that arrived was a first-hand report on the aftermath of Harper's Ferry, as described in a letter by their aunt Clara Horton.

> ...We took the Balt & Ohio railroad. This has recently been in Rebel hands, that is from Harper's Ferry to Cumberland, and showed traces of war's decision. They fired Harper's Ferry, Martinsburg and Hancock; all along the road were the

wrecks of locomotives, and cars, and all the little streams were full of car wheels, rendered useless by fire. The track had been torn up and heaps of charred and blackened crossties lay on every side. The fences were all destroyed and in short it was a scene of ruin.[30]

In September of 1862, Charles Dabney, Jr., was requested for active duty as a Captain of Company B, 4th Battalion of the 44th Regiment of Massachusetts Volunteers. It was with mixed emotions that he made the decision to leave his family, but he decided to go and "since my decision was made amid all the desolation of heart, which has at time almost overwhelmed me, I have never felt that the decision was wrong, nor do I think has Susan."[31]

Susan Oliver Dabney showed her support for the regiment by composing a Battle Hymn for it, "which they seem to like."[32] The melody was that of the "Battle Hymn of the Republic" (which was taken from "John Brown's Body"), but the words had a more personal reference to the soldiers of the 44th regiment.[33] Susan Oliver Dabney wrote the Regiment's Hymn in the same year (1862) as the "Battle Hymn of the Republic" was written by Julia Ward Howe, who was also involved with the Unitarian Church in New England and had some of the same friends and acquaintances as the Dabneys.

The Dabneys of Faial and Massachusetts were strong believers in the cause of the Union and the abolition of slavery.[34] One consequence of this was that the Dabneys of Virginia took offense at the northern branch's beliefs, and the relationship between the two branches of the family, which had not been strong, was virtually eliminated. In a letter to his parents, Charles Dabney, Jr., expresses his, and the family's opinion on the reasons for the war.

> However, we men of this day in America are called upon to do the great work of this country, – and God grant us stout hearts and earnest souls to do it with. Ours will be recognized hereafter as a great era in the world's history, and I trust that posterity will not have cause to say that we were unequal to the occasion.[35]

Charles Dabney, Jr., went for training in New Hampshire, where he and his wife Susan were able to live with a farm family near the encampment.

> Here we are amongst the hills of New Hampshire in a regular old farm house (painted red) with a fine specimen of a Yankee farmer's family – consisting of the old couple and two children, a youth of twenty and a girl of about twelve years. I confess that I had a good many misgivings, as Susan had been so far from strong, and I felt she needed good food as well as good air; food in these farm houses, generally meaning bread made with saleratus [baking soda], plenty of pale crusted pies, pickles, doughnuts, poor vegetables and no meat. At first I was disappointed in the situation, not finding it as high as had been said, however, the air is fine. The fare though better than I feared, still verges upon the objectionable, but we have good bread, butter and milk; everything is neat and nice and all are anxious to make us comfortable.[36]

Here he worked with his regiment, which he believed "is the crack one of the nine months men."[37]

> (...) and the men take care of their discipline themselves, as they put any man in Coventry, who does not behave himself. We have as privates thirty or forty graduates of Harvard. Tuttle the Astronomer, and one of the best Observers in the country, is also in the ranks. One of the drummers is a young man who has been studying music for two or three years in Europe – and so we go. The material of the regiment consists mostly of young men, from 18-25 years of age; almost all of good education and all active and intelligent. They learn very rapidly and all we want is a little time to harden their muscles, to make them one of the best regiments of light troops that can be got up. It is our intention to instruct them properly in the use of the Enfield (we have the last thousand the State had) and this department will fall to me, and as you may suppose I shall be much interested in it.[38]

Charles Dabney, Jr. , described his first war adventures in a letter to his family, which began with a march to Boston after training was over. They stopped there for an hour on Boston Common to say goodbye to their friends and then proceeded on to Battery Wharf. He reported that he had never seen "the streets and Common more thronged than they were that day, even to see the Prince of Wales."[39] Between their troops and the 3rd Massachusetts, 1,500 men were loaded on a ship meant to hold 1,000 comfortably. The Massachusetts troops arrived in Washington, North Carolina, and were prepared for a "secret expedition"[40] to...

> cut off two regiments of the enemy, which were said to be down near Plymouth. This part of the plan failed, owing proba-bly to the delay in our overland forces reaching Washington. An-other object was to take the battery at Rainbow Bluff and destroy two iron clad gun boats said to be building at Hamilton. The for-mer was accomplished, and there was no sign of the latter.[41]

On the way they had skirmishes with the "enemy's pickets" and crossed a ford 80-100 yards wide in waist-deep water while under light fire. They lined up to the left of the 24th Massachusetts to advance on an enemy battery in a file and spent the night in "rifle pits from which we had driven them." The next morning they marched until they arrived in Williamston on the Roanoke River and then on to Hamilton, expecting to meet the Confederate troops. "The men were getting very footsore and weary, and their food was insufficient."[42]

The next morning they arrived at the battery at Rainbow Bluff, which was deserted, and they went on the Hamilton. The next day they went toward Tarboro to within five of six miles of a large force of enemy troops, spent the night and marched back.

> It was a fearful march and I do not like to think of it; the men actually fell down in their ranks from exhaustion and the poor fellows became so haggard, hollow-eyed and changed by fa-tigue and want of proper nourishment that I could scarcely recognize some of them.[43]

They finally got back to their port of entry two weeks after leaving. Two days later they arrived by ship back at their camp in New Hampshire. Charles Dabney, Jr., felt that

> It was a severe ordeal to expose new troops to – the marching being as severe as anything of the kind that has been done on the Potomac, but without the same amount of fighting, whilst the engagement at Smitheric's creek or Rawls Mills was of a nature to try the nerves of the best of veterans – as Gen. Foster himself admitted to us.[44]

Charles Dabney, Jr., was able to return to as much a civilian life as was possible until the Civil War was finally over. He invested some of his time in support of General McClellan's bid for nomination as president.

The Dabneys knew General George McClellan and his family and supported his career and actions, even though others were critical of him. Lincoln had appointed McClellan head of the Army of the Potomac in 1861, but

> ...he was also cautious – exceedingly cautious – it seemed, lethargic. McClellan was over impressed by his reasonable conviction that the South would be a very hard nut to crack.[45]

McClellan was well liked by his troops, and the training he gave them created a high degree of professionalism. "But his caution, his procrastination, his reluctance to move" exasperated most senior politicians, but Lincoln overlooked these faults. Lincoln's staff was demanding more action, and he finally had to give in and had McClellan take his troops to capture Richmond. After a number of skirmishes which culminated in Lee hitting his flank in the Seven Days' Battles (25 June-1 July 1862), Lee defeated McClellan's Army of the Potomac. Several months later McClellan was given another army, and he faced Lee at the battle at Antietam Creek. McClellan lost 12,000 men in his uphill charge and caused Lee to lose the same number, resulting in the bloodiest day of the war, but Lee still held the field at the end of the day. This time Lincoln finally dismissed McClellan for good.

However, the Dabneys supported him against his critics, and Roxana agreed with the opinion printed in the *World* that "if all true, McClellan has been shamefully and criminally thwarted and trammelled; but how difficult to know the truth."

In 1864, the Democratic Party nominated McClellan on a platform that renounced the war, however he did not completely accept the rest of its provisions. In a letter to his sisters, Charles Dabney, Jr., gives his opinion of McClellan's actions.

> I rejoice to say that a great change has taken place within a few weeks. Just before the Chicago Convention there seemed to be a feeling of apathy and despondency over the community generally. Our armies in Georgia and Virginia seemed to be at a dead lock with the enemy, and no prospect of doing much this autumn. Recruiting was not brisk and the draft impending. Moreover, there was an anxious feeling about what was impending in Chicago. From the time that the Chicago platform was enunciated and McClellan accepted the nomination, the spirit of the people seemed to rise up against both.[46]

> We feel generally that McClellan has injured himself as a man, by accepting the nomination as he has, for he either intends to betray his party or the people, it being certain that the people would not vote for him, except for the views implied in his letter, which is entirely at variance with the fundamental "plank " in the platform of the party who nominated him.[47]

> Susan will give you a full account of our visit in Middletown with the McClellans &c. I was glad to see him, though had I read what I have since about his course as Leader of our Armies I should have felt less inclined to do so. We had a very happy visit however... Our Election on the 8th Nov. was all that could have been desired. With all the confidence which we felt, one could not help a little nervous anxiety towards the last it, view of the momentous issue involved; and the relief was immense when it was all over and the desired result so satisfactorily attained.[48]

Far from the war, politics and the U. S., the Dabneys also were touched by tragedy as the year 1862 drew to a close. The Dabney family was struck by "terribly sad times", with three deaths during the month of November. The deaths not only stunned the Dabney family, but also had a great emotional impact on everyone on Faial who knew the family.

The first death was that of six-year old Richard Alsop Dabney, known as Dickie, who was the third child of Samuel Wyllys and Harriet Webster Dabney. For several days he had been suffering from a sore throat, which turned out to be diphtheria, which was prevalent in the islands at the time and had been at a high level in the U.S. for four years.[49]

> Wed. 5th Nov. Dear little Dickie left us a little after eight this morning. How miraculously he escaped from his fall down here last year! He was a fine, interesting child, full of health and spirits, such hones blue eyes and the sweetest expression about his mouth when he smiled. Mother is better to-day, but the shock is very bad for her. Dickie was very fond of his grandmother, she had often spoken of the manner in which he would gaze at her, fix those clear blue eyes upon her.[50]

Less than a week later,

> Mother left us on the 10th November, a most beautiful sort of Indian summer day, calm and peaceful, we remained all day at Mt. Da Guia, and all moved up to 'Fredonia,' in the twilight. All our particular friends had been down, Mr. and Mrs. D'Orey and others. What an influence Mother exerted from her retired little niche; I doubt if there is a person on the Island who would be more generally lamented.[51]

Frances Alsop Pomeroy Dabney, wife of Charles Dabney for 43 years, had not been well for a long time, although there is no specific reference to the problem. She was 65 years old when she died.

The young children had been gathered up and sent down to the "Souza" house not far below Fredonia. It was here that

five-year old Hattie, Harriet Frederica, fourth child of Samuel
and Harriet Dabney was stricken with diphtheria and died in the
early morning of November 12.

> She had been in distress and then suddenly a calm came
> over her, she sat up in bed and opened her eyes and a look
> of awe and wonder came into them – and then such a look
> of rapture, light seemed to stream from them, that her mother
> and I kneeling each side of the couch that we too had a glimpse
> into the beyond; we were awestruck! No one who could have
> witnessed the child's death bed could doubt there was another
> Life beyond.[52]

These three deaths in a one week period – Samuel and Harriet
losing two young children, Samuel and his siblings a mother
and Charles Dabney losing his wife and two grandchildren – dev-
astated the Dabneys on Faial and elsewhere. The deaths also
had a great impact on all those who knew the Dabneys on Faial,
which was virtually the entire population, as well as on the
other islands in the Azores and extended the length of the shipping lanes along which the Dabney ships sailed, in addition to
the crews on those that had visited Horta and partaken of Dabney
hospitality.

There was a large outpouring of sympathy from the wide-
spread community of the Dabney family and friends, as well as
from those who were only casually acquainted with Frances
Dabney, but in some way had been affected by her and felt "the
world is poorer now that she is gone."[53]

The weekly newspaper *Fayalense* published an obituary on
Sunday November 16, which paints a poignant picture of the
three deaths.

> At midnight of the 9th to 10th, the Exma. Sra. Dona Francisca
> Dabney consort of the Illmo. Sr. Carlos Guilherme Dabney,
> Consul of the United States in the Azores died.
>
> Death in robbing the world of this lady, inflicted a terrible
> and cruel blow upon all, who had the happiness of knowing
> her; upon so may poor, friendless ones and especially upon

her family, who loved her so extremely. The most that we could say about her, could not be attributed to flattery, as her exemplary mode of life was generally known in the City, and her multiplied acts of charity, such charity as is enjoined by the Scriptures, testified to the generous qualities of her heart. It is not many years since the population of this Island owed her a singular favor. When famine seemed more and more threatening, at her request a loaf of the bread made of the wild arrowroot ('jarro') was sent to Boston and the sight of this produced the marvellous results of which we were witnesses. Her delicate, womanly instinct comprehended, that by these means, many tears would be dried, many pains alleviated, and many unfortunate ones be snatched from the talons of famine and death.

Such existences, which do so much for humanity, and are the delight and comfort of a family, which has the happiness of possessing them, ought not to end, but since death is the sad end of all humanity, and the Divinity, before which we are all summoned, allows no exemption from it, we can only weep with the family, and with all the poor people, who have met with such a loss, and shed upon her grave tears of grief and 'Saudade.'

As if this blow, which came upon the sudden death of one of her grandchildren (a son of Mr. Samuel Dabney) were not sufficient pain for the family, God saw fit to try them still further by the death of a little girl (daughter of Mr. Samuel Dabney) five years of age, at 6 a.m. on the 12th It suggests the thought that the death of these two grandchildren, whose horizon of life, but a few days since seemed so expanded, were destined by the Divinity, to usher their Grandmother into the 'Celestial Mansions' with their white wings of innocence, one proceeding, the other following.[54]

This image of Frances Dabney being escorted into heaven by her two angel grandchildren was picked up and used by a number of people in their reflections on the deaths. A letter from Charles Dabney, Jr., to his brother Sam gives an indication of how the family pulled together in the face of adversity.

I have no words in which to express to you and Harriet the sorrow and the sympathy I feel for you in the loss of you two sweet little children. I had within a few days heard of your first loss and was about to write to you this morning, when I received letters telling me that you were again stricken, and that our dear Mother had passed away from earth. It seems an accumulation of trial, which I find it difficult for my mind to compass, but it comes in strangely with the temper of our present times, which seem so much out of joint. I will not attempt to offer consolation in your affliction, no human power can furnish that, it comes from above and with time will soften the pain. I know that the children who are left can never fill the gap caused by those who are taken, but they comfort, and when it would seem as if nothing else could; and I feel that grace will be given you to bear your trial, that it will be sanctified to you.

As to the loss we have all suffered in our dear Mother's death, I feel that no words of mine are needed to enlarge upon it. It seems like the breaking up of our old boyish life, with all its happy memories, in which her sweet influence was so blessed, with the thoughts of which she was so closely associated; but grieving for her loss, I feel that it is still more yours, from whose daily life this light has gone out; but the loving bond of brothers and sisters will be a stay and a comfort to each other in this hour of affliction, under God's kind providence; and I trust that He will not yet cut me out of the sheaf, but that I may yet again on earth know the happiness of this sweet intercourse.[55]

In a letter to his cousin Frank Cunningham, Charles Dabney expresses his feelings on his wife's death, as well as the manner in which he dealt with it.

My greatest comfort is in reviewing the happiness, of which she was the primary cause. I have often heard of persons whose fortune has declined, living on the memory of the past; that kind of memory can only be productive of sorrow and regret; whereas the memory connected with my most excellent wife impresses me constantly with gratitude for having been so favoured, combined with the belief that *she* is happy! The Almighty has seen fit to remove her from our midst, but he has most benignantly disposed my mind to bear what otherwise would have crushed me; and to bear in mind that she has left me her share in all those we both loved, which next to the belief that she is receiving the reward of her exemplary conduct is my greatest source of happiness.[56]

All of Charles Dabney's feelings about his wife are summarized in the inscription that he had put on her gravestone – *Unsurpassed*.[57] An entry in the journal of Roxana Dabney summarizes the feelings of the family and the impact that the deaths would have on their future.

A new era begins for us all, though as yet we do not realize it; we are stunned as it were; Death this time seems to have come like a tornado; it seemed at one time as if it would carry everything before it; it did take the 'Pride of our Grove,' with the two tender saplings.[58]

Notes:

[1] *Annals of the Dabney Family on Fayal*, Roxana Lewis Dabney, p. 964.

[2] Roxana Lewis Dabney, *Annals*, p. 968

[3] Roxana Lewis Dabney, *Annals*, p.970.

[4] Roxana Lewis Dabney, *Annals*, p. 970.

[5] Roxana Lewis Dabney, *Annals*, p. 973-74.

[6] Roxana Lewis Dabney, *Annals*, p. 975.

[7] Roxana Lewis Dabney, *Annals*, p. 976.

[8] Roxana Lewis Dabney, *Annals*, p. 979.

[9] Roxana Lewis Dabney, *Annals*, p. 985.

[10] Roxana Lewis Dabney, *Annals*, p. 986-7.

[11] Roxana Lewis Dabney, *Annals*, p. 991.

[12] Roxana Lewis Dabney, *Annals*, p. 996.

[13] Roxana Lewis Dabney, *Annals*, p. 998-9.

[14] Roxana Lewis Dabney, *Annals*, p. 997.

[15] Roxana Lewis Dabney, *Annals*, p. 1146.

[16] "Diary of Roxana Lewis Dabney", Massachusetts Historical Society Microfilm, Roll 2, March 1881 & November 1884.

[17] Document 68, United States National Archives, Microfilm T203, Roll 5, January 1, 1858 – November 9, 1863.

[18] Roxana Lewis Dabney, *Annals*, p. 1152-1156.

[19] Roxana Lewis Dabney, *Annals*, p. 999.

[20] Roxana Lewis Dabney, *Annals*, p. 1000.

[21] Roxana Lewis Dabney, *Annals*, p. 1002.

[22] Roxana Lewis Dabney, *Annals*, p. 1003.

[23] Roxana Lewis Dabney, *Annals*, p. 1007.

[24] Roxana Lewis Dabney, *Annals*, p. 1005.

[25] Roxana Lewis Dabney, *Annals*, p. 1009.

[26] Dabney, Rose Forbes, *Fayal Dabneys*, n. p.: The Author, 1931, p 65.

[27] Roxana Lewis Dabney, *Annals*, p. 1023.

[28] Roxana Lewis Dabney, *Annals*, p. 1074.

[29] Roxana Lewis Dabney, *Annals*, p. 1022.

[30] Roxana Lewis Dabney, *Annals*, p. 1021.

[31] Roxana Lewis Dabney, *Annals*, p. 1044.

[32] Roxana Lewis Dabney, *Annals*, p. 1078.

[33] Roxana Lewis Dabney, *Annals*, p. 1046-7.

[34] Roxana Lewis Dabney, *Annals*, p. 1051-2.

[35] Roxana Lewis Dabney, *Annals*, p. 1044.

[36] Roxana Lewis Dabney, *Annals*, p. 1051.

[37] Roxana Lewis Dabney, *Annals*, p. 1053.

[38] Roxana Lewis Dabney, *Annals*, p. 1054.

[39] Roxana Lewis Dabney, *Annals*, p. 1078.

[40] Roxana Lewis Dabney, *Annals*, p. 1079.

[41] Roxana Lewis Dabney, *Annals*, p. 1082.

[42] Roxana Lewis Dabney, *Annals*, p. 1080.

[43] Roxana Lewis Dabney, *Annals*, p. 1081-82.

[44] Roxana Lewis Dabney, *Annals*, p. 1082.

[45] Hugh Brogan, *The Penguin History of the United States of America*, Penguin Books, London, 1985, p. 333.

[46] Roxana Lewis Dabney, *Annals*, p. 1187.

[47] Roxana Lewis Dabney, *Annals*, p. 1187.

[48] Roxana Lewis Dabney, *Annals*, p. 1188.

[49] Roxana Lewis Dabney, *Annals*, p. 1087.

[50] Roxana Lewis Dabney, *Annals*, p. 1067.

[51] Roxana Lewis Dabney, *Annals*, p. 1068.

[52] Roxana Lewis Dabney, *Annals*, p. 1069.

[53] Roxana Lewis Dabney, *Annals*, p. 1088.

[54] Roxana Lewis Dabney, *Annals*, p. 1070-71.

[55] Roxana Lewis Dabney, *Annals*, p. 1084-85.

[56] Roxana Lewis Dabney, *Annals*, p. 1089.

[57] Dabney, Rose Forbes, *Fayal Dabneys*, 51.

[58] Roxana Lewis Dabney, *Annals*, p. 1068.

16 – THE ALABAMA ATTACKS

The Civil War continued its destruction on the American continent, and Atlantic trade continued under the vigilant eyes of Union and Confederate warships trying to protect their compatriots and destroy the enemy. The Dabney ships safely continued their shuttle between the Azores and Boston carrying their customary passengers and merchandise.

Charles Dabney's efforts to keep Confederate ships from receiving coal at Faial were successful, but the Confederate ships were still able to obtain it, even in the Azores. Two letters from Assistant Secretary of State Seward refer to this and the financial losses the Dabney businesses suffered.

DEPARTMENT OF STATE,
WASHINGTON, Feb. 11th, 1863.
C. W. DABNEY Esq., U. S. Consul at Fayal:
Sir, – The Department has been informed that British vessels trading with Terceira, St. Michaels and Flores, have recently been in the habit of carrying coal to those islands, with the object, as it is supposed, of furnishing it to piratical privateers, or to steamers intending to run the blockade. This indication taken in connection with others, exhibits an apparent purpose of making those islands, perhaps alternating with the Cape de Verdes, the rendezvous for a contraband trade and for armed cruisers to prey upon our commerce. You will see therefore, the expediency and necessity, that our consular agents in those islands should be men of active intelligence, undoubted loyalty, discretion and experience and decision to fill their offices properly, since they may be called upon to act on their own responsibility, and before they are able to receive from you the special and needful instructions, which yon are so well qualified to give.

Entertaining, therefore, entire confidence in your own efficiency and loyal devotion, the Department will be pleased that you will inspire your agents in those islands with something of your own patriotic zeal, and urge them to vigilance in the discharge of their official duties.

I am Sir, & c.
F. W. SEWARD, *Asst. Sec.*

DEPARTMENT OF STATE,
WASHINGTON, April 23d, 1863.
C. W. DABNEY, Esq.

Sir, – It gives the Department much pleasure to transmit to you a copy of a communication received this morning, from the Secretary of the Navy, in which he regrets that the "zeal and loyalty exhibited by you in serving the interest of your country should have been the occasion of your suffering pecuniary loss."

I am Sir, & c.,
F. W. SEWARD, *Asst. Sec*[1].

News of the Civil War continued to arrive in Horta. Those that Roxana considered the most noteworthy for the Dabneys were recorded in her Diary at the end of 1862.

The news of Burnside's defeat was dreadful, but after all it was not quite so bad as we at first supposed, still the loss of life at Fredericksburg was fearful! I had a letter from Mrs. Higginson. Mr. H. is heart and soul in his coloured regiment at Beaufort; he is much pleased with them. The War! We do not hear much that is encouraging certainly – and the escape of the 'Alabama' from the 'San Jacinto' at Martinique is most aggravating. If the French authorities had not lent themselves to it, she would not have escaped.[2]

The Dabney's family friend Frank Higginson was a 1ˢᵗ Lt. In the 54ᵗʰ Massachusetts regiment under Colonel Shaw. This was the much-distinguished "colored" regiment during the Civil War, which was the subject of the 1989 film "Glory".

> Another privateer ('Retribution') out. There has been a suspicious steamer about S. Jorge, she ran down to the 'Açoriano' on her way from S. Miguel to Terceira. Fred Cunningham's journals came, giving an account of the taking of Kingston in a letter from Charles to himself. Burnside resigned, Hooker in command.[3]

> Nothing new of the Army of the Potomac, Stonewall Jackson dead, wounded by one of his own soldiers, by mistake of course (so it is said), but who can believe anything in these days? Stoneman's success much exaggerated.[4]

Every now and then bits of Civil War drama took place in the Azorean archipelago.

> July 17th. A little blockade runner, the Juno,' could get no coal, so left at dinner time, followed by the Kearsarge' [which had been here several days]. We were sorry we did not see them get under way; when we did see them they were near the coast of Pico, going at a great rate; the 'Kearsarge' seemed to gain, but later seemed to be losing. Messrs. Dart and Lane went kindly to John, and told him the news (in the 'World' of July 12) brought by the 'Juno' Lee before Washington with 125,000 men, going on to New York. Eighty thousand men in Philadelphia ready to join him. Grant and Army surrounded – three privateers off Boston burnt forty vessels, and more which I do not remember, and of course we do not believe a word of it all.

> Thursday, July 23d. Father waked Fan and me before six, saying that the 'Kearsarge' was coming in with a prize! There she was sure enough, like a spider with a fly, or as Jacintho said 'like a man bringing along an unruly boy by the ear.' There has been much excitement all day. Father and John took an early breakfast with us, as did Mr. Yeaton (one of the sub-officers of the 'Kearsarge') and then went on board of the 'Kearsarge,'

which was some distance off Mt. Da Guia. Capt. Winslow wished to consult C. W. D. about the 'Juno' for she it was. The reason that they did not take her going out from here was that they were dragging their anchor and fifteen fathoms of chain after them. When I went up to give the little d'Orey children their lessons, saw Messrs. Dart and Lane; people looked after them as if they were some strange sight. Mr. Dart was going off to the 'Juno' as Father and John came ashore. After all they were obliged to let the 'Juno' go – the papers were right, but they had the satisfaction of catching her, annoying the Capt., his Consul and Lloyd's Agent; and the best of all is, that John saw later papers than those they sent ashore, to July 1st. Hooker removed and Meade in command, going to give battle to Lee. Gen. Dix was within eighteen miles of Richmond.[5]

And sometimes the warships brought news about what was happening in America and the assignments of the different ships.

July 31st. Great day! This morning when we looked out there was an English Steamer of war just coming to anchor and the 'Kearsarge' coming down channel. At breakfast came all the letters and papers, among the former a note from Mr. Medeiros, saying he had just come from the 'Kearsarge,' that a little vessel from Portland had arrived at Terceira. Vicksburg had fallen – we had taken 25,000 prisoners, 12,000 of these only soldiers, that Gen. Meade had given battle to Lee at Gettysburg and routed him & c.[6]

Feb. 12th. The 'Sacramento' is nine days from Boston – no letters, for she is on a secret mission – the officers even did not know where she was bound. Mr. Cogly and Mr. Laurie dined here – such mere boys – but they both seem promising.[7]

The major event during the American Civil War as far as the Dabneys were concerned was the marauding of the Confederate privateer, the *C. S. S. Alabama*. A number of books and articles have been written about the *Alabama* and its exploits under Captain Raphael Semmes, however, the perspectives of the inhabitants of the Azores about the Alabama's activities in the archipelago have not been the subject of much consideration.

During its short 22-month career, the *Alabama* sank or captured 65 Union ships and virtually stopped Union Merchant trade in the Atlantic single-handedly.[8] Although the early part of this ship's career began off the island of Terceira, its construction took place in England. The *Alabama* was constructed in Liverpool, England and was originally known as the "*290*". Upon its completion it sailed before the authorities, who had learned of its real owners and mission, could seize it. As required by law, the "*290*" sailed under a British flag with a British crew and with the British Captain Butcher.

The "*290*" sailed to the island of Terceira where it anchored and took on supplies from the British steamer *Agrippina*, and the crew began to convert it to a warship. Before long the British steamer *Bahama* out of Nassau and Liverpool arrived in Terceira where the Confederate officers on board took over the "*290*," and Captain Raphael Semmes replaced Captain Butcher.

On shore it was not clear why these three ships were anchored off the island's coast, and the constant movement of boats between them made their activity suspicious. They refused to submit to customs requests, and the authorities asked them to move their ships to another anchorage. "This latter we did, being too well pleased to find so little required of us, though the change removed us from a still harbor to one of a rough character."[9]

The Terceira newspaper *Lidador* described the events that took place as seen from the island.

> Angra do Heroismo, August 23, 1862.
>
> Sad and unpleasant to us are the impressions caused by what we are about to relate, of the facts witnessed with general indignation by all the inhabitants of this Island. On the 10th of this month the 'Barcelona' of the British Navy, anchored in the bay of the town of Praia da Victoria, situated about 20 kilometers from this City. When she was visited by the Health Department, the Capt. Presented no bill of health, declaring that he was going to remain but a short time to take in some refreshment and repair something in his machinery. In consequence

of this statement the Health Department instituted a quarantine of observation for three days. The quarantine ended and the vessel was admitted, and yet she staid on, under circumstances that seemed decidedly suspicious. These suspicions were even more strengthened by the arrival on the 18th of an English Barque by name 'Agripina,' and no sooner arrived than she began to signal to the Steamer. This vessel not having a bill of health was also subjected to a three days quarantine of observation. All the sanitary and fiscal regulations were treated with contempt, and the Portuguese flag again suffered insult, which had it come from any other nation but the English, our ancient and faithful ally, might have led to a conflict. All that day and night of the 19th and the 20th the Barque never ceased sending cargo to the Steamer (!!!) all this without either of the vessels having entered at the Custom House, nor had they complied with any of the formalities which the law prescribes. What greater proofs could be required to render these vessels suspected? But this is not all – at 2 p.m. on the 20th another English Steamer came and anchored in the bay of Praia, and began exchanging signals with the other two vessels, the result of which was the immediate departure of the first steamer, with the barque in tow. These two vessels passed in front of this bay of Angra, and so close to the coast did they come as to lead to the supposition that they would drop anchor here, but they went on their course, and shortly after, the barque anchored in the port of Fanal close to the Fort of San Diogo, belonging to the Castle of St. John the Baptist. The steamer flew the English ensign, and the barque still had the crane, which had been rigged up to pass cargo to the Steamer in Praia bay. The second steamer was returning to Praia, when she met the other one near the Ilheos; both of them then came and anchored near the barque. There they continued passing cargo to the steamer latest arrived. By request of some of the Authorities, Mr. John Read, British V. Consul in this Island, sent a circular dispatch to the vessels stating that their remaining in the port of Fanal was out of the question as it was an infringement of their fiscal laws, which required that they should come to Angra, whey they could be anchored with more safety. They answer they returned to this was that they were merely taking in some coal and repairing one of the barque's masts, and for this purpose they asked leave to remain 48 hours longer where they were. They said they did not anchor at Angra on account of the high sea running, which was false.

On the 21ˢᵗ another Circular was dispatched by the same V. Consul, ordering them to leave that port immediately under penalty of obliging the Authorities to resort to extreme measures to make the laws of the Country respected. They answered that as they were not allowed the time requested, they should seek some other place; and at once they weighed anchor and after spending the whole day, just outside the village of San Matheos, they came at nightfall and anchored in Angra bay. So unqualified as well as incomprehensible a proceeding, gave rise to all sorts of conjecture; some persons were much alarmed, whilst others conjectured that the vessels only came to these coasts to take in armament and munitions and would then proceed to America. One of the Steamers took in armaments in Praia bay, and the other in Fanal bay, besides which there must have been a large stock of all sorts of munitions of war, judging by the number of iron clamped boxes floating round, which the fishermen brought to land. To palliate, it is supposed, so singular and revolting a proceeding, the three vessels came to anchor in Angra bay and entered at the Custom House, after the usual fiscal visit. The Health Department gave the vessels 'pratique,' merely because they had been in Praia!

What shall we say, what think after all this! We will add nothing more for the present, but will await further information, in order to express our frank and impartial opinion.

This describes the fitting out of the famous "Alabama." She never came to Fayal, but we afterwards heard enough of her doings.[10]

Although the *Alabama* never stopped in Faial, its supply ships did. On November 19, 1862 the *Bahama* stopped over in Horta, as described in Roxana's journal.

> A suspicious looking English Steamer in, said to be the 'Bahama' with supplies for the 'Alabama.' This is the steamer in which Capt. Semmes came to Terceira.[11]

The three ships in Terceira then went "beyond the marine league, and in smooth water, and hoisted on board her armament, placing it 'in battery,' reeving side and train tackles, stowing shot and shell rooms, filling shot-racks on deck, and putting ship generally in fighting trim."[12] Also, "on the morning of Sunday, Aug. 24, 1862, in company with the Bahama, we again put to sea, to unfurl for the first time at the peak of the Alabama, the flag of the young Confederacy".[13]

The men from all three ships were gathered on the "290," and Semmes read his commission and orders, after which a cannon was fired and the British colors lowered. The "290" officially became the C. S. S. Alabama. Semmes described his purpose and the advantages of sailing with him, including higher pay, greater prize share and more grog, as well as warning that by signing on they would forfeit "the protection of the English government."[14] In the end eighty-five British sailors signed on as crew of the Alabama, and she was now ready to take up her task.

> I can truly add that not even the most trifling article necessary to the efficiency of the vessel could be named as wanting. At the period of which we write, the Alabama was the most perfect cruiser of any nation afloat.[15]

> Look at her, reader, from the deck of the Bahama; a long, trim, black hull, elliptic stern, fiddle-head cutwater, long, raking lower masts, and you have the picture of the rover[16]

To the cheers of the Bahama's crew, the Alabama set off on its wave of destruction, sailing northwest toward the island of Flores where the best whaling grounds are located. Twelve days later, on September 5, the Alabama sighted, captured and burned the Union whaling ship Ocmulgee. The Alabama towed the Ocmulgee's boats, containing its crew and their personal possessions and then filled them with "provisions, all their whaling gear and other odds and ends." The men were given the chance to join the *Alabama* crew or be released on parole with a promise not to fight the Confederacy. Those wishing parole would be released on the island of Flores "and soon after be under the protection of the American Consul," that is, Charles Dabney.[17] The *Alabama* followed this procedure with each of the ships that it captured.

While the possessions of the captured crews did not have a great financial value to them, they did represent a lot to the very poor inhabitants of Flores.

> These men, having their entire expenses paid by the United States Government to their respective homes, through their consul, were no doubt rather benefited by the introduction to the Alabama. We have by this time greatly increased the population of the islands, and to the decided gain of the latter; for unlike the mass of the immigrants to our own land, they have been put on shore with, in the estimation of these islanders, untold wealth.[18]

By October 1, the *Alabama* had captured and burned ten ships in the Azores. The second of the ships captured, the *Starlight*, carried female passengers and mail that it had picked up on Faial.

> Among the papers captured on board the *Starlight* were a couple of dispatches from the Federal Consul at Fayal to the Sewards [Secretary and Asst. Secretary of State] – father and son – in which there was the usual amount of stale nonsense about "rebel privateers" and "pirates".[19]

Another of the ships was the *Alert*, which was a ship that Richard Henry Dana had sailed on and is prominently mentioned in his book "Two Years before the Mast". Roxana Dabney's journal entry on September 14 mentions the sinking of the ships and the loss of their correspondence and other entries describe other actions by the *Alabama.*

Sunday 14th. This is dreadful news about the two steamers, probably those that were at Terceira under English colours, burning seven vessels, four last Monday and three Tuesday. Among the first was the poor little 'Starlight' and with all our *letters* on board. The passengers, poor things were landed at Flores, but what became of those, who were escaping the conscription here? Father thinks it probable, that they would enter the Secession service. What a fearful thing this war! Especially when it is brought *home*. And the 'Azor'![20]

Friday, 19th. The 'Hortense' arrived. Same came down and told us the news, Capt. Small (of a whaler) Capt. Doane of the 'Starlight' came up. The Steamer is the 'Alabama,' Capt. Semmes, Jefferson Davis' son 1st Lt. There were seven vessels burnt and one whaling schooner sunk with all on board. Capt. Semmes told Capt. Doane, if he had not seen the women on board the 'Starlight,' he should have sunk her, because it was so long before they hoisted their flag; the 'Alabama' fired twice at her. The 'Alabama' hoists the white St. George's cross;... Capt. Small, as well as all the others, were put in irons, on the deck forward among the men; he felt cold and asked permission to put on some clothes; after a long time, permission was given, but he was obliged to change just where he was. They tried to induce the men to enter their service – one of Capt. Small's men seemed inclined to, but Capt. Small told him, if he did, he would kill him certainly, wherever he met him. They took all Capt. Doane's money and his mate's gold watch – and all our letters – so now they will find out exactly when the 'Azor' is expected. Capt. Semmes told the Capt. Of the 'Water-Witch' (for he boarded her), that he was going to burn the 'Azor,' in revenge for Mr. Dabney not supplying those Steamers with coal. Well! I suppose it is very likely she may be taken, but I have faith that she will escape. She carries a lantern at night to be sure, and two of the 'Alabama's' men were here in the 'Annie Childes' and saw the 'Azor.'

Sat. Sept. 20th. Karl's anniversary. Showery, wintry day. Three more vessels burnt. It is reported that the 'Newsboy' (passenger vessel) was burnt – all our letters, now they will certainly know when to expect the 'Azor.'[21]

The attitude of one of the Alabama's officers toward the capture and burning of Union ships was, at least initially, mixed.

> We witness to-day for the first time the hauling down of the Stars and Stripes – to those of us who served in the old navy, a humbling of the emblem at our hands, carrying with it many a cruel wrench and sad retrospect. To men who in days gone by had stood on the quarter-deck, with the doff of cap, and amid the glitter of uniforms, presenting of arms, and strains of the national air, and daily witnessed the morning ceremony of hoisting this flag at the peak, it was difficult to disassociate the act with desecration.
>
> The writer can never forget the feelings and impressions of this first capture, and the sight later on of the burning ship brought sorrow to the heart. I may almost say shame; but war! Cruel, inhuman war! Soon blunts the sentimental impulses, and what seemed at first sheer ruthlessness became in time a matter of course. It must be acknowledged that after a brief space of time the cry, "Sail ho!" from aloft, was received with the heartfelt wish she would prove a prize.[22]

Other information comes second hand from captives who made it to Faial and repeated what some of the crew had said to them.

> ...The crew are almost entirely English and Irish. Some of them told Capt. Small, that they were heartily sick of this kind of business; they shipped to run the blockade and not to kill people and burn vessels. One of the officers seated himself by Capt. Small one day and said 'I should like to see the bloody old Pirate in H-l.[23]

However, the attitude of Capt. Semmes left no doubt about his sentiments.

> I really felt for the honest fellow [Master of the *Ocean Rover*], but when I came to reflect for a moment upon the diabolical

acts of his countrymen of New England who were out-heroding Herod in carrying on against us a vindictive war, filled with hate and vengeance, the milk of human kindness which had begun to well up in my heart disappeared, and I had no longer any spare sympathies to dispose of.[24]

Obviously, the primary concern of the Dabneys was the safety of their own ships traveling the corridor between Boston and Faial. The ships in the Dabney fleet "were the *Boston, Swiftsure, Sarah, Harbinger, Io, Hortense, Azor, Azorean* and *Fredonia.*" The Dabney ships had become endangered by Charles Dabney's policy not to sell coal to ships suspected of having allegiance to the Confederate States. In early 1862 this decision was supported by the State Department, although not always by his business associates, as was mentioned in the last chapter concerning Mr. F.R. Camroux.

> The Hon. William Seward,
> Secretary of State of the U. S.
> I have the honor to enclose copies of my correspondence in relation to the "Annie Child," Hammer, Master, and to inform you that having heard that she had a small carriage gun on her forecastle, I made known the circumstance to our Civil Governor, and he has kindly assured me that he will use his endeavours to obtain all possible information in relation to her armament and equipage. This vessel having received countenance from Messrs. Dart and Lane (British Consul & Lloyd's Agent) and obtained coal will probably be the prelude to others bearing that flag, and I beg leave to submit for your consideration, the expediency of having a U. S. vessel occasionally appear hear.
>
> With the highest consideration &c.
> Chas. W. Dabney

> C. W. Dabney, Esq. U. S. Consul – Fayal
> Sir, - Your Nº. 6 with its enclosure, relating to your refusal to supply steamers in the interest of the rebels with coal has

been received. The patriotic stand, which you have taken in this matter is fully appreciated by the Department, and is in entire harmony with the long and faithful course of public service, which you have always pursued as an officer of the Government of the United States. The dispatch with the paper accompanying it, has been referred to the Secretary of the Navy. The appointment of Mr. Bartholomew A. da C. Bettencourt as Consular agent at the Island of Graciosa, in place of his father, who has recently been created a Baron, is approved, subject to the provisions of the law and the Consular Regulations.

> I am Sir your obedient servant
> F.W. Seward
> Assistant Secretary.[25]

The *Azor* was expected to return from Boston during the period that the *Alabama* was active off Flores, and the level of anxiety was extremely high among the family and the residents of Horta – "We cannot think of much besides the 'Azor' and 'Alabama'.[26] Charles Dabney had even sent a message to Cadiz for the U. S. warship *Tuscarora* to come to Horta.

> Sometimes in the evening as we returned from town to Mt. Da Guia [the Dabney residence on one of Horta's bays], we would see people going around the Angustias Church on their knees, praying for the safety of the 'Azor.'
>
> The Governor, Mr. Sta. Rita, begged father to move up from Mt. Da Guia, because he said there was no knowing, but that Capt. Semmes might swoop down and bear us all off – and he could do it so easily. He was in earnest.[27]

In a period where news was not available with the rapidity of today, the many days that it took to make the Boston-Horta crossing led to imagining the most negative result, as Capt. Semmes' threat implied, but with hope for the best outcome. Finally the *Azor* arrived amidst surprise, cheers and prayers.

Wednesday, Sept. 24th. God be praised! Will go up from many a thankful heart this morning. The 'Azor' has arrived! Bab waked Clara and me before six saying that the signal boy had announced her. We dressed and went out to take a look. The vessel was far off, looked like the 'Azor', but we did not dare to be too sanguine. Returned and told Fan and George; upon mentioning that there was another vessel off, George's imagination immediately conjured up the idea that Capt. Semmes had brought the Azor up to burn her in sight of the Island, but the other vessel proved to be a whaler and this time when we went to take another look, the 'Azor' had hoisted her ensign, and signal at the fore. George and Fan then came out. We met a widow, who was crying with joy. Such an excitement among all classes! We returned to the house and told our Parents. Father clasped his hands and sank back on his pillow, raising his eyes to Heaven; I think he had had very little hope, although he never said so. Then we went up Mt. Queimado a little way and saw the 'Azor' pass the shell beach, waved our welcome and they dipped the flag. The sea walls all along were crowded with people, we heard. A singular circumstance, we met a man with his hands full of letters that he had picked up on the beach, one of them had an American flag on the envelope, and was quite dry, we suppose from being in the middle of the package, the others were saturated. Upon examining them we haave no doubt that they were letters by the 'Starlight.' George came in while we were still at breakfast with a face nearly down to his waist! 'What is the matter?' we asked and felt almost relieved when he said 'The war news is as bad as it can be.' Capt. Burke was ill all the voyage and had to have ice applied to his head. His first mate, who had never been to the Azores found unexpectedly that they were more than a degree to the south of Flores. It really seemed wonderful. One woman told Clara that the Holy Virgin had covered the 'barca' with her mantle, so that she was invisible to the Pirate. Our letters were filled with clouds.[28]

To avoid further problems with the *Alabama*, the decision was made to change the name of the *Azor*. The initiative to do this was taken by Charles Dabney's representative in America, his nephew Fred Cunningham, in Boston in mid-April 1863. They thought of several options for names, but finally chose *Fredonia* after the name of the house where the Consulate was located. However, they did not realize that the Dabneys had not chosen this name for the house and property, as mentioned earlier in this book, and that Charles Dabney would not be pleased with the change.

> I feel that I must write you a few lines to explain what I fear may be an unpleasant piece of intelligence to you, viz., the changing of the name and nationality of the Azor. You will doubtless see in the papers the proceedings at a meeting of the board of Underwriters in New York at the time of the Azor's arrival. This it was that made me construe the 'I wish you to see how she can be put under English colors' in your letter of the 14th March into a permission to do it, if it seemed expedient...
>
> I consulted with several persons (Frank Parker among the rest) and we looked at the shipping act of 1854 and all said that for a vessel to run on the track between the Azores and the U. S. this seemed the only thing to be done. The change of name was a great drawback, but I see the Shipping Act specially mentions it... [several names were considered]... Suddenly 'Fredonia' came to mind; it seemed like an inspiration, and no one to whom I have mentioned it, but has said at once 'a beautiful name.' I was surprised and quite sorry to learn from Henry Pomeroy that it not thought a pretty name in Fayal, but I hope that may have been some fancied inappropriateness, for it certainly cannot be denied the merit of a musical sound. I hope however that the necessity of the case may excuse my presumption in dealing so summarily with so valued a piece of property as the 'Azor.' I can assure you that I never felt the onus of responsibility more, and I acted with the calmest and most deliberate judgment I could muster. If I have erred it must be set down to my nature and not to my hastiness or inconsiderateness of action. I understood your letter to mean 'I have been thinking that I might be compelled to change the flag of the Azor and I want you to find all about it, so that I can

make up my mind,' but I did not believe you would be dissatisfied to have me make the decision for you, which I felt sure you would make were you on the spot.[29]

The news that Frederick Cunningham had succeeded in his action was received in May 1863

> May 18th...The 'Azor' had been put under English colors and named 'Fredonia'! She was to follow very soon, touch here, go to Teneriffe and then to Beirut, Capt. Burke in her, bringing his wife and children.[30]

After the *Alabama* finished its destructive activities in Azorean waters, it, along with other Confederate warships, prowled the entire Atlantic in search of more prey. For a while the *Alabama* was in the Caribbean from where it escaped in late December 1862 with the alleged help of the French. It was then reported in Jamaica the next February after a battle in the Gulf of Mexico.

> The 'Alabama' in trying to get into Galveston had an engagement with our Transport 'Hatteras' [3 guns only] and sank her, but had sustained some damages herself and had to put into Kingston, Jamaica.[31]

The next sightings of the 'Alabama' had it in the Indian Ocean along with other Confederate warships.

> The 'Alabama', 'Georgia', and 'Tuscaloosa' are committing depredations off the Cape of Good Hope and in the Indian Ocean. The tone of the English journals on American affairs is more favourable, while every day increases the prospect of a war with France.[32]

The remarks of Roxana about the possibility of war with France were based on the fact that the Confederacy had begun to use French ports. Roxana also knew that the *C S S Florida* was being repaired in Brest while the *U. S. S. Kearsarge* was waiting for the repairs to be completed and for the *Florida* to set sail. In the end, France also turned out to be the destination for the *Alabama* in 1864.

In August of 1864 ships arrived in Faial with stories that the *Alabama* had been sunk and on August 21, the *Kearsarge* arrived to confirm the news.

> *Kearsarge* prepared for her fight with the *Alabama* at Cadiz (November 1862-March 1863), then searched for the raider from along the coast of Northern Europe to the Canaries, Madeira and the Western Islands [the Azores]. Arriving at Cherbourg, France, 14 June 1864 she found *Alabama* in port and took up patrol at the harbor's entrance to await Semme's next move.
>
> On 19 June, *Alabama* stood out of Cherbourg Harbor for her last action. Careful of French neutrality, *Kearsarge's* new commanding officer, Captain John A. Winslow took the sloop--of-war well clear of territorial waters then turned to meet the Confederate cruiser.
>
> *Alabama* fired first while *Kearsarge* held her reply until she had closed to less than 1,000 yards. Steaming on opposite courses the ships moved around a circle as each commander tried to cross his opponents bow to deliver deadly raking fire. The battle quickly turned against *Alabama* for the quality of her long-stored powder and shells had deteriorated. *Kearsarge*, on the other hand, had been given added protection by chain cable triced in tiers along her sides abreast vital spaces. One hour after she fired her first salvo, *Alabama* had been reduced to a sinking wreck. Semmes struck his colors and sent a boat to the *Kearsarge* with a message of surrender and an appeal for help. *Kearsarge* rescued the majority of *Alabama's*, but Semmes and 41 others were picked up by British yacht *Deerhound* and escaped to England.[33]

Among the crowds who watched the battle was the artist Edouard Manet, who reportedly watched it from a pilot boat. Manet made a painting of the battle, which is considered his first attempt at portraying a contemporary event.

The *Kearsarge* arrived in Horta to the cheers of every ship in the harbor and all the people lining the shore. The *Kearsarge's* officers were treated as special guests of the Dabneys.

> The sailors of the "St. Louis" manned the yards and gave the most resounding cheers to which the sailors of the "Kearsarge" responded in kind.

> We were truly glad to see them, and they were to see us we knew. And fresh from their victory, it was very interesting to hear all they had to tell us.[34]

The crew of the Kearsarge reciprocated the honors. The Dabneys were able to visit on board and heard some of the story of the battle.

> They beat to 'general quarters' and I [Roxana] fired the big gun. We were shown the slight damages caused by the 'Alabama's' shots. How wonderful that engagement was, and it seems all the more so since we have been on board. Down on the berth deck, I had some conversation with an intelligent man, sergeant of the marines, I believe. He said he was on deck when the 'Alabama's' boat came alongside – one of the men asked, how many killed there were on board of the 'Kearsarge'? none –how many wounded? Two or three' – 'My God! Jack', said he to one of his comrades, there is no blood here, their decks are as clean as if they had just been washed.' The two prisoners were sitting near the forecastle, the one from Philadelphia reading; the Welshman apparently enjoying seeing us go about. Dr. Browne told your aunt Clara about the last shot from the 'Alabama' as she went down, cutting the points which unloosed the flag of Victory on board of the 'Kearsarge'.[35]

In addition, the *Kearsarge* had some of the spoils of battle from the *Alabama*, and "Captain Winslow, to the surprise of all, sold two of the *Alabama's* boats in Fayal; C. W. D. bought them on his own account and sent them as an offering to the

Snug Harbor Fair in Boston."[36] After its short stay, the *Kearsarge* sailed for the east coast of America.

> We all, including Father and George, assembled on the upper veranda and waved our adieus. Such a waving of flags and handkerchiefs, and the 'Kearsarge' fired her big gun at us, and the men ran up aloft and cheered us; the Fort saluted with her flag, so did the Currys, and the 'Kearsarge' exchanged salutes later with those at Mt. Da Guia; and thus disappeared the renowned 'Kearsarge' and her gallant crew![37]

The two boats that Charles Dabney purchased were going to be sent to the Snug Harbor Fair, also known as the Boston Sanitary Fair, as part of the "Fayal Table" that the Dabney family sponsored. It displayed a variety of handicrafts and other items from the island and was gladly welcomed by the Fair Managers. It was so popular that everything was "cleared off in a few hours."[38]

The two *Alabama* boats arrived in Boston just after the *Kearsarge* and, as a result, did not attract the attention they might have. A letter from Charles Dabney, Jr., describes the *Alabama* boats and their presence at the fair, thereby bringing closure to the active involvement of the Azores with the American Civil War.

> BOSTON, Dec. 3d, 1864.
> My dear Father, -The first news I had about the " Alabama's boats was contained in a despatch received from Capt. Burke stating that one of the masts in falling had stove the bows of one Of the boats of the Confederate steamer " Alabama." You may imagine I was somewhat puzzled. The next day I received yours of Oct. 3d, explaining the whole matter. I happened to meet Mr.R. B. Forbes just after receiving your letter, and he was much interested about the boats and said they ought to go to the "'Monitor' enclosure " on the Common. I wrote a note to the Managing Committee into which I copied the greater part of your note to me and told them that the boats were at their disposal, and I would have the broken one repaired

whenever they should think best to have it done. They deputed Mr. R. B. Forbes to receive them, and under his instructions they were sent to the " Monitor" tent on the Common, where they continued one of the attractions of the place during the Exhibition. The destruction caused by the falling mast [*of the Fredonia*] was attributed by the papers to one of the "Kearsarge's" shells, and the injured boat instead of being repaired, was broken and sold in pieces. I do not know yet how your donation resulted, but it was looked upon as a very happy inspiration on your part, and it was quite a matter of surprise that Capt. Winslow should have disposed of the boats at all. I spoke with some of the officers at the dinner, and thought that some of them felt a little sore about it. I think the boats would have attracted more special attention then they did, had they not arrived so precisely at the same time with their Captors. I enclose a copy of Mr. Forbes' note in reply to mine to the Managing Committee. Your affectionate son

CHARLES W. DABNEY Jr.

Notes:

[1] Roxana Lewis Dabney, *Annals of the Dabney Family in Fayal*, comp., n. p.: The Author, 1900, p. 1095-6.

[2] Roxana Lewis Dabney, *Annals*, p. 1075

[3] Roxana Lewis Dabney, *Annals*, p. 1101

[4] Roxana Lewis Dabney, *Annals*, p. 1120

[5] Roxana Lewis Dabney, *Annals*, p. 1123-4

[6] Roxana Lewis Dabney, *Annals*, p. 1125

[7] Roxana Lewis Dabney, *Annals*, p. 1167

[8] "Career of the *Alabama*," *International Herald Tribune*, Feb. 16, 1994

[9] 1st Lt. Arthur Sinclair IV, *Two Years on the Alabama*, Lee & Shepard,?, 1895, p. 12.

[10] Roxana Lewis Dabney, *Annals*, p. 1025-27.

[11] Roxana Lewis Dabney, *Annals*, p. 1071.

[12] 1st Lt. Arthur Sinclair IV, *Alabama*, p. 13.

[13] 1st Lt. Arthur Sinclair IV, *Alabama*, p. 13-14.

[14] 1st Lt. Arthur Sinclair IV, *Alabama*, p. 16.

[15] 1st Lt. Arthur Sinclair IV, *Alabama*, p. 17.

[16] 1st Lt. Arthur Sinclair IV, *Alabama*, p. 18.

[17] 1st Lt. Arthur Sinclair IV, *Alabama*, p. 27.

[18] 1st Lt. Arthur Sinclair IV, *Alabama*, p. 34.

[19] Raphael Semmes, *The Confederate Raider, Alabama: Selections from Memoirs of Service Afloat during the War between the States*, Fawcett, Greenwich, Conn., p. 58.

[20] Roxana Lewis Dabney, *Annals*, p. 1038.

[21] Roxana Lewis Dabney, *Annals*, p. 1041.

[22] 1st Lt. Arthur Sinclair IV, *Alabama*, p. 27.

[23] Roxana Lewis Dabney, *Annals*, p. 1040.

[24] Raphael Semmes, *The Confederate Raider*, p. 60.

[25] Roxana Lewis Dabney, *Annals*, p. 1024.

[26] Roxana Lewis Dabney, *Annals*, p. 1042.

[27] Roxana Lewis Dabney, *Annals*, p. 1042.

[28] Roxana Lewis Dabney, *Annals*, p. 1043-44.

[29] Roxana Lewis Dabney, *Annals*, p. 1093-4.

[30] Roxana Lewis Dabney, *Annals*, p. 1118.

[31] Roxana Lewis Dabney, *Annals*, p. 1101.

[32] Roxana Lewis Dabney, *Annals*, p. 1145.

[33] *Dictionary of American Naval Fighting Ships, Vol. III*, Navy Department, Office of the Chief of Naval Operations, Naval History Division, Washington, D.C., 1968, p. 609-10.

[34] Roxana Lewis Dabney, *Annals*, p. 1181.

[35] Roxana Lewis Dabney, *Annals*, p 1182.

[36] Roxana Lewis Dabney, *Annals*, p. 1189.

[37] Roxana Lewis Dabney, *Annals*, p. 1183.

[38] Roxana Lewis Dabney, *Annals*, p. 1162-3.

Figure 10
Alabama and Kearsarge
by Édouard Manet, 1864, Johnson collection, Philadelphia, PA

17 – CIVIL PEACE

Aside from the attacks of the *Alabama* and the fear they created, life for the people on Faial proceeded normally. Ships continued to stop in Horta to take on supplies, but now the proportion of steamships was increasing. Among these were some Union warships that were patrolling the Atlantic and, specifically, chasing the *Alabama,* such as the *Kearsarge, Merrimac, Missouri, St. Louis, Tuscarora and Vanderbilt.*

Meantime, in the rural areas of Faial, they were having their own small-scale war, this time over taxes. The government had imposed a new form of taxation that the people did not like. As with the *"Maria da Fonte"* uprising in 1844 in northern Portugal, the women led the battle against the authorities.

> Sam told us at dinner that there was a revolution in Castello Branco and we could perceive traces of unusual excitement; the women along the new road all seemed to have come out of their houses, finally we met a soldier with his head bound up in handkerchief, and riding a donkey, followed by two men bearing a hammock. I got George to stop, and asked a woman the meaning of all this? She gave me a very exaggerated account. Further on we met Mr. Avila, and from him learnt that the people had killed three of the soldiers. He was walking out to Castello Branco, where his father in law [the mayor] was at some house. Poor misguided creatures; Father thinks this new system of taxation will really be much better for them.[1]

The revolution finally ended when thousands of people flocked to Horta asking the governor to send a petition to Lisbon regarding their concerns about the tax. He agreed, they broke into cheers and went happily on their way home. Nevertheless,

Charles Dabney felt that they were in error in their actions and that the new system of taxation would have benefited them.

If the *Alabama's* attacks, Union warship patrols and a tax revolution were not enough to shake up Faial, Mother Nature decided to take her turn. In October 1862, there were a total of 120 earthquakes recorded during a 10-day period in the Azores, although none of them was of great magnitude. Earthquakes were not uncommon in the Azores, but their frequency created much concern among the inhabitants of the islands, which moved Roxana Dabney to comment on them.

> We had a very strong shock of earthquake – it lasted so long; there came another while I was undressing. The wind had changed to the southward, very heavy atmosphere and soon it began to blow very hard – such a wild night. I believe there were several slight shocks, but perhaps it was the wind. In the midst of the wind, we could hear many voices chanting, did not know whether they were sailors or not.[2]

These earthquakes varied in strength from little rumblers to shocks that woke everyone, even on the ships. As a result Charles Dabney "put an earthquake house on the west side of the '*eira*' (in the garden)"[3] and many Portuguese moved into tents.

In the midst of the earthquakes, news arrived concerning Abraham Lincoln's Emancipation Proclamation, a declaration that shook America.

> The President issued his Emancipation Proclamation Sept. 22d. After Jan. 1ˢᵗ, 1863 all slaves of Secessionists are to be declared free, and the loyal masters are to be indemnified for theirs!! All Military men are pleased and in fact throughout the country it has given satisfaction, and no wonder; we have come now to the root.[4]

News of the war continued to arrive on the ships stopping in Faial, and visits from the *Kearsarge* did not stop with the sinking of the *Alabama*. On April 25, 1864, the *Kearsarge* sailed into the Bay of Horta one more time, but with a virtually new crew.

Among the members of the new crew invited up to Fredonia was Mr. Dewey, later to become "Admiral Dewey, King of Manila." He "seemed very pleasant, something so earnest about him."[5] He would return a few years later under very different circumstances

The news the *Kearsarge* carried was mixed. The good news was that General Lee had surrendered at Appomattox, and the Civil War was over. They also brought news that Lincoln had been assassinated, a report that was not believed at first.

> Tuesday, April 25th. What news! 'Kearsarge' in ten days from Boston – Richmond and Petersburg, ours – Lee and his army surrendered! The 'Kearsarge' came in while I was at the hotel in the afternoon, but it was not until teatime that John and Sam came up with Mr. Woodward 2d. Lt. Of the 'Kearsarge' so young he is and has seen so much fighting he was at the taking of Fort Fisher and other places. He told us that the report reached Boston the evening they left that Lincoln had been assassinated, but it was not credited. Mr. W. went off and reported to his comrades that it was 'like Boston,' all our excitement over his news.[6]

The death of President Lincoln greatly affected the Dabney family. In addition it also affected many of the residents of Faial and some of the visiting seamen. Charles Dabney wrote his official condolences to Secretary of State F.W. Seward.

> The cruel events of the night of the 14th ult. Were made know to us yesterday [May 7]. If possible, the poignancy of the shock was increased by the distance & we come with all humility to mingle ours with the Nation's Grief, & to commend our cause to Him who never errs!
>
> We pray to the almighty so to inspire our present Chief Magistrate, as will most conduce to his renown & and our National prosperity.[7]

> Friday, May 5th. The 'Laconia,' 16 days from Boston. Sad day for us. Lincoln our Good President was basely assassinated by J. Wilkes Booth, half-brother of the Tragedian Edwin. All that

scene in the theatre keeps rising up before me. What a glorious name in History his! The crowd of people, especially contrabands outside the White House! The coloured people must feel that they have lost their Protector, their Saviour almost. Charles feels so dreadfully – who does not? Rodrigo and José da Silva even had their flags at half mast. The gentlemen of our family wore crape on their hats, we ladies had a band round our left arms. There was a little Russian vessel of war in about that time, and the Currys asked me to go up to Manoel Terra's garden with them – Mr. Curry allowed his daughters to go under my escort. They were not a very interesting set, but one of the younger ones seemed to feel so much about Lincoln; he told Carolina he would like so much to wear a badge of mourning, but it would not be allowed. They were all in sympathy with us, had been in San Francisco and were enthusiastic about that city.

May 23d. We had an interesting morning reading the English papers so full of sympathy about Lincoln. The death of no crowned head (certainly of modern times) ever called forth such feeling, and it is throughout Europe. The Queen wrote a letter with her own hand to Mrs. Lincoln. It is gratifying to see all this demonstration even if not entirely sincere in al cases.[8]

After the end of the years of horror Charles Dabney Jr., writes a long letter describing his and Boston's reactions to the successful (at least for the North) conclusion of the struggle. He brings up some interesting opinions on the length of the war and the reasons for it ending when it did.

To think of what news this vessel will carry you! After four years of weary waiting and disappointment comes the triumphant result, which more than repays it all, because it is so much more complete than success at any earlier period. It seems as if the Rebels had been allowed to remain just long enough to destroy their own institution, by making soldiers of their own slaves, whilst we have been led through the Wilderness until we have been tried, purified and educated by sorrow and suffering to the point needed, to enable us to do full justice to the claims of those who have been so long trampled upon. It now seems as if the end of this terrible struggle were actually upon us, but we have been so long looking for it, and so often disappointed, that it seems impossible that this terrible strain and anxiety of these years which had become a part of our daily life, is to cease; and that we can rejoice with free hearts that we have a country gloriously redeemed – Our own Country, the grandest that the sun shines upon. At the present time all we can do is to thank God devoutly for having vouchsafed us such an infinite mercy.

Although it began to rain before twelve o'clock, everyone was in the streets and kept there. Ladies hurrahed whenever they could get a chance – men went about shaking their acquaintances by the hand, getting up impromptu meetings speaking, singing and I fear in some cases drinking. There were bands of musing, ringing of bells, thunder of cannon, and in the midst of it all, a procession of the steam fire engines, whistling with all their might. In short Boston – staid, puritanic old Boston was moved to the depths, was jubilant, spontaneously, as I never expect to see her again, – and as nearly antic as she is capable of being. But these are days worth living in and for – or indeed, as to that, worth dying for. I think much of how this will seem to May and Zay in future years – and strive to have them get all the vivid impression which the occasion is calculated to produce. It is sad to think how many must mourn in this general rejoicing.

As ecstatic as Boston was with the end of the war, one more act of terror, Lincoln's assassination, made the people feel as low as they had been high.

15th. A sad, gloomy day in our history! How little we dreamed that our rejoicing would so soon be turned into mourning – and in such a way – At an early hour this morning, our milkman brought a rumor that President Lincoln had been assassinated I could not credit it, but at the same time it was a thing so possible. I could not put it aside, and later when I was out in the garden and heard the bells tolling, by heart sank within me and I found it difficult to eat my breakfast. I hurried down with May towards the Station to ascertain the truth, but still discrediting it – but the worst was all confirmed and we have lost the man in whom we all felt such confidence. Of course it is impossible to do anything today. No one pretends to do any business. Again the streets are thronged, and there are meetings, and speaking, but instead of smiles and shaking of hands – men set their teeth hard – and there is a deep resolve in each heart that there shall be no more conciliation with those whose creed admits of such a crime.[9]

Without belaboring the events too much further, I think letters from their family friends the Higginsons are worth including in order to complete the description of the end of the war, the death of Lincoln, and also the beginning of the Presidency of Andrew Johnson and some of the reactions to his presidency.

I often think of Fayal and all of you, of Pico and flowers – and wish myself bake there again for a time. If I had written before the 15th April, it would have been a letter of jubilee, for I have been very well this winter (for me) and very happy and all was going so splendidly with the country – we right on the threshold of peace apparently – when this thunderbolt came out of a clear sky. Never could there have been such a revulsion of feeling before. As victory after victory came, we could hardly contain ourselves with joy. Bells and cannon were resounding through the whole North – but when the dreadful news came of the cruel death of our beloved President, the whole North throbbed as if with one heart. There is no describing the depth and universality of the feeling. No one man seems ever to have been so loved before, and it was his goodness and childlike heart that had caused this love. It can be compared to the feeling of your poor people towards your father. We have lost a good and devoted Father and long will it be before we cease to mourn him. Johnson is showing to great advantage. He has had experience and knows the South thoroughly and is much less lenient than Mr. Lincoln, which is well.

Mary C. Higginson[10]

Dear Friends, – You will of course be anxious to bear how this great blow has been received. Of course the mourning is universal and very simple and touching in its expression. A New York lady writes that the beggar children there now ask for a piece of crape instead of bread or money. But on the other hand it has been a wonderful proof of the vigor of our institutions. There was not an instant's tendency towards anarchy in the faintest degree; - the funds hardly felt a shock – and the first shudder being over, the feeling seemed everywhere instinctive that perhaps such a shock was needed to brave us against the weak impulse of concession of which there seemed danger. Our people are impulsive, and it was said, the leading Republicans in Washington talked of giving experience in public life, you know, than Mr. Lincoln.

Please give my love to your father and the households at Fayal.

Every yrs. &tc.
T. W. Higginson[11]

If the drama of the Civil War in America were not enough, the Dabney family had their own local drama on Faial, actually more of a soap opera, which also occupied their attention. This time it was unusual because it involved the infrequent arrival in April 1865 of a Russian ship, the *Dmitri Donskoy*. Among the officers was Prince Constantin Meschersky, who had the rank of lieutenant and was the ship's paymaster. There were the usual round of dinners and balls for the officers during which Carolina Curry, one of Roxana Dabney's best friends, caught the Prince's eye, much to her surprise. He pursued her relentlessly, even though they did not speak a common language.

Carolina was naïve and did not know how to deal with the situation. "Poor Carolina, there is no end to her troubles, she wishes the *Dmitri Donskoy* would go."[12] Roxana found herself in the middle of the budding relationship as the result of her close friendship with Carolina and her ability to act as translator for them using German as a middle language.

April 18th. The Prince was here this morning to see and urge me to befriend him in his suit; Frisk must have been surprised when he came into the parlor to bring me a note from Carolina to find me sitting on the sofa with the Prince, my hand clasped in both of his and he with tears in his eyes. That note announced her engagement, and we were invited there in the evening.[13]

It being Easter, at just past midnight on Saturday, the *Dmitri Donskoy* set off fireworks and fired its cannons in celebration. On Easter Sunday there was a celebration at the Curry's, which the Dabneys did not attend because of their family rule not to go to social functions on Sunday.

On Tuesday there was an engagement party during which Roxana once again found herself in the middle, and the confusion that was created by poorly understood language continued.

Carolina had a hard time that evening; she had engaged herself on condition that at the end of six months she should give her final answer. I suppose the Prince did not understand entirely, for he went off on board and told the Commander, who said there could be no reason to keep it secret, and so the officers and men began drinking healths and cheering. A cousin of Carolina's mother, Roberto Mesquita, happened to be on board and asked what all the cheering was about; when told, he was amazed! You know that Mr. Curry and Miguel had to act as interpreters, and it is not surprising that the thread became somewhat entangled. They were both much pleased at the engagement though they did not urge it at all.

And so we were all there in the evening. The prince danced the first dance with Carolina, the second with me vis-a-vis to Carolina and Baron Meidell. It is a pleasure to see these Russians dance, they do it with such spirit. When the champagne was brought in, the officers all sang a song with glasses in their hand'; and then surrounded the newly betrothed, klinking glasses and making speeches; there was something impressive and affecting in the whole. As soon as she could,

C. escaped from the room, and made a sign to me in passing, so I followed her upstairs. We sat in a dark room, and presently Dona Anna came up and said that Carolina must come down, for Prince M. wished to return thanks. She protested and declared she would not, but just at this juncture a parrot that Prince Gagarin had given Mary seized Miss Curry by the heel with his bill, and this so diverted C. and all three of us that she acquiesced and went down. Prince M. was waiting for her, and he made a short speech in French in the midst of some agitation on his part. And so her fate is decided.[14]

It was apparent that Carolina Curry felt herself pressured into becoming engaged and was concerned about what she should do about the situation. As a result, like so many others on Faial, she turned to Charles Dabney for advice. Their two letters follow.

MR. DABNEY:

Dear Sir, – The kindness and friendship you have always shown me, makes me wish to let you know the sudden change which has taken place in my life. Roxie must have told you, but I feel as if I must tell you myself, that in a short time Mr. Meschersky will return to Fayal. It will seem strange to you and every one, to think that I have decided on my future in so short a time; it will seem a very inconsiderate step, but Mr. Dabney, be sure it is not; our hearts are mysterious and hard to understand. My decision in accepting the proposals which were made to me will have different interpretations, except the only true one. I should like to have the public sympathy, but I only intend to show my feelings to my friends and so I must tell you with sincerity that *only my heart* decided this important question, only my heart, be sure of this. I acknowledge the risk, and that much trouble may come upon me, but I feel happy with the present, and leave the future to God, in whom I always put my trust. It is very hard to leave my Country, Family and friends and give up my own language! Undoubtedly you will believe that my feelings were strong enough to make me abandon all I have known and loved until now. You cannot believe, I am sure, that I have done so for a caprice or a wish to acquire an independent or better position, only love can oblige one to make such sacrifices. What can I tell you more, only that I need to learn your opinion to be entirely happy. With much respect I am ever your

Thankful and most sincere Friend,
CAROLINA STREET CURRY.

FRIDAY MORNING.

My dear Miss Curry, -On my return from Mt. Carneiro yesterday noon, I found your note of yesterday, the contents of which affords me the very gratifying evidence that you are aware of and appreciate the feelings that I entertain for you. It is true, that Roxie knowing how much we feel interested in your happiness has made known to me the principal circumstances that have occurred in this very remarkable event. At first I confess that I felt alarmed for your happiness, but reflection has led me to the fol. Lowing conclusions. It is a case not to be judged of by the common rules of prudence. The ways of Providence are not to be penetrated by the ken of mortals – a just appreciation of our insignificance forbids the presumption of our being the subject of Divine interposition; but on the other hand, does any one doubt the omniscience of the Almighty? Your case is so extraordinary that His strongly suggestive of superior guidance-and as you have expressed a wish to know what are my feelings in relation to this subject (which desire I fully appreciate), it affords me gratification to declare, that having the most perfect faith in the goodness of the Almighty – I should have acted as you have done.

Renewing to you the assurance, &c., &c., I am,

C. W. D.
April 22d, 1865.[15]

And as Roxa commented,

Father said it seemed providential, knowing as he did the circumstances of the family and the prospect for the future, and he was right.[16]

The Prince had to leave when his ship departed, but in order to be near his betrothed and to begin preparations for his wedding, Prince Meschersky did not wait for its return voyage to the Azores. Instead he arrived on November 24 on the regular Lisbon steamer, much to the delight of the Curry household.

In March, 1868, the Catholic wedding on Faial took place. Carolina Curry wrote to Charles Dabney to be her "Godfather" and Roxana to be her "Godmother" at her wedding. This terminology is a direct translation from the Portuguese and is better expressed in English as Best Man and Maid of Honor.

> 14th March 1868
>
> Dear Sir, – Sure of your kindness and the sympathy you have always shown me, I hope you will not deny me the pleasure of having you as one of the two God-fathers I wish to have assisting on my wedding, tomorrow afternoon at five o'clock.
>
> > Every your respectful and sincere friend
> > Carolina Curry

> C.W.D's answer –
>
> My dear Miss Carolina Curry, – As you have in so flattering a manner avowed your consciousness of my sympathy, you can imagine the appreciation with which I received the high compliment you have bestowed upon me. Be assured, my dear Miss Curry, of the sincerity with which I subscribe myself.
>
> > Your obliged friend
> > Charles W. Dabney

> My dearest Roxie, – I have a favor to ask you, my dear, and that is to be one of my Godmothers to accompany me in my wedding. My Mother and you are *the two* who could only be chosen by my heart in such a time.
>
> > Your most affectionate and devoted
> > Carrie[17]

The wedding cake, using an English recipe, was so large that they had to use the main oven at the bakery. "The cake was a great success". The wedding, which took place in the Church of São Francisco, one of the largest in Horta and it is best to let to Roxana to describe it.

March 15th. What a day of excitement in the town; there were all sorts of stories as to what was to take place on the part of Prince Meschersky. The American vessels were a decked out with flags in honor of the day and of course the flags here and at the cedars were flying.

A great procession from here, all the family but Clara and the little things... Such was the curiosity that many of the ladies went in capotes* to look on.

The wedding party assembled at the Currys'... The Church was crowded, Tomaz da Silva and some others were up in the Pulpit. The capote women crowded so that they scarcely left space for the Bridal party to stand. Carolina did look lovely and appeared so well. The Prince unbuckled his sword and laid it down on his cap. The only difference was that the used two rings, turned them three times, and then put one on the Bride's finger and then one on his own. Carolina knelt down at her mother's knees for a few seconds after the ceremony. What a crowding as we came out; Father had his hat crushed in. The capote women waving their hands to the bride as we drove off. The women servants were all waiting at the head of the stairs for the Bride and Bridegroom. Both Carolina and the Prince kissed them all. I went home with them and helped them a little about the supper table, Gather came in for a few moments, and the rest of the family went home from the Church and came again at nine o'clock. We sang the Russian and the Portuguese hymns, which we had been practicing; the latter, I am sorry to say, was a complete failure. Clara came, but did not look as if she enjoyed it. The supper table was really beau-

---

*A "capote" was a long, black, woman's cloak made of heavy cloth. Connected to it was a very large hood that extended a distance in front of the woman's face so that it hid her from view.

tiful, there were about forty-two people seated. It was the handsomest thing of the kind I had ever seen. Carolina's napkin was in folds, with orange blossoms between the folds, the Prince's had roses. They sat at the head. D. Barbara and Mr. Curry on either hand, I sat next to Mr. Curry, and Father should have be next to D. Barbara, but as he was not there, Clara took his place. There was dancing before and after the supper, and we sang the Russian hymn a second time and left about one.[18]

But the wedding was not yet really over. On May 6, the *Dmitri Donsky* returned to Faial. The Russian Orthodox wedding was to be held on the ship and, again, Roxana best describes the event.

May 8th. The day of the C.'s dinner party. John, Miss Nichols, Katie, Fan George and I went about four, but the dinner was much delayed. The table was just as it was at the wedding; there were upwards of forty guests. Baron Maidell took Carolina and me in first and sat between us, so that I had to speak German all through the dinner and was relieved when it was over. John and Mrs. D'Orey came next to me. The band played all through the dinner which was the best part – pieces from 'Trovatore,' 'Faust,' 'Bravo,' 'Barbiere,' &c. Every time a health was drunk they played a very spirited sort of hymn. Prince M. had many toasts, not much variety in them, he sat at the foot of the table with the Priest. The doctor finally stood up and stumbled through a toast 'aoux habitans de Horta, aux habitans de Fayal, et à tous les Açores – we stood up at each one. After we left the dinner table, the Prince called us out to the garden to hear the band play the Vesper Hymn. The Vesper Hymn was very beautiful, the gentlemen all stood uncovered, it was quite solemn. Afterwards the band played the Russian and Portuguese hymns and then we all sang the Russian hymn. Then the band played a Cossack dance and some of the officers dance to it; such a queer sort of sailor's hornpipe. Our old Spanish dancing master Serráti used to dance something like it he called 'Cossaco Russo.'

We were all ready on the quay about ten, all the family in town, but Father, Sarah and Edie. Besides ourselves and the Antonio Oliveiras, there were only the d'Oreys. I went off with the Bridal party – Mary Curry took me aside on the quay, and asked if I objected to kissing Prince M. that being the custom at their wedding; and then he spoke of it on in the boat. We were taken into the Capt's cabin, the band playing as we came in. The cabin given up to Carolina is delightful. Fanny and I helped her perform her toilette. This time she wore roses instead of orange blossoms. As soon as we came out to the cabin, Baron Maidell offered me his arm, and we went and stood on a Turkish rug. One of the officers handed me a little square bronze fastened to a white ribbon that looked like a chocolate bon-bon I thought it was to keep perhaps as a souvenir, but later I observed that it had the image of Christ upon it, but I was not told what I was to do with it. Baron Maidell had a larger one (gilt) – had clasped hands. The Bridal couple came and knelt in front of us and we were to make the sign of the cross, but I not being told this, merely held the image over their heads as each knelt in turn. Then Mary and the Dr. took their turns. The whole company then went into the Chapel, the Bridal party bringing up the rear. Baron M. took Carolina and me in. There was a raised platform, in the centre of which was the Altar, the Bridal party stood upon this, the groomsmen standing down by our sides, for they could not have stood upright (the Prince was shorter than they were). What heat! The ceremony was a long one. The chanting as we were entering the Chapel was beautiful. First of all the Priest gave the two lighted candles to hold, prayers and chants going on all the time; then came the ceremony with the two rings, changing them and making the sign of the cross each time three times. Then two odd looking crowns were brought made of tin with some crimson cotton velvet, and nearly covered with tamarisk and red and pink flowers. The Prince's had a picture of Christ held to him by the Priest for him to kiss, before the crown was placed on his head. The crown came so far down on his neck that the effect was funny, and I hardly knew where to look. George said John Morrisson *exploded* into his hat,

a

and the officers had hard work to keep their countenances. The Bride's crown was the same, excepting that it had the image of the Virgin and child, which she kissed. On account of her veil and roses, the crown could not be placed upon her head, so Prince Gagarin and two other officers relieved guard by holding the crown over C.'s head. After some prayers and chants, the Priest, followed by the couple and they in turn followed by two of the Officers holding on the crowns, went three times round the Altar, all bending over on account of the ceiling being low; and owing to Carolina's long train, her officer had hard work to get anywhere near her. After this the crowns were removed, and a little porringer with the Sacramental wine was brought, and the Priest held it first to the lips of one and then to the other and this three times until every drop was taken. There was a large light haired man, who intoned in a deep and peculiar voice out of a large book. After this, Baron Maidell whispered to me that I must go with him into the Kajute – 'What next?' I thought, not remembering at that instant that Kajute was the German for cabin. Mary and the Dr. followed us. On the table was a round dish with a great loaf of black bread with a glass salt-cellar on top. The Baron told me I was to hold that in my bands and make the sign of the cross. He had the same gilt image to hold; so we two stood on the rug, and presently the married couple came and knelt before us, and we went through our parts and then kissed each of them. The Prince actually bowed his head to the ground before the Commander. Then the other 'padrinhos' [Best Man and Maid of Honor] went through the same, after which there came a great kissing and shaking of hands. The Prince kissed each of his fellow officers. Such 'smacks', as George said they seemed actually screwed out. Then came champagne and healths were drunk, and then we were taken over the vessel. After we came ashore, some of us went down to call upon the ladies at the Hotel, saw only Mrs. Richardson. The Russian band came ashore at four and played at the Public garden; nearly all of us went, and nearly the whole town was there. The Artistas band was also there, and there was quite a spirit of emulation. We fell in with the Currys going up. The Commander and a number of the Officers were there. Mr. Heredia (who was sent out by the Portuguese Government to inspect the Custom Houses) came therewith Father. Almost all from the Hotel were there. Baron Maidell ordered the band to play the 'Chanson Nationale de Paris' par Gounod. He came and told me about it, and just as they struck up, the Artistas came marching along playing their loudest.

Prince M. and Carolina came up about nine to take leave. Poor C. was much overcome, she asked to see all the servants. Both she and Prince M. went up to see Sam, who was not very well.[19]

And so the wedding couple left Faial. They did keep in touch with Roxana and two years later returned to visit. Carolina wrote one letter from St. Petersburg and she describes the long, rough, tiring trip to the family residence from Moscow in "a dreadful wagon without springs". In another she writes to Charles Dabney.

My God-father and dear friend – I have thought a great many times of writing to you, dear Sir, but while on my voyage and since I am arrived to Kavérinó my time has been entirely taken up… I was so much troubled by leaving my first dear friends and Country. How much pleasure they [letters she took with her] afforded me! I shed tears over those pages of sympathy, and once more I felt how true and strong my love for you all is… I showed yesterday your note to Constantine, who felt very grateful and thanks you for it. He wishes me to present his compliments, and say he offers you his services in Petersburg or Moscow… You will hear from Roxie of our plan for settling for the present at Kavérinó, which is agreeable to me, as I am so fortunate as to meet here a kind family, who seems to love me.[20]

Two years later, the Prince and Carolina paid a surprise visit to the Azores and described their life in Russia. The couple fit right back into the life in Fayal.

I could scarcely believe that Carolina had really come. I went to the head of the quay to greet them as they came up; Prince M. in true Russian fashion kissed my hand, but I did not kiss his forehead, as is done often in Russia. All our party adjourned to the croquet ground...[21]

The following year Carolina gave birth to Prince Sacha. Later in her life Roxana made a visit to the Mescherskys in Russia, but, except for this, there is no further mention of this Russian--Azorean connection in the *Annals*.

For years, Charles Dabney, as well as other businessmen and government officials on Fayal had been trying to convince the Portuguese government to build a breakwater to increase the safety of ships from storms. Finally, the Portuguese "Cortes", a his-torical governmental body made up of the Nobles, the Commons and the Clergy that functioned like a Parliament, at long last ceded some funds. Charles Dabney mentions this in a letter to Secre-tary of State Seward.

You will be pleased to learn that at the last session of the Portuguese Cortes, an act was passed authorizing the construction of a breakwater to render this port secure, which is an important event, materially affecting the interests of all those having occasion to seek refuge in it.[22]

One of the reasons for having this breakwater was to ensure that Faial would be able to attract more ships in comparison with the other islands, principally São Miguel. In fact, Thomas Hickling, Jr., long-time Vice Consul on São Miguel, wrote the State Department in 1865 stating that before Charles Dabney arrived he had been Vice-Consul on São Miguel and was de-moted when the law changed. He presented evidence that trade was greater on his island, although it was mainly with Britain, and it was much richer in agriculture, which was true. He states that Charles Dabney probably never forwarded this information that Hickling's island was of "greater commercial importance" and asked that it he be upgraded to a Vice-Consul and requests that Charles Dabney not be informed of this request – an indi-cation that there was a long-term resentment about Charles Dabney (which had never been openly expressed despite the closeness of the families) having so much power and he being demoted. He also points out that all the other countries have a Consulate on São Miguel.

However, despite Hickling's request, the State Department did ask Charles Dabney for his comments. He documented the reasons for not creating a Consulate on São Miguel, although he found it personally difficult to respond negatively to the request, having known Hickling for over 50 years and it, thus, seeming like personal jealously.

> Time may change the condition of things, but my present opinion is, that the raising of St. Michaels to the grade of a consulate would be unproductive of any advantage to our country.[23]

Hickling complained about Charles Dabney's response and asked for further consideration. The situation was finally resolved in 1868 when Thomas Hickling, Jr. resigned because of "advanced age," and his nephew was appointed Consular Agent.

Notes:

[1] Roxana Lewis Dabney, *Annals of the Dabney Family in Fayal*, comp., n.p.: The Author, 1900, p. 1029.

[2] Roxana Lewis Dabney, *Annals*, p. 1059.

[3] Roxana Lewis Dabney, *Annals*, p. 1061.

[4] Roxana Lewis Dabney, *Annals*, p. 1064.

[5] Roxana Lewis Dabney, *Annals*, p. 1200.

[6] Roxana Lewis Dabney, *Annals*, p. 1200.

[7] Document 36, United States National Archives, Microfilm T203, Roll 6, January 12, 1864 – December 23, 1869.

[8] Roxana Lewis Dabney, *Annals*, p. 1201.

[9] Letter from CWD, Jr., describing Boston's reaction to the end of the war and then Lincoln's assassination, *Annals of the Dabney Family*, p. 1204-6

[10] Roxana Lewis Dabney, *Annals*, p. 1206-7.

[11] Roxana Lewis Dabney, *Annals*, p. 1207.

[12] Roxana Lewis Dabney, *Annals*, p. 1196.

[13] Roxana Lewis Dabney, *Annals*, p. 1198.

[14] Roxana Lewis Dabney, *Annals*, p. 1198-99.

[15] Roxana Lewis Dabney, *Annals*, p. 102-1204.

[16] Roxana Lewis Dabney, *Annals*, p. 1204.

[17] Roxana Lewis Dabney, *Annals*, p. 1238.

[18] Roxana Lewis Dabney, *Annals*, p. 1239-40.

[19] Roxana Lewis Dabney, *Annals*, p. 1244-1248.

[20] Roxana Lewis Dabney, *Annals*, p. 1271.

[21] Roxana Lewis Dabney, *Annals*, p. 1344.

[22] Document 28, United States National Archives, Microfilm T203, Roll 6, January 12, 1864 – December 23, 1869.

[23] Document 82, United States National Archives, Microfilm T203, Roll 6, January 12, 1864 – December 23, 1869.

Figure 11

Bay of Horta with American Whaling ship. Tents for paying out old oil barrels.

18 – RETURN TO NORMALITY

The American Civil War was over, the excitement of the Russian wedding had calmed down and life in the Azores quickly returned to its routine. Now that it was safe to sail without fear of attack, Charles Dabney felt the need to visit the United States. He climbed aboard the *Fredonia* from their small boat the Neptune, and departed on the afternoon of June 13, 1865.

> A great crowd down. We all went off in the 'Neptune.' It must have been hard for Father to leave. What a shouting the beggars made. He has not lived in vain.[1]

During this visit, Mr. Hunt sent him an invitation for a dinner with General Grant. Despite his family's urging, he decided not to go, an event that was to haunt him 4 years later on Faial.[2]

However, the calm was interrupted by an incident in which the *Fredonia* rescued the passengers and crew of another ship. On January 1, 1866, the *Fredonia* loaded with a cargo of oranges being shipped from Horta to Boston came across the British ship *Gratitude*, which was in serious trouble in high seas. Captain Burke stayed with the ship for two days before he could start transferring the passengers. In all, the *Fredonia* took on 273 passengers and crew.

Eleven days they were on board, limited to two crackers (ship bread), half a pint of water and ten oranges a day. Threw over the cargo of oranges to make room for the people. Capt. Burke had to keep four of his best men on guard two and two to relieve each other. The men passengers would steal from each other and even from the children. At one time some of them made a raid upon the bread, and Capt. B. discovering which ones they were had them up in the main top for two hours (severe punishment in cold weather, but it answered the purpose).[3]

Charles Dabney, Jr. , describes the reaction of the entire city of Boston to the *Fredonia's* action in rescuing so many people with the sacrifice of the cargo.

> *Dear Father* – On Sunday the 14th Inst., the city was thrown into a state of great excitement by the arrival of the *Fredonia* with 300 passengers and crew of the ship *Gratitude* in a destitute condition – and having thrown over most of the cargo of oranges to accommodate them. The action of sacrificing the property to save live created a strong feeling and elicited much praise. The proceedings taken in the case you will find in the papers, which I send you. I knew nothing of the event until Monday morning, and while fully sustaining Capt. Burke's action, about which there could be not hesitation, and while also feeling gratified that your vessel had been selected to perform such a memorable act of humanity – I could not at first forbear some natural pangs at the thought of the oranges which had been lost just when I had anticipated making such a handsome return of them... Capt. Burke has fared well in the matter, which I do not think you will regret, and the mates and crew have no cause to be dissatisfied. I out to mention that it seemed to be a matter of general congratulation that this event had occurred with your property, as it was in keeping with your known reputation, and many though the fruit would not have been so readily disposed of, if Burke had not understood his owners.[4]

Captain Burke received great praise for his actions, however the Insurance Board that determined if reimbursement should be paid raised the point that he had voluntarily thrown the fruit overboard and it had not really been lost. After much argument on both sides, the final decision of the Board went against reimbursing the Dabneys for the cargo Captain Burke threw overboard to make room for people who probably would have died otherwise.

Charles Dabney's many friends and the people of Boston felt that an action that saved so many lives should not be penalized. Several people who had been expecting crates of oranges wrote thanking Charles Dabney for shipping them and assuring him they could think of no better reason for them not arriving that to save a life. In the end, Charles Dabney sent everyone the oranges they should have received.

Mr. R. B. Forbes wrote a letter to Charles Dabney that included a brief description of what was going on as the result of the *Fredonia's* actions.[6]

> ...I see the Boston people are doing the right thing in raising money for the "Fredonia" but in what form or for what purpose I know not. Although you lose your cargo and nothing may be got from insurers, you must be as glad as any of us that the Capt. had the chance to do so much good....The Underwriters are bound to save life and could only save it by throwing over cargo. No decent, not to say liberal underwriter ought to take any other view.[5]

Clara Dabney wrote saying the Boston newspapers reported that almost $20,000 had been raised to compensate the Dabneys.

In February 1866, Faial had its own problem with a ship in trouble. During a storm, the crew of the ship *Sandusky* could not keep up with pumping water out. The seas were too rough to land, and Samuel Dabney sent boats to take the crew off and then tow the ship to safety in shallow water. In a letter to the owners, Charles Dabney gave him full credit for doing what was possible for the *Sandusky*.

> To my son Mr. Samuel W. Dabney is mainly due the salvation of the Ship, he having by his ascendancy over the Islanders his example in exposing himself, induced them to go on board and pump, and bail the water out of her. I mention this, not from any mercenary motive, but that he may have the credit of such. The efforts of Capt. Limmekin are deserving of great praise, but from a commander one expects that he will be equal to an emergency, from one not used to hardship, but to the amenities of a high social position, without any obligation, such an act is not of ordinary occurrence.[6]

Some of Charles Dabney's children were leaving the islands and moving to various parts of the United States, mostly to the Boston area, and getting involved with their own businesses. As already described, one of the first was Charles Dabney, Jr. He entered into a partnership with his Cunningham cousins who were the Boston representatives for the products the Dabneys shipped from the Azores. One unifying factor that characterized those that did leave was that they maintained the Dabney traits of industriousness and community involvement. Therefore, it is not surprising that Charles, Jr. got involved in local politics and was made a "Selectman" in the town of West Roxbury, Massachusetts.

> I desire now to inform you, lest it should be too severe a shock for you if you heard of it in any other way, that I have attained the dignity of selectman of the town of West Roxbury. I presume you never anticipated such political distinction for me. The honor is shared, however, with four others, so that I am not so elated as might be. The truth is, I scoffed at the idea as out of the question, when first presented to me, and continued firm in refusing for three months, but finally my conscience overcame me. I have been here for seventeen years and have a considerable stake in the welfare of the town, and if I should not be willing to do my share of the work, I could not complain if the power should fall into improper hands, consequently 'me voila.' I could not possibly have accepted, but the meetings of the board are in the evening. I have just returned from one, which happened, unfortunately for my correspondence, at this time. It is some satisfaction that I have been informed, I was put in by a handsome vote.[7]

As the 19th century progressed, technology began to have a bigger role in people's lives, a trend that increased rapidly and gained in importance. In the area of communications, the first cables began to stretch across the Atlantic, with the first connection between Europe (Valentia Harbor, Ireland) and North America (Trinity Bay, Newfoundland). A number of cities on both sides of the Atlantic were connected around mid-century, including Carcavelos near Lisbon, although news of the connections did not reach Faial until 1866.

Horta was connected a little later in the century and became the main mid-Atlantic cable station. Until that time, the island residents had to continue to rely on information by ship, which wasn't always reliable and took time to confirm: "(…) Louis Napoleon coming to Furnas next June, ordered by his physician. Quite enough news for one night. Oh! and that our President [Johnson] had been impeached, which, to tell the truth, we do not much believe."[8]

Among the miscellaneous news that arrived on Faial was that the William Morris Hunts had gone to France and were staying on the Champs Elysées. One of the pictures they had with them was of Frank Dabney. During his stay, Hunt exhibited in the Universal Exposition of 1867. In addition they met with Prince and Carolina Mechersky in Paris.

Even without a cable or the assistance of a boat, the Dabneys were able to communicate across the Atlantic, at least 5 miles of it. Their residences at Fredonia on Faial and The Priory on Pico were plainly visible to each other, and the family communicated between the two residences by a system of flags that they hoisted on a pole. Usually they were used to communicate about who was making trips back and forth across the channel, but this was also the means used to call people back in the case of urgent situations such as deaths, ship arrivals and ship wrecks.

In addition to representing the United States as Consul on Faial, Charles Dabney also sometimes acted as British Vice-Consul, and John Dabney had the the honor of being Königliche Konsul of Prussia, with Roxana assisting with the translations.[9] A few of the other countries involved in trading also had Consular representatives in the Azores. In addition to the larger countries, there was a small country that had a diplomatic representative in Portugal at this time – the Sandwich Islands, whose Consular representative was Richard Seemann. Today these are better known as the Hawaiian Islands and were annexed by the United States in 1898. During the 19th century and into the 20th, there was talk, and even some negotiating to have the Azores become a dependency of America.

Mr. Roberto asked C. W. D the other day, in case these Islands [the Azores] sent forward a petition to the Congress of the United States, if it would have any effect? A large number would like to be annexed or at least under the Protection of the United States. (C. W. D always predicted that the Sandwich Islands (as Hawaii was then called) would be annexed to the United States, and some day or other very probably the Azores too.)[10]

With the defeat of the Confederacy, the sinking of the *Alabama* and the Dabney ships no longer facing danger, Charles Dabney wanted to change the name of the *Fredonia* back to the *Azor*. He had never liked the name *Fredonia* for the ship from the time it was registered in Britain under the name of his friend Mr. Arklay in order to protect it from Captain Semmes. However, it was virtually impossible to accomplish this because the U. S. Government considered the registration of a ship to that of another country as an unpatriotic act, something that, in reality, did not apply in the case of the *Azor*. In 1867, Charles Dabney petitioned Congress to recover the name *Azor* and American registration. A recapitulation of the entire event is given in the petition.

To the Honorable the Senate and House of Representatives of the United States in Congress assembled.

'The undersigned, your Petitioner, respectfully represents that in the year 1862, being the sole owner of the American Bark 'Azor,' on the 14th of Sept. of the said year, intelligence reached him of the first depredations committed by Capt. Semmes of the 'Alabama' off Flores, where he destroyed seven whalemen, and one merchant vessel, the crews of which were landed on said Island, from whence they were removed by the agency of your Petitioner, to this place. On their arrival here, they proclaimed Semmes' hostility to your Petitioner, for preventing the confederates and their coadjutors from obtaining coal at this Island, and that he had frequently declared, that he would destroy the 'Azor', if it cost him a two months' cruise. The 'Azor' was then on her way here, to convey oil that had been landed from whaling ships to be sent home to the owners, and there seemed scarcely a possibility of her escaping, but (through the 'Grace of the Almighty') she did! The oil, that was here, had been received by your Petitioner with the express understanding, that it was to be shipped on the 'Azor'; more than a year had elapsed since the commencement of hostilities; nothing but the natural consequences of such a state of things had occurred, and your Petitioner would have been perfectly justified in shipping it on the 'Azor,' but he preferred to forego the freight rather than expose the property, to so imminent a peril; and the 'Azor' returned to Boston in ballast. No more oil was shipped under the American flag until after the termination of hostilities.

"The destruction of the eight vessels left eight masters unprovided for and your Petitioner not being legally authorized to afford relief to persons of their grade, he gave them a free passage home. The 'Azor' on her next trip, was insured against the war risk, but no one would ship property on her, or take passage in her, and the crew objected to continue in her; there seemed to be no alternative, and recourse was had to a kind friend, to allow her to stand in his name, under the English flag; no other change was made. The same Capt. Burke (who last winter threw overboard, your Petitioner's oranges, to make room for three hundred and odd persons, that he saved from the sinking ship I Gratitude,' well knowing the satisfaction it would give his owner) has commanded her ever since she was launched (in 1855).

"Your Petitioner has heard that the act of securing property has been by some considered unpatriotic. Your Petitioner is too well aware of the value of your time, to occupy any of it, by a parade of proof of his devotion to his Country, as he flatters himself that his Patriotism is above suspicion. A scrupulous regard for honor has prevented an earlier application to Your Honorable Body. Death having rendered further delay unnecessary, your Petitioner avails of this opportunity to present, what he hopes, will be considered an extraordinary case, and he respectfully prays that you will vouchsafe that the 'Azor' may be restored to her true colors and name."[11]

Unfortunately, Charles Dabney was never to see his ship renamed because Congress did not grant the petition until after his death.

In April 1867, a small group of Dabneys sailed on the *Fredonia* to the United States. Peace allowed them to travel through prior battle areas on to Pomeroy, Ohio, where Charles still had a financial interest in the coalmines with the heirs of his father--in-law. They visited their friends and relatives there and, not unexpectedly, their conversations included the recent war. Some felt things were going to ruin and destruction, and others held a more positive attitude about the future of the reunified nation. They learned about how the "under-ground railway" worked, and their uncle Horton read a letter written by General Pope in 1860 to Jefferson Davis urging him to remain loyal to the United States. They returned east and stayed at Stanhurst, Charles, Jr.'s, home. This was not too long after Charles Dabney, Sr., had sent the figurehead of the General Armstrong, as mentioned in the chapter describing the battle.

In November 1866, Charles Dabney received a letter about a ship's visit in 1867 that would result in Horta being included in a well-known fiction book.

> *Dear Sir,* - It is proposed by about one hundred American Ladies and Gentlemen to make an excursion hence up to various points in the Mediterranean, taking your port on the way. Will you kindly inform me about what would be the actual port charges on a Steamer of about 1500 tons calling only for one day, without cargo, but to give the excursionists an opportunity of looking over your harbor and town. Also, if with clean bill of health and all healthy on board, there would be any quarantine regulations to interfere. Also the prices of Provisions, fruits, &c. By furnishing the above information you will much oblige,

> Truly yours,
> C. C. DUNCAN, *Manager, 117 Wall St.*[12]

About three months later, Charles Dabney responded to the letter and indicated that the ship would be welcome to stop in Horta

FAYAL, 1ˢᵗ February, 1867.

Dear Sir, – The letter you addressed to me having been put away so carefully that I cannot find it will account for my not having your address. In reply to your queries as to the Port charges that a vessel is liable to on entering this Port; pecuniarily it is small, but as this is the first grand Excursion party to the Mediterranean, I beg here that I may be allowed to offer the freedom of the Port to the Ladies and Gentlemen who compose it. It is the first case that I recollect in which the bestowal of the freedom of a place *only* conferred distinction on the bestower. Assure all the members of a cordial welcome from all the Dabneys Lad believe me respectfully yours &c.

CHARLES W. DABNEY.

Mr. DUNCAN.[13]

This was a historically important voyage because it was the first scheduled tourist excursion by ship from the United States to the Mediterranean. The steamship *Quaker City* had advertised its tour to Europe in many newspapers. After it finally had its complement of passengers, it departed from New York on June 10, 1867 and arrived in Horta on June 21 on the start of its approximately five-month journey to Gibralter, Marseille, Naples, Livorno (Tuscany), Constantinople, Sebastopol, Crimea, the Holy Land and return via Alexandria, Malta, Valencia and Bermuda.

Clara Dabney wrote a letter describing the arrival and activities of the cruise tourists to the family still in America.

This excursion steamer came in on the 21ˢᵗ, such a motley collection of people. Alice awoke me about seven to let me know she was at anchor, and at then the parlor was quite full. We took them into the garden and I never saw persons more delighted with flowers &c.; they seemed quite wild in their enthusiasm. One young man had his note book out all the time and remarked as I gave him some verbena, 'I am taking notes as I am a correspondent of a paper.' 'Horrors,' writes C. P. D., 'how we may appear in print'.[14]

Because of the novelty of the voyage, the correspondent referred to was assigned to send back regular reports. This "young man" reporter was Samuel Clemens (Mark Twain) and Clara's reaction was probably justified because Mr. Twain did not find Faial to his liking. Nevertheless, from his description of the visit to the Dabneys, where he encountered the Dabney daughters, indicates that the family impressed him.

> We ploughed through [the crowd at the dock], and like dutiful citizens went to pay our respects to the American Consul, Mr. Dabney. His house is commodious, and stands in the midst of a forest of rare trees and shrubs, and beautiful plants and flowers. The grounds contain eighteen acres and are laid out with excellent taste. The Dabney family are from New England, and have lived here and held this Consulship, father and son, for sixty years. They have grown to be almost the wealthiest people in the island, and are perhaps altogether the most influential and the best beloved. The common people reverence them as their protectors and their truest friends.[15]

Mark Twain was also interested in the family because of their relationship with the Webster family. As a reporter, he would have been better informed about the murder and subsequent trial several years before.

> Two of the junior Dabney's married daughters of Professor Webster, who was executed in Boston twelve or fifteen years ago, for the murder of Dr. Parkman. The girls were very young then, but highly educated and accomplished. The Webster family removed to Fayal immediately after their great misfortune came upon them, to hide their sorrows from a curious world, and have remained here in exile ever since. I remember a print of that day which pictured the young Webster girls in Court at the trial of their father, but I did not recognize them in the fine, matronly, dignified ladies we saw to-day. Their exile was well chosen. In no civilized land could they have found so complete a retirement from the busy, prying world. This island is

almost unknown in America – and everywhere else no doubt.[16]
He did include, however, a number of negative comments about the island in his notes for articles and the book about the trip, his letters to newspapers and in Chapters 5 and 6 of his book *The Innocents Abroad*, which describe the ship's stop at Faial. The excerpts below are from Mark Twain's notes on the voyage that refer only to some of the more interesting observations not included in *The Innocents Abroad*. [17]

> The community is eminently Portuguese – that is to say, it is slow, poor shiftless, sleepy and lazy. There is a civil government appointed by the King of Portugal, and a military governor, who can assume supreme control and suspend the civil government at his pleasure. The islands contain a population of about 200,000, almost entirely Portuguese. Everything is staid and settled, for the country was 100 years old when Columbus discovered America.[18]

Saw no graveyards. They say they do not reverence their dead very highly; only a few graves are well cared for.[19]
The island exports nothing to speak of, and does not import more than double that much. Nobody comes here, and nobody goes away. News is a thing unknown in Fayal. A thirst for it is a passion equally unknown.[20]

> The only species of vehicle they have is a cumbersome cart with a great wicker-work body on it and solid wheels cut from the ends of logs and the axle is made fast in the wheel and both turn together. They have no stoves and no chimneys. They build their fires in the centre of the room a family occupies, and build it on the floor – some of the smoke escapes through channels built in the walls, and a good deal of it don't. Most freight transportation id done on little donkeys considerably larger than a cat, but not larger than an ordinary calf. The donkey and the balance of the family all eat and sleep in the same room. The grass intended for the donkey's breakfast is mad into a pallet for him to sleep on, and if he gets hungry in the night he eats up his pillows, bolster, bed-

ding and everything else. The donkey is not so ignorant as his master, has less vermin, is not so uncleanly, is better informed and more dignified, and is altogether the most worthy and respectable of the two. Neither are allowed to vote, and, doubtless, neither desire it.[21]

Some short excerpts from Chapters V and VI of *The Innocents Abroad* (also included in his notes and articles) will give an idea of his views on Faial and its people by which the public would judge Faial and its people.[22]

A swarm of swarthy, noisy, lying, shoulder-shrugging, gesticulating Portuguese boatmen, with brass rings in their ears, and fraud in their hearts, climbed the ship's sides, and various parties of us contracted with them to take us ashore at so much a head, silver coin of any country.

The group on the pier was a rusty one – men and women, and boys and girls, all ragged and barefoot, uncombed and unclean, and by instinct, education, and profession, beggars. They trooped after us, and nevermore, while we tarried in Fayal, did we get rid of them. We walked up the middle of the principal street and these vermin surrounded us on all sides, and glared upon us; and every moment excited couples shot ahead of the procession to get a good look back, just as village boys do when they accompany the elephant on his advertising trip from street to street.

They principal crop is corn, and they raise it and grind it just as their great-great-great grandfathers did. They plow with a board slightly shod with iron; their trifling little harrows are drawn by men and women; small windmills grind the corn, ten bushels a day....Oxen tread the wheat from the ear, after the fashion prevalent in the time of Methuselah. There is not a wheelbarrow in the land – they carry every thing on their head, or on donkeys, or in a wicker-bodied cart, whose wheels are solid blocks of wood and whose axles turn with the wheel.

The great altar of the cathedral, and also three or four minor ones, are a perfect mass of gilt gimcracks and gingerbread. And they have a swarm of rusty, dusty, battered apostles standing around the filigree work, some on one leg and some with two or three fingers gone, and some with not enough nose left to blow – all of them crippled and discouraged and fitter subjects for the hospital than the cathedral.

As we came down through the town, we encountered a squad of little donkeys ready saddled for use. The saddles were peculiar, to say the least. They consisted of a sort of sawbuck with a small mattress on it, and this furniture covered about half the donkey. There were no stirrups, but really such supports were not needed – to use such a saddle was the next thing to riding a dinner table – there was ample support clear out to one's knee joints...

We started. It was not a trot, a gallop, or a canter, but a stampede, and made up of all possible or conceivable gaits. There was a muleteer to every donkey and a dozen volunteers beside...

It was fun scurrying around the breezy hills and through the beautiful canons. There was that rare thing, novelty about it; it was a fresh, new, exhilarating sensation this donkey riding, and worth a hundred worn and threadbare home pleasures.

The roads were a wonder, and well they might be. Here was an island with only a handful of people in it – 25,000 – and yet such fine roads do not exist in the United States outside of Central Park.... They talk much of the Russ pavement in New York and call it a new invention – yet here they have been using it in this remote little isle of the sea for two hundred years!

And if ever roads and streets, and the outsides of houses, were perfectly free from any sign or semblance of dirt, or dust, or mud, or uncleanliness of any kind, it is Horta, it is Fayal. The lower classes of the people, in their persons and their domiciles, are not clean – but there it stops – the town and the island are miracles of cleanliness.

Despite most of Mark Twain's comments, the vast majority of regular visitors to Faial enjoyed its scenery and way of life and found the people friendly and welcoming. Just after her return from the United States to Faial, Roxana Dabney was at their house at Mt. da Guia and presents a completely different viewpoint of Faial that was shared by the other Dabneys, and most of their friends, and contributed to the family staying for so many years on Faial.

> ...as I sat on the verandah, watching an ox cart come lazily over the beach I had the curious feeling, such as I never before experienced, it was such a complete contrast to what I had left; I think it is owing to snapping off my visit so short. It is all so beautiful, but there is a dreaminess about it all of two or three centuries back. And yet I am perfectly satisfied and happy; and well I may be, for there is every thing but *life* and more congenial outside people. That is the *life* here, must come from within, and I am determined it shall come.[23]

> Sunday, Dec. 15th. I went up to the 'Cedars' to sing, but instead we had a very animated discussion, into which John and Sam entered, upon the advantages and disadvantages of living in Fayal. I think we all agreed that we should probably not be any happier any where else.[24]

However, this did not mean that Faial did not have problems of its own. In September 1867, one of the crew of the *Fredonia* murdered one of his crewmates. Both were known and liked by the Dabneys. The story starts where most shipboard violence started – with both men drinking. Their discussion got loud, and a ship's officer warned them to calm down. At some point it turned into an argument, and one stabbed the other. The man accused of the crime was made a prisoner. The next day, when he sobered up, he said he was very sorry for what he had done. Roxana wrote him in jail, and he said to her, "You have done more with your kind advice, than could ever be done with 'reproof.'"[25] As the U. S. Government representatives, the Dabneys were involved with the investigation. The outcome is not recorded, but in most cases, the accused was sent back to America to stand trial.

Following this incident, the Dabneys had the unusual occurrence of a man entering their house and going upstairs before he was detected When asked what he wanted by one of the family nursemaids, he said, "A light." She told him to leave, grabbed him by the shoulders and escorted him out the door and locked it. "Father says, not one woman in five hundred would have acted as she did."[26] After the family returned, the "insane man," named José Gonsalves, was seen passing by the house again.

"All day the Police had been trying to take him (they were afraid of him)", but John and Sam Dabney caught up with him and told him Mr. Dabney would not want him in their property, at which he laughed. Apparently John had seen him the night before in the same area and had sent him off. After three attempts to enter, they convinced him to come out. By this time 4 or 5 soldiers met him and took him into custody, but he struggled and they pulled out bayonets and clubs, so Sam and John then had to protect him.

His insanity was said to have come from seeing the man who replaced him as lookout aloft fall and die at his feet. He was at first put in prison and then transferred to the Hospital. This concerned the Dabneys because the Hospital windows overlooked the garden at their "Cedars" property. Their concern extended beyond this one man because at this time they were having "hard times with runaway sailors (there were 120 or so here now) and ill-acting Portuguese."[27] As mentioned before, the problem of fugitive, sick and abandoned sailors was something that constantly plagued the Consulate.

Sailors were not the only problem they had in late 1867. In December of the year, a massive storm struck Faial and caused extensive property damage. Needless to say, some of the ships were badly damaged or destroyed, some involving the loss of life. The survivors of one ship on which six people drowned took one of the ship's sails, all that they had left, to the closest church to give thanks for their survival. This type of offering is common among the Portuguese and sometimes includes wax replicas of the part of the body or object that was spared through their faith. Fredonia and Bagatelle suffered moderate damage, with part of Fredonia's wall falling, but the ceiling of the parlor of the Italian Villa fell and there was a fire in Cedars that was promptly brought under control. As usual, the poorest suffered the most from the vagaries of Nature. One of the fishing villages lost all their boats, and the villagers had no livelihood until they were able to replace them. Those most afflicted were provided help by the Dabneys to the extent they could.[28]

To end this chapter on a higher note, a a naturalized American from the Azores named Joseph Davis, a name that he had obviously anglicized, had left Faial 35 years earlier when he was 13 or 14 and now wanted to track down his family. He wrote and asked Charles Dabney if he could give him information about his family. In this instance, Charles Dabney was able to comply, and Davis' mother was extremely happy.

> Never should we doubt the power of God, for in our hour of greatest affliction he aids us. Who would have thought, my beloved son, that when I was thinking most of you, overwhelmed as I was by troubles of all kinds, there entered the Angel of Gladness sent by Mr. Dabney to inform me that my son still lived and asked after his relatives? I could not believe this at first, because in thirty-five years not a word had I heard, and supposed you dead.[29]

This search for past relatives and connections with Portugal, and especially the Azores, continues today on a number of internet sites.

Notes:

[1] Roxana Lewis Dabney, *Annals of the Dabney Family in Fayal*, comp., n.p.: The Author, 1900, p. 1208.

[2] Roxana Lewis Dabney, *Annals*, p. 1413.

[33] Roxana Lewis Dabney, *Annals*, p. 1226.

[4] Roxana Lewis Dabney, *Annals*, 1226-27.

[5] Roxana Lewis Dabney, *Annals*, p. 1228.

[6] Roxana Lewis Dabney, *Annals*, p. 1250.

[7] Roxana Lewis Dabney, *Annals*, p. 1251.

[8] Roxana Lewis Dabney, *Annals,* p. 1276.

[9] Roxana Lewis Dabney, *Annals,* p. 1278.

[10] Roxana Lewis Dabney, *Annals,* p 1363.

[11] Roxana Lewis Dabney, *Annals,* p. 1282-83.

[12] Roxana Lewis Dabney, *Annals,* p. 1290-91.

[13] Roxana Lewis Dabney, *Annals,* p. 1291.

[14] Roxana Lewis Dabney, *Annals,* p. 1292.

[15] Daniel Morly McKeithan, *Traveling with the Innocents Abroad: Mark Twain's Original Reports from Europe and the Holy Land,* University of Oklahoma, Norman, OK, 1958, p. 4.

[16] Daniel Morly McKeithan, *Traveling with the Innocents Abroad,* p. 4-5.

[17] Daniel Morly Mckeithan, *Traveling with the Innocents Abroad,* p. 3-18; Alfred Bigelow Paine, organization, *Mark Twain Notebook,* Harper, New York, 1935, p. 61-62.

[18] Daniel Morly McKeithan, *Traveling with the Innocents Abroad,* p. 16.

[19] Alfred Bigelow Paine, *Mark Twain Notebook,* p. 62.

[20] Daniel Morly McKeithan, *Traveling with the Innocents Abroad,* p. 5.

[21] Daniel Morly McKeithan, *Traveling with the Innocents Abroad,* p. 6.

[22] Mark Twain, *The Innocents Abroad,* American Publishing Company, Hartford, 1869, p. 38-49 (Excerpts from Ch. V & VI).

[23] Roxana Lewis Dabney, *Annals,* p. 1299.

[24] Roxana Lewis Dabney, *Annals,* p. 1318.

[25] Roxana Lewis Dabney, *Annals,* p. 1300.

[26] Roxana Lewis Dabney, *Annals,* p. 1304.

[27] Roxana Lewis Dabney, *Annals,* p. 1306.

[28] Roxana Lewis Dabney, *Annals,* p. 1316-17.

[29] Roxana Lewis Dabney, *Annals,* p. 1318.

19 – LIFE GOES ON

In November 1867, Charles Dabney, Jr.'s house, known as "Stanhurst," burned to the ground. The fire was thought to have begun from the ash barrel, even though they had taken the appropriate precautions. The family was awakened by the cook Mary knocking on the door saying that the house was full of smoke. Despite their efforts, the fire spread too rapidly so they concentrated on saving what possessions they could. Charles, Jr., wrote his father a detailed description of the fire and their actions. Not only does it show how the family reacted, but also shows how the community around them reacted to fires in neighbors' houses.

I hastily put on trousers, dressing gown and slippers and hurried down. The man having been roused came rushing down the back stairs quite wild. The entries were indeed full of smoke, and I felt that the case was a serious one before I saw the fire. Patrick went to the cellar and I to the kitchen, and as I opened the door there was a blaze of light from the little place outside the laundry – a kind of passageway from the back door. The flame was inside. I seized a pan of water in the sink and dashed it on, quenching the flames for the moment, and called to Patrick to come to me. I could see that the fire had got up to the ceiling, and Patrick called to me that it was outside also, and I got my little pump, but there was no one to bring water. Patrick was *wild*, but had got a ladder and placed it, so that I could get on to the roof of the porch and tried to cut in and get at the fire, having nothing but an old spade to work with, whilst I sent Patrick for the axe, which was in the cellar close at hand. He in his confusion lost his light and after an eternity as it seemed to me came back without the axe! I had been calling fire at intervals, and May had run across (in dressing slippers) to our neighbor's. I now heard the flames crackling and roaring inside, so that I knew it of no use to attempt anything more, single handed as it were. Without hat and with really nothing but my night shirt besides my trousers, as the dressing gown was always open, a mass of ice from head to foot, I now gave up the struggle, went up stairs and dressed myself in warm clothing, and then went to work to save books and pictures down stairs.

Susan had had her hands full with the women, who were for the most part beside themselves with terror, and in taking care of Zay, who behaved very well, giving no trouble. Susan was perfectly calm, but so engrossed with the people and so confident that the house would be saved that she did not think of saving her own things, and as I was most anxious about the pictures and some other things below stairs, and not knowing how much time we should have, we saved scarcely anything up stairs, not even our wardrobes. The alarm had at last spread, and people began to come, and after a time the engine, but it was too late; the house was a mass of flames, and all that could be done was to save what still remained in the parlor and dining room. Susan and May had saved most of the silver plate and we were all engaged in saving valuable books, &c. May had done very well throughout.

After burning for about two hours, the house fell in just as the grey dawn was coming on; and it was sad enough to stand amid the wreck and feel that our pleasant happy home had gone forever. All this occurred with the thermometer at 12 above zero.

We were at once taken in at Mr. Cary's, and friends and neighbors vied with each other in kindness. After housing the things saved, I hurried to town to look up quarters and on my return found Susan had gone to William Minot's, where we were to stay temporarily. We were there a week, and then spent ten days with cousin Mary Cunningham, and nothing could exceed the kindness we experienced at both places, as well as from Mr. and Mrs. Forbes, who had May with them, and would hardly let us off from a visit, and of course made it out that we should be conferring a favor by going there. My insurance though not enough to cover at present prices was fair. The terrible loss is in the thousand little things, which money can never replace. All my record of the war time and everything connected with my service, – Susan', May's and Zay's watches, &c. It seems like beginning life over again, and we had never had everything so comfortably and pleasantly arranged and were looking forward with real pleasure to the winter, and having Clara with us. It is certainly, next to the death of dear friends, the severest calamity which can befall a man.[1]

Charles, Jr., did not have enough insurance to cover the actual value of the property. Even more devastating was the loss of a number of items with emotional value.

I had a fair amount of insurance, but not enough, of course, to cover entirely, much less replace at present value; but the sore trial is in the loss of an infinite number of little things – of little money value – but so priceless to ourselves.[2]

The family moved into town and took up residence at Pemberton Square. Unfortunately, Charles, Jr.'s, health, which was not good, suffered as the result of overwork and the residual effects of smoke inhalation from the burning of his house and the fighting during the Civil War. These health problems continued for the rest of his life.

That life in town, coming upon C. W. D. Jr.'s sore trial impaired his health very decidedly; the more so as being near his office, he was often tempted to go there and work at night. He was much troubled with "sciatica" that winter. Susan H. D. thinks the seeds of his fatal malady were laid at the South in the time of the war, but the exposure of that night and his gigantic efforts to save his house, inhaling that smoke all the time, the effects of which showed themselves for weeks after, not doubt increased, if they did not originate the trouble.[3]

Because of the number of Dabneys who had departed for new lives in America, the number of family residences had more space than was necessary to house the family members remaining on the island. Bagatelle, which was still the queen of the family residences, was periodically empty, and when the *Açoria-no* and *Fredonia* arrived at the same time, some of the family and their friends were able to stay there. In July, 1868, the Olivers "settled down to their life at Bagatelle, and very delightful it was to have the dear old house open once more its hospitable doors." However, they left in the early 1870's and finally settled in Santa Barbara, California. Roxana was a frequent guest to their home, as well as at her brother Sam's Fayal Ranch in the San Diego area in later years.

Although the family residence on Pico, known as the Priory, was a summer attraction and a schedule had to be made for summer visits to the Priory, some of the country houses were not visited as often. In January 1868, Roxana made her first visit in two years to Capello on the western part of Faial; visits there were usually hunting trips for the men while the women just relaxed.

In addition to family members leaving Faial, even some of their servants migrated to the U. S. In 1868 Maria Jacintha got married and eventually moved to America and had a "flourishing family" in Southern California.

In 1866-7, Thomas Hickling, Jr., who was quite elderly and who had served as America's representative on São Miguel for more than 50 years, wrote a letter of appeal to the State Department following the refusal of his request in 1865 about his position being downgraded by the State Department to Consular Agent. Hickling felt the position should be upgraded and, in fact, that São Miguel deserved to be made a Consulate on its own.

> It is clear that his Excellency the President, who has the most benign intention, is ignorant of the commerce and important position of this island – and who, if the distress of his poor degraded former Vice Consul to Consular Agent, otherwise he would have extended his fostering hand.[4]

In other letters he describes the commerce and trade movement on São Miguel and says that it has easier access to Europe than Faial. He also once again asks that Charles Dabney not be informed of his communication about wanting to upgrade São

Miguel "as he probably never imparted to Government that in his Department there is an Island of greater Commercial Importance than the one in which he resides".[5]

However, once more the State Department asked Charles Dabney's opinion about Hickling's request. Dabney responded that he disagreed with it; arguing that São Miguel had little commercial importance for the U. S., although he indicates that "Time may change the condition of things", a statement truer than he knew since just over 25 years later, the Consulate, in fact, was moved to São Miguel.[6] The complaints from Thomas Hickling did not continue very long because he resigned because of age and was replaced by his nephew Thomas E. Ivens.

A letter from Samuel Longfellow to Samuel Dabney indicates their still close relationship, gives some historical commentary and reviews the literary highlights in Boston.

> Cambridge, Feb. 26th, 1868
> My dear Sam, – Many thanks for the basket of oranges – I was delighted to get your long letter, full of the account of you family circle… Indeed, my dear Sam, you are greatly blessed in such a home; such a wife and such children ought to make a man happy and thankful and good. I am so fond of children that you couldn't have sent me anything better in your letter than the pea pictures of your circle; and I was glad that you spoke of them all in their places, as an unbroken circle, in the feeling that those who had put off the garments of the flesh were not thereby gone away from your homes and hearts, but held their places forever in both. And is not this undying affection in our hearts, the great assurance of immortality? Your picture, I assure you, awakened in me a strong desire to see you in your home. Some day, I hope, I shall see your boys and girls either there or here. The papers will give you the particulars of the exciting state of Public affairs. Johnson, after putting every obstruction in the way of Congress and its reconstruction measures, and thereby exciting and keeping alive the hopes of the rebels at the South, and their allies, the old Democratic party at the North, has at last, openly and directly violated the law regularly passed by a two thirds vote of the

Congress, that no Executive officer shall be removed during the term for which he was appointed without the consent of the Senate. He has removed Mr. Stanton, who was appointed by Mr. Lincoln for his term of four years, the remainder of which is filled by Johnson as acting President. Of course there was nothing left but to impeach Johnson, which the House have done, and the trial will soon take place. This conflict between the Congress and the Executive has been most unfortunate in hindering the reconstruction, but I do not think the demands of the Congress have been anything but just and liberal. I do not think any other conditions would have given us any guaranty for the future peace of the country.

I went in last evening to hear Mr. Dickens read for the third time. It is very entertaining. He acts, rather than reads, scarcely looking on his book, and using a great deal of descriptive gesture, sometimes very expressive. His face, too, he throws into a great variety of expression, often irresistibly comic. He enjoys his own humor, too, and the appreciation of his audience, and his eye fairly shines with fun. I have heard him in David Copperfield, Bob Sawyer's party (from Pickwick), the "Christmas Carol" and "Boots at the Holly Tree Inn." The Hall is always crowded. I thank you for the "Palavra"; I contrived to pick out the meaning though my Portuguese is rather rusty. It is really encouraging to see such signs of progress. I am to have an article in the March number of the " Radical," which I will send you. I have been preaching for the past year in Boston to the "28th Congregational Society," founded by Theodore Parker, but my engagement with them will cease in the Spring. They have no Church, preferring to hold their meetings in a Hall, the seats in which are free to all comers.

Sincerely and affectionately yours,

SAMUEL LONGFELLOW.

In a little note accompanying the "Radical" a little later, he writes: –

You spoke of Agassiz's opinion on slavery. I am happy to be able to correct your impression. I heard him say not long ago that when he was first in this country, he was indifferent on the subject, or inclined to the pro-slavery side, but that his views had entirely changed.[7]

In May 1868, the island had a surprise visit from Prince and Carolina Mechersky. "Prince M. in true Russian fashion kissed by hand, but I did not kiss his forehead as is done in Russia." "Carolina showed us how she prepared to go out in the winter in Russia."[8] They stayed for an extended period and old friendships were renewed. In 1884 Roxana returned their visit on a trip from the Azores to Russia.

The Dabneys were not the only non-Catholics on Faial. There was also a community of Jewish descent. Most of them had come from Morocco and settled first on the island of São Miguel. Once they were well established there, they spread to some of the other islands. The most prominent of the families were the Bensaúdes. They started out as cloth merchants and extended into other areas of business and became the main competitors of the Dabneys on Faial.

On June 10, which coincidentally was Charles and Frances Dabney's anniversary, there was a Jewish wedding in Horta. It was between Solomon Sabat's niece and Samuel Lerado with rabbi Meyer Pinto officiating. Sam and John were able to go to the synagogue part of the ceremony with "Nimas (a Hebrew), who showed them the commandments on parchment."[9]

The company of the Bensaúdes provided the greatest competition for the Dabney businesses. The competition for customers was strong, but friendly. Both Charles Dabney and Walter Bensaúde were philanthropists, and sometimes they jointly provided funds for projects and programs that would benefit Horta and the people of Faial. The business of both families on Faial decreased as the years passed, but the Bensaúde's remain in the Azores, becoming one of the wealthiest families in the archipelago.

One visitor to Faial in September 1868 was from outside the circle of Dabney friends who regularly visited Faial, but she was soon included in the round of their activities. This was Mrs. Allen who was Commodore Vanderbilt´s daughter, at this time one of America's richest men. She was visiting her daughter-in law who had been visiting Faial. Roxana "found them more like people than I had been led to expect. Mrs. A. Sr. looked as if she had stepped from a fashion plate with her white puffed hair like a French Marquise."[10] Her stay was cut short when she learned of the death of her mother from one of the American newspapers that arrived.

The life and activities of João Brotero, son of Charles' sister Nancy Dabney Brotero, has been described in a previous chapter. However, he was not the only one in that branch of the family to have had significant influence in Brazil. His brother Frederico added his own mark on the country. He had been appointed Judge at Goyaz in the Province of Minas Gerães, and Roxana gives us some excerpts from a speech he made that contained ideas, such as women's rights, a good number years before their time.

> We come here by invitation of the Prince of the Goyano Church... The subject is too vast and the occasion not a fitting one to face on all its sides the formidable problem of popular instruction, which is so intimately connected with the most vital questions of our country, but permit me to bring forward one point – perhaps the most interesting and prolific, the education of women. I rejoice to see that they were not forgotten on this occasion, and that they come with enthusiasm to render this literary festival more brilliant. A pity it is that this should not be of more frequent occurrence in our country, where the majority seem to think that the only mission of woman is to people the world, and be a perfect automaton of domestic accomplishments. A fatal error and fearful injury, which we received from our unhappy and ill-fated Mother country ['Metropole' he calls it] from whom we have inherited with many profitable ideas, much that was false and miserable. By the Grace of God these ideas are disappearing, and it has been said that the "advance of the "Woman's Cause" is that of the Civilization of the human species. She is the only creature, below the Creator, who can say with justice and pride, that she holds in her hands the future and prosperity of the State, as to her is reserved the task of forming citizens.'

[Frederico Brotero speaks with much feeling of the sacred duties of a true mother, and of the calamities to society when woman has not received the education she is entitled to.]

"And who is responsible for these great calamities? We are, we, whom fortune, intelligence, knowledge, chance, family, or duty have placed in the Vanguard of the State. We who form the thinking part should deem it absolutely incumbent upon us to employ all our efforts, each one according to his ability, in every possible manner and without ceasing, for the completion of this great work, the ' Emancipation of Woman,' through education and liberty. We must (without reference to this little spot of our Empire) acknowledge with frankness and courage, that we have everything to do in this our country. What inexplicable inconsistency – Society does not spare sacrifices, it raises sumptuous edifices, pays exorbitant salaries to learned men to turn out Magistrates, Doctors, Diplomats, Military characters; and is so mean and avaricious in creating mothers of families, a 'sacerdócio' superior to all the rest. I do not flatter myself that I have brought forward any new doctrines, or pretend to make proselytes by raising my weak voice in answer to the kind and gratifying invitation of my Friend and Teacher. I but seek to give vent to the sentiments of my soul, which is filled with the beliefs of youth, and the strongest faith in the future of our Country. [The discourse ends with a feeling tribute to the Prelate], who consecrates all his vigils to the welfare and instruction of youth, thus affording a shining example of the union of Church and State."[11]

Relative to women's rights Roxana reports on an argument in 1895, after they were living in America, between Miss Ellen Emerson, daughter of Ralph Waldo Emerson (con), and Mr. Forbes (pro) about women's rights. Roxana pointed out that her father "was a firm believer in the eventual granting of suffrage to women as the just thing."

São Paulo, where Nancy lived, was a rapidly growing city and had added a number of advanced educational and social services.

It is pleasant to think that doubtless Aunt Nancy and her husband had a hand in shaping all this, for they went there in the infancy of the city and province.[12]

Nancy Brotero Dabney died in 1872 at age 69, and José Maria Avelar Brotero died in 1873 at age 76. The accomplishments of this branch of the family were exceptional, and Roxana presents a summary of the family's activities that had been sent to her.

> The Councillor José M. de Avellar Brotero and his wife are both dead; they left seven children, three sons and four daughters. All the three sons had taken the degree of L. L. D. in the University of St. Paulo. The eldest, John, after having been deputy and president of one of the Provinces of the Empire, died of gangrene in one of his legs, as he would not consent to have it amputated. The second, Raphael, is a lawyer in the city of Guacatinguelá in the Province of S. Paulo, and occupies a seat in the Provincial Assembly. The third, Frederico, is at the present time Judge in the District of Itú in the Province of S. Paulo. As to the ladies, they are all married. The eldest married Dr. José Maria de Sá Benevides, Professor in the Law School of S. Paulo. The second one married a son of the Baron of Souza Queiroz, and died in S. Paulo. The third one married Dr. Abranches, who has been twice President of this Province. The fourth is also married, but I am ignorant of the name of her husband, but I believe she resides in S. Paulo.[13]

The Brotero's were not the only connection the Dabneys had with events in Latin America. In October 1868 William Henry Dabney, still Consul in the Canary Islands, wrote to Charles telling him about the revolution that had started in Spain and the actions in Mexico.

> Teneriffe, Oct. 12th, 1868
> Dear Brother, – In my last to John I told you of the escape of the banished Generals in a steamer. It now turns out that she was sent by Prim and Milans del Bosch was on board; they joined Prim in Gibraltar and proceeded to Cadiz; their arrival

being the signal for this wonderful revolution in Spain, which has been accomplished so suddenly and successfully.

On the 5ᵗʰ Inst. the "Cadiz" steamer reached this with the news and immediately a "pronunciamento" of civil and military took place, a "Junta" was appointed and reforms were begun. Their first act was sweeping away all port charges, octroi duties &c. This has since been followed by another, abolishing all duties on cereals and tobacco, and establishing absolute liberty of commerce. We are now in the midst of four days' rejoicing, illuminations, &c., and you never saw a happier people than ours just now. The Revolution was accomplished without an accident. In Canary they attacked the Jesuit's College, took all the Jesuits and sent them to Spain, seventeen in number, completely gutted the building and took all the pictures, saints and crucifixes and burnt them in the yard! They did the same to the Convent of nuns and turned them all into the street. Here they contented themselves with smashing all the portraits of the Queen, and the Royal Arms everywhere.[14]

General Prim who was referred to in this letter was Count of Reus and Marquis of Castillejos and was very important in this revolution. He had visited Faial in 1862 on the ship *Ulloa* accompanied by his wife, a Countess, and their four-year old son (who was a Viscount and had his own boy attendant). The young boy servant had been given to him as a slave, but he refused to accept him as a slave since Spain had no slavery and gave him his freedom. Their ship had left New York for Britain and stopped in Horta for coal. A request was made to Charles Dabney for coal, but he was hesitant because the portion of his coal contracted by the British Government was running very low, and he asked for a day to consider the request.

The next day the *U. S. S. St. Louis* arrived and saluted General Prim, firing 15 guns and raising the Spanish flag. That night the Dabneys had a party for the officers of both ships. In the end Charles Dabney provided the coal requested.

In order to supply the coal required for the "Ulloa,", General Prim had in the name of his Government guaranteed

C. W. D against any pecuniary loss. He sent father a fine engraving, framed, a portrait of himself on horseback with his signature [and a thank you note][15]

General Prim was a Catalonian who fought on the side of Isabella II against the Carlists, had been Governor-General of Puerto Rico in 1817, and in 1861-2 led the Spanish forces that had been sent to Mexico along with the French and British forces in order to collect the debt due from the Civil War which was taking place in Mexico between the liberals, who had elected Benito Juarez president, and the conservatives who did not want any kind of reform. This war was going on when Frank Dabney was traveling there and is the reason for the precautions he took and his surprise that he could travel back and forth between Vera Cruz, which Juarez had made his capital, and Mexico City without incident. The three European countries felt safe in doing this at the time because the United States was involved in its own civil war and was not in a position to enforce the 1823 Monroe Doctrine. The British and Spanish left after they were unable to agree on how to enforce the debt collection, but France remained and occupied Mexico with the support of the conservatives. In 1863 they offered Ferdinand Maximilian Joseph von Habsburg of Austria as emperor of Mexico.

During this time in Mexico, Maximilian, who came from the European liberal tradition, disappointed his supporters. In addition, the U. S. Civil War ended, America began to send arms to Juarez, and France began to withdraw its troops to fight in the Franco-Prussian war. The conservatives began to switch sides, Mexican republican forces defeated Maximilian, and he was executed. Throughout this period, Puerto Rico and Cuba sought their own independence. Instability continued with the involvement of Spain, and eventually the U. S. got concerned with the disputes, the result being the Spanish-American War in 1898.

Starting in 1863, just a year after his visit to Faial, General Prim made several attempts at a military overthrow of Queen Isabella II. In 1868, General Prim and his compatriots were finally successful in the overthrow of Queen Isabella II.

> The Queen of Spain and all the Royal family have gone to join the company of those throneless kings wandering about Europe. And how quietly this was all accomplished.[16]

General Prim was made Prime Minister in the provisional government and was important in the selection of a Hohenzollern Prince as the new monarch. Unfortunately, before everything was settled, Prim was assassinated by his political enemies.

The last couple of months of 1868 were relatively quiet on Faial. The Mescherskys were still in residence and some members of the Dabney family returned for a visit. Thanksgiving was celebrated with 24 at the table, and Christmas with 27 at Fredonia, however, the three main houses were all decorated. Between Thanksgiving and Christmas the family prepared and put on a series of tableaux for their own entertainment. On Christmas night the servants performed a traditional circle dance for the family.

Then there were the end-of-year school exams, which were held orally with the whole family attending, which certainly did not help the students' anxiety level. However, all did well according to their teacher Dr. Adelstein. On December 31, the family had their traditional distribution of gifts to the children of their employees, and on January 1 they tied 81 presents to their tree for the staff of all the Dabney houses.

Ralph Waldo Emerson's daughter Ellen was on a several month visit to Faial. She was included in virtually all the family activities and was well liked.

> Miss Emerson does interest and amuse me [Roxana] so much; I never saw so *perfectly* natural a person.[17]

> Monday evening... the *Fredonia* sailed. I helped Ellen Emerson to bed. I never saw so original a person.
>
> I always remember E. E. remarking on an occasion when we were having a good time playing games with the children, I said, "What a fearful noise the children do make, scraping their chairs over our uncarpeted floors." "Why don't you like it? I think it is the most delightful sound." We all had great enjoyment in her, as who could help it?

In telling of Miss Emerson's visit in Fayal, I omitted mentioning the great pleasure she afforded to your Aunt Clara, she it was who enjoyed the most of Miss Emerson's society. You remember the treasures that used to be brought out of the old wardrobe, treasures accumulated through so many years from all parts of the world one might say. Miss Emerson was shown them all, and heard the histories connected with each. Those mementoes are scattered now east, west, north and south, but have doubtless been bestowed where they were appreciated. It requires a marked and strong character like your Aunt Clara's to be willing to divest oneself of almost every thing one has most valued in life. (I mean, of course, of "belongings.") The friendship of Miss Emerson has been one of C. P. D.'s greatest happinesses since the memorable voyage they made together in 1869.[18]

During Ellen Emerson's stay on Faial, her father wrote a letter to Charles Dabney thanking him for the welcome his daughter had received on Faial and the box of oranges he had received from the Dabneys.

Concord, 22 March 1869

Dear Mr. Dabney, – The "Fredonia" brought me a basket of excellent oranges with my name written on a card. I cannot ascribe the gift to any one but yourself, and please myself with so believing. I have never had the happiness of meeting you, but your kindness and tenderness, and that of every member of your family to my daughter, every day since she has been in Fayal, have made me and all in this house your affectionate friends. Ellen fills all her letters with the praise and joyful anecdotes of your and yours, only saddened lately by the painful accident which befell Miss Roxa Dabney, and which her latest dates reported as no longer alarming. Apart from Ellen's debts of happiness to her new friends, she has interested us all in the glowing picture she draws from real life, of the power for good which sense and character can create and exert wherever they fall. You may be sure that henceforward nothing that concerns you family can be indifferent

to us here in the woods. To Miss Clara and to Mrs. Charles
Dabney, Junior, our thanks, for care and cherishing our traveller,
are especially due. I beg you to present to them my grateful
regards. I remain

your deeply obliged servant
R.W. Emerson[19]

The painful accident to Roxa he refers to occurred when
she jumped out of a small cart and the bottom hoop of her
dress got caught and she hit her head on the ground. She was
too ill to be moved and taken home, and for 11 days they applied
ice to her head. She spent most of the time unconscious and reported feeling great pressure on her head and strange dreams.
After 18 days she recovered sufficiently to be taken home.

In early 1869, one of the 19th century's most famous figures
arrived for a visit. Lady Jane Franklin, widow of Sir John Franklin
stopped in Horta. She had accompanied her husband when he
was appointed governor of Van Diemen's Land, now known as
Tasmania. Sir John was very active in improving the conditions
of life among the people there, as well as promoting educational and cultural activities with the help of his wife. They were
both adventurous travelers and participated in several expeditions to explore Tasmania.

Sir John is best known for his expedition to discover the
Northwest Passage, using as a basis land expeditions led by Sir
John several years earlier. The expedition took place in 1845
with the ships *Erebus* and *Terror*, with 128 officers and men.
When no word of them had been heard by 1847, search parties were sent to find them. Searches continued for 12 years
and in 1857 Lady Jane sent out a search party of her own
because "she felt all the time that the Admiralty and other expeditions did not pursue the right course."[20] This expedition returned in 1859 with news of finding skeletons of the crew and
a written account through April 25, 1848.

In 1846 the ships had been trapped in ice about midway
between the Atlantic and Pacific. Sir John had died before the
journal entries ended, but 105 of his crew abandoned the ships

in April 1848, although none survived. It is possible that some reached a point previously explored by Sir John that was know to connect to the west coast of Alaska. Although Sir John never directly proved the existence of the Northwest Passage, he is generally given credit for proving its existence. Because of her persistence in encouraging searches for him or his body without losing faith, Lady Jane Franklin was given a special place among the distinguished women of the 19th century. Roxa gives a brief description of her meeting with Lady Franklin.

> I remained in the parlor – enter Father with a very short, motherly looking old Lady – she came directly up to me and took my hand, 'We look like dwarfs to you, do we not? but you are accustomed to look down upon people,' and then she added looking up at me with a very sweet expression, 'but you look very condescending.' They admired the flowers very much, and Lady Franklin said, 'I see you soften the corners with flowers.'[21]

> Lady Franklin and niece were here for a few moments just after dinner. Lady Franklin gave me 'Euthanasia,' a poem by Sir John Franklin on discovery of the N.W. Passage. She gave Clara, Harriet, Fanny, and aunt Olivia each some little remembrance, and this book she gave me because she had been told that I once wrote a letter to her for Dr. Kane, and thought I should be interested. How little I dreamed when writing that letter at Brattleboro in 1852 that we should one day have that remarkable woman to dinner.[22]

Susan Dabney, wife of Charles Dabney, Jr., spoke a lot with Lady Franklin and was invited to visit her in London. The offer was taken up and she "gave the Dabneys a delightful dinner party".

> We took leave of these ladies with real regret. They like Americans, they say, because they have so little ceremony. Lady Franklin spoke with much pleasure of seeing uncle William and family in Tenerife.[23]

Because of their isolation, the Azores were slow in keeping up with modern advances. A paragraph from Roxa's diary in 1869 gives a good general picture of one of the technological events that was slowly bringing the Azores up to date.

> May fifteenth. Our City was illuminated for the first time. Two of the bands were out and quite a crowd out to see the *dim* lights. There is a large party opposed to the lighting and much ridicule. Several nights after the inauguration I was coming from the Ferreiras late in the evening escorted by our servant João, and just this side of the Starbucks', I nearly fell flat over a stone on the sidewalk. 'Oh, Sr².' said João, 'eu podia ter trazido a lanterna, mas cuidei que a cidade estava illuminada' (I might have brought a lantern, but thought the city was illuminated). Sam was much amused by this, and would like to have repeated it to some of the wags, but deemed it more prudent not to.[24]

Horta had been trying to raise money for years to establish a system of street lighting. The first lighting there was a lantern that burned olive oil hanging on the city hall. They were offered some more lamps in 1852, but were unable to put them into operation because of a lack of funds. The Baroness of Lagoa donated money for another light, with the condition, however, that it be placed where it would provide light for her residence. The only other lights were small oil lamps, called *perilampos*, which is the Portuguese word for firefly, distributed along the roads. That Horta needed a much better lighting system was unquestionable and was emphasized by foreigners who "walked through the dark streets of Horta... carrying large candles to show the ridiculousness of the state of lighting in Horta".[25]

In 1868, a Portuguese company made a proposal for gas lighting, however, this was considered expensive and a commission decided to use petroleum lights. In December 1868 the decision was made to raise money for 120 street lights and the main contributors were Charles Dabney who donated 70 street lights and Walter Bensaude who furnished the supports to hold them.

The inaugural ceremonies in 1869 were presided over by the President of the commission that arranged for the system and included the local band "*Amantes de progresso*" (Lovers of progress). This system of lighting continued until 1910 when an electric lighting system was initiated.[26]

Once again, the suggestion that the Azores break with Portugal and join with the United States arose. Two events in 1869 prompted further consideration of the idea. One was based on an increase in taxes, the other on the idea of a "*União Iberica*", either under the monarchy of Spain or as a united republic.

> A vessel in from Lisbon. The taxes on property here to be increased 50%! Changes in Custom House and duties increased twenty per cent. It is said that in Terceira they are full of the idea of claiming the protection of the United States.[27]

> Ilha Terceira, Angra do Heroísmo 20 Fevereiro, 1869
> Exmo. Snr., – Will your Excellency [Charles Dabney] inform the American Government that the sons of this land do not wish to be Spaniards, and if they are to lose their nationality they *desire to be Americans*. The general opinion is in favor of this. The moment that there is a Revolution 'Iberica" the American standard will flutter in this land beside the Portuguese.
> "Hespanhões nunca!" [Spanish never]

> The signature has been cut out.[28]

Notes:

[1] Roxana Lewis Dabney, *Annals of the Dabney Family in Fayal*, comp., n. p.: The Author, 1900, p. 1328-9.

[2] Roxana Lewis Dabney, *Annals*, p. 1319.

[3] Roxana Lewis Dabney, *Annals*, p. 1330.

[4] Document 77, United States Archives, Microfilm T203, Roll 6, January 12, 1864 – December 23, 1869.

[5] Document 56, United States Archives, Microfilm T203, Roll 6, January 12, 1864 – December 23, 1869.

[6] Document 82, United States Archives, Microfilm T203, Roll 6, January 12, 1864 – December 23, 1869.

[7] Roxana Lewis Dabney, *Annals*, p. 1336-7.

[8] Roxana Lewis Dabney, *Annals*, p. 1344-5.

[9] Roxana Lewis Dabney, *Annals*, p. 1345.

[10] Roxana Lewis Dabney, *Annals*, p. 1357.

[11] Roxana Lewis Dabney, *Annals*, p. 1367-8.

[12] Roxana Lewis Dabney, *Annals*, p. 1369.

[13] Roxana Lewis Dabney, *Annals*, p. 1370.

[14] Roxana Lewis Dabney, *Annals*, p. 1370-71.

[15] Roxana Lewis Dabney, *Annals*, p. 1017.

[16] Roxana Lewis Dabney, *Annals*, p. 1373.

[17] Roxana Lewis Dabney, *Annals*, p. 1377.

[18] Roxana Lewis Dabney, *Annals*, excerpts from p. 1405-7.

[19] Roxana Lewis Dabney, *Annals*, p. 1398.

[20] Roxana Lewis Dabney, *Annals*, p. 1405.

[21] Roxana Lewis Dabney, *Annals*, p. 1404.

[22] Roxana Lewis Dabney, *Annals*, p. 1405.

[23] Roxana Lewis Dabney, *Annals*, p. 1405.

[24] Roxana Lewis Dabney, *Annals*, p. 1406.

[25] "Lighting in Horta," *O Atlântico*, Anno 7, nº 13, p.4.

[26] Marcelino Lima, "Iluminação," *Anais do Município da Horta (História da Ilha do Faial)*, 3rd Edition, Oficinas Gráficas "Minerva", Vila Nova de Famalicão, 1981, p. 166-8.

[27] Roxana Lewis Dabney, *Annals*, p. 1409.

[28] Roxana Lewis Dabney, *Annals*, p. 1428.

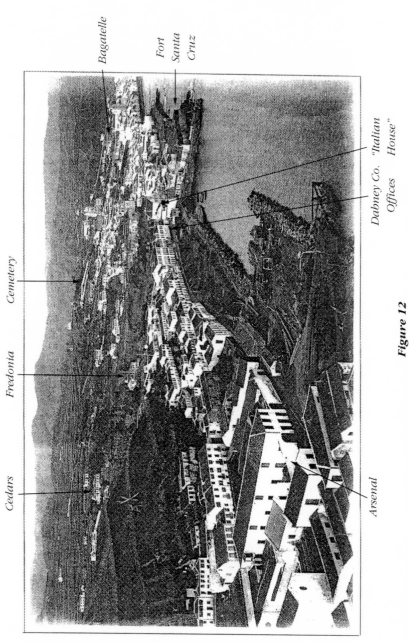

Bagatelle

Fort Santa Cruz

Cemetery

Fredonia

Cedars

Dabney Co. "Italian Offices House"

Arsenal

Figure 12

View from Mount Queimada showing various Dabney properties

20 – ANOTHER EPOCH ENDS

At the end of May, 1869 Charles Dabney, Jr. , and his family left Faial for Malvern Hall (which was the subject of a painting by Constable in 1809) in Warwickshire in central England where they took up residence. His leaving greatly saddened the family, and they were once again reduced in size through the loss of a much-loved son and sibling. As Roxana describes him, "what a beautiful man he is; I never so thoroughly appreciated him before".[1] The same evening "that Charles, Jr., left, the rest of the family walked up to their property at Santo Amaro, and Charles, Sr., as was his custom, stopped in a grotto to visit the tree on which he had carved his wife's initials 40 years earlier.

One of the visitors to Horta in July 1869 was the Portuguese poet Bulhão Pato. While he was there, he attended a party where he recited one of his poems. Today in Portugal he is better known for the dish Clams Bulhão Pato style, a dish consisting of clams cooked in white wine with fresh coriander and a very large amount of garlic – delicious with cold Portuguese *vinho verde* (green wine).

In 1870 Charles Dabney once again sent Ralph Waldo Emerson a box of oranges. However, this time he received a letter plus a gift in return, for which he responded with his own letter of thanks.

Concord, March 4th, 1870

My Dear Sir, – A basket of beautiful oranges was brought to my door a few days ago with no word beyond a card, on which my name was unmistakably written. But the oranges speak for themselves and say "Dabney" and Fayal to every one in this house. I send you my own and my wife's thanks for this unexpected remembrance. We have no sunny fruits to offer you in return, but as I learn that the "Fredonia" sails on Monday, I mean to send you a poor little weed of a book ['Society and Solitude'] which has just grown ripe in this snowy town. Ellen, who is spending some weeks in Milton sends as much good news of your self and family. With Mrs. Emerson's and my own kind regards to them all I remain.

Yours faithfully
R. W. Emerson

Fayal, 9th July, 1870

My dear Sir, – My eyes yet remind me, that I transgress in using them, and being very desirous of prolonging the luxury of communicating with my friends, I have resolved to visit Europe, to try a change. I cannot however leave home without forwarding to you evidence of my reconnaissance for the charming bouquet (by which your not of March 4th was accompanied), fresh from you Intellectual parterre – assuring you that I am grateful to the Almighty for having endowed me with the power of discriminating between our respective gifts.[2]

The major event during 1869-70 was when one more time a non-Dabney American Consul to the Azores was appointed. The first knowledge of the appointment came from the June 4th edition of the Boston *Traveler* newspaper indicating that Mr. J. C. Cover had been appointed Consul to the Azores, replacing Charles Dabney after 43 years in this position. Mr. Cover was a middle-west politician with some political pull, but in "delicate health".[3]

I learn from Senator Mr. H. Carpenter that I have been honored with the appointment of Consul to Fayal, Azores, Portugal – Commission dated 3rd June, which however I have not yet received. Have written to Carpenter to have it forwarded to me.

Am desirous of receiving my instructions at once, so that I can think definitely of what I shall be required to do. Also, am impatient to commence the study of the Portuguese language, and to recover the French, of which I once had a fair knowledge.

J. C. Cover[4]

Newspapers and a letter to Sr. Manoel Garcia, attaché to the Portuguese Embassy in Washington, confirmed this. Without question, it was a profound shock to the Dabney family. The surprising thing was that not any of Charles Dabney's friends and regular sources of information had known of this until they received a letter from Charles, Jr., in England. Finally, the official letter, short and sweet, arrived.

> Executive Mansion
> Washington, D. C., 1st June, 1869.
> You are hereby suspended from the Office of Consul of the United States at Fayal in accordance with the terms of an act approved April 5th, A.D. 1869, to amend an Act regulating the term of certain Civil Officers, passed March 2d. A. D. 1867, and subject to all provision of law applicable thereto.
>
> U. S. Grant
> To Charles W. Dabney, Esq.

And that was all.[5]

Charles Dabney blamed himself to some degree for what happened. In 1865, William Hunt sent him an invitation to have dinner with General Grant. Charles, Jr., and his sister Clara both urged him to accept the invitation, but he tended to avoid events such as these. In 1869, Cover's appointment reminded him of the event and he wrote a letter to Hunt about that dinner.

> My dear Mr. Hunt, – How often have I thought of your kindness in urging me through Charles, to be one of the fourteen to be present at the dinner to be given in honor of Gen. Grant, in the autumn of 65; and I had not an opportunity afterwards of expressing my obligation and regret that I could not avail

myself of my chance. You, of course, are aware that I have been suspended from the Consulate of the Azores. There is nothing but long term of Office that can be brought against me, as I have so many testimonials in the official Despatches from the Department of State highly commendatory to my Patriotism, consideration and judgment on occasions during the last war.[6]

He was right about the support he had for him to remain as Consul and, once alerted to the situation, his usual influential friends wrote letters to the State Department regarding his having been replaced as Consul, possibly for the reason that he had served for so many years. His ardent supporter J.M. Forbes wrote a letter to Massachusetts Senator Charles Sumner, who had been appointed to take Daniel Webster's seat when he became Secretary of State. His letter also sheds more light on Charles Dabney and his service as Consul.

Hon. Charles Sumner, etc. etc.
Boston, July 21st, 1869
Mr dear Mr. Sumner, – I hear with surprise and regret that Charles W. Dabney, our Consul at Fayal is to be *rotated* out. Mr. Dabney, and his father before him have been, it is true, long in office there, but they by their public spirit and hospitality *have been a credit to our Consular system.*

The pecuniary value of the office is nothing, and any hungry expectant will be starved to death there. To a merchant like Mr. Dabney, the prestige of office among the formal Portuguese is valuable. In needful expenses the office costs him double its pecuniary returns.

His father was there when the Privateer "Gen. Armstrong" whipped the British fleet so handsomely, and from that time to the Alabama's day when our present Consul stopped the pirate's coal and drew on himself and his ships Semmes's wrath, no man's record for patriotism and advanced Republicanism has been better than the Dabneys.

In the darkest days of the war, his second son left business – and home and family and went into the active war, at the very time Semmes was cruising especially for his father's ships.

This change, however prompted, is a mistake, which in such matters is worse than a crime, for it discredits the Administration to do such hasty things against us of the Mercantile community, and of the true Republican faith.

Cannot you help us stop it?

How can we make the President and the Secretary see that it is a mistake?

Scores of Mercantile signatures can be had at will against the change, but the mere statement of the case ought to be enough.

Mr. Cushing (Caleb) for instance, if consulted would see and show up the impolicy of this change, but in such a matter I think the Boston Merchants ought to have some weight.

It is only four years since one of Mr. Dabney's ships loaded with oranges, fell in with an Emigrant ship sinking. His Captain *knowing his owners*, threw overboard part of his cargo and saved 300 lives.

Finding the Insurance did not cover it, the Boston Merchants shared the loss with the generous owners, but this incident shows the kind of man you would turn out. Yours very truly,

J. M. Forbes[7]

Another letter from Grant's Secretary of State, Hamilton Fish, to the Reverend Benjamin Haight deals with the change in Consuls in the Azores.

September 10th, 1869

My dear Doctor, – I return Mr. Pomeroy's letter – Mr. Dabney's case is one aspect is a hard one. He has been a good officer and has held the position of Consul for a quarter of a century or more. Under the system prevailing in some other governments, he should have been continued. I do not say but that that system may be better than the system which our people have sought to establish.

While Mr. Dabney has held the office of Consul, the People of the U. S. have six times chosen their chief Magistrate, and on four of the six times have chose a President of different political views from his predecessor. Only once has an incumbent been re-elected – or been a Candidate for re-election. This may not indicate any thing more than that the People insist upon change, and will not have life tenure.

I fear that Mr. Dabney is not the only instance of a very good Consul falling a victim (within the last six months) to the rule of rotation and to the pressure of official position. During the first six weeks after my entrance on office, I saw daily from four to six hundred persons, pressing for Consular or Diplomatic appointments, or for retention in office. Not a word or a line from any one in behalf of Mr. Dabney. The inference was that he was tired of his long service, or was indifferent to the retention of the place. Others sought it, for it was not so small as to be entirely overlooked, and in the press, one got it. Then and not until then was it known that Mr. D. wished to retain it. One tenth of the effort made, since it was too late to be remedied, would have prevented the change. There is an adage about shutting the stable door after the horse is gone.

I certainly am very sorry that a good officer and a worthy gentleman should be disappointed, but remember there were some thousands applying for positions, out of which only a hundred or so could be appointed – the rest were all disappointed and they and their friends are finding fault that more removals were not made. Now I am not arguing – I cannot consent to be on the defensive in this matter. I have heard a great deal about this matter since the removal was made and have testimonials from very respectable parties quite sufficient to have ensured Mr. D.'s retention, or possibly his promotion to the highest Consulate in the gift of the Government, but they came too late. Mr. Cover had been appointed many weeks before I went away. If Mr. Cover, the lately appointed Consul should conclude not to accept the position, I shall be very glad of the opportunity to restore Mr. Dabney. It will be no objection with me that he and his father have held the Consulate during the present century. But having yielded the to prevailing pressure, and the accepted rule of rotation, which the

People have established, it would be an injustice to Mr. Cover now to remove him without cause.

I do not think that Mr. Dabney's friends, who were silent and passive when a would would have sufficed for his retention, have the right to ask of me to do to Mr. Cover the wrong of removing him without any fault of his. I never saw Mr. Cover and have no knowledge of him, except in connection with his application for this office – he is represented to me as a deserving, worthy man capable of the duties of the Consulate. &c. &c.[8]

As shocking as the event was to the Dabney family, they handled it in their customary style and accepted it gracefully as an inevitable occurrence. Charles Dabney invited Mr. Cover to his home and even gave up his own private office for Cover to use, which Mr. Cover accepted, and, as such, "we knew then that Mr. Cover would be guided aright".[9] In addition, recognizing his need for an experienced assistant, Mr. Cover appointed Samuel Wyllys Dabney as his Deputy Consul.

Roxana provides us with the Dabney's first impressions of Mr. Cover.

All agree in saying there is a certain likeness in him to Mr. Lincoln. Clara says, 'He is kindly and dignified'; Alice says, 'Kindly and reasonable'; Harriet says, 'A real American in appearance' (and sentiments, she should think); Francie says, 'The new Consul looks like Lincoln very much; he is kind looking. He was up here this morning in the parlor and I went in without knowing it. He from his waist up seemed to be sitting on the sofa; the rest of him was lolling on a chair – he looked very ugly by the side of Grandpa? (funny child she is).

C. W. D gave up his own office to Mr. Cover and put him *au fait* to all the duties, and made him feel at home. We were all so glad that father had the visit to England to look forward to.[10]

Mr. Cover was welcomed, probably to his surprise, into the extended Dabney family and was provided with valuable assistance including participation in many of their activities. The Dabneys maintained their welcoming character, in spite of the unexpected loss of the Consul position and the manner in which they learned of Cover's appointment as Consul.

In the spring of 1870, Charles Dabney Jr.s' health, which was not good when he left the U. S. began to concern the family. Roxana sailed to England with a group of family and friends to visit Charles, Jr. When they arrived at Newport they were taken on to "Malvern House (on the English lodging house plan)"[11], where they met John Pomeroy and Charles, Jr., and other family members in a "family party". They communicated with Charles, Sr., about what was going on at Malvern. In his letter of response he said he was planning to visit Europe in the spring and included the news that Carolina Meschersky had given birth to a young Prince.

While staying in Malvern, where there were about 12 families living independently, Roxana took the opportunity to go to London to visit friends and returned to Malvern with the Pomeroys, where several other friends showed up during the time they were there. Charles, Jr.'s, health wasn't improving and decided to go with his family to Paris. Around this time, Samuel Dabney and family visited the U. S. for the first time in 19 years.

Roxana and Clara had a long, pleasant stay at Malvern where they made many acquaintances and visited many places in the surrounding area, including Hope End in Herefordshire, the childhood home of Elizabeth Barrett Browning. In the Spring of 1870 they decided it was time to move on, and they went to Paris where they met up with George Pomeroy. When Roxana saw her brother she commented,

I was much shocked to see Charles looking so thin and pale; when he left Malvern he had seemed remarkably well; evidently the climate of Paris did not suit him. We went up that same afternoon to Dr. Lambert's where the Dabneys boarded, found only Charles at home.[12]

Even Charles recognized that his health was suffering. While in Paris with his sisters Roxana and Clara and George Pomeroy, he wrote a letter to his father that included comments on how he was feeling.

We had a pleasant visit of ten days from Roxie, Clara and George Pomeroy, and they left us on the morning of the 24th [May]. It was a little singular that we parted from Roxie in the 'Place of the Palais Royal' at nine o'clock on the evening of the 23d., a year almost to an hour from the date of our leave taking in Fayal. We had *very* hot weather the period of their stay here, and May rather over fatigued herself going about with them... You may hear that I am not very well, but I beg you will not feel any uneasiness on that score. I have had a little of my sciatica lately, and I cannot get rid of a cough, which has clung to me all the time I have been here, though at times it was very slight... I recognize more and more the effect of the strain during and since the war and feel that I did not start any too soon to repair damages. We intend to pass a day at St. Germains, two or three at Versailles and as many at Fontainebleau, so that if our present programme is carried out we shall be on the Rhine about the middle of June...

> Your affectionate son,
> Charles W. Dabney, Jr.[13]

In August 1870, Charles Dabney decided to leave Faial for England accompanied by his sister Olivia. In the meantime a letter arrived from Charles, Jr.'s daughter May

I thank God daily for my strength, for I am able to watch at night and be with Father a good deal in the day and do not as yet feel it; of course I get an hour or two of sleep every night and last night slept steadily, not having to get up every hour. Dear aunt Roxa, I am so sorry to put such a burden on you and to give such a welcome to my dear, dear Grandpapa, but I think, if you think so too, that it would be best for no one, unless Dr. Gully, to know that there is no hope, for after all the doctors may be mistaken, but you must do as you think best, only I do not wish Mother to be written to, until I have told her.[14]

Charles Dabney arrived at Malvern on August 8 and was shocked upon hearing about his son's state of health and wanted to leave for Paris immediately. He was convinced to wait, and two days later they sent a telegram to Paris. Not receiving an answer, he asked Roxana to go with him to Paris on Thursday, the third day after his arrival. That day a letter from Susan Heard Dabney arrived from Paris with better news about Charles, Jr., and they rented the cottage "Oak Lodge" in the area from Mrs. Roberts. After a series of communications "dear Charles and his people arrived at Oak Lodge, the 18th of August". Of course the doctors knew exactly what to do.

Dr. Gully and Dr. Fernie took a more hopeful view of the case, and recommended the water treatment. Their opinion was that the seat of the trouble was the liver.[15]

In the hope that Charles Dabney, Jr., was better, Roxana comments that "Charles is really improving and looks much better." She and her father took a trip up to London to visit friends. When they returned a week later, everything was still fine. After a short stay, Charles Dabney, Sr., took another trip during which he went to concerts at the Crystal Palace. In spite of his being very worried about his son, he did not let anything affect his "Dabney traits". While he was

...at the Crystal Palace concert C. W. D., seeing a lady standing, [went] up and offered his seat. Your Aunt Marianne remonstrated, but he replied, "I can't see a lady standing". That one soon went off, and he offered it to another one. Then he put his handkerchief over his head. Aunt Marianne told him it was not the custom, but he said, "I can't feel the air about my head," They had some amusing times.[16]

He returned to Malvern again in early October and went to Scotland to visit Jessie Paterson, sister-in-law of his sister Emmeline. Her children had grown up and she had remarried, but she was the same enjoyable person that they had remembered. While they were in Edinburgh, they were able to see the Prince and Princess of Wales, the future Edward VII and Queen Alexandra. The Prince was there to lay the cornerstone of the Masonic Temple, and they were able to see all the ceremonies that were associated with this event.

Roxana and charles, Sr., left Scotland for Malvern and encountered a few problems on the train that caused him "to harangue the… officials about, upon the superiority of traveling in the United States, all of which they accepted quite meekly", and to threaten to "publish something about the backward state of England in regard to railway travel!"[17]

Although Charles, Jr., seemed to be feeling better, he seemed prone to bad luck.

> What a narrow escape they had from being burnt out a second time. The maid left the towel rack too near the candle; May showed great presence of mind.[18]

Roxana and the rest of the family convinced C. W. D. to return home after 14 months in England. He was reluctant to leave because of his son's health, but they convinced him that a winter in England might not be good for his own health. At Roxana's insistence they stopped off in Lisbon on their way home. They visited a large number of acquaintances, some of whom were important in Portuguese history. One was the Duke of Bolama, António José d'Avila, who was mentioned in Chapter 16. He was now Prime Minister of Portugal.

> The great man received C. W. D. in the heartiest manner and told him how much he felt that he owed him for his "bons concelhos" when he was a youth in Fayal, and of how C. W. D. had stimulated his ambition rightly. He got into father's carriage and had his own follow him, and nothing would do but that he must alight and accompany C. W. D. to the head of the stairs of the Hotel Central, where he left him as he (the Duke) had much to do, being, as I have said, Prime Minister at that time. This was very gratifying to father.[19]

Other Azorean families living in Lisbon included the d'Oreys and the Ivens. The former introduced them to the Albuquerque family (the family is famous historically for the 2nd Viceroy of India in the 16th century and his son who was first mayor of Lisbon). The d'Oreys introduced them to José Diogo Albuquerque, one of whose sons (Roxa didn't know which) captured the famous African Chief Gungunhana in Mozambique 1896, an act for which several countries decorated him.[20]

As for the Ivens, Thomas Ivens had been appointed to replace Thomas Hickling as Consular Agent on São Miguel. They were related to Thomas Hickling's grandson Roberto Ivens who, along with Serpa Pinto, were the first men to cross Africa from the West to the East, showing Portugal's interest in connecting their colonies of Angola and Mozambique. The British were opposed to this, as were the Germans, and a permanent connection between the two colonies was never made.

The Dabneys left Lisbon for Faial on November 15, 1870, making stops on the islands of São Miguel, Terceira, São Jorge and Graciosa to visit old friends. They finally arrived back in Faial to the pleasure of the rest of their family.

However, their happiness was short lived when Charles Dabney, Jr., died at the age of 47.

In January, 1871, the sorrow came upon us, which our hearts had foreboded.

I find the following notes in your grandfather's [Charles Dabney, Sr.] handwriting:-

On the twenty-second of December, 1870, at Malvern, England, our dearly beloved Charles terminated his earthly career!. A sense of Justice to his memory, and of gratitude to the Almighty, who had endowed him in such manner as to be esteemed by his fellow men, and to be such a Blessing to us, renders it incumbent upon me not to pass over the event without some allusion to the admirable manner in which he acquitted himself in all the relations of life. A good son, devoted husband – good father, good brother and always a favourite with his comrades and teachers. When in College he was distinguished for his high sense of honour.[21]

Charles Dabney, Sr., also referred to some of his son's activities at Harvard and his willingness to serve his country during the Civil War, but was unable to write more. Over the Christmas period his body was laid in an open coffin with pale primroses in one hand and a bunch of holly in the other. John Pomeroy's daughter Edie wrote her mother "what a hallowed Christmas they had had – they had still the beloved form with them, for it was only on Christmas night that the lid was closed over it".[22] Letters and remembrances came from all quarters. An obituary by the Honourable Edmund Dwight, member of the first Board of Education in Massachusetts, summarizes the general feelings and attitude toward Charles William Dabney, Jr.

In Memoriam
Charles W. Dabney Jr.,
Was a man of very remarkable character. It was drawn in distinct and simple lines and with perfect accuracy. One cannot imagine two of his acquaintances differing in opinion about him, any more than about a square or a circle. Was it the completeness of his qualities which made him appear always the same, like a sphere, from whatever point of view? Such a character is hard to describe, – perhaps because its main quality is its absence of imperfection. One would truly say that he combined in a rare degree, gentleness with strength; that he was centered on truth, which radiated to every extremity of his being. Next came unselfishness and warm affection; modesty and courage he had, of coarse. Indeed, all the virtues came very kindly to him and then stayed. While all the parts of his character fitted well together, his scale was large, and he was full of strength and hearty vigor; the most trustworthy of men, in whose hands you would place all you possess, from fortune to reputation. The most sympathetic in joy or sorrow; the most faithful in the performance of all duties; a very rare man, and yet so natural as to be a compliment to his race.
We cannot help being sorry that he is dead; yet there is nothing discordant between death and him. Though so full of life, he was in tone with a life hereafter, and we think of him as one fitly promoted. His 'tenderness, his truth, his purity, his sympathy and self abnegation led him forward, and we cannot wonder that he overstepped the line. We fancy him as a prince just entering a foreign court of a higher tone than ours, and feel that he will be at home and appreciated there, and

without much change from the man we knew. If we arrive, we shall recognize him at once. "Coelum non animam mutant." The old simile of the grub and the butterfly involves too violent a change to suit our ideas of him. His change would rather be as of the same air played in a different key. Here we know only the sad minor, in which all our lives are set, happy if there be some melody or grace in them. But the great Composer has granted him, as we conceive, a new variation set in triumphant key, with richer harmony and nobler instrumentation, but keeping still the air we knew and loved, and all its household sweetness. His life was, for the most part, a fortunate and happy one. He amassed a large fortune of respect and affection, which he invested securely in the memories of many friends, and undoubtedly he has taken some of his investments with him. We dare not speak of the home he created and adorned. His industry was successful, his honor never called in question, for it was his good fortune never to be betrayed and exposed to the criticism of those who never trust. We are glad that he lived; we are grateful that we knew him; we would be like him if we could; we are sorry that he died before us, and we trust we may meet him again.

[Signed with three stars.][23]

The body was shipped to America where family members from the Pomeroy, Alsop and Oliver families that had married into the Dabney family and become an integral part of it met his body at the ship. Services were held in the Church of the Disciples.

With the change from sail to steam, less ships needed to stop at Horta for supplies and repairs, which resulted in an increase in competition for what business remained, particularly with the Bensaúdes. As the result of not having an active business life and not being Consul, Charles Dabney "seemed to have no particular call upon his time."[24] One of his main interests was visiting his property at Mt. Carneiro, which rises up behind the town of Horta, and he still conducted the way he lived according to the three words he considered as guides in life: Toleration, Consideration and Compensation.[25]

He used to go and see different friends a great deal, who always gave him the warmest welcome. Outwardly he seemed the same, but it was with intense pain that we noticed a diminution of physical and mental powers.[26]

Early on the morning of March 7, 1871, he started his day before breakfast by going to Mt. da Guia at the southern edge of Horta to check on "the idiot" Augusto who had fallen into a fire and was badly burned. On his way home he met a "schoolmistress he had befriended" and listened to a long story she told. When he returned home he was quite chilled and "took cold, which developed into an inflammation of the lungs."[27]

On March 12, 1871, "a beautiful Sunday afternoon", Charles William Dabney died, less than three months after his second eldest son.

> ...he left us, after the most touching leave takings, even to his little grandson and namesake, who kept begging to be taken to his grandfather's bedside. (Francie, I think, passed nearly the whole of that day in her grandfather's room.) All the great love that father had for all his children (and I am sure in his heart he never made any distinction between them) came out, and he sent remembrances to every one in all directions. He could not talk much, but he said to Sarah, "There will be compensation" (for those who remain, he meant); and none of us who witnessed that indescribable expression of awe and rapture as he seemed to recognize those to whom he was going, turning his eyes to salute one and another, – can ever forget.[28]

While his strength of body and spirit for which he was known was diminishing, his death was still unexpected. In hindsight there were indications that his will to live was deteriorating, a deterioration that may have begun with the death of his beloved wife Frances nine years earlier.

> After her departure his tie to life must have seemed broken; and since the recent death of his son and namesake, so

well known among us as the inheritor of many of his fine qualities, he is said visibly to have failed.[29]

Added to this was the loss of his position as Consul, more specifically, the manner in which it was done, together with the decrease of his involvement in the Dabney business activities. Needless to say, his death shocked the island's inhabitants. In fact, some of them were not entirely willing to accept the fact.

> The end had come, though many would not believe it. I am sure with some of the more humble, they persuaded themselves that there would be some interposition of Providence, or that there would be some manifestation afterwards.[30]

There was an overwhelming desire among the people of Faial, as well as the family, to have a last look at him. As a result, the family felt it only right to comply with this wish.

> The children kept begging to go and see him, and they brought the brightest flowers they could find to lay upon him.

> So wrapped in his soft, white cashmere shroud, he was placed in the middle of the drawing room, with flowers all about him, and the poor old souls he had befriended seemed to keep back their sobs so as not to disturb him. One of his former employees, of very dignified presence, when he approached, said most impressively, "This is majesty!" One old woman told Dr. Oliveira, "O Sol do Fayal obscureceo-se hontem." [The Sun of Faial was obscured yesterday][31]

During his lifetime, Charles Dabney affected the lives of numerous people in Boston and elsewhere in the United States. In addition, he had an effect on the life of virtually everyone on the island of Faial, as well as on many of those living on the other islands of the archipelago and even some people in continental Portugal. His professional, philanthropic and political contributions have been pointed out numerous times in this book, but Roxana relates two events.

I remember on one day this winter when he and I were walking up to Mt. Carneiro, a persistent, poor old beggar woman followed him all the way up our street, pouring out an endless tale it seemed; when we reached the place where our paths separated, she seized father's hand and covered it with kisses. "What did you give her, father?" I asked. "Nothing, I only listed to her story"; such patience he had.[32]

Returning one day late to dinner C. W. D. encountered in the "Sagão" (as so often happened), a poor woman suffering very much from an inflammation of the eyes. C. W. D. went up and begged the family not to wait for him, and then he went after hot water and a silk handkerchief, bathed the woman's eyes carefully, gave her the handkerchief and told her to repeat the process until she were better.[33]

His granddaughter Rose gives a summary of his life that demonstrates that his real influence was something much deeper and from which all his other contributions arose – understanding and kindness.

Charles William Dabney had a vivid personality with charm and graciousness. He was a man of vision, and not only saw things in a large way but accomplished them in a large way. He carried on the policies of his father, and having unusual initiative and imagination he developed many new business interests. He was keen to introduce activities which might be of benefit to the Fayal people, and as time went on more and more did he become a pillar of strength to the weak and a counselor to those seeking counsel whether in matters material or spiritual.[34]

The newspaper "*Fayalense*" published an obituary written by Miguel d'Arriaga in its March 19th edition, included in its entirety below.

Charles William Dabney is dead!
Is it possible to say more than is contained in this dire simplicity? Needs there more than the utterance of the name,

to produce the exclamation 'a most worthy citizen'? Is it not
enough to announce his death for all to feel at once that there
has been a great and public disaster? No! more than this,
even, said the cries, heard to come repeatedly from the multitude, when his moral remains, covered by the flag of the great
republic, surmounted by a cross and star of flowers, passed
slowly through the streets of this city to the measured and sad
sound of funeral marches; cries which, bursting from afflicted
hearts and dismayed souls, sketched in few words, this spirit
which had departed; cries which are the spotless glory of the
man and a legacy of inestimable value to his family; cries
which on the earth, which he has left, are undying hymns; in
heaven, whither he has risen, are notes which mingle with
the songs of the Seraphim! these cries said, The Father of the
Poor is Dead! What more can be added to this? This is the
greatest eulogy of the man, who on the twelfth day of the
present month, closed his eyes to the light of this world to
open those of his spirit forever before the majesty of the Most
High, where the warm light shed by the sun of immortality
warms without blinding, causing the soul to open like a flower
to pure ideas and heavenly sensations.

Happy the man who is governed by thy lovable inspiration, O divine Charity! Because for him who cheers by his alms
the heart of the poor, those alms will always plead; because
for him who ever finds words of consolation for the suffering,
these words will ever supplicate; because he who loves his
neighbor as himself, fulfils the precepts of the law of Christ,
and he will be among the chosen.

Many and diverse were the forms by which Charles William
Dabney revealed in this Island the goodness of his heart: more
numerous than the deeds of which the public has become
aware, and which have brought him the tribute of well-merited
praise, were the hidden and secret acts, which the right hand
doeth without the knowledge of the left, acts which crept forth
to dry the tears and alleviate the sufferings of many a distressed
yet shrinking family.

Who can now relate all the benefits which his hand scattered with open palm? Who that has been afflicted does not

remember the consoling words which he had ever ready for great sorrow? Who in this land can forget that speaking and sympathetic countenance which so won the hearts of others, for whom it never lacked expressions of comfort or affection? The present generation assuredly will not forget him, and will transmit to future generations the record of the services which this so exceptional a man rendered during his long life to the land, which he loved as if it had been his cradle, to the land, which he adopted as his home, to the land which finally opened its bosom to him like a fond mother, to keep him for eternity. It will not forget him, no! The demonstration of public sentiment on the day of the funeral could not be greater. It was an imposing spectacle which did honor to the city. If Charles William Dabney, by his elevated qualities had acquired a title to the veneration and respect of the population of this island, that population, at the solemn moment when his body was borne to the grave, showed that it comprehended its duty by accompanying on the last journey the remains of him whom the swelling voice of the people, rolling onward, baptised by the touching name of "Father of the Poor".

"Father of the Poor!" Who can now take from him this shining crown of immortality? Certainly no one. It was the hand of the people which placed it on his tomb and there it will remain, as eternally in our hearts will remain his memory and our yearning for him.[35]

His granddaughter Rose describes Charles Dabney's funeral and the reaction of the people on the island of Faial.

Never had there been seen such a funeral of true mourners in Fayal. He was followed to the grave by rich and poor, young and old, in an immense crowd. And well might they mourn, for it was indeed a day to them, they had lost their great benefactor and long will his memory be cherished by them.[36]

Charles Dabney's friend Higginson wrote some memories of his visits to Faial, of which the text below is only a small extract.

It has only once been within the writer's experience to be among the escort of a traveling prince. Since then I have ridden with the staff of plumed major-generals past long lines of glittering soldiers – but I have never beheld another scene like that. And yet the recipient of all this homage was a simple American merchant, dwelling on a foreign island, which had a civil governor and a military governor and whole boards of officials, and yet left room, for him to be its essential king.

He so monopolized the energy, the courage and the statesmanship of that little community, that he seemed to be its force; his sway was greater than that of Rajah Brooke in Borneo, because Mr. Dabney's weapons were those of peace. If he seemed like a feudal lord, it was a feudalism of love. If we can only think of him as The Consul, it is because his personal dignity and demeanour elevated the title, usually so insignificant, into something of its ancient grade. It seemed as if he must be someone of Roman consular dignity, who had somehow lingered on this lonely island, and whose title had been reaffirmed by the President of the United States.[37]

So constant were Mr. Dabney's consular and business cares at that season, that he rarely went beyond the town of Horta; everybody seemed to know in advance that he was going, and that lovely April Sunday became more than commonly a 'festa' day. It seemed as if the whole population were out beside the seaside road, to meet him; the picturesque fishermen, the blue robed women, the graceful black-eyed boys, the old crones, who seemed to have outlived everything but love for him. As we rode along, with the dashing surf of blue ocean on one side, this surf of human emotion seemed to swell and beat and murmur on the other. At every curve in the road new groups sprang up from their expectant waiting; they pressed forward to grasp Mr. Dabney's hand, to kiss it, or to hiss his stirrup; while he with his graceful horsemanship, turned from one to another as he rode, and held always hat in hand for the humblest. He remembered everyone by name and made the sweet Portuguese accents sound sweeter from those kindly lips.[38]

One further comment from Roxana at the end of the *Annals*, which were written to her nieces and nephews, provides a look at a side of Charles Dabney not mentioned by her in any other letters and comments.

> Your grandfather was human and had his faults, may be; the only one I remember I have already alluded to, that perhaps he thought he could judge better for others what was for their advantage; and did not allow quite freedom enough for the full development of individual powers, in those with whom he was acting, but under all the circumstances (he being left with the care of many younger brothers and sisters, etc.) this is hardly to be wondered at. His lead was always gentle.
>
> If I have seemed proud of my father, I wish to say that I am equally so of my brothers, including, of course, the one by marriage, for from my experience they are above the average of mankind in high moral tone and principle – the essentials, in my opinion. And I must in justice record, that they owe an immense deal to the influence of their noble wives. You must often have heard the old Portuguese proverb, "Os Santos da casa não fazem milagres" (Family saints do not perform miracles).[39]

Next in line to head the Dabney hierarchy on Faial was Samuel Wyllys Dabney, Charles' third eldest son. He had been working alongside his father for years in both his Consular and business activities. After the death of Charles Dabney, Samuel received a number of letters of sympathy and support, including one from his long-time friend Samuel Longfellow, a part of which is included.

> While you must hourly and greatly miss your father's presence, you have everything to be grateful for in those virtues of your father's character, which won such genuine and cordial esteem and regard from all who knew him. His beautiful courtesy, which was only the expression of his sincere kindness of heart, his firm principle and unsullied integrity, his high tone of thought and feeling, his large benevolence – while at

time the thought of these will deepen you sense of loss – will always remain as grounds of thankfulness that for so many years you were privileged to know them and have them as your example and inspiration. The tears of the poor were his best requiem, and the profound respect in which his memory will always be cherished in the community his best epitaph.[40]

Notes:

[1] Roxana Lewis Dabney, *Annals of the Dabney Family in Fayal*, comp., n.p.: The Author, 1900, p. 1407.

[2] Roxana Lewis Dabney, *Annals*, p. 1466-67.

[3] Dabney, Rose Forbes, *Fayal Dabneys*, n.p.: The Author, 1931, p. 69.

[4] Document 128, United States National Archives, Microfilm T203, Roll 6, January 12, 1864 – December 23, 1869.

[5] Roxana Lewis Dabney, *Annals*, p. 1411.

[6] Roxana Lewis Dabney, *Annals*, p. 1413-14.

[7] Roxana Lewis Dabney, *Annals*, p. 1414-15.

[8] Roxana Lewis Dabney, *Annals*, p. 1415-16.

[9] Roxana Lewis Dabney, *Annals*, p. 1433.

[10] Roxana Lewis Dabney, *Annals*, p. 1433.

[11] Roxana Lewis Dabney, *Annals*, p. 1425.

[12] Roxana Lewis Dabney, *Annals*, p. 1442.

[13] Roxana Lewis Dabney, *Annals*, p. 1443.

[14] Roxana Lewis Dabney, *Annals*, p. 1444-5.

[15] Roxana Lewis Dabney, *Annals*, p. 1445.

[16] Roxana Lewis Dabney, *Annals*, p. 1450.

[17] Roxana Lewis Dabney, *Annals*, p. 1454-5.

[18] Roxana Lewis Dabney, *Annals*, p. 1456.

[19] Roxana Lewis Dabney, *Annals*, p. 1461.

[20] Roxana Lewis Dabney, *Annals*, p. 1460.

[21] Roxana Lewis Dabney, *Annals*, p. 1467-8.

[22] Roxana Lewis Dabney, *Annals*, p. 1468.

[23] Roxana Lewis Dabney, *Annals*, p. 1469-71.

[24] Roxana Lewis Dabney, *Annals*, p. 1474.

[25] Roxana Lewis Dabney, *Annals*, p. 1484.

[26] Roxana Lewis Dabney, *Annals*, p. 1474.

[27] CWD develops pneumonia, *Annals of the Dabney Family*, p. 1474

[28] CWD's last hours, *Annals of the Dabney Family*, p. 1474

[29] CWD's decline, *Annals of the Dabney Family*, p. 1480-1

[30] Some expecting a miracle of his return, *Annals of the Dabney Family*, p. 1475

[31] CWD's body on display, *Annals of the Dabney Family*, p. 1475

[32] Listening to beggar woman, *Annals of the Dabney Family*, p. 1475

[33] Helping old woman with eye problem, *Annals of the Dabney Family*, p. 1484

[34] Rose's summary of CWD's life, *The Fayal Dabneys*, p. 53

[35] Obituary, *Annals of the Dabney Family*, p. 1476-7

[36] Description of funeral, *The Fayal Dabneys*, p. 70

[37] Comments by Higginson, *Annals of the Dabney Family*, p. 1478-9

[38] Comments by Higginson, *The Fayal Dabneys*, p. 71-2

[39] Final comments by Roxa, *Annals of the Dabney Family*, p. 1484

[40] SL to SWD about C W D, *Annals of the Dabney Family*, p. 1481

21 – BEGINNING OF THE END

Life continued through the 1870's relatively calmly with Consul Cover having to deal with only periodic small disturbances. One that he took much interest in was the abandoned and fugitive seamen who were left on Faial by American ships. One of the problems he had with the seamen was venereal disease "because of the great impurity of women". This resulted in the Consulate having to pay for medical or hospital care. However, Mr. Cover did come up with an interesting solution. "It would pay the Government to keep a dozen or twenty women here – free from disease, for the use of the seaman (!)"[1]

Another of the problems had an interesting twist to it as the result of a change in Portuguese law. Some of the early Portuguese who had emigrated from Faial had been in America sufficient time to attain American citizenship or the 19th-century equivalent of the "green card".

> And these men very often visit their homes of childhood, not as prodigals but as comforters to their aged and always very poor parents, and almost invariably in view of rendering them relief. Three to four hundred comforters are reckoned each year.
>
> Until a late date the possession of a U. S. Naturalization certificate was respected by the authorities a once entitled the holder to a pass from the Azores to the States.
>
> But a recent act of the Portuguese cordes orders the civil governors of Portugal and Dependencies to hold all men returning from the States for the sum of (about) $200.00 to pay for army substitutes; and if they haven't the money, passes to leave Portuguese ports are refused. So they can never get away – unless clandestinely.

> At this time there are lots of naturalized American citizens here in just such a most cruel fix, and having US Citizens papers in their pockets.[2]

Mr. Cover wrote the State Department asking for advice about this problem, however, the problem turned out to last only a short period.

> But in the specific case alluded to, the Governor of the Azores has since yielded all the points by granting the men Passports and ordering their bonds cancelled, thus relinquishing his claims upon them for military service and virtually also for substitute draft bounty; and thereby, recognizing the full power of American Naturalization as held by myself.
> [in some cases $200 for army substitute may be charged].[3]

One incident that had nothing to do with Mr. Cover was the fire in the main Dabney offices in the center of Horta in September 1871. Men, women and children from throughout Horta, as well as the artillerymen from the fortress, gathered to assist in putting out the fire. In addition, Walter Bensaúde quickly provided a pump to aid in extinguishing the fire. On the other hand, the fire department's pump did not function properly, even though they did what they could. Because of all the help, the damage to the property was kept to a low level.[4]

As with Mr. Haight, who had replaced Charles Dabney for a short time, John Cover did not stay long on Faial and submitted his resignation after 5 years. Unlike Mr. Haight who left because he felt the income was insufficient, John Cover's health was deteriorating, and he felt he could not remain in the position. He resigned on June 30, 1872 and left for America on the *Fredonia*. Unfortunately he died on the return voyage and was buried at sea.

> Sir – I have to honor to resign my office of U. S. Consul for the Azore Islands, Portuguese Dominions, on account of bad health; this resignation to be of legal effect at the close of the present official quarter, June 30, 1872.

My thanks for the place, and a pledge of support of your administration and policies.[5]

The good opportunity has offered for sending the quarterly accts, until now and having lately heard of Mr. J. C. Cover's decease on board of the bark 'Fredonia'.[6]

Samuel Dabney was appointed Consul by President Grant to replace Mr. Cover and, once again, a Dabney was Consul for the Azores – this time until Samuel decided to resign and leave Faial in 1892.

At this date I have had the satisfaction of receiving your dispatch of July 23 announcing to me that his Excellency President Grant, with the advice and consent of the Senate, has conferred upon me the honor of the appointment to the post of United States Consul at Fayal.

In expressing my high appreciation of the trust place in me and my thanks for the office, I have to say that on the performance of my duties, so long as I continue to hold the office, that trust shall ever be before me.

In answer to the queries in latter part of dispatch, I beg to say that I was born on the island of Fayal, I have resided here the greatest part of my life. – I was appointed from the state of Massachusetts.

I have to request that all communications to me may be sent to care of John E. Mary, Nº 64 Commercial wharf, Boston. I am with high consideration your obedient servant.[7]

While John Cover was Consul, he appointed his own candidates as Consular Agents on the other islands. On São Miguel he appointed Domingos Dias Machado. Over the previous few years there had been complaints about him, some quite serious, but Cover always defended Machado. After Cover left, Samuel Dabney inherited Machado and, reminiscent of Mr. Hickling several years earlier, information came to Faial that Domingos Machado was attempting to get São Miguel raised to a full Consulate. Samuel Dabney's response to the State Department's

Figure 13

Samuel Wyllys Dabney and Harriet Wainwright Webster Dabney

request for information was that Machado had problems with English and that more American ships stopped at Flores (the westernmost island in the archipelago) than in São Miguel. He also included documents of complaint from the New Bedford Merchants about the prices for whale oil charged on São Miguel. Shortly thereafter he appointed Thomas Ivens to serve once more as Consular Agent on São Miguel, even though he was not American either, giving the reason "there were no Americans there, but his mother was an American". He also appointed his brother John P. Dabney as Vice-Consul on Faial.

Soon after his appointment as Consul, Samuel Dabney asked the State Department for rent for the Consular office located in Fredonia. While it was C. W. D.'s office, no rent had ever been asked. However, after his death ownership of the house was spread among several heirs and the administrator of the estate thought the rent was just. The State Department disagreed and would not allow any rent to be charged.

Samuel responded that the Consul's salary was not very large and that "the American commerce at this port is rapidly declining in consequence of the diminishing number of ships bearing our flag". The State Department responded that rent was only allowed if the office was dedicated to the Consulate and not used for business purposes.

In February 1874, John Pomeroy Dabney, Charles William Dabney's oldest son, died within one-day's sail of Faial. He was returning from Boston aboard the *Fredonia* during a gale and was violently tossed across his cabin striking his head on the swinging shelf and only survived a few days. "His premature death brought sorrow to many hearts for he was admired by all who knew him."[8] After reporting John Pomeroy's death to the State Department, he also indicated that there were no eligible Americans available on the island, and, therefore, he requested that Jacintho Leal, a bookkeeper at C.W. Dabney and Sons, be appointed, for which he received permission. This last occurrence makes it clear that most of the Dabney family had already left Faial.

With the death of his father, along with the departure and subsequent death of Mr. Cover, Samuel Wyllys Dabney stepped into the position of controlling all the Dabney interests on the island of Faial. During his youth he had made many voyages on Dabney ships to foreign countries including northern Europe and Russia. While he was his own man on these trips and acted as he considered the business should be run, with so much influence from his father and family he could not but help carry the tradition of the Dabneys into a third generation on this small island.

> He had the most charming manners that I have ever seen; manners of the courteous gentleman, which were as natural to him as the air he breathed.
> Fond of riding, he was as expert with horses as he was with boats. There was nothing he enjoyed more than a good ride, unless it were a spin over the water in his little schooner "Bayadere".
> He was indeed the "noble heir to his father's distinguished qualities"* ever carrying his responsibilities and duties with the same rectitude and idealism that were characteristic of Charles William Dabney.
> The Portuguese of all classes, from the town aristocrats to the country peasants, loved "Senhor Samuel Dabney".
> *From an article in "The American Foreign Service Journal."9

> Father's and Mother's lifelong devotion was perfect and if ever there was a marriage made in heaven theirs was one. To visualize them we must have some knowledge of their children, for the members of the family were so intertwined in their activities as in their affections that one cannot separate the strands which made up the united life of the home.10

After having spent so many years working at his father's side, he was able to take over the Consular and business operations as if there had been no change in leadership. Unfortunately, some of the problems that his father faced also continued and some became more serious as the years passed.

One of the main sources of income for the inhabitants of Faial was the sale of fresh produce and meat to the whaling and merchant vessels which made a stopover in Horta, regardless of the direction they were heading. The number of whaling ships decreased with the discovery of petroleum in Pennsylvania that provided a source of oil that was cheaper than whale oil. In addition, the change from sailing ships to steam-powered ships decreased the regular number of ships having to make a stop in the mid-Atlantic to seek supplies, and those that did were seeking coal. This helped the Dabney business, but did little to assist the rural Portuguese inhabitants business of providing fresh food since crossings of the Atlantic were much quicker, and ships were able to carry all the supplies they needed.

As for cruise ships like the *Quaker City*, they never became a viable source of income, except for private yachts – perhaps because of Mark Twain's description. Even today, cruise ships very rarely stop in the Azores and then mainly at São Miguel and Terceira. Although there are inter-island ferries, except for freighters, there are no ships connecting continental Portugal with the Azores. Today, Faial's relationship with sea-going vessels is more related to George Crowninshield and *Cleopatra's Barge* than whaling and merchant ships. The large yacht harbor on Faial is a world famous gathering point for trans-Atlantic yachts during the yachting season, and where yachtsmen from the four corners of the world get together to swap stories and information.

The decrease in the major shipping business had a greater effect on the traditionally small landholders than on the Dabney and Bensaúde businesses. The poverty that always lurked just below the surface on Faial and the other islands increased with a resulting growth in emigration to other countries, particularly to the United States. Famine on the islands increased and, following the lead of his father and grandfather, Samuel Dabney did what he could to relieve the problem.

> Several times during S. W. D.'s life, famine threatened the islands, but owing to his far-sighted measures of relief, the calamity was each time averted. He procured corn from abroad as his father and grandfather had done before him, selling it to the poor Fayalese at a low rate – of course foregoing any

profit for himself. "for acts of philanthropy" he received one of Portugal's highest honors: the title of *Comendador*, accompanied by small jeweled decoration and a letter of thanks from the King of Portugal.[11]

However, Samuel did not limit his giving to incidents of poverty, or to money, alone. One example involved "Woodcock Lodge", as the house at Capello in the western part of Faial was named; it was one of Samuel Dabney's favorite places. Being an ardent horseman, whenever he had time he would ride along the coast for a visit, sometimes hunting in the hills for birds, including woodcocks, of course.

The area near their residence at Capello did not have a good source of water available. The people in the area had to climb several miles into the nearby hills to springs in order to fill their water jugs. To do away with this daily chore, Samuel and his brother John Pomeroy Dabney had a large cement and stone cistern with washtubs constructed near the village of Capello. This was connected by pipes to the springs in the hills and was a great benefit to the local residents, including the Dabney servants who lived there throughout the year.

With the Charles Dabney and Sons Company reduced to such a small size, their ability to compete commercially was even further reduced. The breakwater for the Bay of Horta, a project Charles Dabney fought for his entire working career, was funded in 1865 by the Portuguese legislative body. Work began on it in 1876 with the aim of making it safer for ships to enter the Bay of Horta and attracting more trade, a little late to be of much benefit for the Dabneys. Nevertheless, there was one benefit for the Dabneys, at least for the Consulate: there were less abandoned and fugitive seamen on the island for them to worry about as the result of the reduced number of ships arriving.

The Dabney business was not the only one to suffer a personal loss during 1872. In April of 1872 Elias Bensaúde died. As a result the two leading businesses on Faial lost their long-time leaders within the same year. Abraham, Walter and Henrique replace Elias in Bensaúde e Companhia.[12]

In addition to the situations mentioned above, the U. S. Government intervened to create even more problems for the Faial Consulate. They created a classification system for consulates and the Faial Consulate was moved from Schedule C to Schedule B. The effect of this was to prohibit Samuel Dabney acting as both Consul and "from engaging in business as a merchant". The intent of this was to create "professional" Consuls. Samuel requested an extension to sign the Consular bond because recent events, the death of John Pomeroy Dabney and George Oliver traveling in the U. S., had reduced the company to 2 employees.

Having been notified by the Department of State that the Fayal Consulate, among others, had been transferred from schedule C to B, and having later received a bond to sight which prohibits me from engaging in business as a merchant [unreadable], I beg leave to lay before you the following statements and petition.

The primary object of our Government in raising the class and salaries of certain of the Consular Officers, as approved by Act of Congress in June last, being as undoubtedly to ensure faithful, and filling representation abroad. I venture to suggest that the consulate of Fayal is perhaps rather an exceptional one, and that its placement in schedule B with a salary of $1500 may not be conducive to the desired end.

Fayal with its limited area and small population so "out of the world," offers no attraction beyond its climate and scenery to a foreigner as a permanent residence, unless he should have business in?

I have a life long acquaintance with the language and the people of the island, while I have ever cherished the feelings of patriotism towards the United States, of which I am a citizen, which were instilled into me by my parents.

I have had sixteen years of experience as Deputy Consul, and two years as Consul, and I hope I may safely refer to my record for recommendation. I believe that I may claim, without arrogance, that no one occupies a higher social position in this community than mine.

As it is simply impossible for me to five up all connection
with business, and receive on $1500 a year instead. I respect-
fully petition that the Fayal Consulate be relegated to the Schedule C and that I be permitted both to hold the office of United
States Consul and to transact business.

I have the honor to be, sir, with the high consideration.[13]

Samuel Dabney's presentation of the problems he would
face in operating both the Consulate and the family business with
few employees must have reached a receptive ear in Washington
because he was "exempted from the prohibition in regard to
engaging in business". However, in addition to creating "professional" Consuls, it was apparent that the U.S. government
wanted to decrease the number of its consular outposts. The State
Department asked him his opinion about continuing the Consular Agencies on three of the other islands. Recognizing that
they were attempting to reduce costs, he pointed out other functions that the Consular Agencies in the Azores performed.

These agencies, judged by the amount of fees collected at
them, would certainly appear unworthy of continuance, but
there are reasons, I think, of sufficient weight to make their
suppression not desirable.

This group of islands in on the route of a great deal of the
traffic between the two continents, and during the winter
months, there is always the chance that some unfortunate
vessel may be stranded, or driven to seek a port of refuge.
As the only communication, during the stormy season, with
Graciosa and St. George is by the monthly mail steamer, and
this not certain in very rough weather, it is evident that occasions may occur when the services of an agent would be
valuable.

Again, in the summer, whale ships (American) are about,
a few of them touching at all the islands for various purposes.

At all these islands Great Britain has consular offices of various grades, a fact which I mention merely to corroborate my
opinion that there is, if not actual necessity, strong ground in
favor of maintaining our agencies.

My remarks relate more in particularly to Graciosa and St. George; for Terceira, although as yet having but little trade with the United States, is one of the most import islands of the group, being the seat of their Bishopric, as well as head-quarters for the troops.[14]

The government was also concerned with how they could increase income for America from each country they had consulates in and, therefore, they asked about developing or increasing exports from the Azores. Samuel's response indicated that the Azores were not a particularly fertile area for the expansion of U. S. exports.

Taking into consideration the limited market and the relatively large number of speculators endeavoring to force a trade, I think no steps could be taken that would produce a sensible effect.[15]

Over the years, handicrafts were an important export product of the Azores, however their export was severely affected by the American Civil War. One of the biggest selling items was a cotton type of embroidered stockings, which the poverty-stricken women in the villages made around the fire at night. To assist in promoting the sales in America, Clara Dabney acted as the liaison between the villagers and the purchasers in Boston. Straw hats were another popular product made in the rural areas and shipped by the Dabneys. Besides these two major products that the Dabneys were involved in getting to U. S. markets, other handicrafts included lace and small items made from the threads in the leaves of the century plant, cotton embroidery, *crivo*, which was cotton cloth in which the designs were made by taking individual threads out of the material, and, in addition, items, particularly flowers, carved from the pith of the fig tree. While these latter items never reached the export level of the stockings and hats, they are still produced today for the tourist trade. None of these items were major money earners, but they did save many a Faial and Pico family from becoming destitute.

Samuel's reports to the State Department continued to be basically shipping and economics, along with the perennial problem of abandoned and fugitive seamen. However, Portugal created an additional problem relative to this last situation by adopting a law saying that seamen sailing under Articles signed before a U. S. Consulate could be taken off their ship when it returned to Portugal, thereby affecting Portuguese emigrants. Samuel referred this to the State Department for them to handle through negotiations between the two countries.

In January 1877, Samuel Dabney reported that work on the breakwater was underway and he came up with the idea of using the abandoned seamen to work on building it. However, two to three weeks later, the directing engineer said that they were not "fitted for the kind of work required and moreover were troublesome to control".

One item that may be of interest to some and that appears to have escaped documentation, except in specialty railway magazines, was the existence of railroads to help with the construction of the breakwaters on São Miguel and Faial. They were unusual not because they were on islands, but because of the non-standard gauge they ran on. The original rail gauge in Britain was the same as the 4ft $8^1/_2$ ins. (1.436 m) width of the Roman chariot tracks worn into the ground and that is still used in parts of the world. With the advent of the train, disagreement developed over changing the gauge and what gauge should be used as the standard. Narrower gauges allowed for negotiating sharper curves and wide gauges allowed for greater stability and speed. In Britain, the advocates of a narrow gauge won the disagreement. However, two locations with British-built trains used an unusually wide gauge of 7ft 1in (about 2.16 m). These were the trains used on São Miguel and Faial used to carry stone from the quarries to the breakwater construction area. Almost all remnants have disappeared, but on both islands you can still see some support equipment and the rare wide track in a couple of locations.

In 1877, Samuel's son Herbert returned from America to reside in Faial after completing his studies at MIT. Even though Samuel had appointed Jacintho Leal as Deputy Consul after the

death of John Pomeroy Dabney, he now made a request that
Herbert be appointed as Vice Consul, which was approved.
Herbert also worked in the offices of the family business. However, he stayed only a short period of time and then gave up
his position as U. S. Vice Consul, as well as that of German Consul, and moved back to America where he settled in California.
In the mid-1880's he bought property in the San Diego area,
one of which was given the name "Fayal Ranch" and where
Samuel Dabney retired after leaving Faial. He was president of
a small railroad running daily trips between La Jolla and San
Diego. Later he moved to Massachusetts where he remained
until his death.[16]

In November 1879, Nature decided to strike another blow
on the Azores and resulted in international renown for Samuel
and Herbert Dabney. A major storm struck Faial, died down the
next day and returned with a vengeance the following evening.
The regular Lisbon-Azores packet, the *Azor* was dashed to pieces
on the shore. The French ship *Jacques Coeur* from Le Havre
began dragging her anchor, but remained a long way from shore.
The wind and waves remained high, and the ship was sure to
be lost along with the 13 crewmembers that were on board.
However, Samuel Dabney and his oldest son Herbert took it
upon themselves to rescue the crew. The event is described in
detail in an article from the *New York Herald* of January 8, 1880

HEROISM OF A UNITED STATES CONSUL AND HIS SON
Rescuing men in a boiling surf.
To the editor of the Herald:-
It is with great satisfaction that we chronicle a case of marked and unusual gallantry of one of our civil representatives
abroad. On the night of 30th November and 1st December,
1879, there was a very severe gale from the southeast at Fayal,
one of the Azores Islands, and a French bark, the Jacques Coeur,
of Brest, which had entered port that day and could not be
properly moored in time, was driven ashore and eight out her
company of thirteen were lost in the raging surf. Of the five
who escaped four were rescued by the American Consul
Samuel W. Dabney, and his son, Herbert Dabney.

We learn from reliable sources that, unfortunately, neither the Portuguese government nor the local authorities at Fayal have created any organization or made any available provision for saving life in case of shipwreck. An English lifeboat was sent there by the government a number of years ago; but, as it is quite unfitted for the requirements of the place and cannot be launched in a storm it lies rotting in a house which was built for it. For the last half century the late Charles W. Dabney, who was United States Consul at Fayal for more than forty years and his son, Samuel W. Dabney, the present Consul, have been the prominent leaders in saving life and property of all nations at that island and generally the ropes and other appliances necessary have been furnished by the Dabney stores. On the occasion of which we speak no American interests were at stake; but feelings of humanity brought Mr. Dabney and his son to the coast, where, amid a howling storm, torrents of rain and a most fearful surf, the French bark was approaching her doom.

An English bark had entered the bay the same day, but when one of her chains parted, the captain cut away her masts and she was saved. A little steamer belonging to the port, had broken adrift, with no one on board, and was dashed to pieces against the seawall in front of the town, near the spot to which the French bark was drifting, and the fragments of this steamer, dashing to and fro in the surf, had a most disastrous effect upon the unfortunate Frenchmen, as will be seen.

The French captain clung to hope too long, and neither cut away his masts nor slipped his chains. Thus his vessel was driven aground, and when she struck was held by her anchors and could not be washed near enough to the beach for her crew to escape.

On their arrival at the spot the Messrs. Dabney, finding that (though the Vice Consul of France and other Portuguese gentlemen were there, with a number of a lower class, ready to succor any of the unfortunates who might gain the shore) no adequate provision had been made to assist the shipwrecked men while in the water, sent to their stores for a coil of rope, which they speedily cut into lengths suitable for attaching to persons daring enough to go to those struggling in the surf.

The vessel struck! Soon, being old, she went to pieces. Her crew were precipitated into the roaring waves, which, in huge rollers, thundered on the shore with awful force. The ship was stranded perhaps fifty yards from dry land, which seems a short distance for men to swim; but the enormous rollers would dash over her with a forced that swept rocks of fifteen and twenty tons weight from their places, and the beach, of shifting coarse sand, which, with the receding wave would be bare for forty feet, would be the next minute covered with volumes of water in which a strong man was as powerless as a stray. In the boiling surge, constantly swept hither and thither with terrible impetus, were great quantities of wreckage from the steamer and the bark, which increased the danger tenfold and which doubtless caused the great loss of life. No one can be blamed for not venturing within the reach of such fearful danger. But the more honor to those who did!

Mr. Herbert Dabney was the first to bind a rope around his waist and gallantly dash after a receding wave, breast deep into the surf in the endeavor to grasp a struggling Frenchman. For the first and the second he was swept back. By a third daring rush he grappled with an exhausted man and dragged him within reach of other hands. His father, Mr. Samuel Dabney, was scarcely behind him in the gallant race and rescued the French captain, who was quite helpless and temporarily unconscious.

Thus these two, forgetful of their own lives and all dependent on them, fought on in this battle for humanity's sake, to save the lives of foreign strangers, until no more of the unfortunates could be discerned. None ventured so far into the surf as they, and, as we have said, four of the five saved were drawn out of their fearful peril by the Messrs. Dabney. Repeatedly were they in the greatest danger. The ropes fastened to them caught under the floating wreckage, and thus drawn into instead of out of the water, they had to cast them off and regain safety by their own unaided strength and activity. At one time Mr. Samuel Dabney was pinioned by a mass of wreckage which imbedded his leg in the sand, severely bruising him, while a wave passed over him and then nearly swept him out to sea amid a broad quantity of floating driftwood.

ON THE EDGE OF HISTORY   452

Mr. Dabney's age, which lacks but five years of being threescore, and the fact that he has a large family dependent on him and is the head of a commercial firm which could ill spare him must be borne in mind to recognize the especial gallantry of his action.

Americans may well be proud of their Consul at Fayal – the brave son of a brave sire and the brave sire of a brave son.[17]

The whole city resounds the names of Messrs. Samuel Dabney and his son Herbert Dabney. It was they, above all, who at the risk of their own lives plunged into the sea with ropes attached to them and saved five persons, among them the captain, Founier. It was not only the savage of the surf and the distance of the wreck from shore that rendered the work of rescue difficult, but also the large quantity of wreckage with which the water was filled. The peril was so great that at one time much fear was entertained for Mr. Samuel Dabney, who together with a shipwrecked sailor whom he had seized, was completely hemmed in by fragments of wreck… Truth demands that the self-forgetfulness and heroism of those two generous men, Samuel and Herbert Dabney, who did not hesitate an instant to risk their lives to save those of their fellow beings should be proclaimed in the loudest manner.[18]

Despite their valiant efforts, they were only able to save five of the crew. Nevertheless, their bravery was well recognized in both France and the United States. They were each given a medal from the French Ministre de la Marine et des Colonies and also received medals from President Rutherford B. Hayes, as well as from the Massachusetts Humane Society.

The Massachusetts Humane Society has lately had struck from a new die superb massive gold medals, weighing over five ounces each, two of which are designed for Messrs. Samuel Wyllys Dabney and Herbert Dabney, for their noble and persevering efforts… In the terrible storm in the harbor of Fayal November 30, 1879.[19]

Notes:

[1] Document 13, United States Archives, Microfilm T203, Roll 7, January 18, 1870 – December 30, 1874.

[2] Document 30, United States Archives, Microfilm T203, Roll 7, January 18, 1870 – December 30, 1874.

[3] Document 35, United States Archives, Microfilm T203, Roll 7, January 18, 1870 – December 30, 1874.

[4] "Fire in Dabney business offices," *O Fayalense*, Anno 15, Nº 6, September 24, 1871.

[5] Document 64, United States Archives, Microfilm T203, Roll 7, January 18, 1870 – December 30, 1874.

[6] Document 66, United States Archives, Microfilm T203, Roll 7, January 18, 1870 – December 30, 1874.

[7] Document 69, United States Archives, Microfilm T203, Roll 7, January 18, 1870 – December 30, 1874.

[8] Dabney, Rose Forbes, *The Fayal Dabneys*, n. p.: The Author, 1931, p. 77.

[9] Dabney, Rose Forbes, *Fayal Dabneys,*. 93.

[10] Dabney, Rose Forbes, *Fayal Dabneys,*. 105.

[11] Dabney, Rose Forbes, *Fayal Dabneys,*. 96.

[12] "Death of Elias Bensaúde," *O Fayalense*, Anno 16, Nº 35, 14 April 1872.

[13] Document 131, United States Archives, Microfilm T203, Roll 7, January 18, 1870 – December 30, 1874.

[14] Document 5, United States Archives, Microfilm T203, Roll 8, January 10, 1875 – September 2, 1882.

[15] Document 83, United States Archives, Microfilm T203, Roll 8, January 10, 1875 – September 2, 1882.

[16] Dabney, Rose Forbes, *Fayal Dabneys,*. 127.

[17] "Rescue of *Jacques Coeur*," *New York Herald*, January 8, 1888

[18] Dabney, Rose Forbes, *Fayal Dabneys,*. 119.

[19] Dabney, Rose Forbes, *Fayal Dabneys,*. 121.

Figure 14
Roxana Lewis Dabney

22 – ONWARD TO A NEW LIFE

During the rest of the 1880's, the Dabneys last full decade on Faial, life continued pretty much the same. While the decade of the 70's closed with disaster, the decade of the 80's opened with, perhaps, the greatest festivities of the 19th century. This was the celebration on June 10 of the 300th anniversary of the death of Luís de Camões (Camoens in English) who wrote the epic poem "Lusiadas" ("The Lusiads") in English. The "Lusiadas" is often compared with the "Iliad" and "Odyssey" by Homer in combining historical and mythological themes in the description of a voyage, in this case the voyage to India during the Age of Discoveries in the 15th and 16th centuries. The explorers, and later the merchants, traveled a long, dangerous route to India around the southern tip of Africa, having numerous adventures and bringing back spices and glory to Portugal.

The government in Lisbon decided that the 300th anniversary would be celebrated as a special day. In Faial, the leading groups accepted this, and some of them competed with the others for what part they would have in the celebration. The main group that set about organizing the festival was the Grémio Littarário Fayalense, which was involved with instruction in and the love of literature. It recognized that the celebration having just a literary character was not sufficient, and the general population should be allowed to show their recognition for their nation's greatest poet. Therefore, they asked the City Council if they could use the Council's chambers and invited the press to promote the festivities. They planned a public procession, fireworks and an evening presentation by the Grémio in the City Hall.

June 10, 1880 had exceptional weather enhanced by the myriad of flowers that are in bloom at that time of the year added their color and fragrance to the day. All the ships at anchor had their flags out adding their own touch of color.

The celebrations began at midnight on the 10th with the firing of skyrockets. At 1:30 a.m. torchlight marches accompanied by bands passed through the streets and the people gave three cheers for Camões in front of the Grémio. At 5:00 a.m. a cannon was fired from the fort indicating that the festivities were beginning. Around 1,500 persons gathered in the dock area for the beginning of the ceremonies at 10:30 a.m., each person with a bouquet or a laurel wreath, which Camões is always represented as wearing. The whole day was filled with parades, music, speeches, readings, a variety of ceremonies, a 21-cannon salute and, at night, fireworks. The festivities did not stop until dawn of the next day.[1]

In her diary, Roxana Dabney describes the Dabney participation in the celebration. They decorated the windows of the office-sail loft with flowers. They could view the processions from the windows of the office and thought them "very good". Herbert, as German Consul, along with some of the other Consuls, was part of the procession. From the office the family went to the Jesuit College, where the City Council was located and where John Bass Dabney had some wine storage facilities decades before. There they unveiled the bust of Camões with much celebration, and behind it were the flags of the nations. There were laurel leaves around each of the portraits in the senate chamber, including that of Charles Dabney, and under each there was a verse from the "Lusiadas".

Camões is still considered Portugal's pre-eminent poet, and the "Lusiadas" has been translated into a number of languages. June 10th is now a national holiday named Day of Portugal and its Communities and celebrates the fact of being Portuguese both for those living in Portugal and the hundreds of thousands who spread around the world, many living still in almost completely Portuguese-speaking communities. In America, the better known communities are in Newark, NJ, the area around New Bedford and Fall River, MA, Providence RI, the south San Francisco Bay area, California's San Joaquin Valley and Hawaii. Many of these communities have celebrations of their own, some rivaling those in Portugal.

In 1880 there were other events of interest, one of which was the arrival of the ship *Dessong* in São Miguel carrying an Egyptian obelisk meant for the World's Fair in the U.S. In addition to the fireworks of the Camões festivities, Faial was treated to more bright festivities when a cable laying ship stopped in December 1880 and lit its electric lights between 7:00 and 8:00 p.m., the first seen in Horta. The Dabneys and their friends put lanterns on their house railing to acknowledge seeing the lights.[2]

Roxana also reports on a two-wheeled technological marvel and some of the reactions by the local population when Ralph rode his bicycle through Horta in 1883.

> I must tell you a little about my bicycle boy. We were so much amused by the astonishment of the people at the bicycle. Ralph kept just ahead of us so that we could appreciate the sensation he created. Some people were perfectly overcome, and laughed so, they would make us laugh. Others were horrified and one woman stood in the middle of the street with her mouth open saying: "vae-te para o diabo!" [go to the devil] more than once. Another woman said "é o carro da última moda – cá nunca un assim." [it is the latest style vehicle – I've never seen one like it here]. But the best was when Bert was going home. He went ahead of us on account of darkness. A woman called out "o senhor é que concerta tesoiras?" [Is he the man who fixes scissors?]. Bert answered "não senhora" [no, madame].[3]

The last woman may have seen knife sharpeners riding bicycles in Lisbon because even today there are men who travel around the city to sharpening knives and scissors and fixing umbrellas. To attract clients each blows his own tune on pipes-of-pan to attract customers.

There were two sad events during the 1880's. At the end of the 1870's the Dabneys constructed a new ship called the *Azorean* to replace the *Azor* on the Dabney "bridge" – the regular flow of Dabney ships that connected Boston and Faial. The figurehead had the face of a Portuguese peasant woman with a basket of oranges on her head. In reality, the model for the figurehead was Samuel Dabney's daughter Rose in peasant costume. The ship was destroyed in a storm at the end of 1880's.[4]

In the fall of 1881, President Garfield was assassinated,[5] and Samuel Dabney declared a period of six months mourning for the Consular staff. Samuel remained as Consul and was reappointed by Grover Cleveland in 1885.[6]

Among the visitors to arrive in Faial on the *Azorean* in the 1880's was the Dutch-American seascape artist William Frederick de Haas, older brother of the more famous seascape painter Maurice Frederick Hendrick de Haas. He was visiting the Azores because of his poor health. Samuel Dabney befriended Mr. de Haas, Roxana had tea with him, and Clara took time to read to him. Unfortunately, Mr. de Haas died a little more than a month after arriving on July 16, 1880 at the age of 50.

About six months later, Samuel Dabney received a letter from the State Department stating that they had received a letter from a Mr. Taylor (probably a relative of Haas' fiancée Miss Taylor) saying that Dabney had neglected to report the death of Mr. De Haas as required by the Consular Regulations. Haas had been born in Holland, and when asked if he had been naturalized, "he answered unintelligibly". After Haas died, Samuel Dabney and the Dutch Consul spoke and the Dutch Consul asked Dabney to take care of the "funeral and inventory", despite Haas' passport saying he was Dutch. Samuel Dabney had already sent Haas' personal effects to his brother as Haas had asked in a note written just before his death. In response to the State Department's letter, Dabney sent the proper documents to them and the situation was resolved.[7]

There was another ill visitor about this time, although he never came to shore. This was Commander Dewey who, as described previously, had visited Faial as a junior officer. Despite being famous at the time, he became even more famous as the result of his military exploits in the Philippines. His ship made a stop in Horta in December 1882 because the Commander was seriously ill, and the ship left about two weeks later with "Commander Dewey convalescing."[8]

Monsieur Professor Pouchet, who was head of the Museum of Comparative Anatomy in Paris, which had been founded by Prince Albert I of Monaco, made a visit to Faial in 1883. Professor Pouchet desired the skeleton of a sperm whale, and Samuel

Dabney made the arrangements and prepared the skeleton to be sent.[9] In return he received a Sevres Vase about 2 $1/2$ feet tall in "glorious blue".[10] He reported to the State Department that he had accepted it " because he did not regard it as a gift from a government" with which the State Department agreed.[11]

In February 1884, Prince Henry of Germany arrived in Faial as a second lieutenant on the German Steamer *Olga*. The twenty-two year old Prince was the second son of the crown prince and grandson of the German Emperor Wilhelm, as well as of Queen Victoria. He was welcomed to the island by Herbert Dabney, who was German Consul. He spent 4-5 days on the island, and Herbert took the Prince and some of the ship's officers on a hike up to the magnificent Caldeira at the top of Faial's volcano cone.[12]

Perhaps the most exotic visitor to Faial during the 19th century was Prince Min-you-ik of Korea who arrived on the U. S. Warship *Trenton*. His secretary and interpreter accompanied him. He was the first ambassador that Korea had sent to a foreign country and he was coming from Washington, D. C., where he had signed a trade treaty between America and Korea.[13] The Prince wore his traditional Korean Costume while in Horta, where he visited the Igreja do Carmo and had dinner at the Dabney's. It only takes little to imagination to guess the reactions of the general population of Faial who marveled at the strangeness of these visitors. The Prince was considered very progressive in his country and, sadly, he, along with many of his followers, was assassinated by the ultra-conservatives in Korea.[14]

The most important visitor for Faial during the 1880's was Crown Prince Albert I of Monaco who arrived on his yacht *Hirondelle* [*Swallow*] along with his companion Professor Pouchet. The Prince, even after he became ruler of Monaco, spent a large portion of his life, extending into the 20th century, on the sea studying the flow of currents and the sea life in different parts of the Atlantic. He enjoyed visiting the Azores, with Faial being his favorite stopping-off point, and on their visit in 1885, became good friends with Samuel Dabney. One day during lunch at Fredonia, sperm whales were sighted and Herbert and Professor Pouchet rushed to set off in one of the Dabney Company's whaling boats and were successful in capturing one. In later years, the Prince was able to capture one himself.[15] The Prince and his crew left, and later in the same year Herbert shipped a whole fetus packed in a barrel of salt to Professor Pouchet who had indicated he wanted one. Two years later Professor Pouchet sent Samuel Dabney a medal from the Paris City Council for all the help he had given in the Professor's studies on the sperm whale.[16]

A meteorological observatory the Prince had constructed on Monte das Moças overlooking the town of Horta maintains his memory to this day. It bears his name and still functions as a meteorological station and has equipment to measure the many earth tremors that occur in the Azores.

There was one more visitor that made a stop in Horta in 1885. Of all the visitors during the 19th century, her fame has made her an important symbol to the entire world. On June 1, 1885, the French ship *Isere* stopped in Horta with her cargo containing the components of the Statue of Liberty on her way from France as a gift to the United States.[17] Unfortunately it was not possible to see the statue because the pieces were packed in containers.

Portugal also sent a gift to the United States as a gift around this time to be exhibited at the Chicago Exposition. This was the "Long Tom", the cannon recovered from the *General Armstrong* by the Portuguese after the ship was scuttled during its battle with the British in 1814. Samuel Dabney accompanied it on its voyage on the *Vega*.

During the 19th century the number of both whale and merchant vessels stopping in Horta decreased even below the level of a few years earlier. Some of Faial's export products became uneconomical, such as whale oil, which lost out to petroleum, and oranges, so much appreciated by their friends in America, losing to the lower-priced fruit from Valencia and Florida.

As a result, the State Department again raised questions about the need for Consular Agents on the various islands. One of the regulations that they started enforcing more strictly was that a Consular Agent could only act as such for one country and could not represent a company like Lloyd's. This affected the Agent on Flores who was British Vice-consul, the Lloyd's representative and also the Dabney Company representative[18], as well as the Consular Agent on São Miguel, Richard Seemann, who was also the Consular representative for the Sandwich Islands. Samuel Dabney contested this action pointing out how few qualified persons were available for the number of positions on the islands, and he succeeded in getting temporary relaxation of the rule.

None of this stopped the periodic attempts by individuals on São Miguel to move the Consulate there. They based their request on its trade volume and variety, it being the largest island and having a new breakwater. The requests were refused, nevertheless the State Department did move the Consulate there in 1897 under Consul Colin C. Manning, although Manning then decided that it was not a good idea to have moved it. In addition, the Portuguese arrested him for reasons that are unclear, but the U. S. Consul in Lisbon obtained his release. However, the U. S. newspapers published unflattering accounts about the incident with Manning, and the State Department was not pleased with him. Consul George C. Pickerell took over the Consulate, which was once again at Horta, and finally closed the Horta Consulate on April 30, 1899, and moved it to São Miguel.[19]

In addition, the State Department periodically raised questions about the economy of the Azores and the possibility of developing new markets for American Products. Among the suggestions for products U. S. export were sweet potato alcohol, which was already produced in surplus on São Miguel, leather goods and agricultural equipment. Samuel Dabney responded to some of these requests.

> The trade of the Azores with foreign countries excepting the sailing vessels running to the ports of Boston and New Bedford, is limited almost to St. Michaels to England and an occasional vessel from the latter country with merchandize.[20]

> [Regarding] markets for shoes and leather, he reports "at this place I consider there is none. The numerous small im-

porters-shopmen, and the commercial traveller spoken of by
Mr. Seemann [for a Boston Commission house] pay no attention
to this line of goods.[21]

The manner of cultivation is very simple and the imple-
ments in use generally of Azorean manufacture and primitive
in their make.[22]

I regret to say that no Agricultural Machinery worthy of
notice is imported into these islands for the reason that the
farmers yet cling to the old style.[23]

In the late 1880's, Samuel Dabney came down with "a severe illness (probably typhoid)". During his long illness and
recovery he had much time to consider a major decision that
had been in his mind:

...to put into effect the determination that he had made of
moving his family to the United States. The mere thought of
it was a deeper sorrow to him than to anyone else, but he had
in mind the future of his sons and daughters and it seemed
best that they should settle in the Mother land; a strong reason for leaving Fayal being the fact that there were no longer
any Dabneys on the Island excepting ourselves; Aunt Sarah
having moved her family to Cambridge, and the Olivers having also left the Island for good.[24]

This decision was not something that came about on the
spur of the moment. The beginnings probably date back to
shortly after the death of Charles William Dabney. In his will
Charles Dabney divided his business interests among his children
still living on Faial: John Pomeroy Dabney, Clara P. Dabney, Samuel Wyllys Dabney, Roxanna L. Dabney, Frances D. Oliver, plus
her husband who worked for the business, George S. J. Oliver.

Furthermore, considering the decrease in the family's business, their income decreased proportionally. In addition, the
apparent desire by the State Department to not allow Consuls
to have their own business, their desire to increase American

export business, as well as their questioning whether Consular Agents were needed foreshadowed possible changes in the Consular activities. To this was added the persistent requests to have the Consulate moved to São Miguel. As a result, after his illness, Samuel began to implement his decision.

> After this momentous decision, S. W. D. began pulling strings in many directions. The family owned much land and several houses, and although Fayal had become a port of calling and new people were buying and building, sacrifices had to be made and fine properties disposed of at much less than their rightful value.[25]

The Azores was not the only archipelago with a Dabney as Consul who was getting ready to leave. William Henry Dabney, Samuel's uncle, was still U. S. Consul in the Canary Islands. However, he was making preparations to leave and return to America, a decision supported by his daughters. In January 1881 he sent a letter to Roxana asking her to come to the Canaries to keep him and his sister Olívia company while his daughter Frederica (nicknamed Ica) went to America in the "Spring to make preparations for their all removing there in a year."[26]

The decision to leave and start selling property had not been an easy one for the family to make. Some of the property was just empty land or small houses, and there was no reticence in selling these. However, with the larger plots of land, vineyards and particularly the family homes in Horta and their countryside houses, the family had stronger attachments. As a result it was not easy for them to let these properties go, and the family considered their decisions carefully.

> Sam, Sarah, Clara, Bert and I [Roxana] had a consultation as to selling the vineyard at Areia Larga – decided not to let it go at 1900$000.[27]

Nevertheless, piece-by-piece, the Dabney properties were sold. In addition the various components of Dabney Company were either closed down or sold off, much to the sadness of the Dabneys and their friends on the island.

> C. W. D. & Sons have given up the coal business entirely to the Ben Saúdes – made a bargain. Poor Capt. Silveira is terribly cut up about it. Mr. Dart too I fancy. That is the worst of making changes. I am sorry as glad. More glad than sorry, because it may lead to winding up – It is high time for the young folks! Perhaps I may be wrong in wishing this for them – For myself I have no wishes. I shall be taken care of I am sure![28]

In early 1885, Emmeline Dabney, who had been married to Adam Paterson and John Stackpole, suddenly died while her daughter Emmeline was dressing her after her bath. She was 74 years old and this left only Olivia and William Henry from the children of John Bass and Roxa Dabney.

In the early 1880's, Frances (Fan) and George Oliver went on a trip to the U. S., which took them to Southern California where they visited the cities of San Diego, Los Angeles and Santa Barbara. They decided to make their residence in Santa Barbara where they purchased a home they called "Rocky Nook" in Mission Cañon.

In 1884 Samuel and Harriet Dabney went to the U. S. and also visited California. They had received information from the Olivers about their visit and the various areas and wanted to see for themselves.

> And so in one week all was decided, arranged – as they [Sam and Harriet] departed Cara says – it is the beginning of the end![29]

After their visit, they decided that they liked Santa Barbara. Nevertheless, they ended up in the San Diego area in a house that Herbert had bought and named "Fayal Ranch" on land in the eastern part of San Diego County near the town of Jamacha. Today this land is covered with golf courses and expensive suburban homes. On Faial, not everyone was happy with the changes that were coming about. One day in 1889 Roxana and Malcolm Forbes went up to visit the Dabney graves and she -spoke with the Sexton.

> Sexton and I conversed about the Dabneys – he seemed to think things never would have gone down as they have done if Father had lived.[30]

While Mr. Forbes was in Faial, Samuel Dabney was treated to a shock one morning. His wife came downstairs at breakfast time and told him "Rose was preparing to leave in the *Fredonia* at 11:00!! Poor Sam was in dismay".[31] The Dabneys had known the Forbes since the 18th century and the families were very close friends. They stayed in each other's homes when visiting and sailed on each other's ships, whether in Faial or the Boston area. However, this was the first time that Rose had left with them by herself. On July 6, 1892, Rose Dabney married J. Malcolm Forbes and they took up residence in Massachusetts.

Even though it was not the last property sold, Bagatelle was the crown jewel of the family properties. It had been sold to a Mr. Thomas Cardoso who made several payments for it until the final payment on August 21, 1889. With so many memories attached to life at Bagatelle, this must have been a cheerless event for the Dabneys with the remainder of the property sales seeming to be anticlimactic.

> Sam came in this morning. Mr. Thomas Cardoso has paid up the last installment and Bagatelle will now be passed over to them. Sam, H, A and I were up there to see the dear old place for the last time. How many happy days there.[32]

Now that the property was almost all sold, the business virtually closed down and only a handful of Dabneys remaining, the time was rapidly approaching for the remaining family to leave. However, one major task remained for Samuel Dabney before he could depart. On September 1, 1891, he wrote to President Benjamin Harrison to submit his resignation from the position of Consul to the Azores.

I have the honor to inform Your Excellency that, intending as I do to transfer my residence from the Azores to our Country, the time has arrived when I should forward to you my resignation.

The Consulship of the United States for Fayal and its dependencies – with the exception of eighteen months – has been held by members of the Dabney family since 1806: by my grandfather, by my father and by my self – my time of office dating back to 1872.

Permit me sir, as presumably the last of our name that will hold this Consulate, to say with pardonable satisfaction that I have faith that our loyalty to our Country will be recognized by our countrymen and that they will not have cause to find fault with the record we have left in the land of the temporary adoption of our family.

In conclusion, I beg to convey to Your Excellency the expression of my gratitude for my continuance in office on the incoming of your administration.

I have the honor to be sir, with the highest consideration Your most obedient servant.[33]

In response, the State Department sent a letter to Samuel Dabney accepting his resignation "with regret". In turn, Samuel Dabney wrote a letter of appreciation for the comments on the quality of his services.

I have the honor to acknowledge your dispatch of October 28th, N[o] 200, in which you inform me that His Excellency, President Harrison, has, in accepting my resignation of the office of the Consul of the United States in the Azores, wished you to express to me his regret that it was not possible for me to continue to hold the office with which for so many years my family has been connected: and that he further requested you to express his appreciation of my past services, and his wishes for my welfare and prosperity in the future.

These are indeed gratifying words, especially coming as they do to me after a service of nineteen years in a Consulate where my path has not always been strewn with roses, and

I beg that you will kindly convey to His Excellency the expression of my appreciation of his courtesy, and kind wishes for my well-being in the future.

In conclusion, I would add that I expect to leave the Azores about the middle of January.

I am sir with highest consideration, Your obedient servant.[34]

The people of Faial were well aware that the Dabneys were leaving given their actions during the previous few years. Friends expressed their regret individually, and those who knew them only slightly or by sign expressed their esteem and regret collectively.

Our friends all over Fayal and Pico, when they heard that we were going to leave forever, felt terribly and the days grew sadder and sadder as we neared the time for leaving.

For months before we moved away there were articles in the Fayal papers, and countless letters and resolutions from different clubs paying tribute to the family. Bands serenaded our house, and finally the Horta townspeople planned a Regatta in our honor. On the day of the Regatta, the streets leading to the quay were decorated with flags of many nations, the American predominating, and all ships and boats I the harbor were covered with pennants and banners. Everyone who owned a boar, small or large, pressed it into service.[35]

Finally the day came and on January 12, 1892, all the Dabneys remaining on Faial loaded their personal belongings on a ship and departed for America. Rose describes the event.

In January 1892, we bade goodbye to our friends as well as to our loved garden and house, and set forth for New Bedford in a small Portuguese freight steamer (the *Olinda*, under Captain Maranhas), there being no other available vessel to bring us at the time. The family voyagers on the *Olinda* consisted of my Father, Mother, Alice, Aunt Roxie, Ralph and myself. Charles was already in business in Boston.

We had with us besides a goodly amount of luggage, my mother's green parrot "Jacob" and two pairs of Carrier pigeons. Your father J. Malcolm Forbes, met us on our arrival at the railroad station in Boston and was highly entertained over our miscellaneous effects.

Your Aunt Alice Cary had asked us all to make headquarters at her hospitable Milton home, *Bobolink Hill*, until we should start West, and this we were happy to do.

A good many of our larger belongings were sent to California via Cape Horn. The vessel which was carrying them foundered off the Faulkland Islands and all her cargo had to be landed and shipped north by another boat.

While there were Dabneys all over the country, mostly in Massachusetts, the last Dabneys on Faial went to Southern California. Although Samuel died in 1893 on his ranch in California, the others lived a number of years and some continued their new life there and others returned to Massachusetts – but, as the old saying goes, that's another story.

Notes:

[1] Ernesto Rebello, *Notas Açorianas*, Archivo dos Açores, Ponta Delgada, 1885, Excerpts from chapter VI, p. 43-50.

[2] Roxana Lewis Dabneys Diary, Massachusetts Historical Society Microfilm, Roll 1, 16 December 1880.

[3] Roxana Lewis Dabneys Diary, Massachusetts Historical Society Microfilm, Roll 1, 19 August 1883.

[4] Dabney, Rose Forbes, *Fayal Dabneys*, n. p.: The Author, 1931, p. 121.

[5] Document 217, United States Archives, Microfilm T203, Roll 8, January 10, 1875-September 2, 1882.

[6] Document 103, United States Archives, Microfilm T203, Roll 9, October 14, 1882-November 17, 1888.

[7] Document 194, United States Archives, Microfilm T203, Roll 8, January 10, 1875-September 2, 1882.

[8] Documents 10 and 13, United States Archives, Microfilm T203, Roll 9, October 14, 1882-November 17, 1888.

[9] Document 22, United States Archives, Microfilm T203, Roll 9, October 14, 1882-November 17, 1888.

[10] Dabney, Rose Forbes, *Fayal Dabneys*,. 123; Document 40, United States Archives, Microfilm T203, Roll 9, October 14, 1882-November 17, 1888.

[11] Document 40, United States Archives, Microfilm T203, Roll 9, October 14, 1882-November 17, 1888.

[12] Ernesto do Canto, *Archivo dos Açores*, reedition, 15 vol., Ponta Delgada: Instituto Universitário dos Açores, 1980-1985, p. 95.

[13] Ernesto do Canto, vol. 8, p. 94.

[14] "?Korean Prince," *O Fayalense*, Nº 45, June 7, 1885.

[15] Albert I, Honoré Charles Grimaldi, Prince of Monaco, *La Carrière d'un Navigateur*, Paris, 1902; 2nd edition 1905, excerpts p. 219-221; Ernesto do Canto, p. 95-6.

[16] Roxana Lewis Dabney Diary, Massachusetts Historical Society Microfilm, Roll 2, January 17, 1885.

[17] "Statue of Liberty," *O Fayalense*, July 6, 1885.

[18] Document 124, United States Archives, Microfilm T203, Roll 9, October 14, 1882-November 17, 1888.

[19] Consul William F. Doty, *American Consular Service, Historical Sketch of Office*, Consular Despatch Nº 402, St. Michael's, Azores, February 29, 1928.

[20] Document 167, United States Archives, Microfilm T203, Roll 9, October 14, 1882-November 17, 1888.

[21] Document 108, , October 14, 1882-November 17, 1888.

[22] Document 19, United States Archives, Microfilm T203, Roll 10, January 2, 1889-December 30, 1893.

[23] Document 67, United States Archives, Microfilm T203, Roll 9, October 14, 1882-November 17, 1888.

[24] Dabney, Rose Forbes, *Fayal Dabneys*,. 124-5.

[25] Dabney, Rose Forbes, *Fayal Dabneys*,. 125.

[26] Roxana Lewis Dabney Diary, Massachusetts Historical Society Microfilm, Roll 2, 13 January 1881.

[27] Roxana Lewis Dabney Diary, Massachusetts Historical Society Microfilm, Roll 2, 19 October 1880.

[28] Roxana Lewis Dabney Diary, Massachusetts Historical Society Microfilm, Roll 2, 31 December 1884.

[29] Roxana Lewis Dabney Diary, Massachusetts Historical Society Microfilm, Roll 2, 12 November 1884.

[30] Roxana Lewis Dabney Diary, Massachusetts Historical Society Microfilm, Roll 2, 10 June 1889.

[31] Roxana Lewis Dabney Diary, Massachusetts Historical Society Microfilm, Roll 2, 15 June 1889.

32 Roxana Lewis Dabney Diary, Massachusetts Historical Society Microfilm, Roll 2, 21 August 1889.

33 Document 91, United States Archives, Microfilm T203, Roll 10, January 2, 1889-December 30, 1893.

34 Document 100, United States Archives, Microfilm T203, Roll 10, January 2, 1889-December 30, 1893.

35 Dabney, Rose Forbes, *Fayal Dabneys,*. 125.

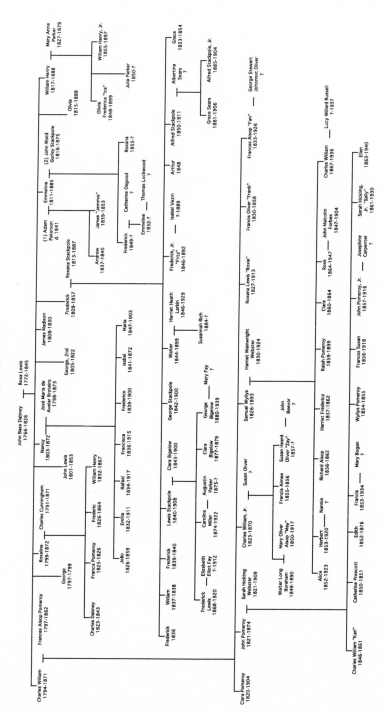

THE DABNEYS OF FAYAL — FAMILY TREE
(born before family left Faial)

BIBLIOGRAPHY

......, Trial of Professor John White Webster......

......, "John Bass Dabney", in *O Açoriano*, 17 January 1992

......, *The Return of William Morris Hunt*, Vose Galleries, Boston, 1986

......, "O Século Dabney", in *Correio da Horta*, Horta (Faial, Azores), 11 January 1992

Albert I,Honoré Charles Grimaldi, Prince of Monaco, *La Carrière d'un Navigateur*, Paris, 1902

Barreira, César Gabriel, *Um Olhar Sobre a Cidade da Horta*, Núcleo Cultural da Horta, Horta (Faial, Azores), 1995

Bensaúde, Alfredo, *Vida de José Bensaúde*, Litografia Nacional, Oporto, 1936

Bombarda, Miguel, *Açores Medico*, 1899

Brotero, Frederico de Barros, *Descendentes do Conselheiro José Maria de Avelar Brotero*, São Paulo, 1961

Buller, Joseph and Henry, *Um Inverno nos Açores e um Verão no Vale das Furnas*, Instituto Cultural de Ponta Delgada, Ponta Delgada (São Miguel, Azores), 1986

Castilho, Júlio de, *Ilhas Ocidentais*, David Corazzi, Lisbon, 1886

Clarke, Robert Henry, *Open Boat Whaling in the Azores*, in the series *Discovery Reports*, v. XXVI, p. 281-354, Cambridge University Press, London, 1954

Crowninshield, Francis Boardman, *Cleopatra's Barge*, Private Printing, Boston, 1913

Dabney, Rose and Hester Cunningham, "Fayal, a Far-off Bright Azor", in *New England Magazine*, New Series, VII, Nº 6, p. 741-749, February 1893

Dabney, Roxana, "A Summer Cruise among the Azores and Canary Islands", in *Harper's Magazine*, XLVI, p. 865-876, Harper's Magazine, New York, 1873

Dabney, Ralph Pomeroy, "Small-boat Whaling in the Azores", in *American Neptune*, XXVIII, Nº 4, p. 284-286, October 1968

Dabney, Francis L, Compiled, *Sketch of John Bass Dabney by his son William H. Dabney of Boston*, 1887

Dervenn, Claude, *The Azores*, George G. Harrap & Co., Ltd., London, 1956

Duarte, Tomaz, Jr., "A Horta em Meados do Século XIX – Subsídios para a sua Análise", in *Boletim do Núcleo Cultural da Horta*, v. 8, Nº 1-2-3, p. 27-44, Núcleo Cultural da Horta, Horta (Faial, Azores), 1985-88

Frutuoso, Padre Gaspar, *Livro Sexto das Saudades da Terra (1963)*, 16th Century

Gomes, Francisco António N.P., *A caça à baleia na Flores*, City Council, Lajes (Flores, Azores), 1988

Guill, James H., *A History of the Azores Islands*, Author's Edition, Menlo Park, CA, 1972

Higginson, Thomas W., "Fayal and the Portuguese", in *The Atlantic Monthly*, p. 526-544, Atlantic Monthly, Boston, November 1860

Holmes, Lionel and Joseph D'Alessandro, *Portuguese pioneers of the Sacramento Area*, Portuguese Historical and Cultural Society, Sacramento, CA, 1990

Howland, Alice Forbes, *The Descendents of John Bass Dabney and Roxa Lewis 1766-1966*, Milton, MA, 1966

Lima, Marcelino, *As Famílias Faialenses*, Minerva Insular, 1922

Lima, Marcelino, "Judeus na Ilha do Faial", in *Boletim do Núcleo Cultural da Horta*, v. 1, Nº 1, p. 5-14, Núcleo Cultural da Horta, Horta (Faial, Azores), 1956

Macedo, António Lourenço da Silveir Macedo, *História das Quatro Ilhas que Formam o Distrito da Horta (Three volumes)*, Direcção Regional dos Assuntos Culturais, Angra do Heroismo (Terceira, Azores), 1981

May, Joseph, Editor, *Samuel Longfellow, Vol. 1, Memoir and Letters*, Houghton Mifflin & Co., Boston & New York, 1894

Melville, Herman, *Moby Dick, or the Whale*,

Morison, Samuel Eliot, *The European Discovery of America: The Northern Voyages A.D. 500-1600*, Oxford University Press, New York, 1971

Nye, Elisa W., "Diário de uma Viagem da América aos Açores no Veleiro "Sylph" em Julho de 1847", in Insulana, v. 29-30, p. 5-106, Instituto Cultural de Ponta Delgada, Ponta Delgada (São Miguel, Azores), 1973-74

Paine, Albert Bigelow, Prepared by, *Mark Twain's Notebook*, Harper & Brothers, New York, 1935

Rebello, Ernesto, Notas Açorianas, Typ. do Archivo dos Açores, Ponta Delgada (São Miguel, Azores), 1885

Rogers, Francis Millet, "St. Michael's Hicklings, Fayal Dabneys, and their British Connections", in *Separate of the Revista Arquipélago. Número Especial, 1988: Relações*

Açores-Grâ-Bretanha, p. 123-148, Universidade dos Açores, Ponta Delgada (São Miguel, Azores), 1988

Salvi, Rejane, *Panorama Açoriana*, Instituto Cultural, Ponta Delgada (São Miguel, Azores), 1990

Schama, Simon, *Dead Certainties: Unwarranted Speculation*, Alfred A. Knopf, New York, 1991

Semmes, Admiral Raphael, *The Confederate Raider Alabama*, Fawcett, Bloomington, IN, 1962

Serpa, António Ferreira de, *A Importância Estratégica do Fayal*,

Serpa, António Ferreira de, *Dados Genalógicas e Biográficas d'algumas famílias faialenses*,

Slocum, Joshua, *Sailing Alone Around the World*, Konemann UK Ltd., London, 1995

Smith, James Wesley, *Sojourners in Search of Freedom: The Settlement of Liberia by Black Americans*, Lanham, MD, 1987

State Street Trust Company (Boston, MA), *Old Shipping Days in Boston*, Reynolds-Dewalt, New Bedford, 1969

Terra, Florêncio, "Dabneys", in *Boletm do Núcleo Cultural da Horta*, II. 1, 23-24, Núcleo Cultural da Horta, Horta (Faial, Azores), 1959

Twain, Mark, *Innocents Abroad*,

Venables, Bernard, *Baleia! Baleia! Whale Hunters of the Azores*, Knopf, New York, 1969

Vermette, Mary Theresa Silvia, *The Image of the Azorean, Portrayals in Nineteenth and Early-Twentieth Century Writings*, Instituto Histórico da Ilha Terceira, Angra do Heroísmo (Terceira, Azores), 1984

Webster, John White, *A description of the island of St. Michael comprising an account of its geological structure with remarks on the other Azores or Western Islands*, R. P. & C. Williams, Boston, 1821

Wheeler, Douglas L., "The Azores and the United States (1787-1987): two hundred years of shared history", in *Boletim do Instituto Histórico da Ilha Terceira*, v. XLV, Tomo I, p. 55-71, Instituto Histórico da Ilha Terceira, Angra do Heroísmo (Terceira, Azores), 1987

INDEX